Indonesian Economic History

Indonesian Economic History in the Dutch Colonial Era

Edited by

ANNE BOOTH
W.J. O'MALLEY
ANNA WEIDEMANN

Monograph Series 35/Yale University Southeast Asia Studies
Yale Center for International Area Studies

Yale University Southeast Asia Studies
James C. Scott, Chairman
Marvel Kay Mansfield, Editor

Library of Congress Catalog Card Number: 89-51449
International Standard Book Number: 0-938692-42-9

Distributor:
Yale University Southeast Asia Studies
Box 13A Yale Station
New Haven, Connecticut 06520

Printed in the U.S.A.

Contents

List of Tables

List of Figures

The Editors

Anne Booth is currently Senior Research Fellow in the Southeast Asian Economic History Project at the Australian National University. She has published extensively on the Indonesian economy in the colonial and post-colonial periods, and edited the *Bulletin of Indonesian Economic Studies* from 1983 to 1989.

W.J. O'Malley has published on several aspects of Southeast Asian economic and social history and is currently analysing Indochinese affairs for the Office of National Assessments in Canberra.

Anna Weidemann was research assistant to the Indonesia Project in the Research School of Pacific Studies from 1980 to 1987; from 1983 to 1987 she was also assistant editor of the *Bulletin of Indonesian Economic Studies*. She is currently a University administrator at the Australian National University in Canberra.

Preface

Most of the papers in this volume were first delivered at the conference on Indonesian Economic History in the Dutch Colonial Era, held at the Australian National University in December, 1983. We are most grateful to Professor R.G. Ward, the Director of the Research School of Pacific Studies, Australian National University, and to Professors W.M. Corden and J.A.C. Mackie, for their support and encouragement, without which the conference could not have taken place. We are also grateful to the Australian Department of Foreign Affairs, whose assistance made possible the participation of several Indonesian scholars in the conference. The typing of the conference papers and their subsequent revision for inclusion in this volume were done with cheerful efficiency by Hilda Heidemanns and Claire Smith. Evelyn Winburn assisted with the final word-processing of the text. Lorraine Dearden prepared the charts. We would like to thank them, and all the contributors, for their cooperation.

Anne Booth
Bill O'Malley
Anna Weidemann

Canberra, June 1989.

CHAPTER ONE

Introduction

William J. O'Malley

A quarter of a century ago, in his contribution to an important symposium on Indonesian historiography, the Indonesian economic historian F.J.E. Tan made a number of points about his field of study that still merit consideration today (Tan 1964). In his brief, somewhat elusive, and rather pessimistic essay, Tan noted:

1. that the economic historian of Indonesia had to be "a kind of hybrid," one who was "at the same time a good theoretical economist and a professional historian" (p. 401);
2. that Indonesian economic history had somehow to keep developments in the village in sight; and
3. that the sociological approach would have to be tied in to economic history if the results were to be adequate.

When taking stock now of the condition of Indonesian economic history, it is useful to bear in mind how valid these points have been. It is also necessary, however, to recall that the writing of that history has not proceeded in the way that Tan had in mind. His view that economic and social questions had to be raised together in considering Indonesia's past is one that few would challenge. But Tan was thinking that economic historians would be stretching themselves beyond their traditional concerns with trade and production figures to include means of social inquiry. Instead, things have generally been the other way around. The major advances in our understanding of Indonesia's economic history, both before Tan was writing and since, have come about not through the innovations or initiatives of economic historians, but through discoveries made by scholars interested in social history who found that they needed to understand the economic side of things better if they were to see more clearly the social changes they were intent on studying. Likewise, the tie between villages and economic history has turned out to be strong in Indonesian historical studies. But, once again, the lead has been taken not by economic historians making efforts to keep village developments in view, but by those interested in the past and present status of villages who came to appreciate the value of economic data—and sometimes the value of economic methods of analysis—in their work.

If Tan got things somewhat back-to-front in his comments on the relationship between Indonesian economic history and sociological, especially rural sociological, research, his observation that an economic historian of Indonesia would need to be both historian and economist,and, moreover, one equipped with splendid language skills (Tan 1964, p. 400), was surely right on target. And among both Indonesians and foreigners who study the country, that "hybrid" combination has ever been rare. To attempt the task of writing economic history demands a certain confidence in one's data-collecting, analytical, and expository skills; to do the job correctly requires those skills plus unusual combinations of training, of abilities, and of experience; to have the results received well means passing the scrutiny of professionals from different disciplines with different standards and different needs. Under these circumstances, it is not surprising that the number of people who would ever have called themselves Indonesian economic historians is minute, and that the economic history of Indonesia is still comparatively backward. What is surprising is the extent to which what we do know of Indonesia's economic past suffuses our general view of Indonesian history. For in fact, far more than is the case with other Southeast Asian countries, the way in which the history of Indonesia is perceived and taught relies heavily on parameters of commerce and of administration established by considerations that are largely economic in nature.

A measure of how deeply ingrained economic considerations have become in the treatment of Indonesian history can be gained by comparing the two most useful introductory textbooks on the subject, J.D. Legge's *Indonesia* (1964) and M.C. Ricklefs' *A History of Modern Indonesia* (1981). Legge's book is analytical in its approach and focuses on issues of immediate interest to economists and economic historians. Ricklefs' book, on the other hand, is essentially a narrative concentrating on political events and political forces, and it has practically nothing to say about the economic side of Indonesian history. In concerning himself almost exclusively with what happened in the political sphere, and with why things happened there in the sequence they did, Professor Ricklefs has produced a book that was badly needed and is very much up-to-date. It is, moreover, a book that is refreshingly different. Different, because Legge and others in recent decades have been directing their efforts not so much at uncovering what happened in Indonesia, but at attempting to understand and clarify how things worked among the people in the archipelago.[1] This aim led Legge to adopt social-science methods of analyzing conditions and developments in Indonesia, whether economic, cultural, or political. It also led him, given the small size of his book (only some 60,000 words, less than half the length of Ricklefs' text), to chart his course through Indonesia's past by fixing on, inspecting, and evaluating the views of earlier authors. Where to Ricklefs the key figures in introducing Indonesian history are such important leaders as Pakubuwana II, Mangkubumi, and Sukarno, to Legge they are such important scholars as van Leur, Boeke, and Wertheim, none of whom Ricklefs lists in his extensive bibliography. Ricklefs, then, was writing outright history, featuring a clear chronology and a detailed narrative, while Legge's work has about it many of the elements of an extended historiographical essay. Educational experts can debate the relative utility of these methods of introducing a new subject to students, but for those interested primarily in economic history, two aspects of Legge's book stand out strikingly. First, in trying to analyze certain important questions in Indonesia's development which have their roots in the past, Legge was compelled to handle issues directly related to economic history. And second, in adopting an historiography-based approach and deliberately tapping into the lode of previous historical writings, Legge was able to mine a wealth of long-standing discussions, debates, and arguments connected with the economic past. For though the number of *echt* economic historians working on Indonesia may have been small, there is nonetheless a rich tradition of valuable contributions made by those writing with the economy in mind.

In the years since Indonesia gained independence, we have seen major changes wrought in the way that Indonesian history before European contact is interpreted. Combining economic ideas with archaeological and linguistic work, prehistorians have set up far more plausible theories to account for the peopling of the islands of Indonesia (Bellwood 1979). Views of the early history of maritime Indonesia have also been turned around, largely through the work done by Professor Wolters on Srivijaya using trade-based sources and considerations (Wolters 1967). And the study of ancient kingdoms, both in Java and outside, has spread from the establishing of dates and the measuring of Hindu influence to questions focusing on means of production and control (van Naerssen and de Iongh (1977); van Setten van der Meer (1979).

Economic considerations have been important in reshaping the study of early Indonesian history, but they are bound to play an even more important part when the history of Indonesia since 1950 is written. The amount of material dealing with the economic conditions and performance of independent Indonesia is already astoundingly large, and it is growing. Daily newspapers in many languages report constantly on all sorts of items connected with the Indonesian economy. Weekly news magazines, both inside and outside the country, regularly cover the economic beat. Official reports—monthly, quarterly, semi-annual, and yearly, from the Indonesian government, foreign governments, international organizations—overflow library shelves. And the number of economists and other professionals who analyze the Indonesian economy in print is on the increase. Problems for future economic historians will focus on the reliability of data and methods for handling a surplus of materials rather than, as has been the case all too often previously, on shortages of sources.

If economic questions and slants have helped recently to illuminate Indonesian history before Dutch rule, and if economic materials are going to pose new and different challenges for those writing histories of Indonesia since Dutch rule, what about the position of the economic history of Indonesia under Dutch rule, which is the subject of most of the essays in this volume? How has this history fared since Indonesian independence? What has been its role in shaping the general way in which Indonesia's past is comprehended?

A distinguishing feature of the economic history of colonial-era Indonesia is that the study of that history had already made considerable strides while the Dutch were still governing the archipelago. Unlike the situation with pre-European economic history, there were both sources for, and concerns occasioning, deeper treatments of economic issues in the colonial era. As Van Niel notes in his essay below, the system of forced deliveries known as the *Cultuurstelsel* (Cultivation System) had already roused sufficient ire among its critics to draw forth, by the second half of the nineteenth century, serious writings on economic developments in Java. Those writings contributed significantly to the record, but they were also generally partisan, and they were limited in their coverage with regard to time, place, and problem. Those shortcomings were not characteristics of the more professional works on the economic history of Indonesia under the Dutch, which began to appear early in the twentieth century.

Pride of place in the more modern school goes to the American scholar, Clive Day. In the way that Raffles' *History of Java* (1817) and Crawfurd's *History of the Indian Archipelago* (1820) are given credit, at least by English speakers, for establishing a worthy precedent that Dutch historians would later follow in contemplating their colony, Day's *The Policy and Administration of the Dutch in Java* (1904) set a certain standard of informed and measured analysis against which subsequent works had to gauge themselves. Day was an economic historian by both training and profession. Though he apparently never travelled to Asia himself, whatever he missed in the way of feel for the colony, he more than made up for with his wide-ranging use of sources and his ability to link economic analysis with a careful chronological treatment. While it is probably fair to say that Day's views were not original—he reflected a turn-of-the-century American belief in free enterprise, and was building on themes already established in more policy-oriented Dutch writings—he nonetheless brought a degree of scholarly detachment to his writing that, for the first time, made the economic history of Indonesia a subject intended to inspire contemplation as well as to stimulate political action.

If Day set a useful example for the writing of Indonesia's economic history, the next major figure to have an impact on the field, J.H. Boeke, managed to draw far more responses in his own time than Day was able to do. This was, no doubt, partly because Boeke was a social scientist rather than an economic historian. Thus he was interested in the past more for the purpose of seeing what general lessons he would discover there than for its own sake. Boeke also drew responses because the most important of those general lessons—one he set out in his 1910 dissertation (Boeke 1910), and tried to adapt and re-apply in the remaining forty-five years of his working life—had serious policy implications. This was the idea that there were difficulties in using general economic laws, laws derived from Western experience and arrived at through Western rationality, to predict or to explain phenomena in Indonesia. Instead, Boeke posited that social rather than purely economic drives motivated many of the economic actions of Indonesians, and that the imposition of an advanced colonial economy on the more primitive local economy had made it impossible for that local economy to evolve along a predictable Westernizing path. What were needed then, in policy terms, were special government programs to coddle Indonesians or to prod them, to preserve them in their cultural shells or to encourage them to break out. In any event, the indigenous peoples could not simply be left on their own to face the storms of the modern world. In the wake of this key observation, Boeke and his critics argued for decades about the roots, the value, and the implications of his discovery (*Indonesian Economics* 1961). But what was just as important for economic history was that, by emphasizing the significance of the impact of Western capitalism on local pre-capitalist societies, Boeke's ideas stimulated new lines of historical inquiry into just how that impact had occurred in the past, and what had thereafter transpired.

A number of important economic-history studies appeared in the years after Boeke put forth his thought-provoking challenge, but the most important of them came from three government officials in colonial Indonesia. Dr. van Doorn writing on Purworejo (1926) and Dr. de Vries studying Pasuruan (1931), produced full-length treatments of economic developments at the local level, and their early interest in regional research has come back into vogue again in the past decade. Another early practitioner of local economic-history research was D.H. Burger, who had already begun in the 1920s to look below the regency level, with which de Vries and van Doorn were mainly concerned, and to explore changes directly at the district and even the village level (Burger 1929; 1930; 1933). Burger expanded his focus in the late 1930s to write a dissertation on Java from the end of the V.O.C. (Vereenigde Oostindische Compagnie) period up to the Great Depression. In that work he combined elements of political, social, and economic history to explore the way in which the expansion of the money-economy affected life in Java (Burger (1939).[2]

At the same time that these strides forward were being made in the study of more recent economic history in Indonesia, a light fueled by economic-history ideas was reflecting glaring defects in the way that earlier Indonesian history had been perceived. J.C. van Leur, in his 1934 doctoral thesis and subsequent essays (van Leur 1955), took issue with the way in which seemingly unanswerable cultural questions and then exclusively Dutch concerns had been given pre-eminence in writings about earlier Indonesian history. By combining economic and sociological insights with a shrewd appreciation of trade data, van Leur was able to take an approach which emphasized processes of change rather than merely static elements in history, and at the same time helped to restore Indonesians to the centre of the stage in the drama of their own past.

Almost simultaneously with van Leur's insistence that the nature of trade and production be borne in mind by those working in Indonesian history, an important move was made in Batavia to insure that such a course could be more easily followed. This was a project initiated by W.M.F. Mansvelt, the head of the colonial government's Central Bureau of Statistics, to compile and publish lists of data connected with commerce and development in the colony. A few of these works, some of them only provisional in nature, had already appeared in print when the Second World War put a halt to this endeavour (*C.E.I.*, Vol. 1, p. 7).

The pre-war advances in Indonesian economic history had been initiated by one English-language writer. They were capped by another. Perhaps it is an indication of how far the field had advanced in four decades that, while Clive Day seems to have felt he could do much of his work on his own in Europe and North America, J.S. Furnivall's work benefited greatly from his being able to rely on substantial amounts of assistance and encouragement both in Indonesia and in The Netherlands. Following a political-economy line of enquiry that stressed the relationship between official policy and socio-economic change, Furnivall wrote a book on the development of the colonial economy. This work still stands out among the best efforts thus far made to describe and explain the changes that Indonesian society had undergone (Furnivall 1944). Furnivall's particular insight was that the Dutch colony, like others he had known, constituted a plural society, one in which different groups of people lived separate social and economic lives under one political unit. This insight enabled him to make sense, within a single framework, of changes occurring in the European, Chinese, and Indonesian spheres of life in the Indies. Moreover, Furnivall's determination to keep both the systems of internal production and the significance of foreign trade in the forefront of his study meant that he could firmly locate the changes occurring inside the colony within the context of changes taking place in the wider world.

In the final four decades of Dutch rule, then, several important contributions had been made toward the understanding of Indonesian economic history, particularly in the study of that period in which Europeans were prominent in the area. Instead of simply broadening the extent of knowledge about the economic past, however, the scholars from Day to Furnivall were progressively developing an appropriate framework for thinking about the colonial period in Indonesian history. They were also setting out something of an agenda for future thought and research. Their framework has been modified only slightly by later writers, and their agenda has had an important influence on post-independence writing and thinking about modern Indonesian economic history.

Because they were dealing with an extended period of European involvement in Indonesia, the major pre-war contributors to Indonesian economic history had to divide centuries of history up into more manageable sub-units. And because they were greatly concerned with economic issues, they made their divisions with the economy and economic policy in mind. Ultimately, they converged toward blocking off the 350 years of Dutch involvement in Indonesia into, sequentially, the V.O.C. period (1600-1800), the period which Furnivall called "confusion" and "uncertainty" (1800-1830), the Cultivation System (1830-1870), the Liberal period (1870-1900), the Ethical years (1900-1930), and the Great Depression (1930-1940). The periodization within this sequence frequently coincides with important administrative, social, or political changes, or even with less easily fixed changes of attitude, either in Indonesia or in The Netherlands. But is largely determined by lines of economy and especially by economic policy. The economic lives of Indonesian subjects did not necessarily change abruptly with the shift from one period to another, but the lines of economic policy in particular help to provide a seemingly firm and clear structure for grasping, and thus imparting, the basic dynamics of each of the periods. For that reason, this periodization—rather than one based on, say, the terms in office of particular groups of governors-general, or stages of urbanization, or changes in patterns of religious belief or indigenous leadership—has, for the most part, been accepted as the standard or most useful one in general texts.

Economic history as it was written during the early twentieth century provided the basis for periodization in general Indonesian history; it also helped to keep the focus of that general history solidly on Java. Day, van Doorn, de Vries, and Burger wrote only about developments in Java. Boeke, though he later drew examples from other locations to boost his theories, was clearly concerned mostly with Java: he drew much of the data for his original thesis from government reports on Java, while the great portion of his professional work with the colonial credit system was done in Java. And Furnivall's idea of "Netherlands India" was also dominated by Java, though he did bring in more material from the Outer Islands and provide additional colony-wide information for analysis as his study moved on chronologically.

In their Java-centricity and their periodization, these pre-war writers helped to shape the way that all Indonesian history was understood, but they also provided an important legacy by setting precedents and establishing guidelines for future work. The idea that research could be and ought to be directed at the regional or village level gained currency through the efforts of some of them. The linking together of international trade and domestic developments was illuminated by others. And the social-science practice of relating local studies to the insights of wider theories so as to cast light on both was already becoming firmly grounded. But perhaps the biggest intellectual legacy of the pre-war writers was the one Tan was still stressing in the late 1950s—the combining of economic considerations with those from other disciplines. For, of the noteworthy authors mentioned above, only Clive Day was a true economic historian. Boeke, ultimately to hold a chair in Tropical-Colonial Economics, had actually been a political scientist before doing his doctoral thesis with Professor van Vollenhoven, the famous *adat* law specialist. Van Leur made his mark by applying Weberian sociological insights to history. Burger had studied broad-based Indology before working as an administrator and then doing his thesis, in jurisprudence, with Professor Boeke as his promotor; perhaps his true feeling for what he was doing is clearest in the title of his final major work: *Sociologisch-economische geschiedenis van Indonesië [Sociological-Economic History of Indonesia]* (1975). And Furnivall is generally thought of as a Fabian political economist. In fact, the only author bold enough to indicate in his title that he was attempting a pure economic history was Dr. G.L. Gonggrijp, Professor of Colonial Economics at both Rotterdam and Amsterdam, whose *Schets eener economische geschiedenis van Nederlandsch-Indië [Sketch of an Economic History of the Netherlands Indies]* went through four editions between 1928 and 1957.

Professor Gonggrijp's work, and the geographer Jan Broek's *Economic Development of the Netherlands Indies* (1942), which leaned heavily towards an analysis of the last decade before the war, provided brief summaries and considerations of the economic changes experienced in Indonesia during the Dutch period. They also provided insights into the difficulties of writing and thinking about straight economic history, as opposed to the socio-economic, political-economic, or other hyphenated-economic work which different authors had been pursuing. Among the difficulties they faced were three which continue to plague those attempting to write economic history today.

First, pure economic historians were confronted with the problem that they had to rely almost completely on official sources for their data. Where scholars whose works had heavy social or political elements could find, either through their mastery of theory or in the use of alternative sources, ways of working around the deficiencies or biases in government-provided materials on the economy, this was rarely practical for economic historians. They were thus, to some extent, prisoners of their material, forced to organize and analyze in print that which was available, and to deplore, perhaps only in private, the lack of that which was not.

Second, they came up against the need in their writing to balance long-term trends against short-term phenomena. In the case of aberrant years or of counter-trends of only very short duration, explanations of idiosyncracy could always be put forward, or hiccups could be removed simply by averaging. But with events that dragged on for longer periods, there were problems for economic historians that did not exist, at least as severely, for others interested in the past. Political economists or socio-economic historians, for instance, could easily leap over the depression of the 1880s in their treatment of the Liberal Period; that depression did not seem to affect the broad lines of government policy in a radical way, and the impact of the depression alone on the bulk of the Indonesian population is difficult to know. For economic historians, however, that depression, coming as it did simultaneously with the devastating diseases which struck at Java's important sugar and coffee crops, can be seen to have had a grievous effect on the economy as a whole that lasted for well over a decade: it influenced investment, the organization of firms, and the location and crop choice of both plantations and indigenous agriculturalists. Should this depression, then, be considered as a major item for analysis? Or should it be quietly submerged within the longer-run picture that is to become the economic history of Indonesia in the nineteenth century? Was it not, in its way, as important a landmark as the Great Depression of the 1930s?

Third, Indonesia is extremely heterogeneous, multi-layered, and complex, and economic historians had to puzzle over the awkward issue of how to integrate information and ideas about developments in different geographical locations and at different levels of society. When, in the 1890s, East Sumatra was experiencing a tremendous export-based boom, Central Sumatra was barely explored, West Sumatra was stagnating, and Aceh was undergoing a devastating war, it hardly suffices to say that on the whole the economic situation in Sumatra looked promising. And yet to cover all the particulars of each place at each time was next to impossible. Likewise, it proved difficult to bring findings at different strata into alignment. Family-level, village-level, district-level, and regency-level research showed signs of being highly fruitful, but what was to be done when the results of those research efforts conflicted with each other or with the broader image of island-wide or colony-wide developments that seemed to emerge from the sea of government figures? Would regional studies and micro-studies, when they were consulted at all, have always to be confined to subordinate clauses or buried in footnotes in the writing of more general works? How could their impact and implications be more convincingly conveyed within the framework of a work with wider concerns?

Facing those problems, but able to build on the established tradition of pre-war scholarship, those concerned with studying the economic impact of the Dutch in Indonesia got off to a fine running start in the early years of independence. A manuscript which Burger had been putting together on sociological and economic history was lost during the Japanese invasion in 1942, but he subsequently reconstructed major parts of that work, published it in eight sections in the journal *Indonesië* between 1948 and 1950, and used ideas and materials from it to serve as the basis for subsequent publications (Burger

1948/50; Burger and Prajudi 1957-58; Burger 1975). Allen and Donnithorne (1954) produced a valuable summary of the history and organization of important sections of the economy, while Reinsma (1955) wrote an important thesis questioning the black picture of the Cultivation System which earlier authors had created and then passed on to each other. And Wertheim (1956) stressed the importance of economic structures in his benchmark study of Indonesian society.

After this auspicious beginning, however, progress tailed off quickly, and, over the course of the next fifteen years, the element of despondency in Tan's historiographical treatment of Indonesian economic history seemed justified. The problem was not that there was, between the mid-1950s and the early 1970s, no interest in the history or the economy of Indonesia. In fact, while the study of those subjects was reaching a low point in The Netherlands, there was a noteworthy expansion in those fields in the United States, in Australia, in Japan, and in Indonesia itself. But the efforts of historians were directed mainly toward the answering of burning questions connected with the political and cultural backgrounds that might help explain the processes of government and administration in independent Indonesia. At the same time, the need for trained economists to involve themselves in planning and evaluating the performance of the Indonesian economy outstripped the supply of those with economic credentials and capabilities. In effect, the special demands of the separate disciplines of history and economics outweighed the fact that there was still interesting and valuable work to be done in combining the two. The only historians who seemed interested in expanding the frontiers of economic history were Van Niel, a social historian who saw a growing need to explain the economic situation in nineteenth-century Java in connection with his work on the Cultivation System (Van Niel 1964c; 1969) and Meilink-Roelofsz (1962), who pointed out that the historical reality was more complex than the sociological picture of merchant society in Southeast Asia painted earlier by van Leur. Fortunately, they were joined in their efforts by the anthropologist Clifford Geertz, who, in a couple of stunningly lucid works based more on social-science theory and techniques than on historical research, raised important questions and posited challenging answers about the links between Indonesia's economic past and her economic present and future (Geertz 1963, 1965). In his *Social History of an Indonesian Town,* in particular, Geertz managed to combine the results of his interviewing, reading, and theorizing in a way that brought a study of local-level economic developments to life, a rare accomplishment for any area and still almost a unique one for Indonesia.

In the early 1970s, Indonesian economic history began to pass out of the doldrums, to reset its course, and to pick up much of the speed and momentum it had lost almost two decades earlier. This turnabout was due to the fortuitous coincidence of a number of factors.

Perhaps foremost among the reasons for this growing interest in Indonesian economic history was the increased accessibility of archival materials relevant to the subject. In Holland, the importance of collections of official documents from the nineteenth century was rediscovered, while in Indonesia new collections were uncovered and opened to researchers. This enabled scholars in both countries to delve far more deeply into local-level economic developments before the twentieth century than their predecessors had been able to do. Administrative materials from the final decades of Dutch rule were also opened to the public, thus making possible glimpses into the formulation and implementation of economic policy. At the same time, increased professionalism among archivists greatly facilitated the work of researchers, and the organization and infrastructural support available to scholars let them reach and use historical materials in a far more efficient manner.

With important new sources at their disposal, those interested in Indonesia's economic history also benefited from a growing world-wide interest in the formative years of Third World countries. The continuing difficulty which many of those countries encountered in trying to improve their economic positions did more than undermine the simple notion of an almost inevitable transformation from a status of backwardness to one of development. Among other things, it brought to the surface the question of exactly how those countries had come to be backward. In the general locus of solutions posed on theoretical grounds, attention was focussed on a number of factors important in Indonesia's past: long-distance trade; export-oriented agricultural production; retarded capital formation; minority-group economic middlemen; stunted social differentiation; and shortages of entrepreneurial skills. This line of questioning presented new ways of looking at the economic situation during the Dutch era and made possible useful comparisons not only with other Southeast Asian countries or with India, which had generally served as standard points of reference in the past, but with countries in South America and Africa as well.

In this new situation, where Indonesia's economic history had rather suddenly become as relevant to the academic and practical needs of the present as social or political history had earlier been, the efforts of one man, the late Piet Creutzberg, to make available to a wider audience important source materials connected with the economy of colonial Indonesia assumed a greater significance. Creutzberg had been a civil servant in Indonesia both before and after the Japanese period, but he had had no further academic or governmental connection with Indonesian studies until he was chosen in the late 1960s to select and edit official documents dealing with colonial economic policy. The resultant volumes (Creutzberg 1972-75), in sifting the crucial documentation on key policy decisions out of literally mountains of files, brought a large number of important issues up for further scrutiny.

By the time his volumes of collected documents had all been published, Creutzberg had become involved in an equally massive task, the expansion and re-working of the statistical information which Mansvelt and the Central Bureau of Statistics at Batavia had compiled some four decades before. With the assistance of Jan van Laanen and others, Creutzberg began to put out a series of statistical source materials, making available to the scholarly community a great amount of vetted economic data organized in a useful fashion (*C.E.I.*, Vols. 1-6). In a tremendous two-pronged effort, then, Creutzberg had managed in the 1970s to solidify the foundations on which future discussions of Indonesian economic history would take place.[3]

A final reason for the rising interest in Indonesia's economic history since the early 1970s has been the situation within that country.

National politics in Indonesia has been forcefully and deliberately shoved into the background since the late 1960s. This has meant both that research concerned with politics, even with the politics of the past, has been frowned upon, and that the relevance of politically-oriented historical research to the present situation in Indonesia is no longer as immediately clear as had been the case in the 1950s and 1960s. Those factors, together with the growing conviction among historians that the advances made in understanding anti-colonial protests and the nationalist movement in Indonesia now needed a firmer grounding in harder economic and social information, worked to shift the major thrust of historical research back towards concerns connected with economic history.

At the same time that the state of politics in Indonesia was acting to inhibit the study of Indonesian political history, the economic performance of the country, and particularly developments in agriculture, worked to push forward the interest in economic history. The stagnation experienced in Indonesia's rural sector in the 1950s and 1960s had helped to lull scholars into accepting a vaguely lethargic image of traditional village society, particularly in Java. The adaptability and flexibility of rural Indonesians in the 1970s to changes (both promising and threatening) in their living and working patterns made scholars seek to re-examine their previously held picture of the past, and to question whether there was, in fact, ever such a thing as "traditional" village society. In the face of rural communities which were quickly adapting to almost frighteningly rapid economic changes, Boeke's social explanations for Indonesia's backwardness—explanations whose predictive capacity and general theoretical applicability had long since been discounted by economists, but whose historical aspects still seemed valid—hardly sufficed any longer as an explanation of past developments. Even Geertz's attractive concepts of agricultural involution and shared poverty, which stressed the fatal way in which Javanese society had accommodated change, began to appear a bit shaky as keys for understanding developments in the past (White 1983). In effect, because they were social scientists Boeke, Geertz, and others had looked to Indonesia's economic history to explain her economic present, to elucidate upon the way things came to be the way they are. With rapid alterations in the 1970s in "the way things are," earlier explanations of "the way things came to be" did not seem as firmly grounded as they had previously.

Under these new and more conducive circumstances, progress has been made on a number of fronts in the last decade.

Sparked by the efforts of Van Niel (1972) and Fasseur (1975, 1977b), a new wave of scholars has moved into a widening re-evaluation of the interplay between peasants and export production in nineteenth-century Java. Concentrating on specific geographical areas and basing their findings on now-accessible archival materials, Elson (1979), Fernando (1982a), and Knight (1980, 1982a)—all contributors to this volume—have looked at local-level developments—in Pasuruan, Cirebon, and Pekalongan, respectively—and have challenged the older general impression that the economic and social effects of Western enterprise were simple, uniform, and almost assuredly negative. Instead, evidence has been accumulating that Indonesians had greater latitude in determining their economic activities than had heretofore been inferred, that developments varied greatly in different places, at different times, and with different crops, and that cash incomes were actually enhancing the position of many people in villages.

As that reconsideration of the historical link between plantations and peasants in Java was getting under way, other scholars were also making contributions to the economic history of that island. Onghokham (1975) wrote an important thesis on change in nineteenth-century Madiun, asserting once again that land was the crucial factor in rural areas, and that the efforts of researchers to focus attention constantly on changes in the control of that vital element would continue to pay dividends. Rush (1977) described and analyzed the system of opium sales, which was both a leading contributor to government revenue in the colony and a major method of capital investment and accumulation among leaders of Java's Chinese minority. And, in a promising development, the economist Booth made the historical situation an integral part of her economic analyses in articles on irrigation and on land-tax in Indonesia (Booth 1974, 1977).

There has also been improvement in understanding the economic history of the islands outside of Java. Thee (1977) studied the rapid economic changes experienced by the East Coast of Sumatra as it developed into a famous plantation zone, and Pelzer (1978, 1982) examined the bases of those economic changes and linked them to social and political difficulties in that area. Dobbin (1974, 1977, 1983) greatly illuminated the role of the economy in the political and social history of West Sumatra around the beginning of the nineteenth century. Van der Kraan (1980), writing on Lombok both before and after it passed under Dutch rule, uncovered the deepening economic exploitation which colonisation brought to that island. And Sutherland and Bigalke, in essays in a collection edited by Reid (1983), brought out the economic and social importance of slavery in southern Sulawesi.

In a different vein, a few Marxist histories with definite views on the colonial economy have also appeared in recent years. Caldwell and Utrecht (1979) wrote a brief general history of Indonesia, intending it to stand out clearly against the mainstream of writings on the topic; the book failed in that respect, but it does provide an activist outline for interpreting Indonesia's past, and stresses the importance of a political-economy approach to that past. Tichelman (1980) also used an analytical method suggested by Marx, that of the Asiatic mode of production, but it is the interplay of social and economic forces—with political elements downplayed—that primarily concerns him in his treatment of the colonial period. Both of these works suffer from an unfinished, almost preliminary, character, but even with that defect they serve to remind economic historians that there are different schools yet to be heard from in the field, and that the current sweep of revisionism in Indonesia's economic history is unlikely to be the last.

Since the early 1970s, then, new sources, new researchers, and new lines of inquiry had become associated with a renewal in the study of Indonesian economic history. It was in order to take advantage of this swelling of interest that a conference was organized in December 1983 by the Australian National University's Research School of Pacific Studies. The Department of Economics in the Research School has for years had a strong connection with the study of the contemporary Indonesian economy (it has since 1965 published the *Bulletin of Indonesian Economic Studies,* many of whose articles have come from scholars associated with the Department), but it is only in the past decade that some members of that Department have extended their research focus backward in time to the colonial period. This kindling of economists' interest in the past has coincided with the involvement of the Department of Political and Social Change in a joint project with Gajah Mada University's Institute of Rural and Regional Research which explores the historical background to social and economic changes in a number of areas in rural Java. Building on this Canberra base, the conference organizers saw an opportunity to bring together a number of scholars working in the forefront of the field. The expectation was that, by exposing those scholars, their research, and their preliminary conclusions to the questions and scrutiny of each other, and of still other scholars professionally linked with Indonesian studies, it would be possible to generate some fruitful cross-fertilization of ideas. At the same time, it was hoped that the conference would act to provide a picture of the present state of the art.

Those hopes were ambitious, but, at least to a satisfying measure, they were fulfilled. Among those attending were not only economists and historians, but demographers, political scientists, geographers, linguists, anthropologists, and librarians as well. In experience, the audience and the participants ranged from Sartono Kartodirdjo, the doyen of historical studies in Indonesia, and Benjamin Higgins, who had been an economic adviser to the Indonesian government in the early 1950s, to students working toward their first degrees. With this great diversity, it came as no surprise that the discussions ranged widely and that a significant number of challenges, many of them from unanticipated angles, were thrown out to those presenting papers. If the discussions went some way toward reaching the anticipated level of interchange, the papers, most of which are gathered together here in revised form, go even further in collectively providing an accurate overview of the way in which the economic history of Indonesia during the Dutch period has moved in the past decade and is now taking shape.

The first three essays challenge an established view. They also challenge each other. For over a century, it was generally held that the Cultivation System—under which the colonial government forced Indonesian farmers to raise crops for export and deliver those crops to itself for sale abroad—was a pernicious experiment which permitted the Dutch to establish the basis for economic progress at home while presiding over the deepening misery of the people they had colonized. Elson looks in some detail at the case usually made against the way the System worked among the Javanese, and he finds both the data and the logic on which that case rests to be weak. His evidence encourages him instead to advance the argument that the material welfare of many Javanese was in fact increasing during the years the System was in operation. Relying on contemporary descriptions of conditions in Java, on statistical data that show money flowing in considerable amounts to Javanese farmers involved in the System, and on evidence of popular responses to broadening economic opportunities, Elson argues that the Javanese in the middle of the nineteenth century had more ability to manoeuvre and make choices than earlier historians have admitted. The Javanese, according to Elson, had a major say in determining their own economic fates under the Cultivation System, and many of them opted to improve their material circumstances.

Following the recent work by Fasseur and by Elson himself, the proposition that the welfare of the Javanese might have risen during the years of the Cultivation System is not as eye-opening as it would have been a decade ago, but Elson puts that proposition here in a clear and persuasive fashion. He does not, however, gain much support from the papers written by Knight and Van Niel. Knight, looking closely at a small area in Pekalongan, still sees the Javanese as being forced into making the economic choices they did, though he notes that economic necessity was as influential a factor in the push towards involvement with wider markets as Dutch coercion. What is more, Knight finds that a closer inspection of the lives of those caught up in the Cultivation System will uncover the fact that their involvement brought hidden financial and labour costs that significantly reduced the incomes that appear to be accruing to them if the only thing taken into account is the official statistics. Van Niel's contribution clashes less obviously with Elson's findings, but it throws down the gauntlet in two ways. First, in his extended sections on cheap labour and on the village economy, Van Niel raises important questions about just how the financial benefits coming from the Cultivation System were distributed; it is clear that many Javanese did improve their situations, as Elson insists, but Van Niel makes us ask "How many?," "Who exactly were they?," and "At what cost, both short-term and long-run, to others?" Second, Van Niel poses the lovely parahistorical question of whether the Cultivation System made any difference whatsoever. His answer is tentatively affirmative, but the question itself forces readers to reflect on the nature and pace of changes which were occurring in the colony quite unrelated to the System. Where Knight, in response to Elson's theme, skillfully puts the local historian's classic position of "It didn't happen that way here, and maybe it didn't happen that way elsewhere either," Van Niel raises the bigger question of "Wouldn't all of this have happened anyway?"

Two further studies on the Cultivation System cover its workings in West Sumatra (Young) and in the coffee-growing uplands of Cirebon Residency in western Java (Fernando and O'Malley). As Young points out, observing the way in which the System operated in an area outside Java can help to bring into better focus certain aspects of the System in Java. In his essay on the adaptation of the principles of the Cultivation System to Minangkabau culture and of the System's initial success and ultimate decline in West Sumatra, Young not only provides a fascinating study of a topic hitherto rather neglected, he also reminds us of a number of things too often overlooked by those concerned with Java. By examining in detail exactly how the Cultivation System fitted in with Minangkabau social and political institutions, he reminds us that simply saying that the System varied in different places in Java is not enough—a deeper explanation of those variations is necessary. By showing how politico-military considerations were important in Dutch considerations regarding the System in West Sumatra, he reminds us how important it was that the Javanese, for the most part, just went along with the System and accepted the demands it placed on them. And by finally placing emphasis on advances in infrastructure, in administration, and in various other fields that were made concurrently with the operation of the System, he strengthens Van Niel's point about the danger of seeing the Cultivation System in isolation.

The Fernando and O'Malley paper also deals with a generally neglected topic, the way in which the Cultivation System operated in less densely populated parts of Java, those where sugar was not the key crop. In this study of government-enforced coffee cultivation on the slopes of the Cirebon highlands in the nineteenth century, it is the continuity between the System and the methods which preceded it which is most striking, while attention is also given to the fashion in which local-level leaders took advantage of the System to cement their position in society. Since coffee was grown by many more people under the Cultivation System than sugar was, and since coffee was responsible for delivering more money into indigenous hands than sugar did, this brief essay can serve as a corrective to the cane-dominated theorizing about the Cultivation System in Java. It can also serve a useful purpose if it sparks still further local studies of various crops raised through forced delivery in other sections of Java. And, read together with Young's paper on the Minangkabau Cultivation System, it raises fascinating questions for comparative work: though the people in the two areas differ so much with regard to social and political organization, their patterns of initial success and then inexorable decline while pursuing forced coffee cultivation run almost parallel, and a combination of ecological and economic factors is cited in both cases to account for that pattern.

Like the papers previously discussed, the Boomgaard essay is firmly rooted in extensive work with material provided by colonial officialdom. But where Elson, Knight, Van Niel, Young, and Fernando and O'Malley have all relied heavily as well on secondary literature and on the insights of colonial administrators, cautiously using tables of figures to support their major points, Boomgaard's is the first paper to rely almost completely on statistical data, which he obtained by scouring various kinds of official sources. With that material, he has computed some ratios for a number of residencies in northern and western Java from 1815 to 1875, presenting a picture from them that appears rather bleak. The trends for this period almost everywhere indicate a decline in arable land per household, and in the percentage of households owning land. At first glance this would seem to render null and void the Elson argument for increasing welfare under the Cultivation System. But a number of things must be recalled. Elson was talking about the total economic position of people, not just about their involvement with subsistence agriculture, which is what Boomgaard's data illustrate. It is clearly difficult to assess the typicality of the residencies on which Boomgaard has so far worked.[4] And at the heart of Boomgaard's paper is the heroic assumption that although the data are, in all probability, faulty, they are faulty in more or less the same measure, so that in arriving at ratios, the errors will be largely cancelled out. As a preliminary paper, however, it certainly serves to stir the pot.

The strong concentration on the Cultivation System in the initial essays of this collection is an indication of the major directional changes the field of economic history has taken in the last few decades. Fifty years ago, it was assumed that enough was known about the workings of the System; the major subject that would have been discussed when the colonial economy was being considered would probably have been the plantation sector, the dominant feature at the time in rural areas in many parts of the archipelago. In this collection, only Knight's essay (which aims to test general hypotheses about the Cultivation System in the area controlled by a single plantation), O'Malley's survey, and the Barlow and Drabble paper devote themselves in large measure to the study of plantations. In the O'Malley survey, some space is given to the varied ways in which plantations interacted with both the government and the indigenous people in their areas, but the paper's chief purpose is to point out when and where major developments in the plantation sector occurred. The result is a more complex picture than we usually have of this vital element in the colonial economy, a picture which considerably reduces the high profile normally assumed by the sugar plantations.

One of the reasons the sugar industry did not completely dominate the plantation scene in the twentieth century, despite its noticeable growth between 1900 and 1930, was the emergence of rubber as a major plantation product soon after the turn of the century. The paper by Barlow and Drabble looks at the performance of this latter industry in Indonesia up until World War II. It inspects the industry from two different angles, comparing developments in Indonesia with contemporary growth in Malaya, and focusing specifically upon the role played by government in determining how the industry would be run. Within the essay itself, this approach enables the authors to bring clarity to important aspects of a key industry, and to comment on the differences between plantation and smallholder production. For the collection as a whole, however, the comparative approach used in the essay has the added value of reminding those primarily concerned with colonial Indonesia that the way things were done there was not the only way—or indeed even the normal way—things were done by colonial powers. Realizing that affairs were conducted differently elsewhere provides two important advantages: it helps to reduce the deadening element of inevitability often connected with considering the past, and it provides another scale for weighing the performance of actors and institutions. (Here it should be noted that compared to the British across the Straits, the Dutch were not doing a bad job where rubber policies were concerned.)

The comparative element also plays an important part in the two essays contributed by Booth. In the first of those, the subject is colonial government revenues and expenditures between the 1830s and the end of the Dutch period, with attention paid as well to official attempts to regulate the colony's economy. An examination of the data provides Booth with an opportunity to point out and comment on important trends that occurred over time, as the government's revenue base and patterns of expenditure changed (both to the relative benefit of the Indonesian population) and as the size of the government's budget and its debts abroad increased. An examination of the data also lets Booth divide the history of fiscal policy in the colonial era into distinct periods with separate dynamics, a division which helps to illuminate other developments in the colony. But it is the comparison of colonial Indonesia's fiscal position with those of other countries and colonies which enables her to come to her ironic conclusion that the Dutch-controlled government was very large by contemporary standards but too small to accomplish what it aimed to achieve.

Booth's second essay is less overtly comparative, but its inquiry into the relationship in colonial Indonesia between expansion in exports and growth in production stems from theoretical considerations that have their basis in the different experiences of the Western countries and Japan on the one hand, and the African and Asian colonies and the Latin American countries on the other. Basically, the question is, "Does an expansion in export trade lead to more general income growth?" Given the difficulties bound to be encountered in applying such a broadly based question to such a long period of Indonesia's economic history (1860-1940), it is unrealistic to expect a completely satisfying answer. But Booth, by subdividing those years into four more manageable segments (1860-1900; 1900-1913; 1921-1929; 1929-1939), helps to clarify the issues which the question raises and is able to offer balanced judgments (and quite different ones) on each of those periods. Furthermore, her considerations regarding the period 1900-1913, the only one in which the answer would seem to be an unqualified "Yes, trade did lead to growth," stress the importance of correctly allocating the benefits of trade if growth is to ensue. It was the colonial government which was chiefly responsible for allocating those benefits in a manner conducive to growth in the early years of this century, but neither world markets nor government wisdom were constant enough in the colonial period to sustain the kind of growth needed.

Writing at a less abstract level, Jan van Laanen sketches an outline of the major institutions concerned with providing credit in colonial Indonesia. These range from the Java Bank, which had some of the attributes of a central bank, through large private institutions serving European agricultural and other commercial interests, to the government programs for providing credit to Indonesians, and finally to less formal arrangements with money-lenders. As van Laanen makes clear, we know more about the workings and the policies of the intermediate-level institutions—the commercial and agricultural banks and the government's organs for providing indigenous borrowers with credit—than we know about the topmost and bottommost levels, those that served the needs of the other banks and the vast bulk of the population. This paper, though providing material in its own right, actually represents a cry for assistance, a cry that deserves serious consideration both because the materials, as van Laanen insists, are there to do so much more, and because it is only by understanding more about banking and credit that we can learn more about the monetization of the colonial economy, which has been much spoken about but little studied since Burger was writing on the subject.

Dick's essay on the integration of the economy of colonial Indonesia makes contributions of two very different kinds. By bringing together information on production, commerce, and shipping, it illustrates how far from a single economic unit the archipelago was throughout the Dutch period, and how little effort the administration put into achieving a unified and coordinated economy. More intriguing than that, however, is Dick's strong concentration on the economic side of things, which he steadfastly puts first throughout his essay. There are places where this is bound to raise some hackles, but it has the great advantage of making us realize how interlaced with non-economic components—political, cultural, geographical, social, ecological—the other contributions to the volume have been.

The final substantive paper is a brief essay by Angus Maddison looking at Indonesia in the 1930s from a comparative perspective. Maddison shows in general how Indonesia's overwhelming dependence on exporting made the Dutch colony more susceptible than others to the ravages of the Great Depression, but he also points out how two aspects of her association with the metropole set Indonesia apart from the position of other Asian colonies. The first of these (reinforcing Booth's point about the comparatively expensive nature of the colonial government in Indonesia) is how strikingly large a role the Dutch played in the Indonesian economy and, just as striking, how large a role colonial incomes played in the domestic Dutch economy. The other factor that Maddison brings out is how Indonesia's colonial tie, more than precluding her from making the right decisions to soften the impact of the depression on her economy, actually linked her to imperial policies (maintenance of the gold standard, trade links with Holland, measures taken to limit Japanese imports) which damaged her far more severely than ought to have been the case.

The individual essays have their own strengths and weaknesses, but if one views them as a whole, a number of features stand out immediately—features generally reflective of the present state of Indonesian economic history of the colonial era.

The most notable characteristic one discerns looking at the essays as a group is the existence of a fault line practically down the middle. On one side are the works of those with serious historical training; on the other, the papers prepared by social scientists, chiefly economists. With regard to approach, concerns, or style, there is no trouble in differentiating between the two. The historians start with a general picture of Indonesia's past in mind; they attempt either to fill in gaps in that picture or to correct aspects of it they see as misleading; they are reluctant to stray from their evidence, which they are constantly assaying. The social scientists begin with a notion of how the society and economy ought systematically to have worked; they search through their data for patterns or anomalies worthy of explanation; they are far more daring at generalizing or simply admitting to shortcomings, and then pushing on despite them. There is also detectable between the two a different level of comfort in dealing with the past: the historians move around in it, accepting it on its own terms, while the economists, in particular, feel safer when they now and then cast a glance back over their shoulders at the present.

A second characteristic, and one associated with the first, is that there is still a high level of wariness and uncertainty connected with the use of figures from government sources, particularly those dealing with population, farmland, and crop production in the nineteenth century. There are in fact tremendous difficulties concerning the reliability of such data, some of them discussed intelligently in the Boomgaard paper, but again there is a notable gap between the way the historians here handle the figures and the way the social scientists do. The social scientists as a rule accept them as the best available, warn about the danger of assuming too much for them, and then proceed to use them as though they mean exactly what they purport to mean. The historians take the other tack, checking the figures against other bits of information, and explaining problems and trying to work through them rather than accepting them or ignoring them. On the other hand, while the historians are cautious in handling statistical data, they are also reluctant to part with them: social scientists from time to time simply discard as useless numbers which cannot be brought into agreement with accepted theories, but historians hang on to those bits of information, hoping eventually to be able to make sense of them or to use them with appropriate caveats.

Another feature of the essays as a whole is that there is a strong concentration on Java. This is not surprising, given the importance of that island and the depth of the Dutch administration there (and therefore the sources available for study) and given the fact that Dutch rule had not yet come to many places in the other islands until late in the nineteenth and early in the twentieth centuries. Still, the result is the reinforcement of the distortingly Java-centric view of general Indonesian history that already exists. The papers of Young and Dick are therefore particularly welcome contributions to the collection.

If the essays are strongly oriented toward Java, they are also strongly concentrated on the nineteenth century, and on the study of the Cultivation System in particular. The concentration on the nineteenth century is not accidental: the conference participants were in the main requested to present work on the period between 1800 and 1940, and at the conference itself, Anthony Reid presented a paper, since published elsewhere (Reid 1984), which ably examined a number of important economic issues in an earlier period of Indonesian history.

But it is inevitable, under these circumstances, that this collection has something of a truncated nature about it, taking off abruptly as it does from an arbitrary (though justifiable) base-year instead of flowing, as it ought, out of a more considered understanding of Indonesia's economic history during the V.O.C. period.

There are problems connected with expanding the coverage of economic history back before 1800—the scope and the nature of V.O.C. involvement with indigenous societies in Indonesia were different from those of the Dutch colonial government, and the information that was recorded and preserved by the Company for its own financial purposes is inevitably less complete than that available in later archives filled with documents compiled for administrative purposes. But those very problems may stimulate some researchers to shift the focus of seventeenth- and eighteenth-century discussions away from the preoccupation with long distance trade which characterizes the work of scholars such as Glamann (1958), and towards issues of production, consumption, and local commerce. Such a change in focus would in turn allow seventeenth- and eighteenth-century economic studies to dovetail more neatly into much of the modern work on the nineteenth century.

The concentration on the Cultivation System is also understandable given the controversy still surrounding the System and the masses of data readily available now to study it. But a result has been, as both Van Niel and Young remind us, a tendency to neglect other developments affecting society between 1830 and 1870, or to see those developments only inasmuch as they relate to the System. This approach has the potential to cause economic history to reflect only the view of the colonial administration, which was naturally enough highly interested in the success of the System, and allowed other economic developments to slide into the background.

A final characteristic of the papers is that there is a fair level of sophistication connected with them. In dealing with the Cultivation System, for example, it took almost a century for the literature on the subject to move from "The System is evil" to "The System was good for Holland and bad for Indonesia." In a fairly short space of time, we have moved from "The System was bad for Indonesia" to "It was good for some Indonesians and bad for others." We are now dealing with a situation where we are confident in saying "The System was good for certain Indonesians in certain places with certain crops and bad for others." This is fairly rapid progress, and it has been possible not least because those working in the field have been reading and thinking about each other's work and letting their ideas compete freely in the literature. Furthermore, there is in all the papers an interest in the long-term effects of the subjects being studied, an interest reflected in the attempts to tie specific conclusions into broader historical and theoretical issues. And, perhaps because of the present situation in Indonesia, there is lurking behind almost every paper collected here, the major question of whether the key factor influencing economic change was government programs or contact with the market and the money economy. That is an issue that is not going to be answered satisfactorily in the near future or in any short essay, but the fact that the authors of this collection are writing with it in the backs of their minds is an encouraging sign for the future.

Notes

1. Among other recent authors, most influential in this regard is probably John Smail, who was responsible for the sections on Indonesia in D.J. Steinberg *et al.*, (1971), the standard textbook on the modern history of the region.
2. Although I treat here the work of only these few administrator-scholars, there were, in fact, many more who turned their attention to aspects of Indonesian economic history. Special mention in this respect should be made of B.J.O. Schrieke, both for the numerous articles he wrote which contained important contributions to economic history (Schrieke 1955, 1957), and for the book he edited with essays by a number of other officials—most notably J.W. Meyer Ranneft, J. van Gelderen, and G.H. van der Kolff—considering different aspects of the subject (Schrieke 1929).
3. For further details of the C.E.I. series, see the bibliography.
4. In a further paper, Boomgaard (1984) has indicated that, for Java as a whole, per capita food availability improved substantially in the last decades of the System, from the nadir reached in the 1840s.

CHAPTER TWO

Peasant Poverty and Prosperity Under the Cultivation System in Java[1]

R. E. Elson

Introduction

This essay seeks to investigate, if only in a preliminary manner,[2] the effect of the Cultivation System on the material welfare of the Javanese peasantry. While the literature on the Cultivation System is vast, and while many of those who have taken up the pen have considered and commented upon this issue, remarkably little progress has been made towards even a moderately satisfactory conclusion. A recently published textbook gives a good indication of the *status quaestionis:*

> For the bulk of the population the *cultuurstelsel* seems to have brought little benefit. Van Niel has shown that in the period 1837-51 there were substantial population movements as villagers attempted to avoid labour burdens and a lack of profit by moving away from agricultural land into towns and larger cities, and out of the interior towards the coast. This produced some benefit, however, for those who remained on the land; such families were left with larger average holdings of land and more livestock. Both the availability and price of foodstuffs improved. But the distribution of such benefits was probably very uneven. Those who prospered under the *cultuurstelsel* included some who held land (or had a share in village lands), but were mostly Chinese entrepreneurs and the administrators and officials, many of whom not only received percentages but also held "official fields" *(ambtsvelden)* by virtue of their office. Although in some areas there is evidence of land ownership widening in order to spread the burdens, in others, land ownership appears to have become increasingly concentrated in the hands of a prosperous village elite. Others gained little, and many exercised the traditional option of flight to escape their burdens. In some areas there was extreme hardship. Defenders of the *cultuurstelsel* formerly pointed to the growth of the indigenous population as evidence of general prosperity. Since population growth had begun before the *cultuurstelsel* was introduced, and has since continued in Java (as in other developing countries) despite extreme hardship, the argument seems spurious (Ricklefs 1981, pp. 116-17).

This account, blurry and provisional in content and halting in style, stands out in a text which is otherwise generally notable for the crispness and dexterity with which evidence is evaluated and conclusions framed. That is no fault of the author, but is rather attributable to the poverty of the sources upon which he relied. In the first place, those sources include widely differing estimations of the impact of the System on the peasantry's standard of living. For example, G.H. van Soest, a liberal fiercely antagonistic towards the System, thundered that "instead of promoting the prosperity of the Javanese [the Cultivation System] unfailingly brought them to ruin" (van Soest 1869-71, vol.3, p.223); after twenty years of its operation, he claimed, "the beautiful island of Java presented a scene of unparalleled wretchedness and misery" (van Soest 1869-71, vol.3, p.223). By contrast, nearly a century later, Reinsma put forward the view that through the Cultivation System "not only was a need awakened among the native people for imported goods, but also a striving to increase possessions and to raise the standard of living in general" (Reinsma 1955, p.115). In the second place, the sources frequently reveal a dearth of empirical data on the way in which the System was actually conducted and how it affected people at various times and in various parts of Java. As Van Niel (1966) and Fasseur (1978) in particular have been at pains to point out over recent years, most of the standard works on the System had only limited and second-hand access to the voluminous archival materials which have become generally available only in the last couple of decades. Thirdly, a good part of the literature is seriously flawed by the particular concerns of its time, and especially by the propaganda ends it was meant to serve; the consequence is that the frailty of empirical underpinning in many works is fortified by a lushness of moral opprobrium and invective (Fasseur 1978, pp.143-45). Finally, these deficiencies have often caused the poverty/prosperity issue to be framed in a blinkered and unenlightening way, which might generally be characterised as the *zegen of vloek* (blessing or curse) approach to things: writers totted up balance sheets of subjectively determined advantages and disadvantages which usually took little account of historical contexts and frequently ignored such questions as the social distribution of rewards.

All this leads me to suspect that it might be useful to dissect this old problem and see whether fresh evidence and different perspectives might cast some new light upon it. The first thing that needs to be done, however, is to clarify just what "the issue" is. The notions of prosperity and poverty are notoriously cloudy ones; often floating within them are clusters of sometimes distantly related ideas: contentment, affluence, leisure, cultural achievement; alienation, want, physical hardship, spiritual misery. The imprecision of the major notions, indeed, has significantly contributed to the fogginess of the debate. I wish, therefore, to limit the discussion purely to the physical conditions of existence, involving consideration of such things as income, expenditure, taxation, food, clothing, shelter, and possessions. While it might be more interesting and informative to analyse peasants' spiritual well-being, or how they felt about the amount and nature of the labour demands imposed upon them, or even the longer term structural impact of the System on Javanese peasant society, these questions do not concern us here. The central question is that of deciding whether the Cultivation System, directly or indirectly, improved the material conditions of life of the peasants upon whom it was practised.

The Evidence for Impoverishment

The Cultivation System, introduced in Java by the Dutch colonial government in 1830, was a classic piece of colonial exploitation. Its sustaining aim was to increase forcibly the productive capacities of Javanese agriculture for the benefit of the Dutch treasury. In these terms, it was an outstanding success, producing large quantities of tropical export goods whose sale in Europe provided progressively greater sums of money to prop up Holland's beleaguered financial situation (Table 2.1).

TABLE 2.1 Financial Results of the Cultivation System, 1840-1859 ('000 guilders)

Crop	1840-1849	1850-1854	1855-1859
Coffee	+64,827	+77,540	+105,599
Sugar	- 4,082	+ 3,385	+ 33,705
Indigo	+15,562	+ 6,759	+ 5,855
Cochineal	+ 499	+ 445	- 44
Cinnamon	- 323	+ 47	- 206
Pepper	+ 191	+ 205	+ 203
Tea	- 2,181	- 1,841	- 2,449
Tobacco	- 95	- 5	- 61
Total	+74,398	+86,535	+142,603

Source: Fasseur (1975, pp. 119-20)

This surge in production and profit came almost entirely from the forced labour of the Javanese peasantry. The colonial authorities provided very little by way of capital investment, and their attempts to improve the techniques of production and manufacture were patchy and generally ineffective (Furnivall

1944, p.127). The reliance on coerced labour to produce returns has, more than anything else, given the Cultivation System a thoroughly bad reputation. The predominant view in the literature has been that the System's success in generating profits went hand in hand with the systematic impoverishment of the Javanese peasantry who were pressed into its service: "So, then, we have the odd phenomenon in Java, that this island annually produces almost 40 million guilders of wealth, but that the population of this same island is unable to provide for its own needs" (van Hoevell 1849-51, vol.1, p.63). Given the currency and persistence of this assessment, it is appropriate to begin the investigation with a presentation and analysis of the substance of this argument for impoverishment. What follows is necessarily generalised; it draws on a variety of sources and a range of views about the workings of a System which was embroidered with a myriad of regional and chronological variations. As such it will gloss over many important local practices and authorial emphases which deserve closer consideration.

Let us look first at the way in which the System operated with regard to the organisation of the forced cultivations. In the case of coffee, the largest and most profitable cultivation, peasants' difficulties began with the fact that the crop grew best in sparsely populated foothill and upland areas. It was particularly successful in the so-called *woeste gronden* of West Java (Priangan), south-central Java (Kedu), and Java's eastern corner (Pasuruan and Besuki). But most of the people required to work it were lowland dwellers whose normal occupation was wet-rice cultivation. This meant that those peasants assigned to coffee cultivation had either to trudge many kilometres every day to the coffee gardens or forest plantations,[3] or, less commonly, to leave their villages for months at a time for coffee service, living in the meantime in rough temporary shelters near the coffee-planting areas.[4] Peasants had to clear forest areas and lay out gardens, plant young trees and tend them to maturity, and, when the time was right, pick the crop, dry it, and shell it.[5] When these tasks were completed, peasants were also required to deliver the produce to one of the small number of government storehouses established in the interior, usually carrying the beans on their shoulders because of the poor state of roads, or because they lacked the animals and vehicles to transport them any other way. For all this endeavour, peasants were paid *f*25 for every *picul* (62 kilograms) of coffee delivered, but from this sum the government subtracted two-fifths as land rent and another *f*3 to meet its own administrative costs and those of transporting the crop from the local storehouses to the major ports for export.[6]

In contrast to coffee, the other major crops of the Cultivation System, sugar and indigo, were grown on irrigated fields which would otherwise have found themselves under rice. Both crops were rotated around the available rice fields, so that before each was planted, peasants had to tear down the intricate arrangement of dykes and channels which normally serviced rice crops, and prepare large garden tracts for planting cane or indigo cuttings; when the fields were returned for domestic cultivation they had to be cleared of roots and reconstructed. In the case of sugar in particular, fields were sometimes organised in large complexes worked by a number of villages together. This required peasants to travel long distances from their villages to the work site; more importantly, it meant that some villages found nearly all their rice land under cane and had to use land in distant villages for domestic cropping.[7] More commonly, as time went by, crop sites were arranged so that each village had its own, but this also caused problems where villages had little or no land fit for cane or indigo; peasants in this situation often had to travel to villages intensively given over to export cropping to fulfill their cultivation duties and surrender a portion of their own rice land to the inhabitants of those villages. In return for cultivating the crop to maturity, sugar workers were paid in proportion to the amount of sugar manufactured from the cane they grew; they received extra payments for harvesting, cane transport, and factory labour, all of which were also usually conducted as forced labour. Where indigo was planted, peasants were required not only to plant and tend the crop, but also to harvest it (three or four times a year), transport the leaves to local factories, and labour at the unpleasant process which transformed the produce into dry cakes of dye. Unlike sugar workers, they received only a single payment for these different tasks, based on the amount of manufactured indigo produced.[8]

One senior official asserted that under the Cultivation System peasants were required to perform as much as four or five times the amount of labour customarily demanded before 1830 (Anon. 1851, p.35). Generally, the returns peasants received in the form of crop and wage payments were in no way proportionate to the extra time and effort demanded of them, far below the market value of the crops, and in the case of export crops grown on village land, much less than the value of the income which could have been expected had the land been used for domestic crops.[9] Especially with indigo cultivation, the moneys received as crop payments were miserably low and the labour requirements alarmingly high. G.R. Knight, for example, has uncovered a *controleur's* report from Pekalongan in 1851 which included an estimation that a peasant indigo cultivator spent 176 days of the year planting, tending, harvesting and delivering indigo, and another 76 days working at the local factory. With 252 days thereby consumed, the *controleur* reckoned that the peasant would need to work 390 days a year if he were properly to cultivate his domestic crops (Knight 1982b, p.22). While the labour demands of indigo were not so arduous in every Residency, it is likely that few peasants escaped with less than 150 days work a year on the crop.[10] As an indication of the payments made, indigo planters in the year of the *controleur's* report received the princely sum of *f*4.15 each—less than 2 *duit* (1 *duit* = 1/120 guilder) per day. Elsewhere things were not much better: the payment in the Priangan was *f*9.42, in Cirebon *f*8.18, in Besuki *f*8.117, in Kedu *f*9.33, in Bagelen *f*7.92 and in Banyumas *f*9.06.[11]

Apart from the additional quota of labour and the scanty recompense they received, peasants encountered a range of other problems associated with the impact of forced cultivations on domestic agriculture. In the first place, as already indicated, the labour demands involved frequently made heavy inroads on the amount of time available for domestic cropping. Despite claims to the contrary, the labour cycles of domestic and export agriculture were not complementary. Sugar and indigo planting, for example, often interfered with rice planting and tilling; the preparation of coffee lands tended to conflict with the harvesting of *padi* (J. & P. Alexander 1979, pp.35-36; van Hoevell 1849-51, vol.1, pp.69-70).[12] Secondly, crops like sugar and indigo took up large areas of the best and most valuable peasant rice land, usually for periods of up to 18 months (Fasseur 1975, p.213, note 93).[13] Thirdly, rice land had to be made available for these export crops at specified times, with the result that peasants sometimes had to forego a second crop of rice or corn or vegetables because there was simply insufficient time for it to mature and be harvested before the land was requisitioned for the export crop. Sometimes, too, the export crop remained in the field at a time when rice would otherwise have been planted, causing damaging delays to the rice-planting cycle. In 1856, for example, the milling of cane in one factory in Kediri did not finish until 8 December, and at another it continued until 19 December.[14] Most frequently, these situations forced peasants to plant quicker ripening but lower yielding *padi* varieties—generally called *padi genjah*—to ensure that they could insert a full crop in the abbreviated time left to them (Anon. 1869, pp.45-96; Vitalis 1851, pp.56-57). Fourthly, export crops grown on peasant land had first use of irrigation water. This was especially burdensome for the peasantry where government sugar was grown, for large amounts of water were needed to irrigate newly planted stands of cane and power mills driven by water wheels during the (dry) milling season. In Cirebon, for example, it was claimed that because of the sugar industry's use of dry season water supplies, only 26,157 of the 350,000 *bouw* of land available could be planted in second crops in 1866.[15] Fifthly, rice crops planted on land previously used for sugar or indigo often yielded significantly lower returns.[16] Sixthly, the Cultivation System multiplied the demands made upon peasants' stocks of cattle. Not only was there a large increase in the amount of field work to be performed with more intensive patterns of export agriculture, but also a much greater need for cattle to transport the fruits of the System from field to factory or port.[17]

These difficulties were part of the normal procedure of the Cultivation System, to be faced year in and year out by the peasantry. But there were other and less regular problems arising from the System's introduction. An important one was the rampant experimentation with new crops and new settings which was especially prevalent in the first decade or so of the System's operations, but which continued on a diminished scale through most of its history. For example, crop failures of coffee in Kedu in the late 1840s were attributed to the choice of unsuitable land and the introduction of new methods of cultivation and fertilisation.[18] Behind this was the government's eagerness to diversify export cropping as much as possible in order to ensure regularity of profits in the face of fluctuating market prices and the possibility of specific crop failures. The result was that local officials—many of them reportedly not very able and most virtually ignorant of the peculiarities and particular problems of tropical commercial agriculture[19]—found themselves encouraged to introduce new crops or experiment with familiar ones in new environments.[20] For example, Louis Vitalis, an Inspector of Cultivations during the 1830s, recounted the tale of about 2,000 coffee planters toiling in one Residency on infertile land for five years to produce three piculs of coffee (Vitalis 1851, p.3). Sugarcane was planted on high ground in Cirebon where it could not be irrigated; it was subsequently damaged by a period of drought.[21] Indigo was tried for four years in Banten before being abandoned (Cornets de Groot van Kraayenburg 1862, p.129). The government introduced exotic crops like silkworms and cochineal with disastrous results for the peasants unfortunate enough to have them foisted on them. Despite promises to the contrary, peasants were not compensated for the frequent crop failures that resulted from the mingling of enthusiasm, ignorance and incompetence (Fasseur 1975, p.23). The best they could hope for was some relief in their land rent assessment.

In addition to the tasks directly associated with the forced cultivations, the Cultivation System levied huge amounts of labour from the peasants—paid for only scantily or not at all—for the construction of public works. These labour services, exacted over and above those which peasants were accustomed to provide for their indigenous leaders or their own communities, were devoted to the infrastructural improvements deemed necessary for the Cultivation System's operation and success. The scheme required road and bridge building for crop transport, the improvement of port facilities, the construction of offices and residences for officials and of factories and storehouses for produce, and the expansion of the cultivated area through the building of dams and the excavation of irrigation channels. Java's growing importance to the Dutch even required the conscription of huge numbers of peasants for work on defence fortifications, the most notorious of which were those erected at Surabaya in the middle of the century (van Hoevell 1849-51, vol.1, pp.204-5).

Taxes in labour were accompanied by taxes in money. Land rent continued to be assessed and collected, even on fields occupied by forced cultivations; indeed these fields usually attracted higher assessments than others (Fasseur 1975, p.25). Moreover, peasants were not permitted to accrue unhindered the benefits, such as they were, which came from their vastly increased range of activities and duties. Land reclaimed by forced labour on irrigation works became subject to land rent after only a short period. The moneys paid to the peasantry in crop and wage payments were frequently hunted down by the government through the simple expedient of progressively raising land rent assessments. The Resident of Rembang, for example, took to his task with such enthusiasm that land rent payments in his Residency rose from *f*301,191 in 1844 to *f*593,635 in 1848.[22] Governor-General Rochussen estimated in 1847 that about two-thirds of crop payments returned to the Government through taxes of various kinds (Fasseur 1975, p.40).

Finally, to bring to an end this litany of criticism of the System and its operations, it is clear that it provided an unusually fertile soil for corruption—at the peasantry's expense—by those empowered to manage it. The purposely vague guidelines governing the utilisation of peasant labour, for example, gave rise to the practice of officials, indigenous and otherwise, using peasant labour for their private purposes (van Deventer 1865-66, vol.2, pp.750-52; vol.3, p.87). More importantly, it was extremely common for officials to use their enhanced powers to advantage themselves in wealth and power. There were numerous cases of indigenous officials and village chiefs withholding portions of the crop payments they were supposed to deliver to the peasantry (Fasseur 1975, p.22); many employed their influence and the threat of coercive state power to intimidate villagers into ceding their land to them.[23] The system of incentive payments for export crop production *(kultuurprocenten)* and the desire for bureaucratic promotion often prompted officials to increase the production of exportable goods at the risk of overextending the land and people in the areas under their care (Reinsma 1980, p.65 ff; van Hoevell 1862-5, vol.1, p.144; Fasseur 1975, pp.16-17, 29).

According to critics of the System, all these impositions and abuses came home to roost in the mid- and late 1840s when a series of catastrophic epidemics and crop failures brought famine and death to thousands of peasants in the north central Java littoral. According to the received view, the famines resulted from a combination of high taxation and overutilisation of land and labour for forced cultivations; peasants found it impossible to produce sufficient agricultural goods to meet their financial commitments and to feed themselves. The resulting desolation was seen by many critics, and especially by the increasingly strident liberals in Holland, as the inevitable consequence of the logic of the Cultivation System. The furor that arose stirred the first waves of indignation and shame that were eventually to bring the System to an end.

The Impoverishment Argument: A Critique

At first glance the argument for impoverishment, based on the evidence recounted above, seems a powerful one. Moreover, variations of it have been presented so often and in so many places that we run the risk of accepting it without demur. In my view, however, it does not provide compelling evidence that the Cultivation System impoverished the Javanese peasantry. My argument has two basic grounds. The first is that the case for impoverishment has serious logical and structural deficiencies. The second is that there is a large stock of countervailing evidence which suggests that the Cultivation System promoted a previously unknown level of general prosperity among the peasantry. Let us consider each of these in turn.

The argument for impoverishment clearly establishes that there were times and places when peasants suffered great physical and material deprivations which were directly attributable to the System's operations or which occurred under its aegis. This, however, is not equivalent to demonstrating a general case of impoverishment. In the first place, much of the evidence and argument is of the "it stands to reason" variety—it stands to reason, for example, that if peasants were required to spend inordinate amounts of time on forced export cultivations, their domestic cropping would suffer; it stands to reason that if peasants lost access to their land and received much less from crop payments than they would have from domestic agriculture, their incomes would decline. In itself, this form of circumstantial argumentation is not invalid, but both the way in which the evidence is mounted and the assumptions behind its use are, in this particular case, questionable. What "stands to reason" might not be borne out in fact, especially when reasoning from circumstantial evidence is used in place of thorough empirical investigation of what actually took place. Indeed, the popularity of this style of argument is indicative of the evidential shortcomings remarked upon earlier. What needs to be shown is not what "stands to reason" but what actually happened, an exercise which frequently reveals complexities, unconsidered variables, and too readily accepted assumptions, and which may serve to alter radically the conclusions arrived at.

In the second place, the argument for impoverishment lacks an historical context. Grounded in the basic assumption that coerced exploitation must impoverish, it pays almost no attention to the situation obtaining in Java before 1830, even though its logic would seem to call for the establishment of some base line around that date against which subsequent standards of living during the period of the Cultivation System might be measured.[24] While it must be admitted that little systematic research into the economic life of the Javanese peasantry during the 1820s, particularly outside the Vorstenlanden, has been undertaken, there are some snippets of information which point to relatively low standards of material welfare in many places at that time. For example, in an 1824 report from Cirebon, we read of a variety of oppressions visited upon the peasantry by their chiefs, a lack of money for trade, and a decline in taxation receipts;[25] in 1823 we read of rice shortages in the Priangan;[26] in Semarang in 1826 there are reports of the deleterious effects of the Java War on the Residency's agriculture;[27] in Rembang in 1829 we are informed that the Residency cannot be expected to provide a high standard of welfare, that it cannot produce enough food for itself, that taxes were in arrears;[28] Pekalongan, too, had insufficient rice for its own needs around that time;[29] and there was little sign of prosperity in Bagelen in 1830 (Anon. 1858, pp.65-84). Whatever the case, it seems desirable that if the argument for impoverishment is to be put, it needs to proceed from the basis of a thorough understanding of the society which existed before the allegedly impoverishing transformations took place.

Thirdly, if the argument for impoverishment is timeless, it is also motionless. By this I mean that the focus of the analysis, the peasants, are portrayed as passive victims of an order over which they have no control and from which they can gather no advantage. Their indigenous sphere of activity is seen as limited and static, their indigenous stock of resources more or less fixed, their range of options circumscribed, their ingenuity and adaptability negligible. When the peasantry's lot under the Cultivation System is painted in these tones, there is a good deal of force to the argument for impoverishment: peasants are a helpless set of objects, expropriated of an increasing portion of the little they have. As we shall see in the second part of my argument, however, this perspective involves a serious distortion of peasant life and attitudes. Seen from a different point of view, in which peasants are actors and managers, the case for impoverishment begins itself to look rather emaciated.

The Countervailing Evidence

Having considered some of the limitations of the impoverishment argument, let us turn to a discussion of the countervailing evidence. I have found it convenient to organise it into three categories: 1) contemporary descriptive accounts or assessments; 2) statistical evidence; and 3) evidence pointing to a radical expansion of the domestic economy, with all that entailed, under the impact of the Cultivation System.

Impressions. The first category of evidence comprises accounts and impressions, mostly from official sources, which indicate improvements in the material conditions of the peasantry in various parts of Java under the System. Many of them come from the eastern half of East Java, an area subject to intensive forced cultivation, but where peasants appear to have gained considerable material benefit thereby. In Pasuruan Residency, for example, Residents' reports point to increasing internal trade, greater circulation of money, great financial profits from the forced cultivations, expanding employment opportunities, improved housing and clothing, the rapid and full collection of taxation, and numerous signs of emerging indigenous entrepreneurship.[30] There seems to be some substance to these claims, because even the harshest critics of the Cultivation System tended to except Pasuruan from their otherwise generally depressing assessments. W.R. van Hoevell, for instance, a trenchant opponent of the actual operations, if not the idea, of the System, found in his travels through Pasuruan in 1847 "nothing but prosperity and welfare ... nothing but activity and industriousness, nothing but contentment and happiness" (van Hoevell 1849-51, vol.2, p.145). Further east, in Besuki, the records contain repeated assertions that prosperity among the people was increasing, with hitherto unknown quantities of money circulating as a result of payments made for labour in the government cultivations.[31] In Surabaya, van Hoevell remarked on "the riches, the liveliness and the bustle in this delightful region" (van Hoevell 1849-51, vol.1, p.171). Admittedly, Besuki and Surabaya, like Pasuruan, were often considered to be exceptions from the situation obtaining generally throughout Java, but there are numerous testimonies to prosperity elsewhere in Java at various times during the period of the Cultivation System. In south central Java, for example, reports from Kedu, Bagelen, Kediri and Madiun spoke of increased economic activity and welfare (Anon. 1849, pp.169-83; Anon. 1862, pp.133-38).[32] In north central Java, the Dutch "demographer" Bleeker remarked on the industry and prosperity of Tegal and Pekalongan after journeying through these places (Bleeker 1849, pp.186-89, 264-67). In 1857, Pekalongan's Acting Resident spoke of a "degree" of welfare brought to the peasantry by the government sugar industry,[33] and in the late 1860s the Resident reported that land rent was collected rapidly and with almost no arrears, and that some people even paid their taxes before they were due.[34] Cirebon appears, by all accounts, to have enjoyed a burst of unusual prosperity in the late 1830s and early 1840s,[35] and despite the deprivations visited on parts of the Residency by famine soon afterwards, by the late 1860s the people were thought to be generally prosperous.[36] Even in Semarang, the Residency most devastated by the famines of the late 1840s, the Resident in 1851 reported a rapid return to well-being and claimed that Semarang would soon be numbered among the most prosperous residencies in Java.[37] Further to the west, in the Priangan, evidence presented by the Governor-General seemed to point to a continuing and improving state of welfare, exemplified by increasing population and cattle stocks, a rapid rate of land reclamation, generally rising food production, and increasing sales of salt.[38]

At a more general level, a little noted enquiry into the economic situation in Java for the period 1856-1868 brought the nearly unanimous response from the Residents that general prosperity had increased markedly in that period. In particular, they pointed to large increases in the amount of land brought under cultivation, a busy commercial life, increases in population and rates of consumption, improvements in housing, food and clothing, and increasing domestic production as evidence for their claims. Summarising their submissions, the Governor-General reported to the Minister of Colonies that "Java in recent years, in a material sense, has advanced and developed to a surprising degree".[39]

All of this sort of evidence needs to be considered with some caution. Not only is it frequently vague and impressionistic, but it usually originated from officials whose careers were not advanced by reporting failures. Nonetheless, it cannot be entirely discounted on these grounds. As the evidence surveyed earlier indicates, officials were not always tardy and deceitful in reporting the unfavourable; we should not, therefore, be too hasty to discard assessments purely because of their positive content, especially given their substantial quantities and geographical diversity. At the very least, they indicate that the view of the Cultivation System as an era of economic disaster for the Javanese peasantry is in need of some qualification.

Statistical Evidence. This evidence is strengthened by a consideration of the second category of evidence, that of a statistical nature. Enumeration in nineteenth-century Java was notoriously imprecise, but assuming that the degree of imprecision was more or less constant from year to year, the available statistics possess a good measure of internal coherence and provide a basis for some instructive conclusions. Let us begin with an examination of the pattern of crop payments and land rent for the major government cultivations (Tables 2.2, 2.3 and 2.4). Tables 2.2 and 2.3 depict the relationship between crop payments made to sugar and indigo cultivators respectively, as well as the land rent levied on the total fields of those cultivators. In the case of sugar, the total crop payments after 1838 were always greater than the total of land rent due from the peasants concerned. Looking at this relationship from a regional point of view, planters in a great majority of Residencies were in a position to clear the land rent owed on all their fields (i.e. not just those subject to government crops) from crop payments alone. Moreover, when one averages things out for individual forced sugar cultivators, the difference between crop payments and land rent became more and more marked in the peasantry's favour as time went by; not only could the average cultivator pay his total land rent bill from sugar money, but he nearly always had a few guilders left over for other purposes. The regular availability of these crop moneys had two important ameliorative consequences for the peasants. First, they provided a regular source of cash, not otherwise available in such quantities and so widely, for the purchase of a great variety of necessities and consumables. Second, they tended to free forced cultivators from reliance on the cheap sale of their *padi* crops as a means of accumulating cash needed to

TABLE 2.2 Relationship between Land Rent and Crop Payments: Sugar, 1837-1851[a]

Year	Land rent levied on cultivators (thousand) (guilders)	Crop payments to cultivators (thousand) (guilders)	Number of Residencies where cultivated	Number of Residencies where crop payment exceeds land rent	Average land rent assessment per cultivator (guilders)	Average crop payment per cultivator (guilders)
1837	1,291	1,262	10	5	10.1	10.9
1838	1,465	1,391	12	6	11.9	11.2
1839	1,409	1,723	12	7	10.1	13.3
1840	1,732	1,990	13	11	11.8	13.5
1841	1,589	2,039	13	10	10.6	13.6
1842	1,734	2,336	13	10	11.0	14.7
1843	1,881	2,417	13	11	11.4	14.7
1844	1,967	2,645	13	11	11.8	15.9
1845	2,225	2,774	13	11	13.6	17.0
1846	2,033	2,816	13	10	13.2	18.2
1847	1,988	2,926	13	9	12.7	18.7
1848	1,938	2,911	12	10	12.7	18.1
1849	2,390	2,907	12	9	15.1	18.4
1850	2,434	3,344	12	10	16.0	22.0
1851	2,218	3,380	12	11	14.2	21.7

[a] I have converted the value of moneys before 1846 into *recepis*-guilders. In columns 4 and 5, I have assumed for Madiun and Kediri, where a fictive rather than actual system of land rent existed, that crop payments exceeded the fictive levy unless the figures clearly show the contrary. Lack of comparable data after 1851 has prevented me from extending the data to 1860.

Source: *Kultuur Verslagen*, 1837-1851.

TABLE 2.3 Relationship between Land Rent and Crop Payments: Indigo, 1837-1851[a]

Year	Land rent levied on cultivators (thousand) (guilders)	Crop payments to cultivators (thousand) (guilders)	Number of Residencies where cultivated	Number of Residencies where crop payment exceeds land rent	Average land rent assessment per cultivator (guilders)	Average crop payment per cultivator (guilders)
1837	863	1,331	10	7	6.8	10.3
1838	905	1,243	10	6	6.9	9.3
1839	1,161	2,215	10	7	6.8	12.8
1840	1,437	2,605	10	6	6.1	12.7
1841	1,455	2,116	11	6	7.2	10.5
1842	1,619	1,738	10	6	8.5	9.0
1843	1,724	1,879	10	6	8.1	9.9
1844	1,190	1,765	9	6	6.2	9.2
1845	2,149	1,711	9	4	11.6	9.2
1846	1,444	1,972	9	7	8.7	11.8
1847	1,671	1,449	9	4	10.5	9.1
1848	1,340	1,331	9	6	10.1	11.0
1849	1,091	1,113	9	5	8.9	8.1
1850	940	732	8	5	8.8	6.9
1851	935	826	8	4	8.9	7.8

[a] Madiun and Kediri are treated here in the same fashion as in Table 2.2. I have excluded Priangan from consideration in columns 4 and 5 because no land rent system existed there. All moneys have been converted to recepis-guilders. Lack of comparable data after 1851 has prevented me from extending the table to 1860.

Source: *Kultuur Verslagen*, 1837-1851

satisfy land rent obligations, something that had pressed heavily upon them in the years before the introduction of the Cultivation System (Van Niel 1981, pp.35-37). Land rent was frequently deducted from crop payments before they were distributed to peasants, or, more commonly in the later years of the System, collected shortly after the full sums had been paid out (Fasseur 1978, pp.148-49). While these practices doubtless helped the Dutch to achieve a more efficient and profitable result from their taxation operations, at the same time it allowed peasants the opportunity (other things being equal) to reap greater profits from the sale of their rice by withholding it until prices improved on the market; this probably contributed significantly to the notable rise in rice prices during the course of the System.

Indigo, in comparison to sugar, was a much less profitable undertaking for the peasantry; as we have seen, it had the reputation of being the most burdensome and impoverishing segment of the scheme of forced cultivations. This notoriety is borne out to some extent by Table 2.3, but not nearly as starkly as might have been expected. It was not until 1845 that the total amount of crop payments for indigo cultivators dipped below the level of land rent assessed against them, and in 1846 and 1849 payments again exceeded the sum due in land rent. Even when levels of remuneration, measured against land rent, went into decline after 1844, cultivators in more than half the Residencies involved were still in a position to pay their land rent obligations with crop moneys and retain some cash besides. For them, and for the good numbers of peasants who were only slightly in deficit, indigo provided cash and opportunity which would not otherwise have been available, for much the same reasons as those relating to sugar. This analysis is not meant to deny that indigo cultivation frequently brought much material hardship and want in those places like Banten and Pekalongan where it grew with little success and reward, but it does indicate on a general level that the impoverishing effects of indigo have been somewhat overrated.

The third of this series of tables, Table 2.4, depicts the situation with regard to coffee. In the absence of data on coffee planters' land rent obligations, it is impossible to construct a table similar to those for sugar and indigo. In its place I have compiled a table which shows the relationship between crop payments for coffee in different Residencies at various intervals in the period 1837-1860 and the total land rent assessed in these Residencies. Accompanying this information are data depicting the number of coffee planting households *(huisgezinnen)* as a percentage of the total number of agricultural households in the various Residencies. With few exceptions (most notably Rembang, where coffee cultivation was a disaster for the peasantry involved from the beginning to the end of the Cultivation System), the table points to a remarkable influx of funds for the peasantry resulting from work in the coffee industry. In Pasuruan, for example,

TABLE 2.4 Crop Payments for Coffee as a Percentage of Total Land Rent Assessments per Residency, and Coffee Planting Households as a Percentage of Agricultural Households per Residency, 1837-1860[a]

Residency	Crop payment as a percentage of total land rent assessment						Coffee planting households as a percentage of total agricultural households					
	1837	1840	1845	1850	1855	1860	1837	1840	1845	1850	1855	1860
Banten	22.2	18.5	13.2	25.4	43.7	20.7	87.1	82.5	29.2	18.1	28.4	21.5
Cirebon	32.1	30.8	21.3	48.9	73.0	32.5	21.9	24.2	23.8	32.0	29.8	30.5
Tegal	49.8	72.9	40.4	77.7	92.4	73.3	18.7	19.9	16.1	20.2	22.4	19.0
Pekalongan	83.1	103.1	51.9	70.3	85.6	143.9	31.8	18.3	23.1	16.8	22.1	27.3
Semarang	50.8	70.3	38.3	150.1	58.0	97.6	41.0	35.0	24.5	27.2	26.3	19.9
Jepara	46.8	21.8	10.7	15.6	9.8	11.9	25.3	13.5	13.3	7.9	7.8	7.3
Rembang	0.2	1.2	2.5	6.2	2.8	0.6	39.8	22.2	5.2	4.3	4.2	1.2
Surabaya	4.9	6.4	8.2	10.0	7.4	9.9	1.3	1.6	2.2	2.4	1.9	2.8
Pasuruan	226.1	205.9	141.0	197.9	218.0	282.3	32.3	42.9	47.5	49.3	47.7	47.9
Besuki	61.7	104.2	64.6	109.7	85.0	74.3	37.7	41.6	42.2	40.5	45.2	38.7
Kedu	207.8	203.0	102.6	123.7	141.3	178.6	100.0	108.8	109.3	103.4	97.3	91.4
Bagelen	34.2	34.1	23.5	51.5	66.0	72.1	14.9	27.9	23.3	27.2	32.2	27.2
Banyumas	107.3	71.0	42.9	26.7	48.2	38.8	58.3	52.6	45.2	47.7	47.8	29.0

[a] I have excluded Priangan, Madiun, Kediri and Pacitan from this table because of the absence of the land rent system in the first and the existence of a fictive system of land rent in the others. The 1855 and 1860 figures include data for Probolinggo Residency, part of Besuki before 1855.

Source: Kultuur Verslagen, 1837, 1840, 1845, 1850; Koloniaal Verslag, 1855, 1860 and 1866, Bijlage I.

where coffee-planting households made up a third to a half of all agricultural households, the moneys received were generally sufficient to pay the total land rent bill of all land-holding peasants in the Residency twice over. The statistics are less spectacular elsewhere, but they have a similar thrust. They indicate the presence, through the forced coffee cultivations, of enormous amounts of disposable income in the hands of the peasantry, something that could not have occurred on so large a scale in the years before 1830.

These conclusions about the financial benefits accruing from forced cultivations for those peasants pressed into their service sit well with a second set of statistics which portrays some patterns of expenditure and consumption during the period of the Cultivation System, set against population figures (Table 2.5,). These figures indicate that, even taking into consideration the rapidly burgeoning population of Java, peasants were able to spend increasing per capita amounts on possessions and consumption. Admittedly, one might question whether the data under individual heads point to increasing prosperity. For example, it might be argued that increasing imports of foreign cloth went hand-in-hand with the destruction of the indigenous textile industry, which must have caused enormous difficulties and labour relocation for the large numbers of women employed in it; again, the growth in revenue from pawnshop farms might be interpreted as a sign of encroaching poverty in a rapidly monetising society. Taking all the figures into account, however, it seems difficult to avoid the conclusion that the spending power of the peasantry had grown rapidly from the time of the introduction of the Cultivation System in the early 1830s.

The third set of statistics looks at domestic cropping or, more specifically, the expansion of cultivable land and the growth of rice production (Table 2.6). Like the data previously presented, it casts doubts on the accuracy of the argument for impoverishment. One of the key features of that argument, as we have seen, was that the Cultivation System robbed peasants of substantial portions of their rice fields and of the time necessary to work them properly. One consequence of this line of reasoning was that whatever material benefits peasants received from crop payments and the like in the forced cultivations were rendered negligible by the damage done to domestic agriculture. But Table 2.6 shows clearly that peasants held their own, and even marginally improved their position with regard to rice production, during the years of the Cultivation System. Despite the growth in population, the per capita area of land put to peasant cropping grew slightly, that land became a little more productive, and as a result, per capita rice production improved quite significantly. These figures, of course, tell us nothing of how this rice was marketed, distributed, and consumed, or whether these activities advantaged some peasants at the cost of others. But they do point to the conclusion that even with a greatly increased regimen of

TABLE 2.5 Some Patterns of Expenditure and Consumption, Java-Madura, 1830-1860

Year	Population (1)	Government revenue from opium farms (guilders) (2)	Government revenue from slaughter-tax farms Cattle (guilders) (3)	Government revenue from slaughter-tax farms Pigs (guilders) (4)	Government revenue from pawn shop farms (guilders) (5)
1830	7,065		97	50	55
1835	?	4,650	191	76	129
1840	?	5,996	250	124	206
1845	9,551	7,655	311	123	271
1850	9,570	5,355	312	110	269
1855	10,916	6,534	479	126	284
1860	12,719	10,539	592	149	350

Year	Government revenue from salt monopoly (guilders) (6)	Value of imports of cloth and cotton goods (guilders) (7)	Value of total imports of goods (guilders) (8)	Numbers of domestic animals Buffaloes (9)	Numbers of domestic animals Cattle (10)	Numbers of domestic animals Horses (11)
1830	?	4,330	11,989			
1835	2,595	4,836	11,453			
1840	3,658	13,373	24,570	1,272	399	271
1845	4,513	11,111	23,349	1,460	531	346
1850	4,405	9,959	21,873	1,425	530	364
1855	4,114	14,571	29,103	1,621	600	387
1860	4,631	21,010	42,249	1,911	758	444

[a] Data do not include information about Bagelen and Kedu Residencies for the year 1850.

[b] The figures are affected by a price rise from f6.81 per picul to f8 per picul in 1852. The price was lowered to f6.80 and then f6.72 in 1856.

Sources: (1) & (7): "Java en Madura. 1825-1869".
(2): Letter Director of Resources and Domains to Governor-General, 30 April 1840; Koloniaal Verslag, 1851, p. 105; 1856, p. 87; 1860, pp. 92-3.
(3): "Opbrengst der verpachtigen."
(4) & (5): Reinsma (1955 pp. 175-6).
(6): "Zout op Java en Madura".
(8 - 11): Reinsma (1955, pp. 175-6).

TABLE 2.6 Cultivable Land and Rice Production, 1837-1851[a]

Year	Population ('000)	Area of land under peasant cultivation (ha)	Area per head of population (ha)	Paddy production ('000 quintals)	Paddy production (quintals per ha)	Paddy production per head of population (quintals)
1837	6,284	891	.14	11,803	13.25	1.88
1838	6,145	897	.15	11,906	13.27	1.94
1989	6,483	909	.14	11,499	12.65	1.77
1840	6,705	913	.14	13,138	14.39	1.96
1841	6,857	980	.14	14,705	15.01	2.14
1842	6,912	988	.14	15,072	15.26	2.18
1843	7,168	994	.14	15,635	15.73	2.18
1844	7,248	987	.14	13,852	14.03	1.91
1845	7,460	1,049	.14	16,483	15.71	2.21
1846	7,470	1,075	.14	15,927	14.82	2.13
1847	7,447	1,066	.14	16,105	15.11	2.16
1848	7,508	1,137	.15	17,200	15.13	2.29
1849	7,460	1,098	.15	15,646	14.25	2.10
1850	7,292	1,098	.15	15,744	14.34	2.16
1851	7,387	1,142	.15	16,080	14.08	2.18

a The data in this table relate only to those Residencies in Java where the Cultivation System was practised. It therefore excludes the Residencies of Yogyakarta, Surakarta, Batavia and Buitenzorg. The land area in column 3 does not include that devoted to forced cultivation or left unplanted. Unfortunately, it is not differentiated into irrigated (sawah) and non-irrigated (tegal) lands, which would allow for more exact analysis. Paddy refers to dry stalk paddy (padi gagang).

Source: Kultuur Verslagen, 1837-1851

activities under the Cultivation System, peasants still found the time and resources to sustain and expand the sphere of domestic production.

The Evidence for Domestic Economic Expansion. This brings us to the third and final part of this survey of the countervailing evidence against the argument for impoverishment. As I have already suggested, the impoverishment critique has tended to consider the material impact of the Cultivation System from an a-historical and static point of view in which peasants are passive victims. I would contend, however, that it is much more useful and enlightening to stress two factors which have generally been ignored in discussions of this issue. The first is the radical change in the rural economy which the Cultivation System's operations both allowed and stimulated; the second is the peasantry's ability and skill in responding and adapting to new arrangements and opportunities. Van den Bosch, the System's creator, frequently asserted that the hoped-for profits from the System would come from capitalising on the labour power of the peasantry, and in particular by bringing into play what he saw as the latent productive capacities of the peasantry.[40] He was proved correct in this assessment, but he did not fully realise the stimulus the System would have in spheres not directly connected with its activities. Some examples might make this point more clearly. In areas of intensive forced cultivation, local shortages of rice often resulted; even along the prosperous northern littoral of Pasuruan, a number of districts could not produce sufficient food to meet their own requirements. The need, however, was filled by the activities of peasant rice growers in areas scarcely affected by the Cultivation System, especially around the Lumajang plain. They saw a new opportunity, and their response was a greatly increased involvement in the commodity production of rice. As a result, these peripheral areas became the rice bowl for this part of East Java, and their inhabitants thereby gained significant material advantages which would not otherwise have been available.[41] Again, more generally throughout Java, the flow of cash and the enormous improvements wrought in irrigation systems and transport networks and facilities stimulated other indigenous commercial activities outside the realm of the forced cultivations. In Kedu, for example, peasants prospered more than ever from the cultivation and sale of tobacco;[42] in Kediri, the Resident reported a 400 per cent increase in native exports from the Residency in the decade after 1845;[43] and in Pasuruan, peasants reportedly planted huge areas in coffee of their own volition because of the crop's profitability.[44] In other words, the conditions necessary for the successful pursuit of the Cultivation System also laid the basis for the development on a substantial scale of other forms of productive activity in a way that had never been possible before. All this activity, of course, had powerful multiplier effects throughout the rural economy, in handicraft industry and trades, in retailing, in transport; its effect, coupled with the more direct consequences of the Cultivation System, was a general rise in the income-producing capacity of the population. There were, admittedly, setbacks and difficulties for some, especially those employed in the indigenous textile industry, but, in general, the economy went into a period of rapid development in size and sophistication which brought enhanced material benefits to the populace at large.

It is a still more interesting and important question to decide just how this prosperity was distributed among the peasant population and how it was used. Unfortunately, in the absence of much firm evidence, it is also more difficult to resolve. From the little research recently done,[45] it appears that, at least in the short term, the material lot of most people improved. More specifically, those who reaped the greatest benefits from the operations, direct and indirect, of the Cultivation System were those at either end of the peasant social scale. Those in positions of authority were able to translate increased political power into greater social and material advantage; those at the opposite end benefited from the multiplication of labour opportunities, especially outside the sphere of domestic production, which enabled them to increase their bargaining power against, and loosen their dependence upon, village-based patrons. This assessment, however, must remain conjectural until it can be further tested against the data that are increasingly being brought to light.

Conclusion

The poverty/prosperity conundrum is a notoriously difficult one to solve, even in societies about which there exist abundant and reliable data and a long tradition of social research. It is all the more tricky in the case of Java during the years of the Cultivation System. Much of the extant evidence, particularly that of a statistical kind, is highly dubious and bafflingly ambiguous. Moreover, the study of the social impact of the System is still very much in its infancy. There is little known about the basic mechanics of social and economic change—how incomes and burdens were distributed among peasants, how much of the money disbursed by the Cultivation System actually reached them, how (and when) it was disposed of, how opportunity and adversity were handled, how and to what extent social structures and usages were transformed.

Notwithstanding these problems, it seems reasonable to conclude that the argument for impoverishment is seriously deficient. Its evidential base shares all those shortcomings of the case for increasing prosperity and its logical underpinnings are far less secure. In particular its ahistorical bent and its tendency to treat peasants as the hapless flotsam of imperial greed betray assumptions about the nature of peasant society that need serious questioning. Behind them lurks the view that times were necessarily better before the imperial age and must inevitably grow worse as the foraging hand of colonialism grows busier. I have attempted to demonstrate that these assumptions do not bear the stamp of indisputable truth, and that, in fact, there is a substantial body of evidence that in the Javanese case during the Cultivation System they are false. To admit them without question is seriously to underestimate the ingenuity of peasants under changing conditions of economic life. The Cultivation System was certainly harsh and oppressive, its aims and methods morally indefensible. But our moral disapprobation should not cloud or hinder our attempts to answer the quite separate question of whether the peasants of Java were materially advantaged or not under the System's operations. In the final analysis the System does seem to have provided, both directly and indirectly and at least in the short term, opportunities for a more secure management of domestic economic life and possibilities for economic growth for a peasant society whose options, up to that time, had been severely limited. Most peasants, I would argue, did not need much prompting to realise and take advantage of this radically new situation.

Notes

1. I should like to thank Dr. J.G. Butcher, Dr. R. Cribb and Professor M.C. Ricklefs for their comments on an earlier draft of this essay, and The Australian Research Grants Scheme for research funding.

2. The research upon which this paper is based is still incomplete. In particular it lacks a thorough grounding in Residency archives and the Archive of the Director of Cultivations, both held at the Arsip Nasional Republik Indonesia, Jakarta.

3. In Madiun, for example, distances from village to coffee-planting area ranged up to seven kilometres, in Jepara up to eight kilometres, in Pekalongan sometimes more than ten, in Cirebon up to twelve ("Inspectie Rapport van den Directeur van Kultures over de Koffijkultuur in de door hem bezochte Residentien van Java in 1854", Archive of the Minister of Colonies [hereafter AMK], Exhibitum [hereafter Exh] 2 March 1858/21, Algemeen Rijksarchief, The Hague [hereafter ARADH], in Surabaya as much as nineteen kilometres ("Nota omtrent de aangelegenheden van de koffij kultuur in de Residentie Soerabaija," AMK, Verbaal [hereafter V] 13 September 1862/17, ARADH), and in the Priangan sometimes up to forty kilometres (Besluit 14 January 1867/12, AMK, ARADH).

4. J. van Sevenhoven, "Over de Kultures op het Eiland Java en voornamelijk van Producten voor de Markt van Europa," AMK, V 8 August 1840/265 Geheim, ARADH; "Algemeen Verslag der Residentie Preanger Regentschappen. 1851," AMK, Exh 29 January 1853/19, ARADH; Letter Resident of Preanger Regencies to Governor-General, 23 April 1865, AMK, Exh 30 May 1865/20, ARADH.

5. In some places, such as Banten, the practice was introduced of peasants delivering their crops to coffee millers for the final stages of preparation of the produce ("Inspectie Rapport," cited in Note 3 above).

6. In 1844 the payment to peasants was reduced from *f*12 to *f*10 per *picul* of coffee delivered (Fasseur 1975, p.21).

7. "Antwoorden der Residenten op de le vraag: heeft de geleidelijk opheffing van bezwaren, vroeger van de Gouvts. suikerkultuur verbonden, de ingenomenheid der bevolking voor die cultuur doen toenemen?" AMK, Exh 11 October 1869/59, ARADH.
8. The Government withheld a small proportion of the crop payments to finance maintenance of the indigo factories (Fasseur 1975, p.27).
9. In 1832 Governor-General van den Bosch had stipulated that peasants were to be paid the market price for the coffee they delivered. A year later, the market price became "market price, to be fixed annually by the Government," a sum nearly five guilders below the actual market price (Anon. 1861, pp.27-28). In the case of sugar, he laid down that peasants must be paid more than if they had used their land for rice (Fasseur 1975, pp.24-25), something that most investigations later showed to be far from reality.
10. Besluit 19 September 1864/3, AMK, ARADH.
11. The data are found in "Kultuur Verslag 1851." These reports are held at ARADH; for their file numbers, see Fasseur (1975), p. 269. An indication of the purchasing power of these sums may be gauged from the fact that the average price of rice in Java in 1851 ranged from *f*1.118 to *f*3.23 per pikul of *padi* ("Kultuur Verslag 1851").
12. See also Letter Resident responsible for enquiry into coffee cultivation to Governor-General, 5 November 1864, AMK, Exh 10 August 1868/20, ARADH.
13. See also Letter Inspector of Cultivations and temporary Resident of Pekalongan to Governor-General, 9 December 1857, AMK, Exh 21 December 1860/2, ARADH.
14. Letter Director Cultivations to Governor-General, 16 March 1857, AMK, Exh 2 September 1857/15, ARADH.
15. "Antwoorden der Residenten," cited in note 7 above.
16. Letter Director of Cultivations to Governor-General, 6 August 1852, AMK, V 4 February 1854/4, ARADH. These lower yields were usually attributed to soil exhaustion caused by the export crops, but they may well have been due to inadequate field preparation or an inability to plant rice at the appropriate time.
17. For example, Letter Resident of Cirebon to Governor-General, 30 September 1835, Collectie Baud, no. 469, ARADH and "Algemeen Verslag der Residentie Cheribon over den Jare 1841," Local Residency Archives [hereafter AD], Cirebon 2, Arsip Nasional Republik Indonesia, Jakarta [hereafter ANJ].
18. "Kultuur Verslag 1850."
19. Van den Bosch was moved to remark that "I am much in need of good Residents; bunglers I have in abundance," letter to J. C. Baud, 20 April 1832, in Westendorp Boerma (1956, vol.1, p.139).
20. "Kultuur Verslag 1834."
21. "Kultuur Verslag 1834."
22. "Korte Schets of Staat der Residentie Rembang zoo als ik die in 1844 heb gevonden en zoo als dezelve thans is," AMK, no. 3066 (1814-1849), ARADH.

23. "Klagten van inlanders over willekeurige afneming van gronden enz." AMK, Exh 13 April 1866/1, ARADH.
24. One exception to this is Bosch (1851, 1868), but his base lines are drawn from highly dubious statistics.
25. "Algemeen Jaarlijksch Verslag omtrent den Staat van de Residentie Cheribon gedurende het dienst Jaar 1814," AD, Cirebon 2, ANJ.
26. "Residentie Preanger Regentschappen. Algemeen Verslag 1823," Collectie Baud, no. 90, ARADH.
27. "Algemeen Jaarlijksch Verslag van de Residentie Samarang 1826," Collectie Du Bus de Gisignies, no. 491, ARADH.
28. Letter Resident of Rembang to Inspector of Finances, 26 February 1829, Collectie Du Bus de Gisignies, no. 326, ARADH.
29. "Residentie Pekalongan. Algemeen Verslag over den Jare 1828," Collectie Du Bus de Gisignies, no. 468, ARADH.
30. For instance, "Residentie Pasoeroean. Kultuur Verslag over 1854," AD, Pasuruan 23, ANJ; "Residentie Pasoeroewan. Algemeen Verslag. 1855," AD, Pasuruan 10, ANJ; "Residentie Pasoeroean. Politiek Verslag. 1858," AD, Pasuruan 1, ANJ; Letter Resident of Pasuruan to Governor-General, 30 January 1867, AMK, Exh 30 March 1867/30, ARADH.
31. "Algemeen Verslag van de Residentie Bezoekie over het jaar 1844," AD, Besuki 5, ANJ; "Residentie Bezoekie. Algemeen Verslag over den jare 1846," AD, Besuki 5, ANJ; "Algemeen Verslag van de Residentie Bezoekie over het jaar 1853," AD, Besuki 6, ANJ.
32. See also Letter former Resident of Kedu to Minister of Colonies, 15 September 1864, AMK, Exh 15 September 1864/F8 Kab, ARADH; Letter Resident of Kediri to Governor-General, 22 May 1857, AMK, Exh 2 September 1857/17, ARADH.
33. Letter Inspector of Cultivations and temporary Resident of Pekalongan to Governor-General, 9 December 1857, cited in Note 13 above.
34. "Nota betreffende den toestand der Residentie Pekalongan bij de aanvaarding van het bestuur door den ondergeteekende," AMK, Exh 15 January 1868/17, ARADH.
35. For example, "Algemeen Verslag der Residentie Cheribon, over het Jaar 1843," AD, Cirebon 3, ANJ.
36. "Nota betreffende den toestand der Residentie Cheribon zooals de ondergeteekende die bij zijne optreding gevonden heeft," AMK, Exh 29 January 1868/17, ARADH.
37. "Algemeen Verslag der Residentie Samarang over den Jare 1851," AMK, Exh [? Oct (?)] 1853/363 Geheim, ARADH.
38. Letter Governor-General to Minister of Colonies, 26 August 1869, AMK, V 29 June 1870/22, ARADH.

39. Letter Governor-General to Minister of Colonies, 25 November 1870, AMK, Exh 14 January 1871/40, ARADH. The Residents' reports are also to be found in this file.
40. See his "Advies van den Luitenant-Generaal van den Bosch over het Stelsel van Kolonisatie" in Steijn Parve 1851, pp.320-27.
41. Letter Resident of Probolinggo to Governor-General, 7 October 1863, AMK, V 25 October 1865/21, ARADH. For a more thorough discussion of a similar phenomenon, see Knight 1982a, p.141.
42. "Nota betreffende den toestand van de residentie Kedoe, zooals de ondergeteekende dien bij zigne optreding heeft gevonden," AMK, Exh 15 February 1870/14, ARADH.
43. Letter Resident of Kediri to Governor-General, 22 May 1857, cited in note 31 above.
44. Letter Resident of Pasuruan to Governor-General, 30 January 1867, cited in note 30 above.
45. In particular that of G.R. Knight and M.R. Fernando.

CHAPTER THREE

The Peasantry and the Cultivation of Sugar Cane in Nineteenth-century Java: A Study from Pekalongan Residency, 1830-1870[1]

G. R. Knight

How was Java's peasantry induced to grow cane for the sugar industry which burgeoned in the colony during the mid-nineteenth century? Before the inauguration of the Cultivation System by Governor-General Johannes van den Bosch in 1830, the processing of cane into sugar for the world market had taken place in Java on only a very limited scale. This was done on Chinese- and European-owned estates in western Java—many of them clustered around Batavia itself—and in the Pasuruan area, in the far eastern tip of the colony, where, for a decade or more prior to the arrival of Van den Bosch, a handful of manufacturers had established a small but apparently viable industry based on the milling of peasant-grown cane (Knight 1980). By the 1860s, all of this had changed dramatically. The estates of west Java had sunk into the background as sugar producers, but elsewhere, in the densely populated and intensively cultivated lowlands of the colony's central and eastern districts, the sugar *fabriek* or factory had become a ubiquitous feature of the rural scene. Around one hundred European-owned factories, powered either by big water-wheels or by steam engines imported from Britain and Holland, produced in excess of 130,000 tonnes of sugar annually. The cane was grown by more than 100,000 peasant households working some 12,000 hectares of irrigated farmland or *sawah*, on which sugar was alternated with the rice and secondary food crops (*palawija*) which formed the basis of peasant agriculture (*C.E.I.*, vol. 1, p.72; Fasseur 1975, p.259).

The creation of this sugar industry was the most striking single achievement of the Cultivation System. In part, of course, it represented the application of modern technology to the expansion of production for the world market. This was made possible very largely by the capital which Van den Bosch and his successors at the head of the Dutch colonial government made available in the form of loans to their "contractors," the manufacturers who agreed to mill cane and produce sugar for the government in return for supplies of material and a percentage of their output, the greater part of which—notionally at least—was delivered to the government in fulfillment of the contract (Fasseur 1975, pp.11-36, 63-76; Fasseur 1977b). The key to the successful expansion of the industry lay, however, in its increasingly assured access to good quality cane, rather than in modernisation within the *fabriek* itself.[2] This hinged, in turn, on arrangements for producing raw material which prevailed in the industry throughout the period of the Cultivation System; in fact, they continued in force for a decade or more after the formal abolition of the System in 1870, under which it was not the contractors themselves who were responsible for organising cane cultivation, but the provincial colonial authorities. Cane was grown by the peasantry of the districts surrounding the factories on orders from the Dutch Resident and his subordinate *controleurs* (in effect, district officers). Those orders were transmitted to the cultivators through the agency of the *priyayi*, the Javanese gentry-officials who, in the course of the mid-nineteenth century, were in the process of being fully incorporated into the Dutch colonial bureaucracy (Sutherland 1979, pp.3-18; Sutherland 1975). In short, the quality and quantity of raw material available to the industry were substantially dependent on the extent to which the Residency authorities were able to coerce, cajole, or otherwise induce the peasantry both to grow cane and to grow it well.

A three-fold explanation of how this was done has been advanced by modern historians of nineteenth-century Java. First, the Dutch architects of the sugar industry used 'traditional' channels of authority in the countryside to secure peasant compliance. Second, this compliance was bought with a regular system of payments to the peasant producers, based on the output of their *fabriek*. Third, the peasantry acquiesced in the production of cane for the burgeoning industry because its demands were less disruptive of the existing rural economy and society than might be imagined.

The first of these arguments has been stated most succinctly by Elson, who writes that the key factor in the success of the Cultivation System was "the decision to utilise traditional channels of authority relationships" in pursuit of expanded production for the world market (Elson 1978a, p.11; Elson 1978b, p.45). Van Niel has come to similar conclusions: "the incentive for growing government crops was the fulfillment of the wishes and orders of the supra-village authorities" (Van Niel 1981, pp.40-41). Fasseur, meanwhile, has stressed the importance not only of the *priyayi* but of the village heads or *lurah* as "the pivots around which the Cultivation System turned," concluding that "the System would not have been possible without collaboration of an important village elite" (Fasseur 1981, pp.7-8). A significant qualification of this thesis touched on by several recent writers, on the other hand, is that there was potential for conflict as well as accommodation between the requirements of the sugar industry after 1830 and the interests of both *priyayi* and headmen (Elson 1978b, p.4).

Recent studies of the industry, however, have emphasised the importance of cash payments—and resultant "prosperity"—as a means of inducing the cultivators to produce cane (or at least to reconcile them to its "forced" production). Writing of the situation in Pasuruan in the 1830s, for example, Van Niel has suggested that "it would be wrong to assume the pressure applied through the traditional native elites was the only [inducement to labour]... the incentive supplied by money was also of primary importance" (Van Niel 1964b, p.4). Reviewing the situation as it had developed by mid-century, Elson has argued in forceful terms that "the most important factor of all in peasant acquiescence... was the prosperity it bestowed upon them" (Elson 1978b, pp.46-47), while Fasseur has repeatedly drawn attention to the role of crop payments (*plantloon*) in sweetening the pill of "forced labour" and in securing the cooperation of the peasantry in the production of sugar. Like most other modern writers, on the other hand, Fasseur has also grasped that the question of the distribution of the "prosperity" brought by crop payments among the highly differentiated peasantry of mid-nineteenth century Java is a vexed one which is susceptible of no easy solution (Fasseur 1981, p.9; Fasseur 1978, pp.149-50).

The third major explanation of peasant compliance with the requirements of the sugar industry during the period of the Cultivation System is that cane cultivation did not unduly disrupt existing patterns of village life. Despite the argument's stress on the continuity of social and economic arrangements among the peasantry of the sugar districts, this is far from being a re-write of the "involution" hypothesis. On the contrary, the fact that peasant society was strongly differentiated on social and economic lines, and far from homogeneous, is widely recognised, and a plethora of historical arguments are advanced *contra* Geertz. What the argument does assert, however, is that peasant society in early nineteenth-century Java was sufficiently flexible to withstand the demands made by the Dutch after 1830 without being more than temporarily pushed out of shape. Elson has argued, for example, that despite the expansion of the sugar industry in Pasuruan after 1830, "peasants remained firmly entrenched in the traditional patterns of production" (Elson 1978a, p.11).[3] In a similar vein, Van Niel has commented that "local arrangements eventually made by the peasants [prevented]... the collapse of Javanese housekeeping arrangements... these adjustments and others made the system bearable" (Van Niel 1981, pp.44-45). In particular (and again largely in the context of Pasuruan), he suggests that "the village responded to new [Cultivation System] pressures in ways determined by existent patterns of village life... the village remains intact and integrated" (Van Niel 1964b, p.6); and "... the growing cycle [of sugarcane] came in many areas to be accommodated within the rice pattern of production" (Van Niel 1972, p.101). On the other hand, it is perfectly clear that none of the writers cited here views the period of the Cultivation System as one of "no change" in rural life. Elson, for instance, has drawn attention to the strengthening of the village elite grouped around the *lurah* as a result of the need of the Residency administrators for village "managers" on whom they could rely (Elson 1978a, pp.28-29). Similarly Van Niel has noted that "as conceived... the [Cultivation] System was supposed to work in and with the traditional pattern; obviously it did not" (Van Niel 1981, p.47).[4]

Such are the main arguments of what might be dubbed the "modern school." This paper is an attempt to review their conclusions about the means by which peasant labour was subordinated to the requirements of cane-cultivation in mid-nineteenth century. It does so by focusing on what we know of developments in the industry which grew up after 1830 in Pekalongan Residency, north Java, and in particular on one large and well-documented *fabriek*, Wonopringo (Wanapringa), on the southern fringe of that Residency's coastal lowlands.[5] In this way, a microcosm of sugar production can be brought to bear on grander arguments about the course of the industry's development. Not that Pekalongan—or the Wonopringo *fabriek*—was typical of the Java sugar industry as a whole in the mid-nineteenth century. Production got off to a very bad start there, characterised by low productivity and a degree of indifference exhibited by peasant and *priyayi* alike to the new incursion into the countryside, so that the industry began to flourish only in the 1850s,[6] a good two decades after the inauguration of the Cultivation System. All the same, this retarded development of the industry serves to point up, more vividly perhaps than in areas where sugar implanted itself with greater ease, the processes involved in inducing the peasantry to work for it.

It is these processes which the arguments developed by the "modern school" seek to explain. To an extent, of course, they do exactly that in a way which blends explanation with a nice appreciation of how much more there is yet to uncover about the means by which the sugar industry grew so spectacularly in Java in the middle decades of the nineteenth century. At the same time, they exhibit certain shortcomings, which stem perhaps from an understandable wariness in pressing conclusions too far on the basis of still provisional evidence. A fundamental problem is that their arguments contrive an uneasy coupling of explanations which stress the Cultivation System's exploitation of traditional channels of authority in the countryside with those which recognise very clearly that new forms of inducement, notably cash payment to the cultivators, were increasingly important. This is not a paradox of which historians of the "modern school" are unaware (Van Niel 1964b, p.4). At the same time, their attempts to resolve it seem, to date, to be unsatisfactory and to rely heavily on the implicit assumption that the mid-nineteenth century was a period of transition during which such apparent contradictions were to be expected. The present paper suggests an alternative solution. On the basis of evidence from Pekalongan, and from the Wonopringo *fabriek* in particular, it argues that the third quarter of the nineteenth century was a period of transformations, which formed the basis for the sugar industry's successful expansion.

Rural Elites and the Production of Sugar Cane

A potential for conflict, as well as for collaboration, between the *priyayi* and Dutch administrators over the development of the government cultivations from 1830 onwards has been noted by Elson and others (Elson 1978b, p.41). It was vividly demonstrated in the case of sugar production in Pekalongan.

The source of such conflict apparently lay in clashes of personality and the unusually straitened economic circumstances in which the "traditional" Javanese rulers of Pekalongan found themselves on the eve of the Cultivation System. Conflict was greatly exacerbated, moreover, by the poor returns from indigo, the major staple of Cultivation System production in the Residency in the 1830s, which meant that the *priyayi* received little in the way of cultivation-bonuses in return for the very extensive work of supervision required of them (Knight 1982a, pp.142-47). At the same time, they had to manage a peasantry growing increasingly restive under a situation of much work for little pay. The early inroads of the sugar industry, meanwhile, did little to modify *priyayi* distaste for the new arrangements. In Pekalongan Regency, for example, the *bupati* (the chief *priyayi* functionary) lost heavily through being the guarantor of a failed sugar-making venture on the site of the later Wonopringo *fabriek*, while the establishment of the big new sugar factory at Kalimatie in Batang Regency embroiled the Residency's other *bupati* in a protracted wrangle with Dutch authorities over the assignment of family lands for the cultivation of cane.[7] There can be little doubt, in these circumstances, that the "indifference" of the *priyayi* (in the parlance of the day) was a major contributor to the slow initial growth of the sugar industry in the Residency.

Whether its final commercial success in the 1860s was attributable in the main to any change of heart by the peasantry's "traditional" leaders is also improbable. To be sure, the successive removal in 1847-48 of both incumbent *bupati* and their replacement by more tractable individuals must have helped. At Wonopringo, for instance, there are signs of the evident usefulness of the *bupati* in the 1850s, when the Pekalongan Regent was to be found accompanying the Dutch *controleur* around the plantations and directly transmitting the latter's orders to his subordinates (Knight 1982a, pp.143-45). Likewise, there is testimony from early in the following decade that the *wedana* of Sawangan (one of the two Javanese District Heads in the area around the factory) had "always been well-disposed toward the *fabriek*"; that his departure through promotion was viewed with some concern; but that his successor was a man of the same family, who could therefore be presumed to be equally malleable.[8] The fact that by 1860, Wonopringo was also generating handsome cultivation-bonuses for the *priyayi* of the area under exploitation *(kring)* must also have had its effect on their behaviour.[9]

All the same, reservations must be expressed about the degree to which the mid-century *bupati* and *wedana* could be of use to the industry in assuring peasant compliance with its requirements for raw material. The general picture of the Pekalongan *priyayi* of the 1860s, at least as it emerges from successive Residents' Annual Reports to Batavia, is anything but promising. They are depicted, in fact, as being notably impoverished, demoralised and lacking in "traditional" aura or authority.[10] Significant, in view of the importance attached in some explanations to their reputed control over labour, was the fact that in 1866 they raised no objections (in marked contrast to what happened elsewhere in the colony) to Dutch proposals to curtail their claims to personal service from the peasantry. They were said to be looking forward only to the higher salaries which would be their recompense.[11]

All of this adds up, in short, to the conclusion that in Pekalongan, at least, the *priyayi* scarcely fulfilled the intention of the Cultivation System's founders that their schemes could be effectively based on "promotion [of cultivation]... by the supra-village authorities (Van Niel 1981, pp.40-41). Was this simply because they were ill-disposed toward the new developments? It might, in this context, be worthwhile to take up Heather Sutherland's suggestion of some years ago (Sutherland 1975, pp.66-72) that there was a tendency "to exaggerate their [the *priyayi's*] coercive and exploitative role" and hence to "minimise their links to the common people," links which presumably have to be perceived as bestowing benefit as well as obligation. If this point is even partly accepted, it becomes possible to see *priyayi* "intransigence" in Pekalongan as reflecting very real difficulties of their own in managing a peasantry which only late in the day, and then (as we shall see) only in a very qualified sense, began to draw some degree of prosperity from the expansion of sugar production.

The role of elites within the village in securing a general acquiescence in the cultivation of cane is a complex one. Some of the Pekalongan evidence appears to support the thesis that the *lurah*, grown rich and powerful under the auspices of the Cultivation System, was the linchpin in the organisation of production in the sugar industry. In addition to supervising work in the plantations, he was both a broker and something of an entrepreneur. Witness, for example, the comment of Wonopringo's British manager, T. G. Edwards, that in the 1850s a "considerable trade in coolies" was carried on by the headmen, who were responsible for supplying the *fabriek* with corvée labour for the Campaign (harvesting and milling season) and who found substitutes (at a price) for those peasant landholders who were not prepared to perform corvée themselves.[12] Again, in the following decade, one Residency report spoke of *lurah* in villages where there was an inverse ratio of population to land who

> ...being in that position,... can enrich themselves through the hire of fields to other, more heavily populated villages. They are then free from worries about cultivation service and corvee, and can almost be considered as landlords.[13]

Though this particular development was in a sense tangential to the Cultivation System, other indications of the growing economic strength of the *lurah* and other substantial peasants were unquestionably a direct consequence of it. It was reported from one of Pekalongan's sugar districts in the late 1850s, for instance, that headmen were contriving to concentrate village landholding in the hands of a "privileged few," on the ostensible grounds that they were the ones who took upon themselves the 'burden' of cane-planting which, if the Resident was correct, actually brought them considerable financial advantage (Knight 1982a, p.138).

We may well be dealing with a situation, all the same, where more than one village elite was either emerging or having its position greatly strengthened as a consequence, direct or otherwise, of the expansion of sugar production under the Cultivation System. Official Dutch sources for the 1860s, for example, mention people who "made a business" out of hiring plough-animals to those cultivators—apparently the majority—who had none of their own.[14] It is tempting to see these entrepreneurs as having accumulated their capital through contracts for cane-haulage entered into with the peasantry by all three of the Residency's sugar factories during the mid-century decades. They were not necessarily *lurah* or other members of village-government: in the Wonopringo area in the mid-1850s, for instance, the *fabriek* came into conflict with village headmen in its attempts to recruit hauliers.[15] Interestingly,—though, given the nature of the evidence, inconclusively—several Residency reports of the 1850s and 1860s depict the *lurah* of Pekalongan as lacking in power, even as being the "playthings" (*Speelball*) of their fellow-villagers.[16] This might again suggest that other elites were surfacing among the peasantry, independent and possibly hostile to the headmen, but still the beneficiaries of the new economy which the sugar industry was promoting. One index pointing in this direction is the sharp increase in the number of *hajis* (pilgrims returned from Mecca) grown rich in trade and moneylending in Pekalongan in the 1860s: in 1868 the Residency recorded 863 of them, whereas at the beginning of the decade there had been only about 240.[17] It is highly likely, therefore, that the success of the sugar industry—and of the

Cultivation System production generally in Pekalongan—owed a lot to the support of one village elite or another. To regard any of those elites as "traditional," however, is to miss the point that they had been radically transformed by the industry's expansion.

Crop-Payment and Peasant Prosperity

On the surface of it, crop payment (*plantloon*) had become, by the mid-1850s, a major inducement to the peasant cultivation of cane in Pekalongan generally and in the Wonopringo area in particular. The background to this was a general reorganisation of the plantation work force in the sugar districts of Pekalongan which made it possible to disburse crop payments in a way which reflected the efforts of particular villages around the factory (and at the same time, of course, enabled their "failings" to be sheeted home to them as well). From the outset of the Cultivation System in Pekalongan, cane had been grown on large, consolidated plantations, amalgamated from the fields of any number of villages. At Wonopringo in mid-century, there were ten to twelve such plantations servicing the *fabriek*.[18] Initially, the system of consolidated plantations had caused considerable problems for the industry, above all because the work force for the cane had been recruited, more or less indiscriminately, from throughout the *kring* (i.e. the *beschikkingskring*, or exploitation area assigned to a sugar factory as part of its contractual arrangement with the colonial Government). This reduced both the possibility of effective labour discipline and the likelihood of crop payment being a realistic inducement to labour. Indeed, in the 1840s it had been a matter of bitter and frequent complaint by the manufacturers that "the maintenance of the [sugar] fields does not take place on a village basis but *en masse*... so that each village headman cannot individually be held responsible."[19]

With the arrival of Resident Van der Eb early in the 1850s, however, big changes were finally made in the organisation of labour for plantation work. Large, consolidated plantations remained the rule, but the village became incontrovertibly the organisation unit for labour. At the same time, each cultivator was assigned a particular section of the plantation for which his household was responsible. Despite some fears that this system would lead to an uneven working of the fields, the results were apparently eminently satisfactory:

> [Field-work] has gone on in a much more regulated way over the last few years [the *controleur* responsible for the Wonopringo area reported in 1856], since the moment that each planter had to look after his own share. And from that flows that the working of the ground, the planting of the cane and maintenance of the [cane] gardens have proceeded with more diligence and care.[20]

As perceived by both *fabriek* management and Residency officials, the root cause of this greater diligence was to be found in the scale of crop payments made by the industry and in the way in which they were now clearly tied to effort. "These ample payments," argued the Resident in 1867, "have brought into existence a prosperity which stands or falls with the factory," while more than a decade earlier the management at Wonopringo had remarked on the cultivators' increasing "enthusiasm" for cane-planting and readily attributed it to the level of crop-payment in the previous year.[21]

It was indeed true that, as far as the peasantry assigned to cane-growing for the Wonopringo *fabriek* was concerned, the gross receipts from crop-payment increased very considerably after mid-century and, from 1854 onward, were well in excess of the land rent which the peasants of the *kring* had to pay into the Residency coffers. This much, at least, can be deduced from Table 3.1.[22]

It is doubtful in the extreme, however, whether this demonstrably favourable ratio between crop payment and land rent implied a general prosperity for the peasant cane-cultivators at large, and hence explained their "willingness" to work in the plantations. Pekalongan evidence suggests that some of the criteria of increasing wealth in the countryside posited by historians of the "modern school"[23] were indeed being met, but that others were more ambiguous in their implications. In 1866, for example, we find the Resident of Pekalongan priding himself on the ease with which he had been able to collect the land rent for that year, despite a stiff increase on the previous assessment, and attributing this unhesitatingly to the "great amount of cash which those (sugar) factories have brought into circulation."[24] On the other hand, some apparent pointers to increasing prosperity in the Residency might better be interpreted as indications of the development of a new economic order in the countryside—very much in the wake of the sugar industry—than as a sign that the peasantry generally was better off. This is particularly true of the apparently blossoming trade in cotton goods and, above all, in rice,[25] for these were arguably primarily indicative of the agrarianisation of the peasantry under the impact of the Cultivation System—leading to a greater reliance than before on imported consumer goods to replace local handicrafts—and of a rice deficit, created at least in part by the inroads of the sugar industry. Large numbers of peasants (as we shall see in more detail below) now depended on their earnings from the sugar industry to finance their purchase of rice, imported in considerable quantities from elsewhere in the colony.

To some extent, of course, increased trade in consumer goods may have represented the increased buying-power of those elites within the village who benefited financially, in one way or another, from the expansion of the sugar industry. For the mass of the peasant landholders of the lowland areas assigned to the industry, on the other hand, "prosperity" was largely an illusion. This was

TABLE 3.1 Crop Payment and Land Rent in the Wonopringo Kring, 1839-1866 (guilders)

Year	Sugar Planting Households	Total Crop-Payment	Crop-Payment per Household	Land Rent paid by the population of kring
1836	2,544	22,880	8.99	12,260
1840	2,253	49,351	21.91	15,985
1841	2,252	24,775	11.00	17,334
1848	3,662	51,590	14.09	-
1849	3.265	29,535	9.05	28,254
1852	2,464	25,936	9.80	28,000[?]
1854	2,908	62,329	21.43	-
1855	2,754	68,310	24.80	25,671
1856	2,975	71,101	23.90	-
1857	3,099	78,249	25.25	26,681
1860	4,261	80,826	18.97	15,991
1861	4,257	80,742	18.97	14,447
1862	3,918	75,404	19.25	18,226
1863	3,918	88,609	22.62	27,592
1864	4,398	88,631	20.15	20,640
1865	4,478	91,925	20.53	35,775
1866	4,590	91,920	20.03	-

Source: See note 22, page 65.

partly because the actual ratio between land rent and crop payment was less favourable to them than it appeared on paper, and partly because there were very substantial hidden costs of cane-cultivation to be set against what the landholders received for their plantation work. The first was a consequence of the arrangements for paying the land rent, which almost certainly meant that individual cultivators paid out significantly more money than ever reached the coffers of the Resident via the intermediation of the village-headmen and *priyayi*, who were his agents for its collection. The village-basis of assessment, which left a great deal to the discretion of the headman, undoubtedly "opened the door wide," as an official report of 1866 conceded, "to all sorts of jobbery and malpractice."[26]

As to hidden costs, these related primarily to the need for the peasant landholders to supply the sugar industry, *gratis*, with labour other than their own, with plough animals, and with fencing materials (Dekker 1978, pp.28-31). On the fringe of the Pekalongan lowlands, where the Wonopringo *fabriek* was established, fencing of the cane fields against the depredations of domestic cattle and wild boar was a major cost item, reckoned in the 1850s to amount to some five thousand guilders worth of materials alone. It therefore absorbed between five and ten per cent of the crop-payment made by the *fabriek* in any one year.[27]

Apart from fencing, other and very significant costs to the cane-growing peasantry stemmed from the convenient assumptions of the Cultivation System that the landholding peasantry came from farms worked by family labour, and that peasants possessed their own tools and plough-animals. Neither of these assumptions was correct, and apart from the expense (in either cash or upkeep) in providing labourers to assist in plantation work, the landholders assigned to cane production also had to provide oxen for ploughing. It was reliably reported from the Wonopringo area in the 1860s, for instance, that many landholders had no oxen of their own (one of the reasons cited was the shortage of grazing land), and were in the habit of hiring them whenever they were required for field work. Costs, in a reasonably successful year, could amount to more than ten per cent of crop-payment received.[28] In short, the supply of fencing materials and plough-animals alone effectively reduced crop payments by between fifteen and twenty per cent, without taking into account other costs incurred by the peasantry—for work on roads and bridges, or for firewood collection[29]—which were less easily expressible in cash terms.

None of this takes into account, of course, the income which peasant landholders of the sugar districts might have been able to earn from their land had they been free to rent it out instead of devoting it to the sugar industry. To be sure, this is in a sense a hypothetical question, since it assumes that there was a market in rented land; in fact, share-cropping seems to have been a more prevalent device, though neither renting nor the sale of land was unknown in mid-nineteenth century Pekalongan. Official investigations into opportunity costs, carried out in the Residency early in the 1870s, however, did at least suggest what the peasantry's potential loss through the compulsory requisition of their land for sugar was likely to have been. Even at Wonopringo, the best-paying of the Pekalongan factories, there was a big discrepancy in favour of the industry. In the few years immediately prior to the investigations, cultivation-payments there had averaged *f*128 annually for each *bau* (.7 of a hectare) of good farmland brought under sugar, while the going rate for the equivalent amount and quality of land and labour among the peasants themselves was about *f*165.[30]

Lack of Disruption or a New Order in the Countryside?

An important dimension to the arguments of the "modern school," as we have seen, has been to stress the way in which the sugar industry fitted into the existing order in rural Java, thereby smoothing the path of its development. As will be obvious from what we have already noted about the rural elites, the main thrust of the present argument, on the other hand, is to emphasise change and transformation rather than continuity in the relations and organisation of production in the Javanese countryside in the mid-nineteenth century. Headmen evolved into village "managers" (*desabestuurders*, in the suggestive terminology of one contemporary Dutch report)[31] and entrepreneurs. At the same time, other and possibly rival elites—rich *santri* amongst them—were also nurtured, though less directly, by the Cultivation System, while the old supra-village elite or *priyayi* became increasingly bureaucratised and divorced from any real control over the means of production.

Simultaneously, and underpinning these developments, there began to emerge in rural Java a new economic order, fostered to a significant degree by the government cultivations introduced in 1830, in which large numbers of peasants became dependent on the sugar industry for their very survival. In the final analysis, it was this fact, over and above pressure from new or old rural elites and any prospect of a new "prosperity," which underlay the Pekalongan industry's increasing success in inducing the peasantry to provide it with cane.

The new economy was itself the sum of rather diverse developments in rural Pekalongan in the middle decades of the nineteenth century. One was the so-called Pekalongan "Padi-Sickness." Another was the expansion not only of sugar but also of a major indigo industry under the aegis of the Cultivation System. And yet a third was an increase in peasant numbers which, unlike the first two factors, was something Pekalongan experienced more or less in common with Java as a whole. Taken together, they produced conditions for the peasants in which their deepening involvement in the production of sugar became a pressing necessity.

The Padi-Sickness—whatever its cause or causes—ravaged the rice crop in much of Pekalongan, with locally varying intensity, from the late 1840s until well into the 1860s.[32] The endemic crop-failure which it caused was only one factor, however, in a deepening mid-century crisis affecting the annual cycle of *padi* and secondary food crops on which traditional peasant agriculture was based. For at the same time, the Government's requirement that large amounts of land and labour be expended first on indigo and then, as that industry became increasingly unprofitable, on sugar, took a toll on peasant resources far greater than a mere recitation of land requisition and labour demand might initially suggest. Not that these figures were trifling: in the early 1840s, at the height of its expansion, indigo occupied nearly ten per cent of Pekalongan's recorded *sawah* area, and by the following decade in the Residency's key sugar districts, cane occupied far more than the one-fifth of peasant farmland notionally assigned to it in the Cultivation System's theory (Van Niel 1972, p.101). At Wonopringo, for instance, cultivation was concentrated in the heartlands of the *kring*.[33] There, in the district of Pekadjangan, immediately to the north of the *fabriek* itself, approximately one third of the *sawah* area was requisitioned annually for cane,[34] resulting in a situation in which some villages lost nearly all their land, something for which they were "compensated" by the assignment of fields requisitioned from other villages, often some distance away.[35]

At the same time, the economic situation of the peasantry was greatly exacerbated, and peasants' prospects either of feeding themselves or of fulfilling their fiscal obligations to the colonial authorities were greatly reduced by the impact which the rotation system of growing cane—which was adopted universally in Pekalongan by the late 1830s—had on the main *padi* crop and on any subsequent planting of *palawija*. The immediate consequence of rotation was that cane, which occupied the ground for from fifteen to eighteen months between planting and harvest, in reality took up to twice as much peasant farmland at any given time of the year than the notional figure for annual requisition implied. At Wonopringo, for example, at the beginning of the Campaign in May each year, there would be some 570 hectares of land under ripening cane, just beginning to be harvested, while another 570 hectares was in the process of being planted for the following year's Campaign. As the Campaign was not finished until October or November, it could be the end of the year, and time for preparation of land for the main *padi*-crop, before all farmland requisitioned for sugar in the previous year had been returned to the peasantry.

This long growing season for cane had far-reaching effects on the *padi-palawija* cycle. Either land was unavailable for second cropping or else the crops were jeopardised by the need to divert dry season irrigation water to the newly-established cane plantations (the dry season began in May and extended to November or later, depending on the vagaries of the monsoon). Worse still, at a water-driven *fabriek* like Wonopringo, the farmland up-country of the factory was deprived of irrigation water so that the *fabriek's* millstream could be maintained at full spate. As mountain-fed streams dried up in the later months of the dry season, this put the peasant's *palawija* seriously at risk.[36] As for the main *padi*-crop itself, the basic problem in the *kring* was that land assigned to sugar needed to be cleared well before the normal time for harvesting rice. In Pekalongan in the 1860s, as is plainly attested from official reports, this led the peasantry either to ripen the *padi* prematurely by early draining of the *sawah* or else to plant quicker-maturing but lower-yielding varieties. In either case, there was a major drop in the productivity of the fields.[37]

Conclusion

The evidence from Wonopringo—and from Pekalongan generally—suggests the need for substantial rethinking of the means by which the production of raw material for the burgeoning sugar industry was secured in mid-nineteenth century Java. Previous analyses have concentrated attention, as we have seen, on the utilisation by the responsible Dutch officials of traditional channels of authority in the countryside, as well as on the new prosperity which sugar notionally brought to the cane-growing peasantry. In fact, the first of these arguments is ambiguous, in that the rural elites involved in the management of cane production were themselves being radically transformed in the mid-nineteenth century: they had ceased to be 'traditional.' The second argument, though it may well explain the attitudes of those elites toward the requirements of the industry, posits a general prosperity generated by the expansion of sugar production which is far from proven. The present argument does not seek to deny that the subordination of labour to capital in this sector of world market production in nineteenth-century Java was a complex and evolving process, in which *priyayi*, headmen and crop-payments played a significant part. On the other hand, it does point to the need for a far broader appraisal than has been attempted hitherto of the impact of government cultivations on the agrarian economy of Java generally, and of the consequences of this for the development of labour in the export industries. As the Pekalongan case indicates, the development of government cultivations—first indigo and then sugar—had implications for the rural economy which extended far beyond the effects of the flow generated by the increasingly substantial crop payments made to the cultivators. Indications are that in this part of the north Java littoral, at least, the expansion of production for the world market had a highly deleterious effect on the cycle of *padi* and *palawija* which had earlier constituted the basis of "peasant" agriculture, and that this, in conjunction with the "Padi-Sickness" and the increase in peasant numbers, created a new rural economy in which sugar was king and in which peasants became willing cane planters, essentially because they saw no other way of securing their livelihood. This remains, of course, a scenario greatly in need of quantification and probably of further qualification. Its appositeness for Java's other major sugar districts also needs to be worked out. It forms, nevertheless, an important dimension of our understanding of why peasants grew cane, a dimension which, whatever the problems involved in further investigation, cannot be neglected.

Notes

1. An earlier draft of this paper was given at the Conference on Indonesian Economic History in the Dutch Colonial Period, Ursula College, the Australian National University, Canberra, December 16-18, 1983. I am grateful to the participants in that Conference for their comments. My thanks also go to the University of Adelaide for continuing financial support for my research and to my patient typists who have seen this through several wearying drafts. In addition, I am indebted to the staff of the Arsip Nasional in Jakarta (particularly Mona Lohanda) and to LIPI for facilitating my research there.
2. For example, the British manager of the Wonopringo *fabriek*, one of the best-equipped in Java, commented that it was "nothing but a bad cultivation" which stood in the way of improved productivity there in the mid-1850s. Edwards to Nederlandische Handel Maatshappij's (NHM) Batavia Factorij, 4.2.1854 [-extract], in Batavia Factorij to NHM Amsterdam, 25.2.1854/271, Algemeen Rijksarchief, The Hague [hereafter ARADH], NHM Archive 4887. It was also the opinion of the Director of Cultivations in the Batavia Government that "the greater output of sugar must be ascribed to the cultivation, which is improved through its greater popularity with the native population...". Director Cultivations to Governor-General, 14.7.1856/2303, Exh. 3.9.1857/4, ARADH, Archief Ministerie v. Kolonien [hereafter MK] 636.
3. Out of context, of course, remarks like this could be mistaken for Geertz. See, for example, the latter's statement that "what is striking about this development [of the sugar industry] is not how much it affected the general pattern of village economic life, but how little" (Geertz 1963, p.94).
4. These statements should be compared with the much more radical arguments of J. and P. Alexander (1978; 1979).
5. Brief details of Wonopringo can be found in W. M. F. Mansvelt (1925-26, vol.2, pp.363-65). Wonopringo was owned from 1844 until 1870 by the NHM (Nederlandsche Handel-Maatschappij), the largest European commercial concern operating in Indonesia during the late colonial era. Founded in 1824 under governmental patronage to wrest control of the Java trade from British hands, it became under the Cultivation System the "Crown Agent" and banker of the Dutch colonial government and the shipper of the government's share of the output of the System. By mid-century, it also had direct investments of its own in the sugar industry, among them Wonopringo.

6. Monographie Fabriek Wonopringo, B/II/G, Exh. 24.5.1862/40, ARADH, MK 1181; Jaarverslag NHM Factorij Batavia, no. 41 (1865-6), p.214, ARADH, NHM Archief.
7. Vitalis to Director Cultivations, 10.3.1834/25, Exh. 13.3.1834/761, Arsip Nasional, Jakarta [hereafter ANJ], Archief Cultures [hereafter AC] 333; S. van Deventer 1865-6, vol. 2, pp.704-5; Besluiten Governor-General, 5.10.1837/7, ARADH, MK 2575.
8. Batavia to Amsterdam, 16.3.1861/940 and 2.5.1861/951, ARADH, NHM 4891.
9. In 1860, the Dutch administrators and Javanese *priyayi* were drawing a total of 12,397 guilders annually from the sugar industry of Pekalongan in the form of *cultuurprocenten*. Around 75 per cent of this came from the Wonopringo factory. See Opgave ... Kultuurprocenten [1858-1860], ARADH, MK Supplement 32; Staat ... Verschillende Kultuurinrigtingen ... Pekalongan, 1861, ANJ, AC 1624.
10. For example, Politiek Verslag Pekalongan, 1857, ANJ, Pekalongan 1.
11. Resident Pekalongan to Governor-General, [?].12.1866/Lett. A, in Governor-General to Minister of Colonies, 12.1.1867/Kabinet no. 1/Lett. A, Exh. 29.3.1867/11, ARADH, MK 1894.
12. Edwards to Batavia, 19.3.1859, in Batavia to Amsterdam 26.3.1859/2583, ARADH, NHM 4889.
13. Politiek Verslag Pekalongan 1863, ANJ, Pekalongan 2 [emphasis added].
14. Inspector Cultivations Sijthoff to Director Binnenlands Bestuur, 25.4.1867, Exh. 11.4.1868/91, ARADH, MK 2064.
15. Edwards to Resident Pekalongan, 24.1.1857/1100 and Batavia Factorij to Director Cultivations, 31.1.1857/48, in Batavia to Amsterdam 11.3.1857/533, ARADH, NHM 4888.
16. Politiek Verslag Pekalongan 1857 and 1864, ANJ, Pekalongan 1 and 2.
17. Politiek Verslag Pekalongan 1861 and 1869, ANJ, Pekalongan 2.
18. See, for example, Kultuurverslag Pekalongan, 1834, 1-4, ANJ, AC 1624; Batavia to Amsterdam, 26.1.1858/619 [which shows nine big plantations], ARADH, NHM 4889.
19. Besluiten Governor-General, 9.11.1841/16 and 2.2.1843/11, ARADH, MK 2635 and 2642. As early as 1836, the arrangements for sugar planting in Pekalongan had drawn critical comment from one of the *controleurs*. He claimed that in contrast to the situation in "successful" Pasuruan, where the planters in effect "owned" the cane up until its harvest, the system in Pekalongan meant that the growers "had to work like day labourers" and consequently had little interest in the quality of the cane which they produced. See Van Stralendorff to Resident Pekalongan, 18.1.1836, Exh. 22.2.1836/383, ANJ, AC 353.
20. Kultuurverslag Pekalongan 1856, ANJ, AC 1624; [Fragment] Kontroleur Afdeeling Pekalongan to Resident Pekalongan, 4.8.1856, ANJ, Pekalongan 74.
21. Resident Pekalongan to Director Binnenlands Bestuur, 20.2.1867/674, Exh. 11.4.1868/91, ARADH, MK 2064; Batavia to Amsterdam, 10.7.1855/384, ARADH, NHM 7887.

22. The information in this table is derived from the Kultuurverslagen Pekalongan and Algemeen and Jaarverslagen Pekalongan for the relevant years, all in ANJ, Pekalongan Archief, Archief "Pasar Ikan" and Archief Cultures and from Aantooning Uitkomsten Wonopringo, 1856-1865, Exh. 11.4.1868/91, ARADH, MK 2604.
23. Most notably by Fasseur, who discusses a range of criteria, including the price at auction of the colonial government's opium farms together with its various other revenue farms (i.e., markets, cattle-slaughter, etc.); the number of cattle owned by the peasantry; the degree to which the land rent was in arrears; the value of imports of cotton goods; and the government's income from the salt monopoly (Fasseur 1981, pp.10-15).
24. Politiek Verslag Pekalongan 1865, ANJ, Pekalongan 2.
25. See, for example, the information on trade in Politiek Verslag Pekalongan 1860 and 1866, ANJ Pekalongan 2.
26. Nota over de Aanslag der Landrente ... [Pekalongan] 2.4.1866, Exh. 15.1.1868/35, ARADH, MK 2021; Politiek Verslag Pekalongan 1864 and 1870, ANJ, Pekalongan 2. For abuses involved in the collection of the land rent in Java generally, see S. van Deventer (1865-66, vol. 3, pp.266-71).
27. Batavia to Amsterdam, 10.12.1856/511, ARADH, NHM 4888; Monographie Fabriek Wonopringo, B/II/K, Exh. 24.4.1862/40, ARADH, MK 1181. According to the "Monographie," fencing had to be made anew each year; old fencing was only suitable for protecting second crops. There was, as one of the Pekalongan *controleurs* pointed out in the 1860s, no such thing as "free" resources in the countryside. All timber and bamboo came from land claimed by one village or another and had to be paid for. [*Priyayi*, too, expected to be compensated for infringement of their rights over the Residency's natural resources of timber, etc.]. See the information supplied by A. van der Gon Netscher, *controleur* of the Bandar division of Pekalongan, cited in *Tijdschrift voor Nederlands-Indië*, 1867 (2), p.88.
28. Inspector Cultivations Sijthoff to Director Binnenlands Bestuur, 25.4.1867, Exh. 11.4.1868/91, ARADH, MK 2064.
29. Batavia to Amsterdam, 15.2.1864/1233, ARADH, NHM 4893; Edwards to Batavia, 4.2.1854, in Batavia to Amsterdam 25.2.1854, and Edwards to Batavia, 19.9.1854, in Batavia to Amsterdam, 11.10.1854/320, ARADH, NHM 4887.
30. This calculation is based on (a) the average crop-payment made at Wonopringo between 1869-1870, less the ten guilders land rent assessed on each *bau* of cane, and (b) the figure calculated around 1870 by an Indonesian government commission as the "going-rate" in the countryside of lowland Pekalongan for the hire of a *bau* of land and the labour to go with it. [Extract] Besluiten., Governor-General 26.12.1871/19 and 21 and Governor-General to Minister of Colonies, 11.5.1872/726/Bij1.B, Exh. 20.11.1872/27, ARADH, MK 2543; Director Binnenlands Bestuur to Governor-General 5.9.1871/6453, in appendices to Mailrapport 556/1871, ARADH, MK 6353.
31. See note 28 above.

32. By way of introduction to this complex issue, see Boutmij (1868, pp.129-33), and de Vriese, (n.d.). On "mentek," see van Hall and van de Koppel (1946-50, vol. 2A, pp.53-63).
33. Batavia to Amsterdam, 24.4.1852/138, ARADH, NHM 4886; Monographie Fabriek Wonopringo B/II/G, Exh. 24.4.1862/40, ARADH, MK 1181; Van Below, Verslag ... Opname der Suikerriet Aanplanting ... Wonopringo ... Oogst 1861, Exh. 17.9.1863/10, ARADH, MK 1381.
34. In the late 1850s, in that part of Pekadjangan which belonged to the Wonopringo *kring*, approximately 334 hectares were requisitioned annually for sugar from a total recorded 1008 hectares of *sawah*. As a result of an expansion of the *kring* itself, the proportion of requisitioned land to fields left to the peasantry declined after 1860, so that by the late 1860s the annual requisition for sugar amounted to approximately 334 hectares out of a total of 2,100 hectares of *sawah*. (As will be argued in the text, these requisition figures should be doubled to get the amount of land actually taken out of peasant use for much of the year). The figures for requisition used here are 20 per cent higher than the notional ones in the *Kultuurverslagen*, etc., since it was standard practice in Pekalongan to allow an "excess" requisition of twenty per cent for drainage ditches and roadways in the plantations area. Inspector Cultivations Boutmij to Director Cultivations, 16.8.1858, Exh. 21.12. 1860/2, ARADH, MK 1015; Inspector Cultivations Sijthoff to Director Binnenlands Bestuur, 25.4.1867, Exh. 11.4.1868/91, ARADH, MK 2064.
35. Kultuurverslag Pekalongan 1856, ANJ, AC 1634.
36. Sijthoff to Director Binnenlands Bestuur, 25.4.1857, Exh. 11.4.1868/91, ARADH, MK 2064. In the case of the Wonopringo factory, it was calculated by Inspector of Cultivations, Sijthoff, in April 1967 that no harm would come to peasant *palawija* if the mill had first call on the *kring's* water resources up until the end of July each year. This was after nearly three decades during which the Campaign at Wonopringo had almost invariably continued into October or November.
37. Secretaris Pekalongan to Director Binnenlands Bestuur, 14.5.1867/1747, Exh. 11.4.1868/91, ARADH, MK 2064. Quicker-maturing padi was usually identified in Pekalongan as belonging to the *gendjah* or *gogo* varieties. Their substitution for the more usual (in the lowlands) *dalem* varieties is confirmed from contemporary evidence from adjacent Tegal. *Dalem* was said to take 115-120 days to ripen, whereas the comparable time for *gendjah* was only 90 days. The latter, however, yielded on average one-third less rice and was planted only on poorly watered *sawah* "or on fields assigned for tobacco and sugar." See Anon (1856).

CHAPTER FOUR

The Legacy of the Cultivation System for Subsequent Economic Development

Robert Van Niel

Would it have made any difference to the economic development of Java if the Cultivation System had never been instituted; if, instead of introducing Van den Bosch's scheme in 1830, the government had simply carried on with the direction sketched by Du Bus in 1827? I cannot, of course, answer these questions because they are purely suppositional, but simply asking the questions causes me to reflect on long-term as opposed to short-term trends. When I do this, I tend to find all sorts of reasons for thinking that the Cultivation System made very little difference at all, and that things would have been much the same no matter what. These thoughts are not totally satisfying, for the System quickened the pace of change. I would certainly not be the first to say that the Cultivation System used and built upon social and economic patterns already present in Javanese society. In a very real sense, that is precisely what Van den Bosch said he was doing. But then Van den Bosch said so many things. Truth be told, I think that he and other Hollanders had much less influence in affecting in any way the fundamentals of Javanese life throughout the nineteenth century than they thought they did.

In any event, I shall not beg the question. I am not prepared to argue that the Cultivation System was revolutionary in what it did, but will take three areas of change in which I think the Cultivation System did influence economic matters with important consequences. The three areas are: (1) capital formation, (2) cheap labour, and (3) village economy. Before I begin discussing these, I must devote some consideration to the manner in which writers have regarded the Cultivation System over the past century and a quarter. These earlier writings, of which there are many, reflect the feelings and attitudes of another day about the System. Though not uniform in their views, they form a body of received knowledge which has shaped out thinking about the Cultivation System and about the entire course of change in nineteenth-century Java.

The Historiography of the Cultivation System

The historiography of the Cultivation System can, for my present purposes, be divided into three phases. The first phase dates from the later years of the

System, that is from the 1850s and 1860s, and extends to the early 1920s. This is a rather long period in which there were diverse types of writings about the System. Nevertheless, I propose it as a single phase because it was imbued with an optimism about how much better things could and would be once the errors and terrors of the Cultivation System were out of the way, and saner economic principles were allowed to prevail. As with the other two phases, these writings may tell us more about their authors and the notions of their time than about the Cultivation System. Soest (1869-71) and Deventer (1865-66), writing in the 1860s, highlighted the abuses which the System visited on the Javanese people and sought a restoration of liberal economic principles; they also felt that they knew all there was to know about the System and that it was mostly bad. Some liberal writers such as Pierson (1868) and Cornets de Groot van Kraayenburg (1862) were less bitter and absolute in their condemnation, but felt that the System went wrong in practice, and that a more enlightened economic policy which promoted private enterprise would help matters. Clive Day's classic account is an English-language version of this kind of thinking and optimism (Day 1904). In the early twentieth century, writers were more inclined to ignore the details of the Cultivation System, labelling it merely "exploitative," a black page of the past which had now been turned. Hasselman (1912) and Stokvis (1922) are examples of this kind of scholarship. In the area of archival publications, the endeavours of van Deventer, de Roo, and van der Kemp to extend the great documentary publication of de Jonge never reached beyond the 1820s (Jonge 1862-1888; Deventer 1891; Roo 1909; Kemp 1890-1920).[1] Transitional to the next phase is van Vollenhoven who condemned the Netherlands' policy for the entire nineteenth century, especially in its impact on the landholding rights of the Javanese village (Vollenhoven 1932). Van Vollenhoven provides much of the raw data and fundamental viewpoint of the second phase.

The second phase of writings about the Cultivation System dates from the 1920s to the end of Dutch colonial rule. Not only had van Vollenhoven's writings and polemics about land policy raised questions about all aspects of Dutch policy over the previous century, but De Kat Angelino's *magnum opus*, in the philosophical spirit of the time, displays a synthesization and aloofness which takes the sharp edges off the whole of the Dutch impact in Java, thereby providing a blandness that is almost unreal (Kat Angelino 1929-30). The striving for balance is best found in the classic work of Furnivall (1944). While exposing how the Cultivation System diverted and undermined Javanese village life, he shows some of the positive changes which the system promoted. At the same time, Burger, in his sociological-historical studies, attempted to detail how western ideas and institutions had penetrated into the interior of Java, resulting in a defeudalization and opening of Javanese society (Burger 1939, 1948-50, 1975). Detailed historical studies of nineteenth-century Indonesian history using archival source materials began to appear in the University of Utrecht dissertations directed by Gerretson (*Utrechtsche Bijdragen* 1932?-1950?). In Batavia, the writings and statistical pamphlets of Mansvelt on nineteenth-century economic developments began to raise some questions about the impact of the System, for it became evident that some rather positive economic changes had occurred; these materials have been reissued and updated by Creutzberg in the *Changing Economy in Indonesia* series. A number of developments in the economic and political arena during the 1920s and 1930s tended to make people aware of the impact of colonial policy and practices on Javanese society and also somewhat more conscious of the role of government in economic life. When combined with a growing interest in socio-historical theorizing, these developments tended to steer writers toward a mixed view of the Cultivation System. While recognizing the advances made by the System in the growth of the export-oriented sector, they became more severe in their criticism of the impact of the system on Javanese society and more theoretically consequential in their condemnation of European imperialism. Not one of these writers, however, would have gone as far in trying to change the earlier view of the system as Gerretson (1938) when he wrote that: "The Cultivation System was the greatest benefaction bestowed by the Netherlands on the Indies."

The third phase begins after Indonesian independence and is still going on today. More so than in the earlier periods, it represents a worldwide interest in Indonesian studies. During this phase new questions are being asked and new historical evidence is becoming increasingly available. In both the Netherlands and Indonesia, archives are gradually being opened and the new materials which have come to light enable historians to penetrate more deeply into the workings of the Cultivation System than had previously been possible. Pioneering in this phase of writings about the Cultivation System is the work of Reinsma (1955), which offers some startling, revisionist ideas, especially as regards the general prosperity in Java during the time of the System. In other respects, however, Reinsma's work leans heavily on ideas from the previous period, especially those of van Vollenhoven and Burger. In 1960-61, while in the Netherlands, I began my research into the early years of the Cultivation System, and in the early 1970s Fasseur began to examine the economic effects of the System, both in Java and the Netherlands (Fasseur 1975). Both of us were then still much influenced by the second phase authors, but we had new materials with which to work and new questions to ask, so gradually we began to diverge further and further from these earlier ideas (Fasseur 1977a, 1977b, 1978, 1981; Van Niel 1972, 1976, 1981, 1982). In the mid-1970s, the study of nineteenth-century Indonesian history gained popularity, especially in the Netherlands, where a group of young scholars began exploring anew their colonial past. In Australia, too, Indonesian studies and economic history were combined in a most fruitful way. These studies gained access to historical evidence at a local level, closer to the actual operation of the System than had earlier been possible. This resulted in a further advance along lines suggested in the 1950s and 1960s, as well as in directions not previously considered (Van Niel 1966). The overall effect of this third phase of historical writing has been to initiate a robust revisionism of the first two phases of writing about the Cultivation System.

The three economic legacies of the System mentioned above, namely capital formation, cheap labour, and village economy, have been differently viewed—or not viewed at all—in earlier writings about the System; other legacies, which I will mention only in passing, were considered more worthy of attention in earlier times than I am now willing to accord them. As our knowledge of nineteenth-century events increases, it becomes concomitantly more difficult to make broad generalizations for all of Java or even for those parts of Java where the Cultivation System was operative. From the very first, the Cultivation System made local adaptations in order to achieve its desired goal of exportable products which could compete on world markets. The very word "System," in fact, is misleading, since it implies a higher level of co-ordination than existed. The phases of historiography reveal a spectrum of ideas about the System, from severe condemnation, to selective criticism, to a broader social perspective, to the discernment of positive social changes, and finally to the perception of economic developments within Javanese society. No one is prepared to say that the System worked without entailing hardship and ill treatment of the Javanese peasantry, but increasingly the historical view seeks to reveal the broad framework of socio-economic change which forms the background for the current state of affairs.

Capital Formation

Before the introduction of the Cultivation System in 1830, there were efforts by Europeans to break away from the system of forced deliveries and contingents which had characterized the operation of the United Dutch East India Company (VOC). The potential producers of exportable agrarian commodities in the years before 1830 were:

1. Javanese villages which controlled lands on which they paid an assessed landrent.
2. Private planters, chiefly European, who used "waste" land for which they paid the government a rent.
3. Private planters, chiefly European, who contracted with Javanese princes for the use of their appanage holdings in the Princely Lands.
4. Owners of private estates, chiefly European, who had seignorial-like rights over their lands and the people on them.

Each of these forms of production had great difficulty in attracting capital with which to expand and improve its operations. European capital, the only capital available at the time, had had varied experiences with colonial agrarian enterprises and was not attracted to investment in Java because of the high risks.

Among the four forms of production arrangement, only the second, the private planters working lands rented from the government and making individual labour arrangements with the local population, seemed to have any potential for attracting capital. The Javanese village was totally outside the realm of capital economic involvement and showed no interest in the area of cultivation for export. Left to its own devices, it focussed on its own subsistence, producing rice, cotton, indigo, and other products for daily use. Moreover, since the normal western legal procedures had little application to village matters, there was no protection for capital investment. Experience between 1815 and 1830 had shown that where export cultivations, such as coffee gardens, had been turned over to village control, they were neglected or abandoned. Such export products as were obtained during this time came from private planters on rented lands, from appanage holdings, or from areas where forced delivery arrangements remained in effect (Van Niel 1981). Private planters on lands rented from the government could not attract much capital because they did not have title to the land. What they could and did do was to work with export-import houses (mainly Dutch and British) in Java, obtaining money from them in return for export crops which they produced. Not only was this a precarious existence, but it provided barely sufficient capital for ongoing operations, and none for expansion or improvement. Private planters in the Princely Lands at the beginning of the century appeared to have the best potential for growth and expansion. For reasons which are not fully clear, this did not occur. Perhaps their expansion was restricted by the appanage arrangements and the manner in which they drew upon land and labour through traditional obligations. Or it may have been that they had adopted the Javanese lifestyle which surrounded them and were satisfied with the level of operation which they had reached. In any event, they remained throughout the century at roughly the same size and level of profitability which they had achieved by 1830. Finally, the owners of private estates seemed not to be much interested in export cultivations or in expanding their economic operations. Increasingly such estates became more prestige than economic items; their greatest economic value was as real estate. Many of their owners had tied up most of their revenue in their estates and did not want to involve themselves with outside interests. A few of these lands, such as the P & T Lands in Krawang, did obtain outside financing and subsequently expanded and grew. This was an exception, however; most of these private estates became increasingly anachronistic as the century wore on.

The Cultivation System had the primary goal of stimulating the production and export of agricultural commodities which were saleable on world markets. The government realized early that any processing which these products required would have to be developed by inputs of capital which the government itself undertook to supply. It loaned money to persons contracted to construct mills for processing agricultural products supplied by the villagers. Such contractual arrangements were tried for various crops, but only with sugar did they become a significant factor in the development of expansion capital. In coffee and indigo production, the other two profitable export crops, contractors were either not used at all or became superfluous because of the small scale of production. In sugar processing, however, the government-sponsored system seemed to be just right. Government contractors not only received the capital needed to build their facilities, but also had the help of the government in obtaining the raw cane and the necessary labour. The contractor was obliged to sell his processed sugar to the government to repay the loan made to him, but sugar in excess of the amount needed for loan repayment could be sold privately by the contractor for his own profit. There was money to be made here and within a few years, the resale value of these sugar contracts rose greatly in value.

The village lands which supplied contractors with their raw materials were in the same general areas as the former wastelands used by the private planters who had rented lands from the government before 1830. This is understandable, for, being dependent on an adequate labour supply, both drew upon land tracts in the vicinity of population concentrations. The lands planted for the government cultivations were in close proximity to those of the private planters. Over the years both did rather well, and both expanded at about the same rate, the private planters maintaining a constant ratio of about one-fourth of the land area planted by the government. As contractors gained wealth, they either expanded their operations as private planters or assisted family members in opening up new areas of cultivation to other crops. Government restrictions periodically limited private expansion into profitable cultivations such as coffee, sugar, and indigo, while less-profitable cultivations such as tea, tobacco, and nopal (cochineal) were turned over or left to private planters. The role of the private planter in the growth of capital has been amply expounded by Reinsma (1955), with further explanation and correction by Fasseur (1975). The political clout and the capital which were needed for this agricultural expansion insured that government contractors, private planters, import-export houses, and members of the Dutch civil service in Java came to be closely linked through family ties. During the Cultivation System the capital base of the agro-economic export sector expanded many times over, largely through the interconnections of the European families in Java (Van Niel 1964a). Much of the annoyance with the system expressed by Hollanders in Europe after the middle of the nineteenth century was directed against the nepotism and personal influence exercised in the awarding of contracts and land rights. Outsiders to the Java clique saw the lucrative nature of the system and wanted part of the action. The development that had occurred, however, was attributable to a capital build-up stimulated by forces internal to Java, not from outside.

The Cultivation System, through government injections of capital and through the expanding cultivation of products for the world market, had stimulated the formation of private capital, which in substantial amounts was invested in further expansion of the export agrarian sector. The very success of this process created problems. One has already been noted, that is, annoyance with the special privilege accorded to a group of intimates. Among Javanese planters, too, there was a growing feeling that they could expand even faster and operate more efficiently if the government would remove itself from the cultivations. Traditional wisdom in the first two historiographic phases regarded the Cultivation System as opposed to all private enterprise and restrictive of capital formation. It was long thought that private capital which suddenly flowed into Java from outside during the 1850s and 1860s forced the dismantling of the System. This is not correct in any of its parts, as Reinsma has pointed out. Expansion was generated mostly in Java, and the amount of outside capital remained relatively small until the 1880s. The close alliance among government contractors, private planters, import-export houses, and government civil servants is at the heart of the matter. It is a subject that awaits a great deal of historical research; fortunately, much of the needed evidence is available. The formation of capital among Chinese planters and entrepreneurs was, I am quite certain, also occurring at the same time. I know much less about the available evidence here and am less certain of the prospects for historical investigation.

Cheap Labour

A cost-effective and ample labour supply was a prime requisite to export-oriented cultivations. For the nineteenth century, control over labour was more crucial than control over land, for the latter seemed in oversupply; the former, if not in short supply, was difficult to manage and exploit. The Cultivation System addressed this problem by utilizing, in a new way, the traditional mode of Javanese labour exploitation which required the Javanese peasant to deliver a portion of his production to a higher authority and work part of each year at tasks designated by his superiors (Naerssen 1977). He was not paid for this labour [corvée], for the work was viewed as an expression of social solidarity and supportive of the hierarchical social order. By the early nineteenth century, before the Cultivation System, a tax on the produce of the land, known as landrent, had been substituted for the delivery of produce. The village had been designated as the unit for collecting this tax and also as the unit for supplying the cost-free obligatory labour service. From both an economic and a socio-political point of view, these changes were disruptive to Javanese society, for such matters had been handled differently in earlier times (Breman 1980). This will be discussed in greater detail in the following section.

The colonial government of Indonesia, as the VOC before it, viewed itself as successor to the Javanese sovereigns and laid claim to all rights previously accorded to Javanese higher authorities. This included the right to labour service, which was used on an unprecedented scale to develop an infrastructure of roads, fortifications, waterways, irrigation projects, and public buildings, all at a minimal cost to the government. Obligatory labour service for Javanese superiors and for village headman also increased, despite the professions of the government to check abuses. In fact, the Javanese headmen at the village and supra-village level were so essential for tapping the available labour supply and for collecting taxes, that the government could not have done without them and so was obliged to leave restrictions on their duties unenforced. Everything was to remain as it always had been, or was thought to have been. The Javanese peasant was to work under the orders of his immediate headman and superiors while regarding this work as his traditional tribute to higher authority. Even private planters who managed to hire labour for wages had to buy off the corvée value of that labour. Others obtained labour by paying the taxes of a village, and in this way obtained quasi-seigniorial rights to labour service.

Since obligatory labour was the substance of cultivating export crops, the Cultivation System now added some new wrinkles to the practice of forced labour. In the Fundamental Law (*Regeerings Reglement*) of 1830, Article 80, the practice of obligatory labour in the forests of Java, formerly imposed by the government for either a wage or for a remission of landrent, was extended, at the government's discretion, to use in areas other than forests. The System planned to use one-fifth of the village's land for the cultivation of export crops. The value of the produce grown on this land was supposed to be enough to pay the landrent (tax), which had earlier been assessed at two-fifths of the production of the chief crop. In this way the village was calculated to be better off under the new System. In practice, I hasten to add, things did not quite work in this way, but the point here is that the government set aside a proportional amount of the peasant's labour, that is one-fifth of the year or 66 days, for government use and designated this as *cultivation service*. This cultivation service was really a substitution for the amount of landrent (tax), which earlier had been a substitution for the obligatory delivery of produce. This cultivation service was not a substitution for corvée service imposed by the government, but in addition to it. Since the peasant, or rather his village, was paid for the crops produced by the cultivation service—however inadequate that payment may have been—the cultivation service was always considered by the government to be quite separate from the corvée service. It was also separate from the personal services extended to village headmen and supra-village superiors (Van Niel 1976). The work on the government crops was, however, coerced by the government in the same manner as other obligatory services. To the Javanese peasant there was no distinction in the type of obligatory labour; there was only a marked increase in the amount.

The amount of forced labour required of the Javanese peasant during the time of the Cultivation System cannot be weighed or measured because no rule or consistency prevailed, even within a single village. Already before 1830 there are indications that within villages there were divisions of labour that had some people working much of the year on government corvée while others worked the land. After 1830 there were persons who worked consistently in government cultivations or in the nearby processing establishments. There had always been persons who worked as day labourers or tenants for other villagers. In all such circumstances, some form of monetary payment was usual, and there was thus some movement in the direction of specialization and a wage system. But wage-payment must not be overestimated, for wages were generally not adequate for survival. The individual or his family remained bound to the village and to the traditional obligations which had to be fulfilled. The Javanese peasant did not become accustomed to an open wage system and did not generally see wage labour as an exclusive means for satisfying wants and desires. Instead, he continued to view labour within the context of obligatory service to higher authority which had to be fulfilled. Increased demands for labour were accompanied by an increased use of coercion by officials tied into government service. With the growth of population and the pressure on land in areas of government cultivations, the extra money from wages became increasingly essential to the survival of the poorer peasant. Writings in the first historiographic phase make much of the fact that from the 1840s on, planters and contractors claimed that wage labour worked better and more efficiently than forced labour. This is undoubtedly true, given the tasks it was assigned. But, in the late 1850s, efforts to introduce wage labour into areas normally covered by corvée labour had to be abandoned because no labourers were forthcoming for the kind of wages that the government was prepared to pay (Schoch 1891, p.64). The masses of the Javanese peasantry had not learned to value work as a means toward an end, but continued to view their labour as a burden to be endured and suffered. Extending forced labour in burdensome amounts throughout wider sections of the population may have taught the peasant how to work in new cultivations. It did not, however, stimulate any personal interest in these export crops, for the context in which labour was viewed by the Javanese peasant remained unchanged.

In the 1860s and 1870s when private planters began to institute labour- and land-contracts with individuals and villages, it was evident that the Cultivation

System had not done much to prepare the way for a free and voluntary labour market. Instead, it had attached a negative value to labour by keeping the compensations minimal through continued use of traditional authority patterns. It had also created a need for supplementary incomes in those areas where export cultivations could flourish. For the private planters, this had both advantages and disadvantages. The advantage lay in the fact that the prevailing wage level was low, and they could thus continue to compete on world markets. The disadvantages, which for a while outweighed the advantages, arose from the problems in attracting and keeping labourers. In this period a number of devices were tried to overcome these problems, but in one way or another, they all involved a return to coercion and to the use of traditional authority figures as intermediaries in the process. Labour recruiters were often village headmen or other powerful figures. Money was advanced to attract labour, but frequently the labourer did not come to work as agreed. Consequently various pressures had to be applied. The regular courts were slow and inadequate; more effective was the use of strong-arm men to coerce the labourer. Sometimes the planters could persuade administrative officials to assist in coercion, but there were limits to this. Eventually force of circumstances rather than any particular device solved the dilemma. By the 1880s, the pressure of population growth was becoming evident in the reduced amount of land available and in the limited capacity of villages to produce all of their basic food requirements; some people had to find sources of income outside village production. At the same time diseases struck both the sugar and the coffee plants in Java, causing a sharp decline in sugar and coffee production, and reducing income from wages and crop payments, on which many Javanese villagers had come to rely. At this very moment sugar prices became depressed internationally because of beet sugar competition; as a consequence planters lowered the wage rates offered to hired labourers and the amount they were prepared to pay to rent land. These factors in combination resulted in a reduction in the amount of money available to Javanese society, which had to respond with a greater readiness to take on wage labour at prices, and under conditions, not previously acceptable (Elson 1982). Current research into prosperity in Javanese villages tends to support the idea that there was more material wealth in Java during the Cultivation System than in the years following its demise.

Cheap labour was only partly a legacy of the Cultivation System. Powerful forces, beyond policy restrictions, were at work to keep the cost of labour down in Java. It is a fact, however, that population growth was more rapid in the Princely Lands and in areas under government cultivation than in other parts of Java. Why this should be so has led to much discussion. Population was already most dense in these areas before 1830, and the economic stimulus of the System led to a faster influx of migrants and population increase than elsewhere. Over the years of the Cultivation System, these areas became more accustomed to costs of traditional village activities being supplemented with outside injections of money. As will be pointed out in the next section, these were also the areas which witnessed the greatest socio-economic evolution: increased powers of the village elite and diminution in the power of the supra-village groups. Even if there was no stimulus to move out of the traditional context of labour, a climate developed for a concentration of available labour, which also provided mechanisms for aggregating that labour for use in export cultivations. Earlier historiographic accounts were certainly not unaware of the impact of forced labour on Javanese society. If anything, they tended to underestimate the magnitude of the number of labour days coerced out of the population, for the government rarely exposed itself by lumping corvée and cultivation services into a single statistic. Truly the System was a tax in labour. Multatuli's famous condemnation of the administration for burdening the Javanese, which appeared in 1860, laid the blame on the doorstep of maladministration (Douwes Dekker 1860). His experience, ironically, was in parts of Java not affected by government cultivations. In his later writings he saw clearly the failure of wages to attract labour in a free and open manner. Boeke, writing early in the twentieth century, saw a division between the village household economy of the Javanese and the export-oriented, capital-intensive economy of the government (Boeke 1910; *Indonesian Economics* 1961). His observations, which involved cheap labour as part of the distinction, were astute and comprehensible. The reasons he assigned to this were quite unacceptable, however. The Javanese was not oblivious to personal advantages or gain, but the demands made upon him within the context of the arrangements in which he lived did not make it possible for him to react in ways that a liberal economic system would find appropriate.

Village Economy

One of the aims of the Cultivation System was to use the traditional authority patterns of Javanese society to induce the peasantry in selected areas to work on the production of export crops. What was supposed to happen was that the village headmen and their supra-village superiors were to use their authority to induce persons to work in new ways and to surrender the use of part of their land for government cultivations instead of rice production. This was supposed to keep Javanese society static. In fact this did not happen. The economic impact of the System induced changes and speeded up tendencies already present. The traditional ruling patterns of supra-village superiors had already been disrupted at the beginning of the nineteenth century; the Cultivation System could restore these only in an artificial way. Authority figures were placed under increasing pressure by the demands which the System made upon them. The European civil servants came in time to find them more a hindrance than a help and proceeded to bypass them while working to improve the cultivations. In the areas where the government cultivations were applied, the supra-village Javanese were forced to adjust to new circumstances which gradually eroded their prestige in the eyes of the population at large (Sutherland 1979; Van Niel 1981). This was such a slow process, varying from place to place, that one cannot really speak of a loss of power on the part of these groups until early in the twentieth century. However, there were changes both within the supra-village groups and in its relationship to the villages.

More significant as a legacy of the Cultivation System, in my estimation, is the change which occurred where the System touched the Javanese villages. Earlier writings make the point that the Cultivation System destroyed the Javanese village. Such charges had already been made during the first phase of writings about the System, but in the second phase they became a major theme. The Cultivation System was thought to have forced a communalization of landholding rights upon the villages and thereby destroyed older individual rights to the land. Landholding rights were of special interest to the private entrepreneurial groups intent on replacing the System with their own form of exploitation. The investigation into land rights launched in the 1860s was supposed to provide the raw data to support this argument (Eindresumé 1876-96). Vollenhoven (1932, pp.3-28) brought this landholding issue into sharper focus by tracing the evolution of indigenous land rights and demonstrating how government policies had destroyed an evolutionary trend toward private user rights. Writers of the 1920s and 1930s used this evidence to explain the economic and social disintegration of the village into a sort of gelatinized egalitarianism under the impact of European imperialism. While Furnivall and Burger are eloquent spokesmen for this trend, the clearest unfolding of this argument in English is found in Clifford Geertz's study of agricultural involution (Geertz 1963). Drawing upon the evidence and conclusions of these earlier writers to explain the developments since the introduction of the Cultivation System, he found that a social homogenization occurred in the Javanese village which resulted in "shared poverty." Given the climate of opinion at the time, these earlier writings probably made sense; but recent writings, reflecting contemporary observations, tend to portray the Javanese village as a vital social unit with clearly defined and commonly understood social differentiations. It would seem that accounts of the disintegration and demise of the Javanese village were exaggerated. What then seems to have happened and how does current historical research and writing explain the evolution of the Javanese village?

Our knowledge of the origins of villages in Java or elsewhere is based mostly on speculation and theory. However, Van Naerssen and others, working with inscriptions recently found in Java, have developed a historical sequence which ties the settled agricultural community and its irrigated lands into the process of higher state development governed by the magical-religious sanctions which bound the order together (Naerssen and de Iongh 1977; Kulke 1980; Mulherin 1970-71; Setten van der Meer 1979; Wisseman 1977). The social distinctions between village and supra-village were vague, with an uninterrupted hierarchy of family connections and client (or bondage) relationships from top to bottom. The centers of authority (*negara*) drew labour and produce from the lower groups, but the relationships were loose and flexible and could change rapidly in the struggles for power. The distance between state and village was not always great. Not surprisingly, individuals moved back and forth between *negara* and *desa* (village) as their fortunes and the occasion warranted (Sartono 1972).

The village was, in the first instance, a cluster of agrarian families with ties to the surrounding fields, but it also might serve as a residence of families tied into the supra-village power groups, or of merchants from inside and outside the village, or of craftsmen and artisans of various sorts. Such a village was not isolated from outside contacts and was autonomous only to the extent that it might regulate some internal functions such as rituals, land arrangements, etc. The actual tribute of produce and labour which the peasants were obligated to deliver was probably channeled through patrons rather than through the village *per se*. Family clusters or corporate households were headed by a patron who was in turn attached to a higher authority. These patrons exercised influence over diverse socio-economic matters in addition to the tribute deliveries. For instance, they would arrange for opening new lands, introduction of new crops, movement of produce to market, and reassignment or relocation of clients.

In Mataram times, a firmer bureaucratic control had fixed many of these relationships in a more rigid pattern. To judge from the development of the Javanese language, social distinctions become sharper and more formalized. Retainers of the *negara* were rewarded in units known as *cacah*, which, while possibly a land measure in origin, had come by the eighteenth century to signify corporate households or production units under a single head. These *cacah* were originally expected to deliver produce and labour in varying amounts and of different sorts. The higher retainers subdivided these *cacah* units among their subordinates or clients (Rouffaer 1906; Moertono 1968). Everyone was tied into this hierarchy except for "free" villages, which were attached to religious institutions or temples and thereby freed from service and delivery to the government. Such "free" villages were, I suspect, far fewer in number after Islam gained control in Java. By the late eighteenth century, the obligations of *cacah* had been converted to a monetary equivalent in the interior Mataram areas; thus they paid a sort of tax known as *pajeg*.

This process of monetization in the interior seems to have resulted from an increasing amount of bullion in circulation after the sixteenth century, from a growth in European and Chinese mercantile activity, from an increasing amount of imported luxury goods which affected the lifestyle of the upper classes, and, above all, from the loss of Mataram lands to the VOC. The VOC government in the coastal areas continued to collect produce and labour officially, but private dealings were often in money. As the Java wars from 1679 to 1755 disrupted life in the interior, there was a migration of population to the coastal areas under VOC control. This population shift continued into the early nineteenth century resulting in heavy concentrations of people in and around some coastal cities and the abandonment of some interior areas considered unsafe.

In the coastal areas it was evident to many European administrators at the end of the eighteenth century that the traditional *cacah* system of assessing deliveries of produce and labour was no longer an accurate appraisal of the human resources of the area. As the wars against Napoleonic France cut off Java from the Netherlands (1795-1816), the VOC servants were thrown onto the local economy for consumables, particularly rice, and corvée labour for the building of roads and defences. A sudden concern was evinced with how Javanese society functioned, generating a number of reports on social organization at the grass-roots level (Ysseldyk 1799; Rothenbühler 1798, 1812a, 1812b; Waterloo 1806, 1811; Salis 1809; Daendels 1814; Engelhard 1816; Knops and Lawick van Pabst 1812). While these reports were not always as clear as we would wish, they do provide more information than is available for earlier periods. Along the coast between 1800 and 1812, wage labour was used in the cultivation of some fields; village lands were rotated periodically among a large labour pool; lands were share-cropped under the control of *cacah* heads; and some landless persons who hired themselves out to do corvée for others were almost constantly employed in this fashion.

Well before the introduction of either the Landrent System or the Cultivation System, then, the Javanese peasantry was making flexible adjustments to the needs of the locality in which they found themselves. These qualities of hard work, individual capacity, and flexible adjustment to change are much the same as Selo Soemardjan noted in the 1960s (Selo Soemardjan 1970). The supra-village authorities knew of all this and worked out the details with their *cacah*, whom Hoadley, examining the Cirebon and Priangan regions, sees as bondsmen of these higher authorities (Hoadley 1983). This adjustment allowed supra-village heads to meet the government requirements for produce and labour while also meeting their own expanding needs for labour and for more cultivated land. Under their direction, the use of available land was regulated and adjustments were made. Possession rights or control rights over land were in the hands of the *cacah* and other local elites; peasants usually worked a regular plot from which they received a portion, usually half, of the produce. This plot they might consider "their own" in the sense that they worked it regularly and that the fruit of the land was theirs in part, but they did not own the land and could be moved off it by higher authority if this were warranted. The new pressures being visited on the peasantry forced modifications of peasants rights, but did not have much effect on the rights of the *cacah* or of the supra-village heads.

The supra-village heads were upgrading their lifestyle in the coastal areas, modeling their living arrangements on the courtly styles of the interior. They built larger houses, expanded their retinues, adopted non-local dress and furnishing items, and were more aloof in their social pretensions. The *bupati* as a sort of rustic country squire was disappearing from the scene. The new lifestyle was supported either directly from the labour of the population under their control or indirectly by trading or selling the products derived from the population. These supra-village heads involved their people in the production of coffee, indigo, and cotton which they delivered to the VOC in exchange for imported goods. Since bullion was ever in short supply, many of the transactions with the VOC were in the nature of bookkeeping arrangements in which private interests on both sides often took precedence over official requirements.

It was this sort of activity that raised concern among some European reformers at the turn of the century. Hogendorp, Daendels, and Raffles were the most noted of these, but many others also expressed concern over the burdens being placed upon the Javanese peasant. Since there was a great deal of slack and flexibility in the Javanese production and delivery system, and since the Europeans could only with difficulty penetrate the surface of Javanese society, there was little solid and reliable information on which to formulate change. In the first instance, the reformers thought of applying the then prevailing European economic wisdom, which favoured free and open markets along with individual economic advantage rather than the older monopolistic and mercantilistic system of the VOC. In the second instance, they thought in terms of responsible administration as they knew it in the Europe of their day—in Raffles' case also the reformed Indian administration—which in practice involved either eliminating or reforming the parasitic, exploitative supra-village authorities so that the Javanese peasant could be freed to seek his own best economic advantage. Neither of these concepts of reform took much cognizance of the socio-economic dependency arrangements and delivery systems of Javanese society.

Efforts by Europeans to alter the structure of the Javanese socio-economic system began with Daendels in 1808 and continued throughout the entire Dutch colonial period to 1942. It is not my intention to trace this process here, but only to focus on the initial changes aimed at the Javanese village. Raffles, by introducing the Landrent System in 1813, set out to "restore the autonomy" of the basic Javanese production unit, the village, with the elected headman becoming the basic revenue-collecting deputy of the government. In "discovering" the village and restoring it to its rightful place, Raffles actually discovered more than there was to be found (Soetardjo 1965, p. 212). The village as residential complex had never performed the functions or filled the position which was now conceived for it. Small wonder that the remainder of the nineteenth century saw many colonial administrators and policy makers trying to fit an idealized notion of a primitive agrarian social unit to the changing reality of the village as it emerged.

It was probably because the Landrent System—the leasing of lands by the government/owner to the village, the collection of revenue (or products) by the village headman, and the elimination (or alteration) of the supra-village heads—was so far removed from the socio-economic realities of Javanese society that it could be introduced without overt resistance. The personalized control arrangement through the *cacah* system was unaffected and the Javanese continued to see relationships as personal, not territorial. The restoration of the supra-village heads even in Raffles day, to positions of salaried revenue and police officers may also have contributed to keeping them both satisfied and in a position from which they could exert their old influence. Finally, the designation or election of the *cacah* heads to positions within the village leadership, which occurred quite widely, kept the dependency relations as well as the land control arrangements intact. The nuclear villagers, under the various names by which they came to be known, were a continuation of the old *cacah* heads. Over the next couple of decades, there were some realignments in this group as government interfered to meld hamlets into villages and to lay a hand to some land control arrangements, but in the main, the upper elements in village life remained a continuation of the previous order. With government support, they now had more power than previously in controlling matters within their village, but they also had new responsibilities.

When the Dutch government regained control of Java in 1816, it took over the Landrent System with some modifications. This decision consciously severed ties with the old VOC system in which the Company had been both government and merchant. The expectation was that private initiative from all sides, European, native, and Chinese, would now take up the role of merchant and that the government would finance itself from revenues from the land and from import and export duties. The disenchantment with this ideal during the years before 1830 has already been discussed. The expectation that the Javanese villages would now freely turn to the production of marketable export crops also came to naught. The Javanese village, when left to its own devices, produced mainly consumables, which were also very marketable; the only way in which it was involved in export production was through the intervention of higher authority (either alone or in conjunction with a European or Chinese entrepreneur). This was just as it had been earlier. Within the village the nuclear villagers remained in control of most of the land, with some small but independent peasants continuing to control their traditional plots. The real power in the village lay clearly with the nuclear group.

It was upon this agrarian base that the Cultivation System was introduced in 1830. Its purpose was to obtain commodities which would be saleable on world markets and to this end the System was to use the land and labour of the Javanese villagers, persuaded (or coerced) by the supra-village heads. This was to take place within the confines of the Landrent System (Van Niel 1964c). Interestingly enough, Van den Bosch spoke still of the *cacah*—perhaps a residue of his earlier experience in Java in the first years of the century—and seemed quite conscious of the vertical ties in Javanese society. These, as already indicated, he planned to use, but they were actually twisted rather out of shape during the years in which his System operated. There continue to be references to *cacah* until the end of the 1830s, after which the concept is abandoned in favour of dealing with individual households in order to tap more labour.

Recent historical research presents information about what happened in villages after 1830, when the government began to arrange for new production patterns; this information puts a different interpretation on events than that presented in earlier writings. Evidence from Cirebon, Pekalongan, Jepara, and Pasuruan—all areas where government cultivations were introduced—shows that the village leaders managed to take advantage of the demands of the government in order to strengthen their hand and make personal advances within their village structure (Elson 1979, 1984; Fernando 1982a; Knight 1982a, 1984). By using their land rights, both personal and official, and especially by manipulating the forced labour which was under their control, they were able to make internal adjustments. In this way they gained a double advantage: satisfying the wants of the government, on the one hand, and prospering from the crop payments which flowed into the village, on the other hand. It was up to them to distribute money from the government in whatever fashion they thought best, a fashion that frequently did not coincide with what the government officials thought should be done. As the System proceeded, European civil servants were constantly attempting to regulate and control the monies which went to the village for its participation in the System. Usually these attempts had little effect in the face of the devices employed by the village leaders to keep the major benefits in their own hands.

Certain cautions are called for. Although a modification seems in order, I am not prepared to call for a total abandonment of the old views. Not all villages reacted in the same way; not all cultivation arrangements were the same; and not all changes occurred at the same time (Fernando 1982b). Yet when all this is considered, the new research affords explanations which make more comprehensible than the old view the present village household arrangements in Java. Quite simply put, present-day villages in Java manifest a definite social distinction between wealthy villagers and poor villagers. They do not exhibit either a social levelling or the social homogenization which the Cultivation System is supposed, according to earlier writings, to have induced. Also, villages today show a strong cohesion, something which would not normally be described as an after-effect of disintegration.

If this view of both the social differentiation and the economic staying power of the village has any merit, then two related matters must be considered. These are the question of landholding rights within the village, and the continuance of traditions and social bonds among the villagers in the face of sharper economic differentiation. In earlier writings, landholding rights received a great deal of attention, though mostly within a western rather than a Javanese context. The communalization of village lands, in the sense that an increasing number of villagers gained rights to use a piece of land, undoubtedly occurred both before and during the Cultivation System. Since in many, but not all, parts of Java, the right to use a piece of the village lands and the obligation to perform work service in all its varieties were tied together, the broader distribution of rights to use land was a natural way of enlarging the labour pool in order to meet the growing requirements of corvée and cultivation services. Evidence indicates, however, that much obligatory labour was also imposed upon persons who had no land rights throughout the century (Schoch 1891; *Historische Nota* 1905; Fokkens 1901-02). To the western observer, especially in the latter part of the nineteenth century, the growing communalization of landholding seemed socially destructive of the village order. It also seemed to present difficulties for individual contractual arrangements for rental of land. But this matter of landholding was deceptive on both counts. Communalization arrangements often did not involve the ultimate right to the land, only to its use, and thereby the right to its product. Village leaders, who had never, or hardly ever, directly worked the land under their control before, during or after the Cultivation System were able to retain their ultimate control of a substantial portion of the village's lands. They had a wide variety of contractual arrangements at their disposal for keeping what they had, while letting others do the work both on the land and elsewhere. Small independent peasants who were not part of the village inner circle or who had run afoul of the village leaders might have their lives made miserable. Such persons must have lost out economically and could even have been forced off their land and out of the village. The households and labourers who had always been landless were not much affected by the growing power of the village head and his associates, since they had always been someone's client anyway. So it came to pass that communalization, while appearing to blot out social distinctions in the village, did not do so. Nor did it present particular difficulties to private planters who wanted to rent village lands; here again the headman generally had control of the situation, and some sort of agreement could always be reached.

This shifting in the social and economic class structure of the village did not totally alter the ties which held the village together as a social entity and as a productive unit. While villagers understood social and economic differences, the village also remained the core of the subsistence system for a large part of the population. True, persons migrated to towns and took up non-agricultural types of work, while others became attached to an agrarian enterprise which operated in the export sector. Most Javanese remained within their villages, however. Even some of those who appeared to be totally apart retained ties with their village in various ways. This somewhat ambivalent arrangement was, obviously, one of the foundation stones of the kind of cheap labour arrangements which benefited the export sector of the economy. The village, which aggregated and managed this cheap labour supply, had to retain its traditional ties and bonds in order to fulfil this function which was not eliminated by transforming forced labour into wage labour, for the low level of the wages depended on a continued symbiosis between private-export and village economy. It was in this context that the village leaders had to build and expand their power. The realities did not require them to become independent market-oriented farmers, though in this area they did perform some intermediary functions. They could not abandon the social relationships of the village, for it was the village on which they relied as their sole institutional base for the continued acquisition of power and wealth. In the context of a labour-intensive economic system, the village leaders, for their own economic advancement both within the village and with the export-oriented sector, had to maintain traditional ties and social obligations.

Summation

Conceptions registered before World War II still prevail in present-day writings about nineteenth-century Java and the Cultivation System, despite publication in the past thirty years (and especially during the past fifteen) of some robust revisionary research that greatly expands our understanding of the operation and impact of the Cultivation System on Java. To illustrate how some of this recent research is changing our knowledge and insights into the Cultivation System, this essay has focused on three areas which are undergoing reinterpretation. These are: (1) capital formation (2) cheap labour and (3) village economy. These topics are central to the Cultivation System, but they are not by any means the entire System nor are they meant to tell the whole story. Nor are the new views and arguments presented in this essay meant to alter the moral perception of the System. The Cultivation System was, in the main, brutally exploitative, and it was managed by greedy, power-hungry persons whose values were shaped by their respective cultural backgrounds. What should become evident, however, is that the System functioned somewhat differently than has formerly been thought; that the System worked its wiles in a socio-economic environment that was more sophisticated and complicated than has been conveyed by traditional writings; and that the System consequently had a rather different impact on Javanese society than earlier authors have believed.

Capital Formation. With regard to capital formation (which is an aspect of colonial history involving Europeans and Chinese much more than Indonesians), I follow the lead of Reinsma and Fasseur in overturning the traditional view that it was enterprise capital in Europe that forced the dismemberment of the government-controlled Cultivation System. The evidence before us today shows that the essential capital formation leading to the expansion of Javanese cultivations occurred in Java itself, and that it occurred during and as part of the Cultivation System. The government sugar contractors were undoubtedly the leaders in this capital formation, but agency houses, which had never ceased to exist in Java and actually thrived under the Cultivation System, were also able (along with retired government servants) to expand into areas in which the government and its official agent, the Netherlands Trading Company (*Nederlandsche Handel Maatschappij*), either could not make a profit or simply were not interested. In short, the Cultivation System, through a sort of government-endorsed bootstrap operation, managed to generate capital (out of the hides of the Javanese, one could say) where there had formerly been none, or too little. The controllers of this capital (and there were some private injections from Europe) ultimately came to the conclusion that they could do the job better under liberal, private-enterprise arrangements than by working through the cumbersome, patronage-ridden government system, and they were able to win support in the Netherlands parliament for this. Major capital inputs from Europe into Java occurred only after 1880, when the Cultivation System was already well into the process of being officially phased out of existence.

So what was the impact of capital formation under the Cultivation System on the subsequent economic development in Java? There was capital in Java before 1830 (though not enough) and a great deal came into Java after 1880, so the answer to this part of the question must not be too extreme. What the Cultivation System did was to show explicitly that Java could produce certain agricultural commodities cheaply enough to compete on world markets. Once this had been shown to entrepreneurs inside and outside Java, the island became an attractive field for capital investment. It was, however, the Java-based entrepreneurs who were first aware of this and who were most intimately acquainted with the devices which the government used to make this possible. Therefore; it is not surprising that the growth of capital investment in Javanese agriculture should have its origins among the close-knit group of entrepreneurs, civil servants, and agency houses living and working in Java. The path that they opened was expanded in the late nineteenth and early twentieth centuries into a highroad for worldwide capital investment in Java, and eventually the rest of the archipelago. The initial path, however, was made possible through developments in Javanese society which I discuss under the rubrics of cheap labour and village economy.

Cheap labour. Cheap labour was a feature of Javanese life long before the Cultivation System made its appearance. Part of the duties of the lower classes to persons of higher status and authority took the form of labour obligations. Dependency relationships, bordering on bondage in many instances, were a key determinant of social distinctions in the society. As the Dutch gained control over the north coast of Java in the eighteenth century, they found it both pleasant and profitable to make use of labour at either no cost or very minimal cost, and to accept delivery of products without payment or far below cost. Such products, naturally, were the result of labour done by Javanese peasants for Javanese officials or patrons at very little cost, and they were certainly obtained without payment of a monetary wage. The intermediate and higher levels of Javanese society knew very well how to exploit this labour and how to play the market process in gaining the most out of the products at their disposal. Since there were no fixed rules or any equity in the exaction of labour, it is not possible to estimate the number of work days provided in this manner, but it was increasing. By the beginning of the nineteenth century, there were some persons who worked half of the year on required labour, for themselves and others, with little or no wage payment but often with some sort of subsistence arrangement. Obligatory government service (corvée) was in place long before the Cultivation System existed, for the Europeans in authority had always assumed the sovereign right to such labour in the territories under their control. The amount of corvée seems to have increased greatly in the early nineteenth century as the government came to make extensive use of it for infrastructure development. The Cultivation System left this corvée in place, and added to it something called *cultivation service* which was the required work on the government cultivations. Theoretically this cultivation service was compensated in the form of crop payments, but more often than not the persons who did the actual work did not receive the payments. So far as these lower classes were concerned, work in the government cultivations seemed to them to be done for their headmen and chiefs just as all required labour had always been done. While some groups in Javanese society benefited from the Cultivation System, the lower classes became more dependent on traditional authority, and they worked with very little gain beyond the provision of their subsistence and security. So it came to pass that the symbiotic relationship between cheap labour and the provision of life's basic subsistence grew ever stronger, while the concept of working for a wage on which one could survive was never generated among Java's poorer peasantry.

Village Economy. It was the village economy and village political structure that in the course of the nineteenth century aggregated the socio-economic realities of Javanese life, transforming the crop production and cheap labour into a functioning arrangement. The villages of Java as residential units had always contained social distinctions. They were the source from which labour and produce were drawn, though only from some of the villagers. In the early nineteenth century, the upper groups in the village were strengthened by the assignment of new functions and competencies which enabled the village headmen and their associates to collect in their hands control of land, labour, and produce to a greater degree than ever before. Though the government, under the Cultivation System, appeared to work through the supra-village elite, in actuality the village leaders were increasingly the ones with whom government officials, Dutch and Javanese, came to deal in order to accomplish the set production goals. While it is difficult to generalize about this, what seems to have happened in the areas of the government cultivations is that the upper village groups gained strength and wealth at the expense of the middle class of villagers, whose small individual holdings were sacrificed. The lower class of villagers remained as they were, serving and dependent upon the better-situated groups. To win cooperation from all concerned and to make the system work properly, the village became closer knit so that the increasingly complex land arrangements and complicated work assignments could include an ever greater number of the village inhabitants. While this might have appeared egalitarian to earlier writers about the Cultivation System, the social distinctions within the village were never obliterated. Moreover, they were well known and clearly understood by the villagers. The Cultivation System continued the process of making the Javanese village into the lowest unit in a centralized administrative system; it added to this process by making the village the basic production and subsistence unit of Java's entry into the world market economy. This function continued after the Cultivation System faded away and it remained the basis of economic life in Java during the colonial period.

Finally, in responding to the original question of whether the Cultivation System made any difference in the subsequent economic development of Java, I feel that the answer should be a tentative "Yes." Yes, because the System influenced the socio-economic growth and development of all social groups in Java, but tentative, because this pattern of change was already established before the founding of the System in 1830 and continued on after its demise in 1870. There was more continuity than change in the operation of the System, especially if one accepts the revisionist views that have been proposed in the past two or three decades. In past historical writings, the System has been viewed as a radical departure from the prevailing flow of colonial policy. Because of this, it was thought to have had a destructive impact on Javanese society. This view of the past no longer seems tenable. The System introduced some tactical changes which made colonial exploitation more effective, but it was part and parcel of a longer historical process involving the integration of Java into a system of market economy.

Notes

1. Between these dates, van der Kemp produced some eighty books and articles which drew upon archival sources, chiefly the Ministry of Colonies archive. Unfortunately these writings are almost unusable since he interspersed interpretations and opinions with sections of documents without clearly indicating where one began and the other left off.

CHAPTER FIVE

The Cultivation System in West Sumatra: Economic Stagnation and Political Stalemate[1]

Kenneth R. Young

Through the work of Professor Fasseur and that of a number of scholars represented in this collection, we have come to see the Cultivation System not so much as a single system but as a variety of revenue-raising techniques, all of them dependent on political intervention and on control of major sectors of agricultural production and exchange. Almost all of this literature has been concerned with the workings and the effects of the Cultivation System in Java, which was the prized holding of the Dutch in the region and the chief source of government revenue, as well as the site of the System's greatest triumphs and worst abuses. It is important, however, not to lose sight of the fact that the Cultivation System was also applied outside Java. A study of non-Javanese variants can help to illustrate its essential characteristics.

In Sumatra's West Coast, home of the Minangkabau, forced coffee cultivation and deliveries were successfully instituted in 1847 and continued to be a major economic and political factor for over six decades. The Minangkabau themselves are one of the most thoroughly researched ethnic groups in Indonesia, but the crucial changes wrought in Minangkabau society by the Cultivation System have to date attracted little attention.[2] I have treated developments among the Minangkabau in the nineteenth century at greater length elsewhere (Young 1983), but here I will attempt to summarise the way in which the Cultivation System was applied in West Sumatra and show how its imposition led to stagnation in the previously vigorous economic life of Minangkabau society, a situation compounded by political stalemate in the last decades of the nineteenth century. Such a summary should raise still further questions about the working of the Cultivation System as a "system," while casting light on the background of many problems which were carried forward into the twentieth century.

In this essay, the historical outline which introduces the main discussion will be confined to a brief overview of the major developments in these decades. I will then discuss the situation that existed in Minangkabau at the time the System was introduced, noting the political and economic conditions which largely determined how the System would work and identifying the politically most significant elites. Next, the functions of the most elementary socio-economic units, peasant households, will be presented through a discussion of their structure and economic functions. With these general features clarified, the operation of the System will be examined. I will then establish the interconnected reasons which account for why the System worked and why it failed. To conclude, I will summarise the effects of the System within Minangkabau villages and within the region, and then note the internal contradictions of the monopoly which led to its failure and to more than two decades of economic stagnation and political stalemate in the late nineteenth and early twentieth centuries—an impasse that was resolved only with the abolition of the System, economic liberalisation, and the introduction of a small tax on incomes in 1908 (measures which paradoxically triggered a popular rebellion against the Dutch in that same year).

Historical Overview

Prior to the nineteenth century the Dutch had never ventured into the populous heartland of the Minangkabau, which lay in the mountainous highlands of West Sumatra. In the two preceding centuries, the United East India Company's presence had been limited to a few enclaves on the narrow coastal littoral, where it attempted to dominate trade in pepper, gold, and towards the end of the eighteenth century, coffee. Those enclaves on the coast were taken over after 1795 by the British, and it was only in 1819, following the British withdrawal, that the Dutch (government officials now, for the VOC had been bankrupted) returned to the coast (Joustra 1923, pp.48-50; Dobbin 1983).

When they reappeared, the Dutch found that a protracted and continuing civil religious war, the Padri conflicts, was disrupting the highlands. These conflicts gave the Dutch the opportunity to intervene. By opposing themselves to the Islamic Padri reform movement, they could move toward control of the entire region. Joining the conflict in the 1820s, they overcame the last centre of Padri resistance only in 1837 (Dobbin 1972, 1974, 1977, 1983).

Johannes van den Bosch, the chief architect of the Cultivation System on Java, had visited West Sumatra in 1833 with the aim of regulating trade in Sumatran products for the profit of the Dutch Crown. He made a series of recommendations about how the government could win revenues from the lucrative Minangkabau coffee trade. Many of van den Bosch's schemes failed initially, but his suggestions finally led to the launching of a successful system in 1847 (Lulofs 1904, p.1636, p.1642; Kielstra 1888, p.1610ff.). That system, which is to be discussed here, lasted until 1908, when its replacement by a small tax on incomes set off an anti-colonial uprising. After 1908 the region was thrown open for trade and investment. Spectacular economic booms, notably in smallholder cash-crop production, followed. These years were also a time of prolific expansion in indigenous political organisation, a time when movements grew which were to have a continuing influence up to and beyond the Indonesian independence struggles. Again, the turning points of regional history were punctuated by political conflict, the post-1908 political freedoms being stifled after the communist rebellion of 1927 (Schrieke 1955; Abdullah 1971; McVey 1965; Geertz 1963).

The system discussed here, then, was the principal source of government revenues in the region in the years between 1847, a decade after the termination of the Padri conflicts, and 1908, the year of the anti-tax rebellion. Before examining the organisation of peasant production under the system, it will be useful to comment briefly on the situation in the region prior to the implementation of the system and the distinctive characteristics of the domestic economy of Minangkabau in the nineteenth century.

Minangkabau on the Eve of the System

The coffee trade originating in the Minangkabau highlands was clearly the principal factor which spurred Dutch attempts to dominate the region. Even before the Dutch established themselves in the highlands, coffee cultivation and processing were already the work of individual planters and small household enterprises there. Coffee made its way through a multiplicity of small traders down to coastal brokers, who in turn dealt with international buyers (Dobbin 1983, chs. 2, 3, 6). It was this profitable trade that stimulated the colonial ambitions of the Dutch, and it was this individualised household production that they were to strive to regulate under the Cultivation System.

To achieve their political and economic objectives, the Dutch had to break the influence of the leaders of the Padri movement, who possessed a significant capacity to mobilise Minangkabau resistance to Dutch demands. The Padris' weakness lay in the fact that while all of their leaders were morally united against the Dutch, the personal authority of any individual Padri leader was limited to only a particular part of the Minangkabau world. Thus, groupings of Padri communities under different paramount leaders could be, and were, separately engaged by the Dutch, so that over time, incremental Dutch gains were made because of the absence of effective pan-Minangkabau resistance by the Padris.

Prior to Dutch intervention in the 1820s, these Islamic leaders were the focus of the most effective form of territorial power that remained in Minangkabau in the early nineteenth century. The core of Padri support was among those social groups and those villages which were most involved with trade and production for exchange, especially coffee production. By contrast, the authority of the alternative elites, those associated with the Minangkabau Royal

Family, had been severely diminished, above all because of the near exhaustion of gold lodes in the area. Revenues from gold mining and trading had long been the economic mainstay of the Royal system, whose remaining supporters were largely concentrated in the rice-growing villages of the Tanah Datar plain. It was these communities which most vigorously resisted the complete takeover of the Minangkabau heartland by the Padris (Dobbin 1977, 1983).

In this period, neither those villages loyal to Padri leaders nor those associated with the Royal system (nor, in fact, the goodly number of villages connected with neither rival group) could be characterised as forming a well-developed political hierarchy possessing a centralised focus of territorial authority. The authority exercised by the two foremost political groupings in the region depended, apart from their religious and ideological claims, on their ability to protect and regulate trade and trade routes in the interest of particular Minangkabau communities. At the more basic economic level, land and labour in Minangkabau were barely influenced at all by higher authorities; instead they were regulated largely within individual communities *(nagari)*, principally by the councils of lineage leaders whose prerogative the domestic government of these settlements remained.

In the aftermath of the Netherlanders' suppression of the Padris, the victors attempted to locate and work through a local elite capable of organising land and labour on their behalf. They soon discovered, however, that there was no such ruling stratum, and extracting surpluses on the Javanese model was difficult in the absence of local allies who could command servile labour or tribute. The political feebleness of the remaining notables of the Royal system was readily apparent. An alliance with any of the Padri leaders was neither feasible nor ideologically acceptable. What remained was the authority of lineage leaders in each individual community, a customary authority deriving from association, consensus and reciprocity unsuited to organising social labour within the kind of tribute system the Dutch wanted to establish. A pseudo-traditional elite (*tuanku, laras, panghulu kepala, panghulu suku rodi*, etc.) was thus grafted onto these institutions, but it remained a foreign body possessing little legitimacy among villagers, who were disposed to reject the transplant of new political hierarchies (Schrieke 1927; Kielstra 1890, pp.320-23; Dobbin 1983, p.233ff).

Politically, then, the Dutch saw no option open to them other than indirect rule through customary *(adat)* heads of lineages *(panghulu)*. Outside of this awkward alliance, the influence of independent religious authorities persisted. Based on their specialised schools of religious learning (called *surau*),[3] these leaders continued to be regarded with suspicion and often with apprehension by government officials. The enduring contradiction embedded from the start in Dutch attempts to regulate the growing and sale of coffee lay in the political necessity of relying on an elite of *panghulu* who would not or could not effectively sustain the economic demands made by the government.

Within existing property relations and the organisation of social labour in Minangkabau communities, each peasant household possessed a significant degree of autonomy in its economic life. When this is more fully understood, it is not surprising that, notwithstanding pressure and positive material incentives from the government, the *panghulu* were able neither to claim nor to assert sufficient authority to direct the labour process, nor were they capable of organising production in large cooperative groups on consolidated tracts of land. An appreciation of the structure and function of the elementary economic units (households) is also essential for understanding the methods which were eventually developed and which helped, for two decades at least, the Cultivation System to flourish in West Sumatra.

Minangkabau Peasant Households

Peasant households are, in many societies, described as being simultaneously the basic unit of production and the basic unit of consumption (Chayanov 1966; Shanin 1971). One of the things that was distinctive about Minangkabau households in this period was that, while they were the units of consumption, production was yet more specialised, with different household members concentrating on particular types of work.[4]

Moreover, the operation of these distinct units of production was adapted to plural property relations. The great majority of households were engaged in both subsistence and commercial sectors. In the subsistence sector, access to the crucial resource of wet-rice land *(sawah)* was regulated by the matrilineal inheritance system *(adat pusaka)*. In the commercial sector, where village and clan controls were relatively loose, private property rights, mediated through markets, prevailed.

The labour which was contributed to units of subsistence production in cultivating rice came predominantly from the women of the household, each of whom typically held, for her own use and for her lifetime, a piece of lineage *sawah* (Hasselt 1882, p.252f.). For much, if not all, of the year, therefore, male householders were relatively free from subsistence tasks connected with lineage property, and they could thus engage in other productive activities (Hasselt 1882, p.254). They were also geographically mobile and were encouraged to exploit this freedom profitably in accordance with the cultural tradition of *merantau*[5] (Verkerk Pistorius 1871, p.168; Stibbe 1901-02, p.517). While women also participated in the commercial sector, the units of production and exchange there tended to be predominantly worked by men, especially in such fields as trade, transportation, craft production or mining.[6] The gains from successful commercial ventures tended to be consumed by household members, to be used to acquire livestock or additional wet-rice land (under "pawning" arrangements), or to be dissipated in the accumulation of cultural capital (religious, ceremonial, etc.) (Verkerk Pistorius 1871, p.131ff, 153; Hasselt 1882, p.252ff., 303ff.; Stibbe 1901-02, p.519ff.). Lineage property could be and sometimes was used to stake commercial ventures (Dobbin 1983, p.30ff.). At the other extreme, some of the most successful entrepreneurs, especially merchants, were known to have invoked Islamic practices to evade the inheritance rules of *adat pusaka* (Dobbin 1983, p.30ff.; Benda-Beckmann 1979.[7]) The generalised picture is that of degrees of engagement with the subsistence and commercial sectors by households, with the great majority of them active in both.

Peasant units of production were therefore involved in a considerable range of economic activities, both subsistence and commercial (Hasselt 1882, ch.12). Wage labour was not established to any significant extent among the Minangkabau in the nineteenth century (Verkerk Pistorius 1871, p.155; Stibbe 1884). What was significant was the interdependence of these seemingly autonomous units of production. Whether in the subsistence or commercial sector, these units coordinated their economic behaviour through jointly fulfilling the consumption needs of their households, and it was such household-centred objectives, rather than the optimisation of particular enterprises, which apparently determined their economic choices. Therefore, our estimations of the conditions under which, say, a tobacco grower or a buffalo-cart haulier would enter or leave a market, or calculations of what prices would be acceptable to them, cannot be made simply by analogy with capitalist enterprises operating entirely through the market.[8]

Dutch observers frequently remarked on the highly individualised patterns of production and on the relative lack of village- or even clan-based groups engaged in cooperative labour (Couperus 1856, p.290). Even in rice production, group effort was minimal, and, when it was unavoidable, arrangements tended to be *ad hoc* and labour was compensated for in kind (Verkerk Pistorius 1871, pp.147-48; Stibbe 1901-02, pp.503-6). Households also had dry-field plots and domestic gardens, fish tanks, fruit trees, domestic animals and so on (Hasselt 1882, p.258ff.; Stibbe 1901-02, p.514). Notwithstanding these resources, villagers in the populous heartland were dependent for many essential items of consumption on what they could buy in local markets (Veth 1881, p.197). Textiles, salt, salted fish, ornaments, tools and a remarkable range of other essentials were acquired through markets (Veth 1881, p.197).

Trade was always important, even in the period of the coffee monopoly. As a nineteenth-century Dutch scientific observer noted in the 1870s: "Trade is lively everywhere; the Malay [Minangkabau] is no less a trader than he is a cultivator" (Hasselt 1882, p.360). The scope of exchange networks was simultaneously inter- and intra-village, intra-regional and international (Hasselt 1882; Veth 1881; Stibbe 1901-02; Graves 1980; Dobbin 1983). Production for more extended markets (crafts, cash crops, etc.) was well established in specialised centres, credit and currencies were widely used, and trade and production for exchange provided a diversity of occupations for household members in almost every village. Here, too, economic activity was quite individualised (Young 1983, p.313ff.).

The commercial sector was therefore well developed and vital for the livelihood of most rural households (Veth 1881, p.197). The well-known commercial flair of the Minangkabau and their confident use of markets, money and bargaining are undoubtedly of venerable origin. The well-established trade-based division of labour, the various levels of specialisation within households, villages and local areas, and even beyond the region itself, indicate that these were long-settled patterns of economic activity. The importance of markets and the individualised property rights prevailing in the commercial sector might encourage the view that an incipient capitalist mode of production was developing in rural Sumatra. Such a view would be unfounded. Because lineage property rights in land remained strong and could be defended in the political realm, and because land remained relatively plentiful, no significant class of wage labourers was formed. Nor was there a clear pattern of capitalist accumulation. For the commercially successful, there were a number of uses for wealth—obtaining land through pawning; buying buffalo, horses and cattle; making the *haj;* building mosques; acquiring status in the community through costly *panghulu* ceremonies, etc. There is no sign in this period of genuine capitalist accumulation—the systematic re-investment of surpluses in production, technical innovation, etc.

Now that the nature of the social organisation of economic life in village Minangkabau has been reviewed, and the internal political situation on the eve of the System noted, we are in a position to see how it worked, why it temporarily succeeded and why it ultimately failed.

The Operation of the Cultivation System

Christine Dobbin has provided an admirable treatment of the beginnings of free coffee cultivation in West Sumatra in the late eighteenth and early nineteenth centuries and has covered the vigorous expansion of that cultivation and its broader social significance (Dobbin 1983). What is of most interest here is the way in which key techniques employed in that free cultivation prior to Dutch colonization were very much the same as those which marked the Cultivation System, especially in its most successful phase (Nahuijs 1826, p.65; Raffles

1835, vol. I, p.394; Swieten 1863; Lulofs 1904; Dobbin 1983, p.40; Young 1983, chs. 8 and 9).

Between 1820 and the late 1840s, the Dutch had made a number of attempts to control the Minangkabau coffee trade either directly or indirectly. Van den Bosch had advocated the use of taxes and financial incentives to encourage the sale of coffee to the Netherlands Trading Company (NHM). Other officials, such as de Stuers in 1825-28, Steinmetz between 1840 and 1844, and van den Hart as late as 1848-49, tried to control production more directly (Lulofs 1904, p.1642; Kielstra 1888, p.1610ff.; *De Vrije Arbeid* 1855, p.92ff.; Dobbin 1983, p.229). Their attempts to set up large plantations worked by supervised, obligatory communal labour all failed (*De Vrije Arbeid* 1855, pp.92-94), and it was only with a return to some of the earlier principles that the Cultivation System moved towards success in West Sumatra.

The most important characteristics of the early free coffee cultivation were:

1. It was lavish in its use of land. Within indigenous property systems, individuals and households had easy access to land for cash-crop cultivation (Dobbin 1983, p.34ff.), and they made use of that access to plant coffee on wide stretches of land, both near household compounds and in more distant forest areas.

2. It was sparing in its use of labour. According to Dobbin, "coffee growing expanded with relatively little effort ... [it was] a crop which was very little trouble for the planter" (Dobbin 1983, p.107).

3. Household specialization in coffee was never total. Instead, cultivation of this commercial crop was blended together in households with other commercial and subsistence-oriented activities, even in those areas which accounted for much of coffee production (Dobbin 1983, p.34, p.37, p.108).

4. Coffee was raised only in those parts of the highlands most ecologically favorable towards it (Dobbin 1983, pp.36-41).

5. Market prices on the coast were quite a bit higher than those paid to growers by the numerous petty traders who transported the coffee down from the highlands (Dobbin 1983, pp.107-8).

In essence, the Cultivation System as it operated after the late 1840s attempted to retain the first three of those characteristics, in order to ensure continued production, and to alter the final two, in order to benefit the government. That is, coffee was still to be raised by non-specialized households in a way that utilized much land and little labour. Now, however, it was to be grown by every village in the highlands, not just by those situated where conditions were most suitable for coffee, and the difference between world market prices and the returns gathered by local producers was to accrue not to small traders but to the government.

The techniques employed by the Minangkabau to produce coffee were simple. Some coffee bushes were grown in hedges, or closely planted clusters, in the immediate surrounds of a dwelling. These hedges were much more densely packed than the two to three metres between bushes recommended for maximum production per bush, but since the hedges were close to the houses, women and children could tend them (Nahuijs 1826, p.65). Most of the coffee gardens, however, were planted outside the villages on forested land, and ideally on hillsides (Couperus 1856, pp.301-2). This "forest coffee," as the Dutch called it, was worked by individuals rather than by larger cooperative groups (Hasselt 1882, p.344; Couperus 1856), and to minimise the effort required for travelling or transport, the forest gardens were set up as close to villages as possible. In these areas, a selection of forest trees would be felled, with the remainder left as shade trees. In the cleared area, holes were dug with a pointed stick and seeds were then deposited into the holes. Those plants which subsequently flourished were pruned and tended, while the remainder were simply weeded out.

This technique guaranteed that the amount of work put into preparation and maintenance was kept to a minimum, but it did require wide stretches of land as the cultivation expanded. Fortunately, this was not a major problem. Negotiations with *panghulu* over uncultivated village lands were no great obstacle to any villager intending to start a garden, and, once it was established, the garden and its products were the personal property of the individual or household that set it up (Hasselt 1882, p.307). These coffee gardens, then, like units of production for other cash crops, were largely outside lineage control once the issue of access to land was settled (Couperus 1856, p.299; Nahuijs 1826, p.65; Lulofs 1904, p.1638; Dobbin 1977, p.26).

Taking advantage of these favorable conditions and of the fact that during the time men were involved in the clearing, planting, tending or processing connected with coffee production, they would be supported through the complementary efforts of other household members, the Dutch in the late 1840s made it compulsory for every able-bodied male in the Minangkabau highlands to raise coffee. The finished yield from the coffee bushes had to be delivered to government coffee warehouses, where the growers exchanged their product for cash at a low fixed price. The Government then shipped the collected coffee down from the highlands and auctioned it to international purchasers, pocketing the difference between the low purchasing price it paid for the beans and the fluctuating world-market price.

Over the next sixty years, this Cultivation System worked with little change in West Sumatra, and as Figure 5.1 and Table 5.1 make clear, it caused a great expansion in coffee production in the first four decades after its introduction. The causes of that expansion, and of the decline that set in after 1870, are

FIGURE 5.1 Analysis of Trend of Coffee Sales in West Sumatra, 1840–1907, Five Year Moving Average

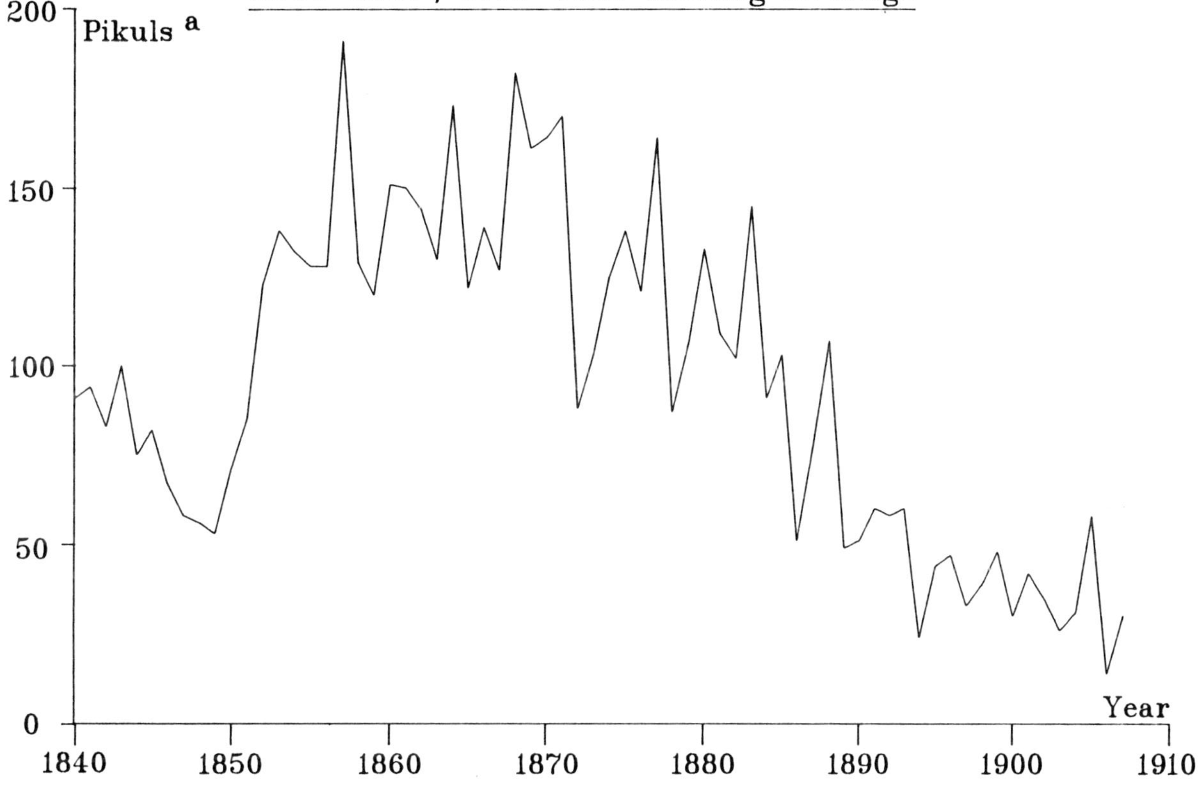

[a] 1 pikul = 61.76 kg

Sources: As for Table 5.1

TABLE 5.1 Government Coffee Sales, West Sumatra, 1842-1906[a]

(million kg)

Five Year Period	Total Sold	Average Annual Sale	Range
1842-1846	25.1	5.0	2.0
1847-1851	20.0	4.0	2.0
1852-1856	40.0	8.0	1.0
1857-1861	45.8	9.2	4.4
1862-1866	43.7	8.7	3.1
1867-1871	49.6	9.9	3.4
1872-1876	35.5	7.1	3.1
1877-1881	37.0	7.4	4.8
1882-1886	30.4	6.1	5.8
1887-1891	21.2	4.2	3.6
1892-1896	14.4	2.9	2.2
1897-1901	11.9	2.4	1.0
1902-1906	10.1	2.0	2.7

[a] Quantities sold in five year periods

Sources: Lulofs (1904, pp.1660-61); Kielstra (1888, p.1674); Bosse (1895, pp.124-28); Graves (1980, p.58); Oki (1977, p.37)

treated below, but in order to understand those causes it is necessary first to take note of further details connected with the actual working of the System.

For the government, the costs associated with the Cultivation System in West Sumatra were not insignificant. Close supervision of every step in coffee production was simply not feasible, but even intermittent supervision of growing, plucking, processing, and delivery demanded the development of a small stratum of paid Minangkabau officials working under more highly paid Dutch *controleurs*. Warehouses had to be built to receive and store coffee, and these also had to be staffed by paid officials. The transport of coffee to Padang required not only contracts with private hauliers but also the construction and maintenance of a widespread, quality road network. Above all, the element of compulsion behind the production and delivery of coffee meant that the government had to be prepared to use coercion to enforce the System at any time, and this in turn necessitated a standing military and police capability. The System, then, demanded a significant expansion in the body and the tasks of the government in West Sumatra. It also supported that expansion: in the years after 1847, the returns from government coffee sales were sufficient to meet these local outlays and to make substantial contributions to the colonial treasury as well (Paerels 1949, p.90; Furnivall 1944, p.208).

Though the Dutch referred to coffee as a "people's crop," the raising of it under the Cultivation System was not primarily intended to benefit the people. All other things being equal, the fixed delivery price made it possible for any Minangkabau to expand his cash income through extra amounts of land and labour devoted specifically to coffee production. But direct work in the coffee gardens was not the only labour extracted by the System. Much of the effort required for the construction and upkeep of roads and government buildings was garnered through village corvée labour. And the work put into raising coffee had, at least in the short run, to be offset by additional work performed by other household members in the subsistence and commercial spheres. Furthermore, by appropriating the coffee trade to itself, the government forced those local people who had earlier been involved with the marketing of coffee to turn, willy-nilly, either back to the land or to alternative, and less profitable, mercantile activities.

The essence of the Cultivation System in West Sumatra was the connection between the colonial government and the Minangkabau farmers, but those were not the only elements touched by forced coffee production in the highlands. The independent religious leaders with their strong bases in Islamic schools seem not to have been much affected by the forced coffee cultivation, but the other key elite groups, the *panghulu* who headed clans or lineages and the pseudo-traditional leaders whom the Dutch expected to coordinate higher-level activities for them, found themselves put into strained positions by their association with the System.

The newly created supra-lineage elites among the Minangkabau owed their existence to the Dutch need for respected leaders through whom the colonial administration could work effectively and inexpensively. This was in line with the model followed in Java, and as was the case with the Javanese *bupati, wedana,* and other officials, the Minangkabau *tuanku laras, panghula kepala,* etc., enjoyed a share of the revenues accruing from coffee production in their areas. But since they had no power or legitimacy deriving from the pre-colonial past, and since the authority they did exercise was due almost entirely to Dutch support, these officials were commonly identified only with the Cultivation System. They thus had no hope of being popularly accepted as leaders, and, because they never had sufficient power to enforce the System effectively, they were considered weak as well.

By contrast, the authority of the *panghulu* did not depend on the Dutch presence. They had an established position in society long before the Europeans came to the highlands, and their authority over important matters was unquestioned within the family units they headed. Those matters, however, had little to do with mobilizing clan members as a workforce, and their Dutch-imposed responsibility to encourage their followers to comply with the System put them into an uncomfortable, compromised position. In dealing with the outside world, they were obliged to protect the interests of their clan members. Yet the Dutch provided them with political, material and moral support in order to entice them to enforce the System with vigour. This placed them in an unenviable situation. From the Dutch point of view, the *panghulu* were considered unreliable allies and ineffective agents. To their followers, the privileges and small commissions accorded them by the Dutch signified that their loyalty to the clan was being eroded.

The Cultivation System, then, brought great changes to West Sumatra. The environment underwent a massive facelift, with vast tracts of forest replaced by coffee gardens. The bureaucracy expanded, and the colonial presence penetrated deeply into political and economic life. The allocation of tasks within almost every household had to be altered to permit work directed toward the delivery of coffee. And the secular elites found themselves manoeuvred into potentially dangerous positions. Yet this was all successfully accomplished, with practically no resistance from a notoriously fractious and resolute people, within the space of twenty years. How was this possible?

Why the System Succeeded

For the first twenty years after it was introduced in West Sumatra, the Cultivation System experienced notable success. As the records of the quantities of coffee sold annually by the government demonstrate (Table 5.1), coffee production reached new high levels and stayed at those levels for some time. Large amounts of money were dispersed among the farming communities. And still larger amounts were retained by the government. Though an element of coercion was connected with the lucrative expansion of coffee production, that element was not the crucial one in the working of the System. Force, after all, had been applied and found ineffective in Dutch attempts to spur coffee production before 1849, and a capacity for force was unable to prevent the decline of coffee production after 1870. Instead, the success of the System in its early decades was due to three main factors, all of them connected with the Minangkabau economy.

The first of these factors was the fixed price paid for the coffee. The government had estimated that under the earlier conditions of free cultivation, growers were receiving only a small and uncertain amount of cash for the coffee they raised. When the international price of coffee was *f*20 per *picul* (about 32 cents per kg), it was estimated that duties, storage, transport, and middlemen took some 80 per cent of this price, leaving the farmer a return of only *f*4 per *picul* (six cents per kg). When the market price declined precipitously in the 1840s from some 20-30 guilders per *picul* to less than *f*9, the amount received by farmers was so meagre that they simply began to abandon their coffee gardens (Swieten 1863, pp.206-10; Couperus 1856, pp.296-97; Kielstra 1888, pp.1629-30, 1467-68).

Faced with this situation, government officials reasoned that if they were prepared to pay a fixed, moderate price for coffee in the highlands, they could encourage production, with the government perhaps absorbing losses when world prices were abnormally low but more than recouping those losses when prices rose again (Kielstra 1888, pp.1612-13). The price they fixed upon, *f*7 per *picul*, appears to have helped spur production in the early years of the Cultivation System, when that price provided much higher returns than farmers had been getting for their beans in the immediately preceding period. The price also proved beneficial to the government's coffers, for as the world price passed *f*30 per *picul* in the 1850s and eventually reached *f*50 per *picul*, the revenues from the sale of Minangkabau coffee became handsome indeed. The stable price may also have appealed to the peasants' inclination toward risk-avoidance, something to which Scott (1976) has drawn attention; the government's returns from coffee may have been high, but it was taking on itself the risk of market fluctuations, leaving Minangkabau farmers with the safer position of receiving guaranteed prices and fairly predictable cash incomes from coffee.

The second factor behind the success of forced coffee production in West Sumatra was its continued small demands for labour. The initial effort to get the System under way must have been considerable: forest had to be cleared; coffee bushes planted; roads and buildings constructed. The element of coercion involved was strong and was consistently applied, and the System in West Sumatra could not have been implemented or have functioned thereafter without it. But this push was taking place at a time when the guaranteed price was raising farmers' returns from coffee much higher than they had previously been, and after this initial effort the labour required for the crop was minimal, precisely because the methods of production followed were those of the earlier period of free cultivation. The Minangkabau system of household-provided labour apparently had sufficient flexibility to meet the initial heavy workload demanded by the System, and thereafter the steady income from coffee sales probably provided adequate recompense for the small additional work entailed in plucking, drying and transporting the coffee beans.

The third major factor leading to the success of the Cultivation System between 1850 and 1870 had to do with the wider West Sumatra economy in that period. The commercial sphere had long been a basic part of Minangkabau life, with the importance of trade and exchange taken almost for granted, and the cash incomes earned by farmers under the old system of free coffee cultivation had undoubtedly helped to whet appetites for trade goods.[9] But during the Cultivation System the importance of cash and of exchange increased still further, and though the System was often referred to as the "coffee system," it would be more accurate, though more clumsy, to call it the "coffee-cloth-salt-rice system," for there was an important intertwining of the marketing of these products at the heart of the Cultivation System in West Sumatra.

Cloth and salt were channelled into West Sumatra through a small number of private firms, mainly located in Padang. The merchants in charge of those firms, who were mostly European though there was some subsidiary involvement of Chinese, stood to gain substantially from their control of importing and initial sale of these consumer necessities before they percolated through the reticulation system of indigenous petty traders into village markets (Veth 1881, p.99; Swieten 1863; Lulofs 1904). With Minangkabau households dependent on markets for the supply of these essentials, the government quite consciously supported the cloth and salt oligopoly in Padang, recognising that villagers would need the cash they received from their coffee crop to acquire these commodities (Swieten 1863, p.222, p.224; Lulofs 1904, p.1642; Kielstra 1888, p.1633; Dobbin 1983, p.215ff). It has been argued that villagers had a surplus of cash under the System (von Benda-Beckmann 1979, p.287, p.366), but other evidence, particularly the vociferous complaints of villagers about their lack of cash when they were threatened with an income tax payable in money (*De Gouvernements Koffiecultuur* 1904, p.63)[10] indicates that people were short of cash and therefore had to participate in coffee production in order to be able to purchase items they needed.

To make acceptable the low price paid for coffee and the artificially high prices paid for cloth and salt, it was essential that rice, the principal subsistence crop, be plentiful and cheap. Accordingly, official intervention into rice production and rice trade became necessary, and this eventually reached a scale almost comparable with State attempts to regulate the coffee growing. In the long run, this created troubles: by the turn of the century, government regulations, limitations on trade, demands for village self-sufficiency, and outright blunders by officials brought about a situation where rice actually had to be imported into the area (Steinbuch 1917, p.67; Schrieke 1955, p.97ff; Frijling 1917, p.95ff; Stibbe 1901-02, vol.2, p.506ff). This situation was alleviated only by the 1912 abolition of these restrictions, which led to a boom in rice production (Schrieke 1955; Oki 1977). In the short run, however, the restrictions helped to keep the terms of trade between coffee and rice favorable to coffee growers during the years of the System's greatest success (Couperus 1856, p.304).

Since coffee cultivation required small amounts of labour which were indirectly subsidized by those raising rice, and since cash returns from that labour were both predictable and necessary to pay for other essential goods, it is not surprising that forced coffee production succeeded among the Minangkabau between 1850 and 1870. But the success did not last, and by the end of the century yields from the Cultivation System had fallen below even the disastrous levels of the late 1840s.

Why the System Failed

During the period of the Cultivation System, government purchases of coffee expanded from 58,000 *piculs* (3.5 million kg) a year to 173,000 *piculs* (over 10.5 million kg) in 1864 (Lulofs 1904, p.1660). Yet within a decade of this new peak, coffee production was heading inexorably downhill, a decline which the government proved incapable of halting. There were a number of contributing factors.

First, the best land for raising coffee was becoming exhausted. The Minangkabau style had been to use large areas of conveniently located land for planting coffee bushes and then to exploit the bushes for as long as possible.[11] As early as the 1850s, the need to plant new bushes was becoming apparent, for many of the best forest gardens were "reaching the point of exhaustion through old age" (Couperus 1856, p.302). But with the soils in the older, best-situated areas depleted, it would be necessary to lay out new gardens in different areas. And not only would this mean a repetition of the temporarily unproductive work of clearing, planting, and culling, it would also entail continued extra effort, for the new areas would have to be further from the villages than the ones they were to replace, thus increasing travel and transport difficulties. Like the earlier free cultivation, the forced-delivery System had been built on a foundation of minimal labour requirements. Renewing the System would involve changing that foundation, and the Minangkabau did not respond.

Second, a devastating leaf disease struck the coffee bushes. In the 1870s, *hemilia vestatrix* attacked the *arabica* species of coffee grown in West Sumatra and decimated many of the gardens (Ultee 1949, p.10; Paerels 1949, p.90; Scholz 1977, p.58). Gardens above one thousand metres were not affected (Paerels 1949, p.96, p.109), and it was possible to plant new areas with the *liberica* species which was not susceptible to the disease, although using only higher areas or planting new gardens in new areas would mean further increases in the amount of labour demanded for coffee production, an option the Minangkabau had already found unappealing.

Third, after 1873 the Dutch colonial government was involved in waging a long, costly, and periodically intense war in Aceh. Because of the strong Acehnese resistance, which was fuelled by Islamic sentiment, the willingness and capacity of the Dutch to muster the coercion needed to change Minangkabau behaviour by force was probably more limited than it had been a quarter of a century before.

In addition, official attempts to counteract the decline in yields were not helped by the technical shortcomings of those entrusted to take Minangkabau coffee production in a different direction. In 1875-76, an experienced agricultural specialist from Java, Inspector Ples, visited West Sumatra in order to lay out guidelines which would establish coffee production there on a new scientific basis and thus enable far more intensive cultivation. Failing to appreciate the uniqueness of the highlands, Ples urged the industry to take up methods which proved deleterious. The shade trees he recommended to protect the young coffee bushes turned out to be harmful, and his lack of attention to the ecological differences between the Minangkabau territory and the lower terrain in which much of Javanese coffee was raised posed still other difficulties, thus weakening any faith in a more scientific approach to coffee cultivation.

But the major reason for the long-run failure of coffee under the Cultivation System was that the only method which might have worked in West Sumatra could not be implemented among the Minangkabau people who lived there. At the heart of Inspector Ples's reforms were not only his scientific approach but also his perception that coffee really ought to be grown on a different basis altogether. If coffee production were to be sound, expandable, and lasting under the Cultivation System, it would have to be pursued through the constant use of the land best suited for it, through a continuous cycle of replacing less productive bushes with new plantings, and through more careful tending of the bushes and the gardens. In effect, what was needed was a plantation system. This insight might well have been right. But recommendations stemming from it were not feasible. Plantations had been tried, even with coercive backing, in the years before 1847, but they had inevitably failed. Given the Minangkabau household-production system and political arrangements, there simply was no way to mobilize the villagers for work as plantation labourers. Under these circumstances, any plantation scheme was doomed.

For as long as the Cultivation System provided modest cash rewards for light inputs of labour, and encouraged the need for these rewards by controlling the distribution of essential goods, it could succeed. Changes, whether they involved higher labour inputs or different labour arrangements, were unacceptable to the Minangkabau, and, with the old System faltering and change unacceptable, decline was inexorable.

Conclusion

The Cultivation System, in its final form, lasted for six decades in West Sumatra. During that time it was an important influence in effecting change among the Minangkabau, both within villages and in the wider region.

In their local communities, the Minangkabau were not transformed by the System. Contact with the wider world through involvement in trade as both sellers and purchasers had long predated forced coffee cultivation in West Sumatran households, and the patterns of agricultural labour demanded by the System—patterns marked by sporadic concentration on a single effort—were not dissimilar to those already in effect in the region. Yet there were important changes within villages. Lineage heads, losing more from their association with the colonial authorities than they gained, saw their influence wane and their active positions ossify, particularly as the Dutch began to codify and regulate *adat*. Rice production and rice trade, crucial elements in village life, were hampered by their intimate connection with the System and suffered major setbacks. And many villagers, despite the flexibility accorded them by household economic arrangements, began to show signs of timidity and reluctance to take on the risks of new cash crops, fearing that government attention would inevitably cut short the profitability of new ventures (Young 1980).[12]

Changes in influence and in attitude brought about by the Cultivation System were not confined to the smaller communities. Though the pseudo-traditional elite whom the Dutch established in order to help them run the System did not gain the solid footing that had been envisaged, they were still in place in 1908, with at least the strength that decades of institutionalised existence provided them. They had been joined in their elevation to higher status by those Minangkabau who had moved into government service through positions in the administration of the System itself; clerks, inspectors and warehouse supervisors had seen opportunities, gained education, and entered the respected salariat through the workings of the forced-delivery system. And the System, by focusing attention on Padang as the ultimate destination of coffee and the point of origin of important trade goods, helped to shift the commercial orientation in West

Sumatra from the rivers leading eastward toward the Strait of Malacca to Padang, now grown into the administrative, marketing, and transport hub of the region.

These changes, both in villages and in wider Minangkabau society, did not always flow smoothly and unimpeded. Difficulties were caused not least by three contradictions inherent in the Cultivation System in West Sumatra, contradictions connected with economics, with politics, and with property.

In the economic sphere, villagers were becoming increasingly dependent on trade items, and particularly on salt and cloth purchased for cash. The coastal merchants' monopoly of those items made possible a distorted high price for them, and this helped compel farmers to produce coffee for cash. But eventually the System's low returns for coffee, and for rice, in turn depressed producers' incomes to the point where purchases of such goods as cloth and salt had to be cut back. This reduced profits among the coastal merchants (Bosse 1895; Kamerling 1895). Thus one of the prime beneficiaries of the System began to lead complaints against it.

Politically, the System could run with the bare minimum of expensive coercion only if local leaders could act to mobilize the necessary manpower. But neither the traditional *panghulu* nor the pseudo-traditional officials had the ability to compel peasants to work. All they could do was encourage participation. In order to elicit that encouragement, however, the Dutch had to offer financial rewards to the local leaders, and the widespread knowledge of the existence of those financial rewards undermined the ability of local leaders to mobilize manpower without expensive coercion.

At the heart of Minangkabau involvement with coffee cultivation was the property system. Property rights were basic to the organisation of production, and through them land was used by independent individuals and households. This was fine during the early years of the System, but as it became clear that larger collective units were needed if the government were to organise and supervise large, rational plantations, plans for this clashed with the very system of individual rights which had made the initial success possible. Changing property rights would have entailed either the complete undermining of the local leaders who provided the System with some guidance, or the use of coercion at a level where the expense incurred would have outstripped the potential returns to be gained under the System.

Whether in Java or in West Sumatra, the Cultivation System was an unequal struggle, entailing the extraction of surplus from peasant communities by an expanding colonial State apparatus. It is misleading, of course, to talk of one single Cultivation System for all of Java, given the important differences that existed with regard to crops and methods on that island. In West Sumatra, the regional political and socio-economic conditions which the government had to face made the System diverge even further from the idealised model than the various Javanese cases did. The Minangkabau were predominantly a sedentary, wet-rice cultivating peasantry, but in dealing with them, the Dutch found that the mechanisms developed in Java for taking surpluses were clumsy at best and ultimately ineffective. Large profits were eventually taken from the region, but only through an unwieldy, unstable, and, in the long run, unworkable system whose form owed as much to Minangkabau preferences and predilections as it did to Dutch plans and coercion. It is arguable, indeed, whether the marriage of force and economic incentives directed at small enterprises of individual peasant households can correctly be termed a "System" at all. And in any event, the System ought not to be seen in isolation, for in nineteenth-century West Sumatra it was not an isolated phenomenon. Instead, it was in operation at a time when other important developments were taking place. Those developments—in transportation, urbanization, education, standardization, and administration—were helping to change the orientation of the area and the very meaning of being Minangkabau. Some of those developments were caused by the System, others came about despite the System, still others emerged regardless of the System. It is only by taking all of these together that the materials for a meaningful picture of change among the Minangkabau in the nineteenth century can be collected.

Notes

1. The archive documents cited here are from the former Netherlands Ministry of Colonies kept in the General State Archives in The Hague. They are all classified using *verbaal* codes. *Verbalen* were ministerial decisions or minutes, and nearly all documentary material relevant to a particular decision has been filed according to the number of the decision. The number consists of the date of the decision together with other auxiliary codes (numbers, letters). Thus V:6.3.1907.27 stands for the *verbaal* of March 6, 1907, number 27.
2. The period between the final 'pacification' of the region by the Dutch (the end of the Padri conflicts in 1837), and the anti-tax rebellion of 1908 has not attracted much research. Graves (1980) is an exception. The excellent work of Dobbin (1983) provides, in its final chapter, by far the best coverage of this period, but her book deals fully only with the period 1784 to 1847.
3. In Minangkabau, *surau* is also the term for the elementary religious schools which double as dormitories for unmarried males in every settlement. It is important to differentiate between the two.
4. Using historical materials from the late nineteenth and early twentieth centuries, I have developed (Young 1983) ideal types of Minangkabau households which identify both the structural features and constraints which influenced their economic behaviour and also the underlying tendencies to transformation active during this period.
5. The Minangkabau custom of encouraging young men to leave their home village to win fortune outside (in the *rantau*).

6. It would be tempting to simplify the intra-household division of labour here as simply male:female. However, it is clearly more complex. Furthermore, even if there were a consensus among government observers of a division of labour based on gender, one would need to take care to establish that this really was the case, and not an ideological construct (Stivens 1983).
7. See also the 12 June 1907 Letter of Governor Heckler, which specifically refers to such merchants. The letter is to be found in Verbaal [hereafter V] 11.10.1907/21, Archief Ministerie van Kolonien [hereafter MK], Algemeen Rijksarchief, The Hague [ARADH].
8. These arguments are further developed in Young (1983).
9. It is notable that the sketchy figures available for the earlier period all indicate that the value of imported goods destined for village consumption consistently exceeded the money received by coffee growers (Swieten 1863, pp.210-11; Lulofs 1904, pp.1658-59; Vinne 1842).
10. See also V: 8.10.1895/86 and V: 16.6.1895/35.
11. According to Couperus (1856, p.303) and Ochse (1961), coffee bushes in the Minangkabau area were still producing after thirty or forty years; normal productive life on commercial plantations was fifteen to twenty years.
12. Further documents supporting this observation are to be found in V: 6.3. 1907/27.

CHAPTER SIX

Changing Measures and Measuring Changes: Regional Agricultural Growth in Java, 1815-1875

Peter Boomgaard

Introduction

Java in the nineteenth century has often been regarded as an agricultural success story. Export crops such as coffee, sugar and indigo show an enormous increase after 1815, and population growth, although not as high as the official figures suggest, was still a respectable 1.0 to 1.5 per cent per year on average. Figures for rice production, livestock and area under cultivation show an almost continuous upward tendency.

It is also universally acknowledged that Java's nineteenth-century statistics are unreliable, especially those from early in the century. Van Niel has found evidence for the period 1837-1851 that the figures recorded for population and for arable land both represented over 75 per cent of the actual values in those regions where spot checks were carried out (Van Niel 1972, p.109).[1] This is a problem, but if it were true that the recorded values of all variables are, for each period, underestimates of the same order of magnitude, then dividing one variable by another would result in a fairly accurate quotient. So if, for instance, both the population and the rice production in 1820 are off by 25 per cent, the figure obtained for rice production per capita, the result of dividing one by the other, will be a good estimate of the real value. In this chapter I shall test these assumptions by presenting a number of "annotated" ratios for five residencies in Western and West-Central Java (Banten, Priangan, Cirebon, Tegal, Pekalongan).

The four variables that will be considered are:

1. population
2. rice production
3. area under rice
4. buffaloes

After a short discussion of the statistics used, I shall try to establish for all calculated ratios what the chances are that the assumption of similar underestimates for all variables (for every period) is not true, and what that implies for the calculated trends and averages. I shall also try to give an explanation for those trends that seem to be reliable. A separate section compares demographic and agricultural indicators for the five residencies. Finally I shall confront my findings with current historiographical opinion and practice.

As I am not interested in year-by-year variations, but in change over a long period of time, I have used, as much as possible, five-year averages. Figures based on one or two observations in a five-year period will be indicated as such.

Sources

The Dutch were not the first to count, or at least make an intelligent guess of, people and arable land in Java. Javanese rulers, primarily interested in tax, war, and "feudal" tenure, had from time immemorial kept some sort of record of their subjects and their land, expressed, respectively in *cacah* and *jung*.[2] Both units varied from one another, and hard-pressed rulers did resort from time to time to crude methods of increasing tax returns and the number of potential "feudal" holdings by halving the size of both *cacah* and *jung*. It was not until 1795 that the Dutch organized a "modern" survey of a large part of the island, the Pasisir. The surviving documentation of that "census" contains, by regency, the number of villages, the population—specified as to age (adults or children) and sex, the traditional *cacah* figures, the numbers of *jung*, and the number of buffaloes. The registered numbers of both people and buffaloes are evidently the result of a real census of sorts, but the *cacah* figures, and in some cases the arable land figures as well, represent traditional notions.

Nevertheless even the *cacah* figures must have been the product of a recent reassessment by Javanese power-holders, because the figures are not rounded off to hundreds or thousands, as they were under the old rulers, and they differ perceptibly from earlier figures. In many cases the number of arable *jung* are half or a quarter of the number of *cacah*, but not always. It is not known whether *cacah* figures were derived from *jung* or the other way around. For the north coast from Brebes to Tuban, the correlation coefficient between *cacah* and *jung* by regency is 0.9, that between *cacah* and people 0.76. There were twenty people to the *cacah* for the same area, but individual regency ratios range from 9:1 to 65:1. That alone should warn us against any easy conversion from *cacah* to population figures. At that time the Dutch were probably more interested in people than in the area under cultivation, because they needed corvée labour and conscripts, whereas the deliveries of rice, the main crop of Java, were the responsibility of the regents.

In 1802 another survey was carried out in the same region. The data registered were more or less the same, but there were a few extras. Coffee trees and coconut trees, areas under indigo and cotton were new, while *cacah* were not mentioned any more. Arable land figures were still expressed in old *jung* but they all differed from the 1795 figures, so they were apparently readjusted. We must again assume that the Dutch officials were predominantly interested in accurate population figures.

Our documentation on the survey carried out in 1808 is rather scanty, but it seems that it was carried out along the lines of the 1795 and 1802 work. To my knowledge these three surveys have never been analysed before, and only the final totals of the population data of 1795 and 1902 are quoted in the literature. The exception to this statement is Bleeker, who published the 1802 population figures in detail and used them in comparison with later data (Bleeker 1870).[3]

As the 1795, 1802 and 1808 data are lacking for three out of the five Residencies dealt with in this chapter, our real starting point is Raffles' 1815 survey. The earlier data will be used, however, to evaluate Raffles' survey for the other two regions. Raffles' census—as it is often called—is well known, and the population statistics from it are widely used. Unfortunately these are not the best part of the survey, because Raffles was more interested in land than in people. The obvious reason for this statistical *volte face* was the change in tax policy that he introduced: a land tax, or land rent, was to be substituted for forced deliveries and corvée labour. It was therefore necessary to have a fairly good estimate of both the area under cultivation and the productive capacity of the soil, because both irrigated *(sawah)* and dry *(tegal)* fields were to be classified into three categories and taxed accordingly. The *jung* was standardized at 2,000 square Rhineland rods or 2.8 hectares. In the course of the nineteenth century, it became accepted practice to measure agricultural land in *bau,* which equalled one quarter of a standardized *jung* or 0.71 ha. Potential rice production was expressed in *amat padi,* or unhusked rice, except for the Priangan where *cains* were used. In this paper, all measures have been converted to kilograms.[4] Unfortunately we do not know how Raffles' survey was carried out. The instructions published in Raffles' *History* (1830, II, appendix L.2) are explicit enough: "Every householder shall have a number given to him," and "even the smallest quantity of land must be accounted for." It was, however, virtually impossible for Raffles and his small corps of collectors to have counted everybody or measured all cultivated lands, and a report from the Inspector General of Land Rent Revenue from 1818 was highly critical of the results.[5] Yet, in one way or another, landed property was assessed for the first time with standardized measures, and as this assessment was to be the basis for the Land Rent System, statements from village headmen would not simply have been accepted at face value. With regard to the population,

Raffles was interested only in householders paying land rent or tenement tax and not in the exact number of household members.

A source at least as bountiful as Raffles' *History* and its tables, and one certainly more bulky but far less well known, is the collection of statistics ordered by Governor General van der Capellen in 1820. Its only flaw in comparison to the 1815 survey is its vagueness about area under cultivation. Its population data, however, are better that Raffles'. In 1826 Governor-General Du Bus set up the Agricultural Commissions in order to stimulate and coordinate the cultivation of cash crops for the European market. In 1828 and 1829 the Central Agricultural Commission presented, for the first time, statistics on production of and area under commercial crops for the European market, and probably, as an afterthought, added material on rice and on total area under cultivation. This also reflects the preoccupations of that period: Java was not living up to expectations as far as the production of cash crops was concerned, and nobody was very much interested in total arable land and rice production, both by that time a matter of routine for the land rent collectors. Fortunately annual reports from the Residents—the so called General Reports (*Algemeen Verslag, or AV*)—yield population data for these years.[6]

The series of annual Cultivation Reports *(Cultuur Verslag, or CV)* starts in 1834. The last CV available to me was that of 1851. A description of the contents can be found in Van Niel (1972, pp.94ff.). From 1854 onward the same data can be found in the (published) annual Colonial Reports *(Koloniaal Verslag, KV)*. The CV and KV statistics are, in a sense, by-products of the Cultivation System introduced in 1830 when land rent and forced village export crops were combined into one system. Because the rice price was one key factor in the assessment of land rent and estimated rice production, based upon the quality and size of peasant holdings, was another, it was to be expected that policy makers would be interested in good statistics on both the area under cultivation and rice production. No less importance was attached to population figures, because they ultimately determined whether past policies concerning export crop cultivation had been successful and whether cultivation could be expanded. A growing population was regarded as proof of good administration, while a declining population indicated migration and high death rates, both products of oppressive rule (or, as most Residents would have preferred to argue, of acts of God).

Counting and Measuring

How reliable are the data on population, arable land, rice production, and cattle recorded in the sources mentioned above? As far as I could find out, there was no real cattle census in the period under consideration; European administrators gathered the data provided by village headmen and sent them on to Batavia.

Occasional spot checks could have been carried out, but cattle statistics were never an important issue before 1880 and no fuss was made over their accuracy.

Rice production statistics were, in fact, a by-product of arable land statistics. Land rent assessment was based on an estimate of area under cultivation (subdivided into four to six categories) multiplied by an estimate of average rice (or maize) production per hectare for each category.[7] The land rent collector presented his estimate to the village head, who usually succeeded in getting a rebate. Land rent assessments were highly sensitive to political pressure. In 1836 when van den Bosch, as Minister of Colonies, suggested to the authorities in Batavia that land rent could be increased, a rather steep rise in revenues resulted, after a relatively long period of stagnation. The reverse occurred after the disasters of the late 1840s: the Residents were told to take it easy with assessments, and, lo and behold, revenue was more or less stabilized at the 1846 level for the next ten years. Thereafter it increased slowly from year to year, and made another upward jump when Governor-General Mijer told the Residents in 1869 that land rent was too low. During the early seventies this policy was backed up by a new assessment of the productivity of the soil in the residencies by sampling yields of the various categories of *sawah*.

This does not mean that variations in rice production as recorded in the sources are entirely fictitious. If we find very high or very low figures, they usually coincide with bumper crops and crop failures respectively, and can be established from the General Residential Reports. Good examples are Cirebon in the 1840s, Tegal between 1820 and 1855, and Pekalongan between 1850 and 1865. It should, however, be kept in mind that the annual production figures do not tell us much about the absolute level of actual production; understatements of between 25 and 50 per cent can be expected (Boomgaard 1984, pp.15-16). If corrected for the above-mentioned alterations in land rent assessment policy, the calculated five-year averages can, however, be used to discover relative changes in production levels.

Following the heavy criticisms of Raffles' assessment of the area under cultivation, an Inspector of Surveys was appointed in 1820. He started a cadastral survey in Kedu, and a beginning had been made in Rembang when the Inspector died. It was then realized that carrying out such a cadastral survey in all residencies would overtax the resources of the understaffed survey service, and it was decided that a less ambitious program should be initiated under the responsibility of the local land rent collectors (Resolution 14.6.1825, 19). It is not clear whether this Resolution was carried out in all residencies. Of the five residencies under consideration here I found traces of new surveys only for Cirebon and Pekalongan. In a report dated 1827, Vitalis, then the collector of Majalengka in Cirebon, stated that he conducted a survey of one third of the arable land in his division in 1824 and 1825.[8] The only other example of early surveys is that in Sukabumi, a private estate in the Priangan created under British rule and bought back by the Dutch soon after their return. The landowner, de Wilde, measured the *sawah* on the estate (De Wilde 1830, p.204).

In 1840 Batavia ordered the Resident of Cirebon to organize a survey of the area under cultivation, and over a two-year period the survey uncovered about 40 per cent more *sawah* than had previously been thought to exist. The outcome of the Cirebon survey whetted Batavia's appetite, and Governor-General Merkus told Java's other Residents that they should conduct similar surveys (Nahuijs 1847, pp.90ff). There seems, however, to be no proof that this order was ever carried out. A new epoch began when it was finally understood that a real cadastral survey was beyond the grasp of the local authorities. In 1853 the centrally organized Cadastral-Statistical Survey was launched in Cirebon. At then end of the 1870s, after the survey had been completed in nine residencies (twice in two of them!), the Cadastral-Statistical Survey was abolished because it was too expensive and too slow. Of the five residencies considered here, Cirebon had been measured twice (1853/60, 1870/76), and Tegal and Pekalongan once each (1865/71 and 1865/69 respectively). The results are given in Table 6.1 together with those of the earlier survey in Cirebon.

Although the Cadastral-Statistical survey was not in operation in Banten and the Priangan, it is clear from the data collected that figures from those Residencies were corrected upwards several times, probably as a result of local initiatives. In the Priangan, there twice occurred a ten per cent increase over a two-year period (1855/57 and 1863/65) against an expected three per cent. In both the Priangan and Banten we find corrections during the early 1870s (Banten 1873, 17 per cent; Priangan 1871/73, 15 per cent), probably part of the Java-wide attempt to obtain better arable land and rice production statistics, and because land rent was being introduced in the Priangan.

Finally we should look at the population statistics. In Table 6.1, the differences are presented between expected growth and the increases actually recorded in the Cadastral-Statistical Surveys. The surveys were certainly not the only reassessments of the population during the period under consideration, but they were more thorough and better organized than earlier attempts. Appendix Table 6.1 gives an overview of the years of excessive increases, mostly attributable to a better "census." In many though not all years of excessive increase, the General Residential Reports mention a new census. Often a reassessment was held after years of harvest failures, rural unrest and migration due to the introduction of the Cultivation System or epidemics, so that recorded increases were not results only of the reassessment but also of returned migrants. The figures from Appendix Table 6.1 show that population statistics for the Priangan before 1830 are virtually worthless.

TABLE 6.1 A Comparison between "Expected" Growth During the Years a Survey was Conducted and the Recorded Increase over the Same Period[a] (per cent)

	Sawah			Population		
	Recorded Increase	Expected Growth	Difference	Recorded Increase	Expected Growth	Difference
Cirebon						
1840/43	44	4.5	39.5	11	4.5	6.5
1853/60	23	10.5	12.5	46	10.5	35.5
1870/76	7	9	-2	18	9	9
Tegal						
1865/71	38	9	29	46	9	37
Pekalongan						
1865/69	46	6	40	30	6	24

[a] A normal growth rate of 1.5% per annum is postulated in order to find the increase attributable solely to the survey. From the 44% increase in the arable land figures from Cirebon between 1840 and 1843, 5% has to be subtracted because a 1.5% increase per annum can be regarded as normal. The 1840 figures were therefore 39% off the mark.

Source: Algemeen Verslag, Kultuur Verslag, Koloniaal Verslag, various issues.

I shall conclude this section on an optimistic note: there were also "census" years without excessive increases!

Trends

Area under Rice per Household. Household size as reported in the sources varies roughly between 3.5 and 6.0 persons per household. Most residencies, however, show averages of between 4.5 and 5.5. As the criteria used to define a household are not clear, I have standardized household size for my calculations, using an average number of five people per household.[9] For the area under rice, I have used the total arable land under peasant cultivation for all years before 1856. I subtracted a small percentage (0-10) for that part of the area under peasant cultivation which, according to data for 1856-1865, was planted with *palawija* (dry crops). After 1856 data for the area under rice are available. From 1866 onward I have subtracted area under rice as a second crop. Table 6.2 shows the resulting ratios, in hectares, per household.

TABLE 6.2 Area under Rice per Standardized Household[a]

(hectares)

Five year period	Banten	Priangan	Cirebon	Tegal	Pekalongan
1795/99	n.a.	n.a.	n.a.	(0.55)	(0.92)
1800/04	n.a.	n.a.	n.a.	(0.56)	(0.78)
1805/09	n.a.	n.a.	n.a.	(0.53)	(0.78)
1810/14	n.a.	n.a.	n.a.	n.a.	n.a.
1815/19	n.a.	n.a.	(1.07)	(1.03)	(1.11)
1820/24	n.a.	n.a.	n.a.	n.a.	n.a.
1825/29	n.a.	n.a.	(0.67)	0.98	(0.64)
1830/34	n.a.	n.a.	n.a.	0.92	n.a.
1835/39	0.55	0.43	0.73	0.84	0.61
1840/44	0.58	0.44	0.86	0.71	0.57
1845/49	0.56	0.50	0.87	0.78	0.63
1850/54	0.56	0.51	0.89	0.84	0.61
1855/59	0.55	0.55	0.74	0.72	0.58
1860/64	0.51	0.56	0.74	0.64	0.52
1865/69	0.49	0.57	0.73	0.59	0.43
1870/74	0.48	0.60	0.67	0.55	0.46

[a] All values between brackets are based on one or two observations only.

Source: As for Table 6.1

It is clear that, if 1815 is used as a starting point, the trends in Cirebon, Pekalongan and Tegal are all downwards; thus it must be concluded that average arable land per household was declining over the entire period 1815-75. However several factors almost certainly lead to an overstatement of this decline; Raffles' population figures were worse than his arable land data, which in turn were more understated in the late 1820s (especially in Cirebon) than were the population data. Furthermore, large-scale migration in the late 1840s and 1850s resulting from famine and epidemics caused a temporary fall in population, whereas reported area figures changed much less markedly. So a gradual decline in average cultivated area per household would be the outcome if the ratios were corrected. For Cirebon, we have three measuring points with a rather high degree of accuracy, namely the three years after the completion of the surveys (1843, 1860, 1876). The ratios of the area under rice per household are 0.81, 0.69 and

0.58 respectively, which, at least for the period 1843-1876 can be accepted as proof of declining average arable land per household. Unfortunately no such reliable measuring point exists before 1843.

In Cirebon, Tegal, and Pekalongan, the differences between 1815 and 1875 are too large to be attributed solely to a disproportional understatement of population figures in the earlier decades. In the case of Banten, the decline is not large enough to enable us to draw clear conclusions. In the Priangan, there is an upward trend, but that could be a result of the fact that the area under rice was relatively more understated than the population data. Population data there had been corrected several times between 1825 and 1835, and it may be that the population figures for 1835 are not too bad. Before 1855 the area figures do not show excessive increases, probably because there were no reassessments. Land rent had not been introduced in the Priangan, and figures on rice production and arable land were reported by the regents, who received as tax one-tenth of the rice produce. Reassessment of these figures was much less important to the colonial government than in those residencies where land rent operated. Between 1855 and 1873 there were three upward corrections of the arable land data which could be called excessive, and only one upward jump in the population data. So arable land data in the 1830s and 1840s was relatively more off the mark than population data, and the increase shown in Table 6.2 was partly or even entirely fictitious.

Finally, one example of grossly overstated area figures should be mentioned, because this case has been cited as proof of the unreliability of early nineteenth-century statistics. I am referring to the Cadastral and Statistical Survey carried out in Cirebon in the late 1850s. In 1857 the KV statistics mention 178,595 *bau* of arable land in Cirebon, but in 1858, after the Survey had been completed, 514,967 *bau* were reported. This incident has been quoted as proof of grossly understated early arable land figures. What in fact happened is that the reporting survey personnel had included 300,000 *bau* of uncultivated but cultivable land in their figures. It was not until 1873 that this error was discovered and corrected. So in this case the later figures were in fact much more overstated than the earlier figures were understated.

As far as the pre-1815 data are concerned, it can be said that low averages are to be expected, because the traditional arable land figures, grossly understating the actual area under cultivation, are divided by rather accurate population data. And even then, the pre-1815 data for Pekalongan are still higher than those of 1855-59 onward.[10]

Rice Production per Capita. In the four residencies where statistics for 1815 or 1820 are available, rice production per capita was higher than 1870/74 (Table 6.3). There are more similarities: after 1815 (or in one case 1820) there was a steep decline; a trough was reached between 1830 and 1845. Production per capita then increased in all five residencies, reaching relatively high levels between 1840 and 1865. Thereafter another downward trend is visible. Only in Pekalongan was that downward trend neutralized by an equally strong upward movement after 1865. It has been mentioned already that, outside the Priangan, all rice production figures were produced by the land rent collectors, after a bargaining session with the village headmen.

The rice production figures were therefore based not only upon area statistics and an assessment of the crop, but also on political guidelines from Batavia. Some of the fluctuations should clearly be attributed to these guidelines, as for example the increased production figures in Cirebon and Pekalongan in 1840/44, the lower or stable figures after 1849 in Banten and Pekalongan, and the upswing in Banten, the Priangan (where land rent was introduced in the early 1870s) and Pekalongan after 1869.

TABLE 6.3 Rice Production Per Capita[a]

(kgs of unhusked rice)

Five year period	Banten	Priangan	Cirebon	Tegal	Pekalongan
1815/19	n.a.	(353)	n.a.	(431)	(310)
1820/24	(246)	(286)	n.a.	n.a.	(174)
1825/29	n.a.	292	(245)	232	(173)
1830/34	184	188	n.a.	235	(172)
1835/39	185	194	241	226	136
1840/44	179	261	333	195	145
1845/49	198	293	264	262	148
1850/54	195	283	311	277	110
1855/59	212	297	233	334	81
1860/64	190	300	258	273	71
1865/69	157	238	239	267	80
1870/74	166	258	236	234	132

[a] All values between brackets are based on one or two observations only.

Source: As for Table 6.1

Differences in timing of revisions of area and population statistics can explain other fluctuations, such as the steep decline in the Priangan after 1815 (caused by corrected population statistics) or the sharp increase after 1839 in Cirebon (where several large corrections of population figures were done between 1824 and 1837, followed by large corrections in arable land between 1840 and 1843).

A third possibility is that corrections of one factor are much larger than those of the other, which was the case with the upswing after 1864 in Pekalongan (where arable land corrections were larger than population corrections) and the downswing in Tegal after the same year (where population corrections were larger than those of the area statistics).

But not all fluctuations are caused by political decisions or statistical corrections. An all-time low in the Priangan during the five year period 1830/34 reflects a series of harvest failures, and a severe drop in Cirebon after 1844 can be explained by the harvest failures of the late 1840s. Several series of harvest failures in Tegal between 1820 and 1854, combined with migration and epidemics, explain the deep trough between 1825/29 and 1850/54, and the same observation (numerous harvest failures due to the *ama mentek* disease between 1850 and 1864) applies to the Pekalongan trough (Table 6.3).[11]

Finally, as a warning against uncritical acceptance of early nineteenth-century statistics, the statistical peculiarities of the Residency Tegal between 1827 and 1847 should be mentioned. Although Raffles had expressed arable land data correctly in standardized *jung*, after the British interregnum Dutch officials reverted to pre-1815 practices and reported figures expressed in *ribu*, a local name for old *bau*. The Cultivation Reports treated these figures as if they were new *bau*, thereby underestimating the cultivated area by at least one third. When the error was finally discovered in 1847, both area data and rice production figures were almost doubled from one year to another. As land rent also went up (but only by 15 per cent), part of this increase might have been real, but probably not all of it. In 1849 the rice statistics were more or less back to normal, so the high figures for 1847 and 1848 could have reflected a bumper crop, but given the then rampant epidemics this is not very likely. An alternative explanation could be that it was realized after two years that the usual multiplier was valid for *ribu* but not for *bau*. Nevertheless, rice production per capita between 1825/29 and 1845/49 could have been higher than is suggested in Table 6.3.

Where do all these corrections and explanations of fluctuations in per capita production leave us? If, again, we use Cirebon, with its three good measuring points, as a test case, the downward sloping curve still stands. Production of unhusked rice per capita dropped from 349 kg in 1843 to 255 kg in 1860 and 237 kg in 1876. It may be assumed that the same trend applied to the other residencies as well except Tegal, because reported ratios in 1870/74 were lower than those of 1840/44, and the early ratios were an understatement of production per capita because area statistics were subjected to larger corrections between 1840 and 1875 than population figures. But how real are high ratios of 1815/19 (and 1820/24) compared to those of 1870/74? Even if we accept an understatement of the population in the early years of 50 per cent, as against 30 per cent for the area statistics, ratios for 1815/19 and 1820/24 are still higher than those of 1870/74. Comparing 1815/19 (and 1820/24) to 1840/44, it can be said that the differences are so large that even disproportionate population corrections do not erase them.

My conclusion is that all residencies for which we have early data experienced a drop in rice production per capita between 1815/19 (and 1820/24) and 1870/74, and that Cirebon experienced the same between 1843 and 1876.

Finally, three things should be kept in mind before these figures of rice production per capita can be used as estimates of food consumption per capita. First, even though the statistics improve during the early 1870s, they were still underestimates of actual production; second, rice was imported into areas of structural shortage, and seasonal migrants from these areas went to surplus areas to help with the rice harvest; third, rice was not the only food crop, and maize, cassava, sweet potatoes, taro, yams, soyabeans and various other beans, often collectively called *palawija,* were planted on dry fields *(tegal)* as a first crop and on *sawah* as a second crop. These constituted between 25 per cent and 40 per cent of the diet (in calories), but unfortunately there is not much detailed information on *palawija* before 1870 (Boomgaard 1984, pp.25-28).

Rice Production per Unit of Land under Rice. The most obvious feature of this series is that there is not a clear trend; for three residencies a 10 per cent drop between 1815 (or 1825) and 1870/74 is suggested by the data, but given the quality we cannot draw firm conclusions (Table 6.4).

All residencies keep their relative positions over the period shown; Priangan and Tegal were rather high relative to the other three, although not relative to residencies in East Java which are not examined in detail here. I am inclined to regard these ratios as indicators of "natural" soil fertility. After 1880, "technical" irrigation (as opposed to indigenous or "wild" irrigation) would change these fertility levels considerably by increasing the area under permanent irrigation, thereby reducing the possibility of large-scale crop failures. Before 1880, the area under permanent irrigation increased only gradually, and a large percentage of *sawah* depended on rainfall. Short-term fluctuations should thus be attributed largely to harvest failure (especially in Tegal 1825/54 and Pekalongan 1850/64).

Some other similarities can be mentioned: all residencies experienced a (relative) trough between 1830 and 1840, whereafter things brightened up in Banten, Priangan, and Tegal. All three reached a peak between 1855 and 1865. In Cirebon there is no trend at all, and in Pekalongan the opposite picture is found, no doubt as a result of the series of harvest failures already mentioned.

Due to the peculiar way in which the local officials of Tegal dealt with area measurements, the ratio of rice production to cultivated area is probably too low between 1825 and 1850. Real yields per hectare, however, were certainly low because of the harvest failures between 1820 and 1854.

A look at test-case Cirebon does not help this time; production per unit of land was 2,141 kg/ha in 1843, 1,861 in 1860, and 2,061 in 1876. The difference between 1843 and 1876 is hardly significant, but the earlier figure was probably an underestimate relative to 1876, because in the early 1870s repeated sampling had taken place in order to arrive at the "real" values of soil productivity. This would, again, point in the direction of decreasing production per hectare, but the evidence is not very strong. I have demonstrated elsewhere that the all-Java average increased between 1815 and 1875; the decreasing or stagnating productivity in West Java and the western part of Central Java was thus atypical.

Buffaloes per Household. In Banten, the average number of buffaloes per standardized household (of five persons) increased perceptibly between 1815 and 1875. In Tegal the increase was much smaller. In the Priangan the number was fairly stable throughout the period. In Cirebon and Pekalongan the average number of buffaloes in 1870/74 was slightly below the 1815 figure, but there is no clear trend. So only for Banten can it be said with some confidence that the average number of buffaloes per household increased. A look at the pre-1815 figures for Tegal and Pekalongan does not yield surprising results. It can only be said that both the slight downward trend for Pekalongan and the upward trend for Tegal are confirmed (Table 6.5). The only similarity between the five residencies is that after about 1850 (in Banten rather later) the average number of buffaloes did not increase.

Explaining the trends. In summation it can be said that arable land per household and productivity of labour (rice production per capita) clearly declined between 1815 and 1875; in Banten and the Priangan these developments are less marked than in the other three residencies. Productivity of land might have declined slightly, but it could also have been static. The number of buffaloes per household was also more or less static, except for Banten where it was increasing.

If we take the productivity of the soil, a more or less natural given, as our starting point, we must begin by trying to explain why there was a clear drop in productivity between 1815 and 1850. The solution is relatively easy: during the first decades of the Cultivation system, 1830-1850, a lot of energy was withdrawn from the indigenous agricultural sector. After local protest movements and migration in the 1830s and the disasters of the 1840s, the percentage of households performing cultivation services dropped sharply and land rent

TABLE 6.4 Rice Production per Unit of Land under Rice [a]

(kgs/ha of unhusked rice)

Five year period	Banten	Priangan	Cirebon	Tegal	Pekalongan
1815/19	n.a.	n.a.	n.a.	(2,100)	(1,400)
1820/24	n.a.	n.a.	n.a.	n.a.	n.a.
1825/29	n.a.	n.a.	(1,833)	(1,182)	(1,357)
1830/34	n.a.	n.a.	n.a.	(1,273)	n.a.
1835/39	1,700	2,262	1,662	1,343	1,111
1840/44	1,535	2,953	1,945	1,378	1,269
1845/49	1,755	2,905	1,511	1,681	1,172
1850/54	1,745	2,747	1,753	1,644	893
1855/59	1,930	2,689	1,593	2,308	700
1860/64	1,879	2,674	1,740	2,129	676
1865/69	1,597	2,093	1,632	2,284	941
1870/74	1,731	2,167	1,771	2,133	1,432

[a] All values between brackets are base on one or two observations only.

Source: As for Table 6.1

TABLE 6.5 Average Number of Buffaloes per Household[a]
(of five persons)

Five year period	Banten	Priangan	Cirebon	Tegal	Pekalongan
1795/99	n.a.	n.a.	n.a.	(0.73)	(0.84)
1800/04	n.a.	n.a.	n.a.	(0.66)	(0.96)
1805/09	n.a.	n.a.	n.a.	(0.79)	(0.83)
1810/14	n.a.	n.a.	n.a.	n.a.	n.a.
1815/19	(0.73)	(0.91)	(1.00)	(0.68)	(0.73)
1820/24	(0.62)	n.a.	(1.06)	n.a.	(0.63)
1825/29	n.a.	n.a.	(0.64)	n.a.	(0.58)
1830/34	0.77	n.a.	(0.75)	(0.70)	0.50
1835/39	0.82	0.85	0.80	0.84	0.58
1840/44	0.87	0.97	1.07	0.79	0.66
1845/49	0.86	1.00	1.16	0.73	0.71
1850/54	0.95	1.00	1.15	0.85	0.80
1855/59	1.05	0.98	1.01	0.81	0.97
1860/64	1.11	1.00	1.04	0.82	0.93
1865/69	1.12	0.97	1.08	0.83	0.82
1870/74	1.11	0.93	0.95	0.77	0.69
1835-75 average	0.99	0.96	1.03	0.81	0.77

[a] All figures between brackets are based on only one or two figures per five year period.

Sources: 1795-1809: See footnote 3; 1815: Raffles (1830);
1820-1834: Algemeen Verslag; 1835-1851: Kultuur Verslag;
1854-1874: Koloniaal Verslag.

payments per household were lowered and thereafter kept stable (Table 6.6). This resulted in improved land productivity, although in Pekalongan the trend is still downward, because of the series of harvest failures caused by *ama mentek*.

TABLE 6.6 Average Percentage of Households Employed for Cultivation Services, 1835-1870

Five year period	Banten	Priangan	Cirebon	Tegal	Pekalongan
1835/39	99.9	65.2	85.8	45.7	69.1
1840/44	103.7[a]	63.2	74.9	35.8	69.4
1845/49	52.8	66.2	52.1	38.9	59.4
1850/54	33.6	64.7	44.6	38.8	47.2
1855/59	28.4	56.8	34.0	27.5	44.7
1860/64	24.9	51.0	32.0	23.9	32.3
1865/69	23.3	47.3	32.3	23.7	28.3
1835-70 average	52.4	59.2	50.8	33.4	50.1

[a] As I have taken standardized households of five persons as 100, it is possible that in Residencies with a (perceived) mean household size of less than five, figures of more than 100 appear

Sources: For number of households: Kultuur Verslag and Koloniaal Verslag; for total population: Algemeen Verslag and Koloniaal Verslag.

Differences in the rate of expansion of irrigation networks could have been one factor in the diverging trends after 1860. Cirebon, which does not show a downward trend in land productivity after 1860, saw the largest expansion of irrigation canals (KV 1871, p.155) of the five residencies discussed here. Trends in land productivity ran parallel with changes in arable land per household in four of the five residencies; this should not surprise us, given the differences in population density between the various residencies. Sparsely populated Banten and the Priangan had less difficulty expanding their arable land area compared with Cirebon, Tegal and Pekalongan.

Tegal is something of a special case in that yields per unit of land did not increase perceptibly in spite of declining availability of arable land per household. Failure to expand irrigation was probably the main reason; between 1856 and 1868 the number of irrigation canals constructed was quite low in comparison to Banten, Priangan and Cirebon (KV 1871, p.155). Another way of describing the relationship between land productivity and cultivated area per capita is to correlate trends in the two variables over time; in four of the five residencies there was a significant negative correlation (r was between -0.5 and -0.7). Only in Pekalongan was no correlation found.

The next trend to be explained is that of the decreasing area under cultivation per household, measured over the whole period 1815-1875. We saw that this tendency was most marked in Cirebon, Tegal and Pekalongan, and much less so in Banten and the Priangan. We already touched upon a factor that could explain the differences between these two groups of residencies: population density. Another possible explanation is the fact that in Banten and the Priangan *sawah* was individually owned, whereas in the other three residencies communal ownership with periodic redistributions was the predominant form of tenure. It could be argued that communal ownership gives peasants less incentive to invest time and money in the expansion of their arable land than individual ownership.

Within these two groups of residencies—slowly declining Banten and the Priangan, and more quickly declining Cirebon, Tegal and Pekalongan—differences in the rate of decline seem to be explained by the differential weight of the Cultivation System. Within the group where decline was most pronounced, Tegal's rate of decline was slower than elsewhere; its percentage of households obliged to perform cultivation services was also lower than that of Cirebon and Pekalongan (Table 6.6). If we compare Banten and the Priangan, it is the Priangan where the decline was minimal. It has often been said that Priangan was never brought under the Cultivation System, and although that is rather exaggerated—apart from coffee which had long been there, there were new crops (indigo, tea and silk) introduced under Cultivation System-like arrangements—it must be admitted that the burden per household was probably less than in other residencies, particularly where sugar and indigo were the most important crops. It is my impression that the Priangan had had its darkest hour comparable to that ensuing elsewhere after the introduction of the Cultivation System between 1795 and 1805, when several Commissioners of Native Affairs tried to increase coffee production per capita. By 1815, the most excessive features of the system had been removed, and the population there was accustomed to growing coffee, having incorporated it into their agricultural routine. This might explain why the Priangan hardly experienced any decline in acreage per household, compared to the other residencies examined. Indeed the evidence in Table 6.2 shows some increase.

The overall downward trend, however, must be connected with the high demands placed upon labour by the Cultivation System, especially during its early years. The relatively low levels in Cirebon and Pekalongan as early as the late 1820s could be explained by sloppy statistics, but it is also possible that demands on labour were already increasing there even before the Cultivation

System was introduced, especially if increasing exports of sugar and indigo from those two residencies between 1825 and 1830 can be used as indicators.

It can, of course, be argued that arable land per household is not a good indicator for measuring agricultural change, and that area per land-owning family would be much better. In the case of Java these figures are not available on a regular basis, so a trend cannot be calculated. Fortunately, we do have data on land-owning households around 1815-20 and around 1870 (Table 6.7). If these figures are to be trusted, the average percentage of land-holding families in the five residencies concerned dropped from 65-70 per cent around 1820 to 50-60 per cent around 1870. So it is likely that the average area per land-owning family dropped less than the average for all families, and might even have increased slightly in the Priangan. The effects of this are, however, more or less the same for all residencies, so their relative positions do not change. Nor does it invalidate the trend we had established. Productivity of labour, expressed in kilograms of rice per capita, shows the same downward trend as does arable land per household, with similar fluctuations and similar differences between residencies. The explanations for the trend, the fluctuations and the differences are also partly the same. There was a sharp downward trend after 1815 or 1820 connected with the introduction of the Cultivation System. Recovery occurred after 1850 because the sharpest edges of the System were removed. The final downturn might be explained by pointing out that the newly opened lands were probably of poorer quality than the fields already under cultivation and that irrigation probably lagged behind. Pekalongan has, again, a different pattern after 1845/49 for reasons already discussed.

Tegal and Pekalongan experienced a larger drop than Banten and the Priangan (Cirebon data for 1815 or 1820 are not available). That was to be expected, because in densely settled areas land available for clearing with good soil was scarcer than in sparsely settled ones, a factor which has a negative influence on labour productivity, other things being equal.

Population and Agriculture

An interesting pattern emerges if we compare agricultural production indicators and demographic data (Tables 6.8 and 6.9). At first sight, the demographic indicators in columns 2 and 3 seem to contradict those in column 4. Banten and Pekalongan are growing slowly if the figures in columns 2 and 3 can be trusted, and yet they have a high percentage of children. This contradiction can be reconciled if we assume that emigration of adults took place on a perceptible scale. The opposite applies to the Priangan and Cirebon, where higher population growth and lower percentages of children could have coincided, if it can be assumed that those areas received large numbers of adult immigrants. Tegal seems to take up a middle position: high population growth, and an intermediate position as far as the percentage of children is concerned, which could mean that some adult immigration occurred.

Unfortunately, there are hardly any (independent) data on migration before 1880, but the percentage of landless agricultural families (Table 6.9) could be used as an index for migration. I assume that residencies with a high proportion of landless agricultural families received more migrants than they produced, whereas a low percentage indicates net out-migration. This tallies with the demographic data: Banten and Pekalongan, with high percentages of children and slow population growth, have small percentages of landless peasants. On the other hand, quicker growing Priangan and Cirebon, with low percentages of children, have high proportions of peasants without land. Tegal takes up an intermediate position in both categories.

TABLE 6.7 Percentage of Agricultural Families and Land Owning Families, 1815/30 and 1870

	1815/30		1870	
	% Agricultural families	% Land owning families	% Agricultural families	% Land owning families
Banten	84	71	68	63
Priangan	86	n.a.	76	56
Cirebon	88	66	80	58
Tegal	87	68	65	49
Pekalongan	90	72	67	56

Sources: 1815-1830: Raffles (1830) and *Algemeen Verslag*; 1870: *Koloniaal Verslag*.

TABLE 6.8 Demographic Indicators

	Population density in 1867 (per km)	Estimated average annual population growth 1830-80	Average annual natural increase 1820-80	Average percentage children 1835/70
Banten	75	1.5	0.2	49
Priangan	44	2	0.7	39
Cirebon	143	2	-	38
Tegal	180	3	0.8	41
Pekalongan	209	1.5	0.3	45

Sources: For population density: Bleeker (1866); other data: *Algemeen Verslag*, *Kultuur Verslag*, *Koloniaal Verslag*.

TABLE 6.9 Agricultural Production Indicators, 1835-1874

	Area under rice per household (ha)	Rice production (kg/capita)	Yield per hectare under rice (kg)	Percentage landless agricultural families, 1870
Banten	0.54	185	1,734	5
Priangan	0.52	266	2,561	20
Cirebon	0.78	264	1,701	22
Tegal	0.71	259	1,863	16
Pekalongan	0.55	113	1,024	11

Sources: *Kultuur Verslag* and *Koloniaal Verslag*.

If rice production per capita is an indicator of productivity of labour, there is a strong relationship between low productivity of labour and emigration on the one hand, and high productivity and immigration on the other. In Pekalongan and Priangan, the productivity of labour seems to be fully explained by soil productivity, which was low in Pekalongan and high in the Priangan. In Banten, Cirebon, and Tegal, productivity of the soil is neither high nor low, but differential labour productivity could have been related to the differences in average area under rice per household. Diminishing returns to labour are more likely in regions with relatively small peasant holdings (Banten), than in areas with larger holdings (Cirebon, Tegal). It is logical that residencies with high productivity of land and/or labour should attract migrants, whereas regions with low productivity of land and/or labour should produce migrants. A look at Table 6.7 confirms these findings: Banten and Pekalongan, with low productivity of agricultural labour and large numbers of out-migrants, had a large proportion of the population outside agriculture. Priangan and Cirebon, with high productivity of agricultural labour, retained a much larger proportion of the population in the agricultural sector. Tegal was the exception to this rule, but that is not so amazing, given its ambivalent position on most scores. Perhaps the fact that the Cultivation System kept a smaller percentage of families busy in Tegal than it did in other residencies (Table 6.6) can supply part of the explanation for Tegal being the "odd man out." With more time to spend on its own farm, a peasant family needed less outside (adult) help and under such circumstances, an extra child could be fed, who in time could add to the family earnings. Marginal productivity of agricultural labour was high enough to justify an addition to the family labour force. This is, admittedly, all rather speculative, and the family that found itself burdened less with forced labour under the Cultivation System could also prefer more leisure to more children and more income. But it is the only explanation—as far as I can see—that fits all the facts. This hypothesis should be tested, of course, along with the others formulated here, with material from other residencies in Java.

Finally the data on cattle (Table 6.5) should be related to the variables discussed here. The average number of buffaloes per household was lowest in Pekalongan, which is not strange, given the low productivity of land and labour there. Priangan and Cirebon, with high labour productivity, had a high average number of buffaloes per household. In fact, we can calculate the average number of buffaloes per land-owning family; such a calculation would yield averages of 1.57, 1.71, 1.78, 1.65 and 1.38 for Banten, Priangan, Cirebon, Tegal, and Pekalongan respectively. This calculation does not change the relative positions of the Priangan and Cirebon (high) and Pekalongan (low), but it does put Banten and Tegal in their proper places: Tegal somewhere behind the Priangan and Cirebon, and Banten between Tegal and Pekalongan. The reason that Tegal has fewer buffaloes per land-owning family than Cirebon, though its productivity of land and labour is on the same level, could perhaps be found in the fact that fewer transport services would be required in Tegal because of its lower involvement in the Cultivation System.

Summing up this section on the relationship between demographic and agricultural indicators, it can be said that poor Banten and Pekalongan have low natural increase and net emigration, whereas better-off Priangan, Cirebon, and Tegal have net immigration, and, at least in the Priangan and Tegal (for Cirebon there are no data), a high rate of natural increase. These data lend some tentative support to the so-called "labour demand" hypothesis. It has been suggested before that this hypothesis might explain Java's nineteenth-century population growth (White 1973; Boomgaard 1981, p.6).

Conclusions

The overall patterns seem clear from this data: declining acreage per household; declining productivity of labour; slightly declining, but perhaps static, productivity of land; and, except in Banten, a static number of buffaloes per household. If land-owning families are substituted for total households, the trend of the average number of buffaloes is converted from a static into an upward one. So the idea of "static expansion," first proposed by Boeke, and popularized by Geertz, should be qualified for the period under consideration (Boeke 1953, p.175; Geertz 1963, p.79). Nor would one like to speak of "static expansion" when the percentage of landowners was obviously declining and a large rural and urban proletariat was created during a relatively short span of time.

It also will not do to judge the results of the Cultivation System by pointing out that absolute amounts of arable land, food production, and tax receipts were increasing (Reinsma 1955, p.177; Burger 1975, I, p.128; Fasseur 1981, pp.13ff). What I have tried to prove is that one should study ratios. Even if the variables used do not always underestimate the actual values by the same percentage, some trends are so pronounced that differences in accuracy do not invalidate them. As long as we are able to establish, source by source, which variables have been measured with a certain degree of reliability and which must be regarded as gross underestimates, even unreliable sources, going back as far as 1795, can be used.

It should also be clear that statistics for the period under consideration can be used only after their reliability has been tested, residency by residency. Only when all residencies (for which statistics are available) have been evaluated, will it be possible to draw conclusions for the whole island of Java.

Notes

All archival material in this article is obtained from the Arsip Nasional Republik Indonesia in Jakarta (ANRIJ), and the Algemeen Rijks Archief in The Hague (ARADH), especially the Archive of the Ministry of Colonies (AMK). Research in the ANRIJ was made possible by a grant from the Netherlands Foundation for the Advancement of Tropical Research (WOTRO) and by the Vrije Universiteit, Amsterdam. I have made liberal use of comments graciously supplied by Anne Booth, Bob Elson, Wouter Hugenholtz, Bob Van Niel, and Judith Van Oosterom. Where their warnings went unheeded, the fault is mine.

1. Some of Van Niel's examples are problematical. The 145,000 inhabitants, he cites, must refer to the regency and not the residency, of Cirebon; for the residency, checks carried out between 1840 and 1843 showed only 6 per cent more people than could be expected. The 1,515,436 *bau* of Cirebon in 1842 are another riddle: the residency did not have more than 164,704 *bau*.
2. Both *cacah* and *jung* are notoriously tricky notions. A *jung*, as a rule, can be regarded as a measure of landed property. When a new, standardized *jung* (2,000 square Rhineland rods, or about 2.8 ha.) was introduced around 1815, it was found that the old *jung* varied between 1.5 and 12.5 new *jung*. From Tegal in the west to Banyuwangi in the east, the old *jung* became progressively larger, which could mean that its size had something to do with population density and access to markets. In the older literature it is often stated that 1 *jung* equals 4 *cacahs;* by 1795 that was certainly not universally valid any more. *Cacah,* in fact a classifier, has often been translated as "family," but that is misleading. It would be better to regard is as a unit a taxation for which one household, not necessarily a nuclear family, was responsible.
3. The 1795 survey can be found in Collectie Nederburgh, No. 387, ARADH. Some of the 1802 population data were published by Bleeker (1866), while other data from this survey are in Collectie Van Alphen/Engelhard, No. 1900, 226, ARADH. The 1808 data are scattered in various Residential Archives in ANRIJ, and a summary of the data on the eastern Pasisir was found in the "Pasar Ikan" Cultivations Archive, No. 38, ANRIJ.
4. One *amat* is 2 *piculs;* 1 *cain* is 10 *piculs.* A *picul* is roughly 62 kilograms.
5. Report Van Lawick van Pabst Van de Graaff to CCGG, 19.2.1818, Collectie Schneither, No. 74, ARADH.
6. Raffles' statistics are published in his *History* (Raffles 1830, II, pp.268-332); the 1820 statistics, with some gaps are in Collectie Schneither, No. 83-100, ARADH; the reports of 1828 and 1829 are in Verbaal 10.4.1830, 29, AMK and Collectie Du Bus de Gisignies, No. 371, ARADH.
7. Total land rent included also an assessment of arable land under crops for the European market, house tax, and some other, relatively unimportant, categories.
8. Exh. 24.10.1861, 209a Geheim: Memoir, Vitalis, 1827, AMK, ARADH.
9. The sources use the word family *(huisgezin)* without an explanation. I prefer the word household because in most cases it was almost certainly not a (nuclear) family which was meant. *Bujangs* (labourers) were probably included; the same

applies to in-laws and widowed parents in residence. Household size as recorded was not stable over time, and we may miss some clues by standardizing, but for comparative purposes standardization is the best choice.

10. All pre-1815 area data provided by the sources were multiplied by 6 to get standardized *baus:* the traditional *jung* in these areas was about 1.5 times as large as the standardized *jung* of 2,000 square rods, and there were four *jung* to a *bau*. Between 1827 and 1847 area figures for Tegal had to be submitted to the same procedure, because they still were being expressed in "old" *jung* and *bau!*
11. Most data on harvest failures are from the AV and the KV; on *ama mentek* in Pekalongan see: Commission De Vriese, No. 237, AMK, ARADH; I am indebted to Bob Elson for this reference. See also the paper by G.R. Knight in this collection.
12. The same proviso, formulated for the term "family" as found in the sources, obtains for "agricultural family" and "landowning family"; we do not know what the criteria were. My impression is that members of the village council were not counted as "agricultural", but I am not sure that that was always the case.
13. Demographic data can be found in the AV, CV, and KV. For the calculation of the figures in column 2, I have used rough estimates of the percentages by which the population figures in 1830 were underestimated.

APPENDIX TABLE 6.1 Excessive Population Increase Between 1815 and 1875[a]

Residency	Year	Percentage Increase	Comments from the General Residential Reports (AV): author's comments in brackets
Banten	1819	26	(Raffles' 1815 'census' had been the first ever held in Banten)
	1822	15	
	1847	14	(Sharp decrease in 1843)
Priangan	1827	75	
	1828	20	A better census in 1826 and 1827
	1833	10	(Migration in 1830/31 caused by introduction of indigo)
	1834	13	A better census in 1833 and 1834
	1868	8	Partial counts from 1864 onward
Cirebon	1824	10	
	1825	35	A census in 1824 and 1825
	1837	8	A new census (migration from 1830-33)
Tegal	1839	8	(Unrest caused by introduction of sugar, 1833/35)
	1845	9	(Migration in 1844)
	1855/59	40	(Normal natural growth during the same period is assumed to have been 6%; from 1848 to 1850 large scale migration had occurred)
Pekalongan	1829	7	(Migration in 1828)
	1860	13	New census (bad harvests in the late 1850s

[a] Growth of over 6% per annum is regarded as excessive. Whereas average natural growth over the whole period cannot have been more than 1.5% per annum, incidental natural growth rates of 3 or 4% are not entirely impossible. Another 2% for normal immigration should be added. For good measure, it should be added that there were also years in which a 'census' was held, not resulting in excessive increases (Banten 1854, 1866/67; Priangan 1829, 1836, 1851/54; Pekalongan 1830/31, 1839/41).

CHAPTER SEVEN

Plantations 1830-1840: An Overview

William J. O'Malley

Introduction

For over a century, plantations were the dominant feature in the economic landscape of colonial Indonesia. The unabashed purpose of the colony was to serve the interests of Holland; those interests were deemed to be served best by yielding a significant export surplus; an export surplus was most easily and consistently achieved in the archipelago through the production of agricultural commodities for the world market; and plantations proved to be a highly effective way of producing the desired agricultural commodities. First in Java and then in certain parts of the other islands, large-scale, export-oriented production of crops came to be a major concern of government and the major concern of private capital. The pattern of organization, of crop choice, and of location changed considerably over the period from 1830 to 1940, but the plantation industry as a whole remained the keystone of the Indonesian economy. In that position, it seriously affected not only the colonial balance of payments, the fate of Western entrepreneurs, and the policies of the Indonesian government, but the economic activities and social organization of a great number of the people of the islands as well. For many Europeans—visitors touring the archipelago, school children studying it, and managers working there—plantations were almost all that was known of the colony. This is no longer the case with economic historians, but plantations had much to do with shaping colonial Indonesia even as scholars know it. A survey of the growth of the plantation industry and of its connections with government and with local people provides a necessary background against which to see many other topics in proper perspective.

The concept of plantation embraces a number of components—land, labour, capital, technology, scale, organization, and purpose. Within the plantation system, all of these factors could and did differ considerably, measured by a variety of yardsticks, both over the course of time and in any given period. Plantation land, for example, could be leased for long periods from the government, from local self-governing entities or from others with claims to it; it could be rented for short periods from its indigenous owners; it could even be (as in the case of the *particuliere landerijen* or the *Mangkunagara's* plantations) owned outright. That land could be permanently under one plantation crop, in transition from one plantation crop to another, rotated with peasant agriculture through a number of systems, or even set aside as plantation reserve. It could vary in size from only tens of hectares on some hillsides in Java to up to tens of thousands of hectares in the great rubber areas of Asahan. Most of the other components likewise varied along many axes, and rather than attempt at length to bend all of those variables into a definition that could clearly differentiate those agricultural enterprises that were plantations from those which were not—an effort bound in any event to produce a result arbitrary, controversial, and unsatisfactory to almost all concerned—it seems best simply to accept the idea of a plantation current at the time under study: large-scale, market-directed, export-oriented agricultural production which was organized and run for the purpose of making profits. Even this necessarily blurred idea leaves some loose ends unaccounted for. Is the *Prianger-Stelsel* part of the plantation network? What about the organization of the Cultivation System in West Sumatra? Why were the rice-producing efforts of the *particuliere landerijen* not considered plantations? What happens to smaller enterprises, or those producing largely for the domestic market, whose directors might well have thought of themselves as plantation managers? These are questions with which many studies on plantations in colonial Indonesia have lived and with which this paper also will not concern itself any further.

Neither bulk exports nor plantations were new to Indonesia in 1830. Kristof Glamann (1981) and M.A.P. Meilink-Roelofsz (1962) have looked in some depth at the trade statistics and trade patterns connected with Batavia and other local ports in the days of the Dutch East Indies Company. Their research provides evidence already in the seventeenth and eighteenth centuries of substantial quantities of agricultural exports and surprisingly high figures for the Cultivation System's dominant crops of coffee and sugar. Not all of those crops were raised by smallholders, either. Both Westerners and Chinese had become involved, profitably, in agricultural enterprises on wide stretches of land in Java. Scholars have become cognizant of this because of the connection between Chinese sugar planters in the environs of Batavia and the outbreak of the massacres spreading out from that city in 1740, and because of the link between rental advances on plantation land in the Yogyakarta region and the beginnings of the Java War in 1825. 1830, however, marks a useful starting point for the serious consideration of plantations in Indonesia for two interconnected reasons. The first is that the records provided by the deepening colonial administration enable a surer monitoring of agricultural and business activities than is possible for the previous period. The second is that the statistical information becomes more reliable and uniform after that date.

Java Crops

Sugar. Because of the influence of sugar growers on those concerned with governing Indonesia and the influence of Clifford Geertz's *Agricultural Involution* (1963) on those concerned with understanding it, the cane industry ordinarily takes price of place is discussions of plantations. And so it should, for it was a profitable, a leading, and in some ways a model industry for a century after it helped to spark the forced-cultivation export boom in the 1830s.

Though the actual way in which sugar cultivation was pursued and supervised under the Cultivation System varied widely in different areas, it had come in important senses into general conformity with the guidelines proposed in Batavia.[1] This meant that Javanese farmers in some locations were directed by the government to plant a percentage of their land under cane. They were then obliged to yield up the harvest to a mill in the region, receiving in return a cash payment dependent upon the quantity and quality of the crop. The mill in turn processed the cane into sugar which was sold to the government-connected trading company, the Nederlandsche Handel-Maatschappij. The company was responsible for transporting the sugar for auction in Holland. The system permitted numerous scandals and abuses—the percentage of local land under sugar frequently violated the maximum amounts supposedly allowable; labour was often harshly recruited for cultivation and transportation; payments to farmers were not always in line with the harvests; mills, first legally and then illegally, involved themselves privately in sugar marketing—but it did put money, though in varying quantities, into the hands of almost all connected with sugar production. Javanese farmers and labourers found some remuneration for their substantial efforts in production and transportation of cane. Dutch and Indonesian officials were given payments for their supervisory roles. The mills—supported by government advances, guaranteed sufficient cane at low cost, and offered automatic sales at higher prices—soon turned into gold mines. And the government after deducting those costs and other expenses, reaped the difference between low production costs in Java and high market prices in Europe.

Under these conditions, the government-sponsored sugar industry did well, though unspectacularly, in the period between 1840 and the Sugar Act of 1870. A general picture of the industry in that period is reflected in the data compiled in Tables 7.1, 7.2, and 7.3, but a number of items stand out from that background. The first is that, following some sporadic experimentation, the government estates system had by the 1840s settled down to approximately the same structure that it would retain until 1870.[2] The number of mills, the amount of land under sugar, and total production at government behest all changed remarkably little in the quarter of a century following 1845. Second, the major sugar-producing areas under the Cultivation System mainly associated with the littoral area of the northern coast, were already staked out as cane territory by the mid-1830s. Third, the number of Javanese families involved in sugar production, the amounts paid to them, and the average return for an amount of land under sugar cultivation all continued to increase even when the industry ceased growing. And fourth, particularly after the late 1840s, government sugar production was being outstripped by private producers in the principalities of South Central Java, on the *particuliere landerijen,* and on private estates.

The Sugar Act of 1870 embodied the resentment which had been growing in Java and the dismay which had been arising in Holland against the operation of the sugar industry under the Cultivation System. In keeping with the tradition of compromise, the Act provided for the gradual abolition of compulsory planting, and beginning in the late 1870s, the old system was reduced in annual instalments until it disappeared in 1892. By 1895, despite the fact that the economic conjuncture had not been propitious since the early 1880s, estates in the directly ruled area of Java had come to work comfortably with a system in which the government was only marginally involved in arranging land and labour for them. So great, in fact, was their comfort working with hired labour on rented land that they expanded in number, in area under cane, and in production far beyond the total of both private and government enterprises a quarter of a century before (Tables 7.3, 7.4 and 7.5).

Between the turn of the century and the eve of the Great Depression, sugar plantations continued to prosper, but the expansion in numbers ceased and was in fact gradually reversed. What was expanding were the average size of land under cane for each mill and the productivity per area, both of them resulting from improvements in technology which permitted more rapid transport, more efficient milling, and the development of new varieties of cane (POJ 2878, introduced in 1924, was the most important of these). The prosperity the industry had known in the first three decades of this century, clearly evident from Tables 7.3 and 7.6, came to an abrupt end in the early 1930s. The world depression, which squeezed Java's sugar out of its markets in India and China, drew an organized response from the colony's sugar firms, which acted in concert with the government to slash production and the amount of land under cane. The figures in Table 7.7 tell much of the story of that unhappy decade, though it is necessary to point out that the reductions were not applied uniformly to all plantations; instead, entire mills were closed, some of them for good: in 1929, 180 mills were working, in 1934 only 45, in 1940, 85 (Allen and Donnithorne 1954, p.85).

The sugar plantation industry, then, was a great commercial success story up until the 1930s depression. By the 1840s, it had already concentrated itself in those regions which were to form the heart of sugar cultivation for the next century: the northern Pasisir region stretching from Cirebon to Semarang and then south of Gunung Muria to Juana; the Vorstenlanden; the Madiun and Kediri

TABLE 7.1 Government Sugar 1836-1870: Number of Mills and Area under Cane (ha)

Residency	1836	1840	1845	1850	1856	1860	1865	1870
Cirebon								
Number of mills	4	6	5	8	10	10	10	10
Area under cane	1,185	2,037	2,064	3,034	3,331	3,005	3,139	3,033
Tegal								
Number of mills	2	2	6	8	9	9	9	8
Area under cane	756	994	2,271	2,583	2,343	2,286	2,218	2,093
Pekalongan								
Number of mills	3	5	3	3	3	3	3	3
Area under cane	238	1,100	1,100	1,064	1,064	1,064	1,135	1,135
Semarang								
Number of mills	2	3	4	4	4	4	4	4
Area under cane	292	1,114	1,490	1,519	1,490	1,306	1,703	1,703
Japara								
Number of mills	10	9	12	13	9	9	9	9
Area under cane	2,413	2,854	4,232	3,773	3,030	2,629	3,207	3,065
Rembang								
Number of mills		5	2	2	2	2	2	1
Area under cane		565	394	334	348	213	355	207
Surabaya								
Number of mills	23	23	17	16	18	18	20	20
Area under cane	2,964	4,127	4,971	5,311	5,688	5,698	5,734	5,547
Pasuruan								
Number of mills	17	17	18	18	17	17	17	17
Area under cane	4,827	4,642	5,153	5,139	4,308	4,259	4,308	4,308

TABLE 7.1 (cont.)

Residency	1836	1840	1845	1850	1856	1860	1865	1870
Probolinggo								
Number of mills					10	10	10	10
Area under cane					3,549	3,330	3,529	3,529
Besuki								
Number of mills	7	9	11	13	5	5	5	5
Area under cane	2,159	2,920	4,209	4,684	1,561	1,419	1,419	1,407
Banyumas								
Number of mills		1	1	1	1	1	1	1
Area under cane		111	284	284	256	227	284	224
Madiun								
Number of mills	-	5	2	-	3	2	2	2
Area under cane	1,056	1,540	1,526	568	568	568	568	568
Kediri								
Number of mills	1	13	10	9	4	6	6	6
Area under cane	509	612	568	904	923	1,348	1,348	1,348
Madura								
Number of mills						1	1	1
Area under cane						213	284	284
Total								
Number of mills	-	98	91	95	95	97	99	97
Area under cane	16,399	22,626	28,262	29,197	28,459	27,565	29,231	28,451

Sources: *Kultuur Verslagen*, 1836-1850; *Koloniaal Verslag*, 1856-1870

TABLE 7.2 Government Sugar Industry, 1836-1870[a]

Year	Number of households	Payment in guilders	Payment per household	Payment per hectare
1836	118,959	1,132,152	9.52	68.78
1840	148,247	1,990,348	13.43	87.35
1845	165,092	2,774,296	16.80	97.00
1850	154,836	3,343,697	21.60	114.58
1855	172,182	3,940,891	22.10	135.92
1860	190,525	4,345,445	22.81	157.72
1865	196,670	4,769,673	24.25	164.46
1870	221,924	5,517,834	24.86	194.76

[a] All money has been converted to recepis-guilders

Source: Kultuur Verslagen

TABLE 7.3 Total Sugar Exports (1840-1940) and Sugar Production on Government Estates (1840-1870) ('000 tonnes)

Year	Exports (5 yr average)	Production on Government Estates (5 yr average)
1840	59[a]	40.6
1845	76	54.7
1850	95	60.7
1855	109	55.7
1860	129	56.0
1865	142	64.6
1870	172	66.5[b]
1875	217	
1880	255	
1885	384	
1890	414	
1895	547	
1900	786	
1905	1,063	
1910	1,327	
1915	1,528	
1920	1,640	
1925	2,112	
1930	2,893	
1935	913	
1940	1,528[c]	

a Average for years 1840-42

b Average for years 1868-71

c Average for years 1938-40

Source: C.E.I. Vol. 1, Tables 5 and 7

TABLE 7.4 Sugar Mills Working with Government, 1870-1890

(Land area in hectares)

Residency	1870	1875	1880	1885	1890
Cirebon					
Number of mills	10	10	10	9	9
Government-arranged area	3,033	3,033	2,822	1,478	419
People's land under sugar	-	-	-	48	781
Land rented by plantations	-	71	417	1,196	1,390
Tegal					
Number of mills	8	8	8	8	8
Government-arranged area	2,093	2,093	1,932	1,125	319
People's land under sugar	-	-	-	-	-
Land rented by plantations	-	286	649	1,654	2,852
Pekalongan					
Number of mills	3	3	3	3	3
Government-arranged area	1,135	1,135	1,048	610	173
People's land under sugar	-	-	-	-	-
Land rented by plantations	-	52	131	463	800
Semarang					
Number of mills	4	4	4	4	4
Government-arranged area	1,703	1,490	1,377	802	227
People's land under sugar	-	-	26	28	353
Land rented by plantations	-	16	119	742	937
Japara					
Number of mills	9	9	9	9	9
Government-arranged area	3,065	3,065	2,829	1,649	469
People's land under sugar	-	-	26	-	4
Land rented by plantations	-	182	594	1,817	2,905
Rembang					
Number of mills	1	1	1	1	1
Government-arranged area	207	213	197	114	33
People's land under sugar	-	-	26	-	-
Land rented by plantations	-	-	-	170	225
Surabaya					
Number of mills	20	19	19	19	19
Government-arranged area	5,547	5,408	4,990	2,905	824
People's land under sugar	-	-	-	343	-
Land rented by plantations	-	752	1,001	3,381	6,130

TABLE 7.4 (cont.)

Residency	1870	1875	1880	1885	1890
Pasuruan					
Number of mills	17	17	17	16	11
Government-arranged area	4,308	4,027	3,717	1,996	396
People's land under sugar	-	282	21	-	-
Land rented by plantations	-	114	532	2,051	2,673
Probolinggo					
Number of mills	10	10	10	10	9
Government-arranged area	3,529	3,357	3,141	1,829	466
People's land under sugar	-	-	67	-	213
Land rented by plantations	-	432	495	2,053	2,597
Besuki					
Number of mills	5	5	5	5	5
Government-arranged area	1,407	1,375	1,269	739	213
People's land under sugar	-	-	-	-	-
Land rented by plantations	-	151	300	1,227	1,570
Banyumas					
Number of mills	1	1	1	1	1
Government-arranged area	224	284	262	153	43
People's land under sugar	-	-	-	-	13
Land rented by plantations	-	28	50	149	295
Madiun					
Number of mills	2	2	2	2	2
Government-arranged area	568	568	524	305	87
People's land under sugar	-	-	-	-	-
Land rented by plantations	-	45	59	207	771
Kediri					
Number of mills	6	4	6	6	6
Government-arranged area	1,348	1,348	1,244	724	206
People's land under sugar	-	50	23	153	168
Land rented by plantations	-	6	197	1,072	1,930
Total					
Number of mills	96[a]	93	95	93	87
Government-arranged area	28,167[b]	27,396	25,352	14,429	3,875
People's land under sugar	-	332	189	572	1,532
Land rented by plantations	-	2,135	4,544	16,182	25,075

[a] Excludes one mill operating in Madura

[b] Excludes 284 ha in Madura

Source: Koloniaal Verslag for the appropriate years

TABLE 7.5 Private Sugar Estates, 1875-1895

Residency	1875	1880	1885	1891	1895
Cirebon					
Number of private estates	11	11	8	7	12
Number owned by Chinese	4	5	2	3	3
Number owned by corporations	-	-	-	-	6
Area planted (ha)	n.a.	1,138	1,343	666	4,521
Tegal					
Number of private estates	5	5	4	3	10
Number owned by Chinese	1	-	-	-	-
Number owned by corporations	2	3	3	2	5
Area planted (ha)	541[a]	994	892	597	4,401
Pekalongan					
Number of private estates	2	2	2	2	5
Number owned by Chinese	-	-	-	-	-
Number owned by corporations	2	2	2	2	4
Area planted (ha)	260	369	454	480	1,772
Semarang					
Number of private estates	-	-	-	-	4
Number owned by Chinese	-	-	-	-	-
Number owned by corporations	-	-	-	-	4
Area planted (ha)	-	-	-	-	2,003
Japara					
Number of private estates	1	5	3	3	12
Number owned by Chinese	-	3	1	1	-
Number owned by corporations	-	-	2	2	8
Area planted (ha)	195	470	707	414	4,496
Rembang					
Number of private estates	1	3	3	2	3
Number owned by Chinese	-	1	2	-	-
Number owned by corporations	-	-	-	1	1
Area planted (ha)	337	691	455	511	1,016
Surabaya					
Number of private estates	12	10	16	20	39
Number owned by Chinese	6	2	3	4	8
Number owned by corporations	2	2	4	8	21
Area planted (ha)	504[a]	1,608	3,961	5,453	15,160
Pasuruan					
Number of private estates	2	3	3	6	17
Number owned by Chinese	2	2	1	4	8
Number owned by corporations	-	-	-	1	2
Area planted (ha)	47[a]	355	593	1,406	4,914
Probolinggo					
Number of private estates	4	4	4	4	14
Number owned by Chinese	-	-	-	1	-
Number owned by corporations	-	-	-	2	11
Area planted (ha)	624	872	1,069	1,030	5,549

TABLE 7.5 (cont.)

Residency	1875	1880	1885	1891	1895
Besuki					
Number of private estates	-	-	3	4	12
Number owned by Chinese	-	-	-	-	-
Number owned by corporations	-	-	1	3	9
Area planted (ha)	-	-	580	1,238	4,611
Banyumas					
Number of private estates	-	-	-	2	4
Number owned by Chinese	-	-	-	-	-
Number owned by corporations	-	-	-	2	4
Area planted (ha)	-	-	-	253	1,803
Bagelen					
Number of private estates	3	3	4	2	2
Number owned by Chinese	3	3	4	1	1
Number owned by corporations	-	-	-	1	1
Area planted (ha)	a	45	53	442	704
Madiun					
Number of private estates	1	1	3	3	6
Number owned by Chinese	-	-	-	-	-
Number owned by corporations	-	-	1	2	6
Area planted (ha)	a	312	862	791	2,055
Kediri					
Number of private estates	-	-	2	6	12
Number owned by Chinese	-	-	-	3	4
Number owned by corporations	-	-	1	2	7
Area planted (ha)	-	-	569	1,170	4,370
Kedu					
Number of private estates	3	1	-	-	-
Number owned by Chinese	3	1	-	-	-
Number owned by plantations	-	-	-	-	-
Area planted (ha)	a	10	-	-	-
Madura					
Number of private estates	1	1	-	-	-
Number owned by Chinese	-	-	-	-	-
Number owned by plantations	-	-	-	-	-
Area planted (ha)	153	118	-	-	-
Total					
Number of private estates	46	49	55	64	152
Number owned by Chinese	19	17	13	17	24
Number owned by plantations	6	7	14	28	89
Area planted (ha)	a	6,982	11,538	14,451	57,375

a Incomplete data

Source: Koloniaal Verslag for the appropriate years

TABLE 7.6 Number and Area of Sugar Plantations in Java, 1900-1929

Residency	1900	1905	1910	1915	1920	1925	1929
Priangan							
Plantations	1	-	-	-	-	-	-
Area (ha)	35	-	-	-	-	-	-
Cirebon							
Plantations	15	12	13	14	13	9	11
Area (ha)	7,133	8,458	8,871	9,227	8,766	7,942	11,831
Tegal							
Plantations	11	-	-	-	-	-	-
Area (ha)	6,276	-	-	-	-	-	-
Pekalongan							
Plantations	4	15	15	18	18	18	17
Area (ha)	2,497	9,850	10,751	15,089	16,015	17,224	17,870
Semarang							
Plantations	3	12	12	12	12	11	11
Area (ha)	1,973	8,343	8,453	8,630	9,600	10,495	11,089
Japara							
Plantations	11	-	-	-	-	-	-
Area (ha)	5,868	-	-	-	-	-	-
Rembang							
Plantations	-	-	-	1	-	-	-
Area (ha)	-	-	-	375	-	-	-
Surabaya							
Plantations	41	40	40	36	36	36	35
Area (ha)	19,955	23,763	25,308	26,103	26,931	28,395	29,045
Pasuruan							
Plantations	18	29	29	31	29	28	27
Area (ha)	6,562	14,825	18,930	22,313	23,687	26,543	26,896
Probolinggo							
Plantations	13	-	-	-	-	-	-
Area (ha)	6,948	-	-	-	-	-	-

TABLE 7.6 (cont.)

Residency	1900	1905	1910	1915	1920	1925	1929
Yogyakarta							
Plantations	15	15	18	18	17	17	17
Area (ha)	5,380	6,161	7,932	10,399	10,716	14,079	16,085
Surakarta							
Plantations	16	17	17	16	16	16	16
Area (ha)	5,886	6,803	7,546	10,000	11,298	14,487	17,983
Besuki							
Plantations	13	11	11	10	9	9	12
Area (ha)	5,515	6,336	6,286	6,561	6,571	6,904	14,498
Banyumas							
Plantations	4	4	5	6	6	5	5
Area (ha)	2,246	2,823	3,107	5,164	4,974	5,751	7,176
Bagelen							
Plantations	1	-	-	-	-	-	-
Area (ha)	495	-	-	-	-	-	-
Madiun							
Plantations	6	6	6	6	6	6	6
Area (ha)	3,611	3,982	4,391	6,997	6,581	8,271	9,756
Kediri							
Plantations	17	17	22	23	21	21	21
Area (ha)	9,101	11,792	13,817	21,521	20,271	24,291	21,658
Batavia							
Plantations	-	8	6	-	-	-	-
Area (ha)	-	270	92	-	-	-	-
Kedu							
Plantations	-	1	2	2	2	2	2
Area (ha)	-	778	1,629	3,655	3,707	4,200	4,715
Indramayu							
Plantations	-	-	-	-	-	3	-
Area (ha)	-	-	-	-	-	2,971	-
Total							
Plantations	139	187	196	193	185	181	180
Area (ha)	89,431	104,184	117,113	146,034	149,117	171,553	188,602

Sources: 1900-1925 Kolonial Verslag; 1929 Personalia (1930/31)

TABLE 7.7 Sugar Estates in the 1930s Depression

Years	Area under sugar (ha)
1930	198,007
1931	200,831
1932	166,138
1933	84,343
1934	34,211
1935	27,578
1936	35,572
1937	84,494
1938	84,829
1939	94,947
1940	90,765

Source: *C.E.I.* Vol. 1, p. 76

regions; Besuki Residency; and the two great East Java clusters, one running in an arc from Probolinggo through Pasuruan to Malang, the other from Surabaya southwestward to Jombang. Backed by the products, the profits, and the taxes wrung from that base, the sugar industry could demand and then utilize first an expanded road—and then a rail-transport network. It could claim much responsibility for the rise of the great port cities of Surabaya and Semarang and the emergence of major towns in a dozen other places. And it could boast of itself as a major employer of skilled European and indigenous labour and as the primary provider of assistance into the monetized economy for the Javanese (as an indication, cash payments provided to the indigenous sector by sugar plantations in 1920 are listed in Table 7.8.[3] Most important, however, in terms of the plantation industry as a whole, sugar provided an example of organization, financial strength, technical progress, efficiency, and profitability that helped spark a boom in large-scale agriculture in other products that outpaced the cane industry even in the years when sugar was succeeding most notably.[4]

While sugar remained by far the largest export crop by volume, it did not completely dominate the plantation scene in the colony. In Java alone, and even before the painful dismantling of the sugar industry in the 1930s, other plantation crops provided serious challenges, in many aspects of production, to any claim of pre-eminence that sugar might have had.

Coffee. Coffee, even more than sugar, was the successful trade item of the Cultivation System. Like sugar, it was raised by indigenous farmers in Java because they were compelled to do so by the government.[5] Unlike sugar, it was not usually raised on normal cropland, interspersed with food crops. Instead, the Government's intention was to use previously uncultivated land, which meant that farmers had frequently to travel some distance to plant, tend and then harvest their coffee. Because the market preparation of coffee consists merely of drying and cleaning the picked beans, this was left completely to the indigenous farmers and there are thus grounds for excluding this particular form of cultivation from the topic of plantations altogether. To the farmers involved, however, the differences between the two categories would not necessarily be meaningful, while the numbers and distribution of households caught up in the compulsory growing of coffee and the sums paid out to them help to place the government sugar industry into perspective.

Between the consolidation of the Cultivation System in the mid-1830s and the 1870 date usually given for the System's demise, coffee was quite clearly the major export crop in Java. Table 7.9 gives a picture of the number of households involved in coffee deliveries in Java and of the sums provided them for their efforts in the final six decades in which coffee was compulsorily raised. A comparison of the 1850s-1860s figures with equivalent data for sugar in Table 7.2

TABLE 7.8 Payments to Indonesians from Sugar Plantations in Java, 1920

('000 guilders)

Residency	Number of plantations	Wages, etc.	Land rentals	Rice provisions	Extras	Total
Cirebon	12	4,853	648	13		5,514
Pekalongan	18	9,560	1,565	48		11,173
Semarang	12	6,026	814	8	114	6,962
Surabaya	36	17,921	2,068	211		20,200
Pasuruan	29	13,765	1,760	27	2	15,554
Besuki	9	4,442	590	1		5,033
Banyumas	6	3,037	590	-		3,627
Kedu	2	2,198	552	2		2,752
Madiun	6	4,292	440	25		4,757
Kediri	20	11,459	1,347	128		12,934
Yogyakarta	18	5,681	1,375	22		7,078
Surakarta	15	7,196	2,355	39		9,590
Total	183	90,430	14,104	524	116	105,174

Source: *Koloniaal Verslag* 1921

TABLE 7.9 Government Coffee on Java

Year	Number of households	Payments to planters ('000 guilders)	Total local payments ('000 guilders)
1856	455,229	4,866	6,857
1860	466,207	9,278	11,251
1865	520,661	10,405	12,615
1870	616,636	11,298	13,240
1875	675,397	5,982	7,080
1880	725,977	6,719	8,321
1885	547,113	6,665	8,078
1900	184,598	2,974	3,526
1905	152,155	1,006	1,351
1910	152,431	417	686
1915	190,917	903	1,151

Source: Koloniaal Verslag for appropriate years

TABLE 7.10 Government Coffee on Java: Households per Residency, Selected Years

Residency	1856	1875	1900	1915
Bantam	33,440	20,406	56,688	82,830
Krawang	1,595	2,201		
Priangan	93,998	20,092		
Cirebon	22,528	52,096	1,485	
Tegal	7,727	20,885	15,268	
Pekalongan	8,187	15,905	6,547	15,494
Semarang	30,411	49,971	14,152	13,549
Japara	5,101	9,308		
Rembang	3,021			
Surabaya	2,805	6,988	3,567	
Pasuruan	29,216	38,147	36,886	66,495
Probolinggo	14,210	17,909	15,744	
Besuki	25,924	36,271	16,488	3,140
Banyuwangi	3,495	3,910		
Banyumas	25,925	74,034	5,612	
Bagelen	26,705	38,401	n.a.	
Kedu	69,310	70,594	2,370	2,395
Pacitan	11,674			
Madiun	14,170	42,892	9,791	7,014
Kediri	25,787	55,387	n.a.	
Total	455,229	575,397	184,598	190,917

Source: *Koloniaal Verslag* for appropriate years

TABLE 7.11 Value of Government Exports of Coffee and Sugar from Java, 1835-1870 ('000 guilders)[a]

Year	Coffee (5 yr average)	Sugar (5 yr average)
1835[b]	10,353	4,760
1840	18,571	6,975
1845	15,610	10,428
1850	16,955	11,756
1855	26,896	12,825
1860	27,239	13,260
1865	31,554	12,923
1870	25,965	8,416

[a] All money converted to *recepis*-guilders

[b] 1835-37 average only

Source: *Handelsstatistiek Java 1823-75*, Tables 10-11, pp. 39-41

shows that in terms both of the number of people involved and of the cash distributed, coffee substantially outstripped cane in its impact on the indigenous population. What is more, Table 7.10 indicates that coffee production under government direction was spread throughout the width and length of the island, while sugar cultivation was territorially limited. An inspection of Table 7.11 also reveals that the value of coffee exports under the System was much higher than the value of sugar. It has been noted that, up to the point where sugar-growing under the System began to be reduced, coffee contributed 80 per cent of the profits accruing to the government (Robequain 1958, p.319).

As was the situation with sugar, there were also private estates producing coffee in Java during the years of the Cultivation System, with exports from those estates amounting to some 30 per cent of the value of coffee exports in 1870 (Allen and Donnithorne 1954, p.89). As the forced deliveries of coffee slowly ground to a halt (the System was not done away with completely until 1918), private coffee estates—many of them established through the long-term leases of government lands made possible through the Agrarian Law of 1870—proliferated to take their place. After the great coffee blight of the mid-1880s, which severely cut Java's production potential, the private plantations in the island regularly outproduced forced-cultivation growers. By the turn of the century the balance was well in the plantations' favour (Caldwell 1964, Table IX, p.82), though they never exceeded the forced deliveries' one-year high total of some 78,000 metric tons produced in 1879 (*C.E.I.*, Vol.1, Table 12, pp.107-12).

Sugar and coffee were successful crops in the Cultivation System years both for private entrepreneurs and for the government, and the two continued their success, though at different levels, under the regime that followed. Other crops were also tried under the forced cultivation system, but were less successful. Indigo was a major crop early in the period but fell into high disfavor with its producers and was dropped (see the land under indigo cultivation in Table 7.12).[6] Cotton, cinnamon, silk, pepper and cochineal also had trials under the Cultivation System and were found wanting, to the extent that serious attempts to exploit them through private plantations were never made in the years after 1870. There were crops, however, that were relatively unsuccessful when raised through forced deliveries but which achieved much higher levels in Java under private enterprise plantations later on. The two most important of these were tobacco and tea.

Tobacco. Because of the care which tobacco demands, the way it exhausts the soil, its relative fragility in the face of the vagaries of weather, and its notoriously uncertain markets, it proved a risky venture under the Cultivation System. When private Western entrepreneurs took both a greater personal interest in supervising and a greater technical concern to the tasks of organizing wide-scale tobacco growing, the risks were still there, but they were reduced considerably. Over the

TABLE 7.12 Java - Area of Estate Lands

(hectares)

Year	Sugar	Coffee	Tea	Rubber	Indigo	Tobacco[a]
1835	12,357				14,810	
1840	22,701		1,868		30,396	808
1845	27,346		2,937		29,506	2,616
1850	29,204		1,643		19,488	1,241
1855	28,816		1,952		13,368	1,162
1860	27,976		1,820		11,743	1,248
1865	30,760		n.a.		6,532	901
1870	32,347		3,082			
1875	32,520		4,429			
1880	37,483		5,776			76,553[b]
1885	42,597		6,041			65,105
1890	44,020		7,747			73,048
1895	77,116		9,173			71,792
1900	91,049		n.a.			93,768
1905	105,761	79,706[c]	n.a.	10,117[d]		137,346
1910	126,525	51,231[c]	49,439	63,943		151,533
1915	151,165	33,053[c]	73,886	109,215		159,484
1920	153,366	105,886	78,247	157,299		129,302
1925	176,267	95,357	84,682	180,478		165,261
1930	198,007	97,520	98,589	228,923		182,169
1935	27.575	96,460	104,415	230,162		173,686
1940	90,765	83,081	104,967	240,956		173,037

a Includes both estates and smallholders

b 1881 data

c Data are for government cultivation only

d 1906 data

Source: C.E.I. Vol. 1, Tables 7, 8, 10, 12, 13, 17

course of time between 1870 and 1940, tobacco plantations were established in such places as Kedu, Kediri, and the limestone areas stretching between Semarang and Surabaya, but the most successful ventures were those launched around Klaten in the Vorstenlanden and around Jember in Besuki.[7] The tobacco grown in these two places differed considerably in many respects (including cropping patterns, cultivation time, and curing processes), but the plantation systems worked out there had much in common (Beets 1989; Jaeggi 1949). The important element was the distribution by the firm of tobacco seedlings to trained local farmers who would then raise the plants in carefully tended fields, closely monitored by the company, and sell their final product to the company for payment commensurate with its quality. In both places as well, it became customary, even necessary, to alternate the tobacco crops with food crops, and the tobacco plantation industry in Java thus came to resemble in some ways the sugar-cane system there. Under those conditions, and helped by the technical ability the industry developed to produce new seeds, to master the use of fertilizers, and to combat pests and disease, tobacco plantations flourished in Java, more than tripling production between the 1890s and the 1920s (*C.E.I.* Vol.1, Table 13). Though the industry was hurt by the depression of the 1930s and affected by the gradual shift in preference away from cigars towards cigarettes, it was still in respectable shape in the last years before the war.

Tea. Like tobacco, tea cultivation had not prospered under the Cultivation System. In private hands, it grew steadily, though without any impressive signs, from the 1860s until the 1890s. In that decade, a spurt of growth coincided with a mastery of certain techniques and with downturn in the prices of crops—notably cinchona and coffee—that competed with tea for lands at certain altitudes (Allen and Donnithorne 1954, pp.100-102). Once it had established itself in the highlands of southwestern Java, tea was quite successful there, grown on wide plantations that depended heavily on male labour for their establishment in the first place and then on female labour for much of the work of plucking, processing, and sorting the leaves. The enormous expansion of the land given over to tea plantations between 1895 and 1935 is evident in Table 7.12. Production on those estates leapt forward as well, from less than 3,500 metric tons in 1890 to 12,500 in 1910 and 46,000 metric tons in 1930 (*C.E.I.*, Vol.1, Table 8, pp.81-84). Production continued to expand through the depression, even when prices fell considerably (Allen and Donnithorne 1954, p.103-4). The tea plantation industry remained firmly anchored in West Java, but it also featured plantations in the highlands of various residencies in Central and East Java, which together accounted for some 10 per cent of the industry in Java in 1939 (Emden 1949, p.124).

Rubber. In the first decade of this century, there sprang up in Java, as in many tropical locations, a new crop which also did well on plantations—rubber. Fuelled by the incorporation of that product into many manufactured goods and by the needs of the new automobile industry, the demands for rubber expanded rapidly, and those places suitable for its growth experienced something of a bonanza. Java was no exception, and the crop's extraordinary profitability at the time meant not only that new lands for its planting were taken out on lease, but that plantations previously given over to other products were planted in rubber trees as well, with the older plants—chiefly coffee—usually eliminated as the rubber trees reached their productive life (Maas and Bokma 1950, p.253). In Java, rubber plantations were run much like the coffee and tea plantations. Located in sparsely populated areas, they needed large work forces, often attracted from other regions, to set them up and then smaller groups of labourers, resident on the plantations or immediately adjacent to them, to do the actual work of exploiting the producing plants and processing the yield. The rapid expansion in the amount of plantation land under rubber in Java (see Table 7.12) was reflected in the gains in rubber production as the trees reached maturity: from only 200 metric tons in 1910, Java's rubber plantations leapt upward to export-production levels of 27,000 tons in 1920, 67,000 in 1930, and 99,000 tons in 1940 (*C.E.I.* Vol.1, Table 11, pp.93-94). This catapulted rubber to the position of Java's second largest export producer by volume, behind sugar. However, unlike the highly localized sugar-growing areas, rubber plantations were far more evenly spread around the island.

Sugar, coffee, tobacco, tea and rubber were the major plantation crops in Java, but there were as many as twenty crops being grown on estates in the island (*Koloniaal Verslag* 1926, Appendix V), and two of those other crops were also quite substantial.

Cinchona. Cinchona, or Peruvian bark, which was marketed for the quinine it yielded, got off to a slow start under government direction in the late 1850s, but by the turn of the century, largely through the efforts of private planters and despite the fact that the government long retained its interest in the crop, it was pressing tea in terms of the total quantities being exported (*C.E.I.*, Vol.1, p.143). Raised mostly in the Priangan highlands of West Java, but with smaller stretches in many regions across the island, cinchona by 1930 was planted on some 16,000 hectares in Java, yielding perhaps 12,000 metric tons a year; in the depression decade that followed, those figures dropped by only small amounts (*C.E.I.*, Vol.1, Table 9, p.90).

Coconuts. The growth demand, both worldwide and within Indonesia, for coconut products was largely met by the efforts of smallholders, but this crop also proved to be adaptable to plantation exploitation. By 1920 there were some

10,000 hectares of plantation land under coconut trees in Java, the chief centres being the residencies of Batavia, Semarang, and Kediri. The amount of land planted with coconut trees fell off in the late 1920s and 1930s to a figure of some 7,000 hectares just before the war, but the fully productive and selected trees on that plantation land were turning out some 6,300 tons of copra and high quality oil per year, more than four times what the yield had been twenty years previously (*C.E.I.*, Vol.1, Table 14, pp.129-30).

Other plantations in Java—raising cacao, sisal, various essential oils, etc.—were less impressive on their own, but collectively, in terms of land area under cultivation and of yields produced, they amounted to figures that were not insubstantial.[8]

Java Summary. By drawing together the data and the individual crop sketches provided above, it is possible to put together a picture of plantation developments in Java that, without denying the importance of the sugar industry in the island, goes some way towards reducing that industry in scale. Within the bounds of the Cultivation System, coffee not only produced substantially more in the way of profits than sugar, it also reached more people and provided them with more cash. It is true that sugar expanded in importance after 1875 while coffee languished in the 1880s as a result of the blight, but even in the final years of the nineteenth century, tobacco, tea, and cinchona plantations began to expand rapidly, a situation which never left sugar as the only important estate crop in Java. The continued growth of tea and tobacco plantations, the recovery of the coffee industry, and the phenomenal rise of rubber cultivation meant that even as sugar more than doubled in area (Table 7.12) and quadrupled in productive capacity between 1900 and 1930 (Allen and Donnithorne 1954, p.292), it did not come to dominate completely the plantation world of the island. And while no plantation crop could boast of escaping the depression unscathed, none was as badly damaged, structurally and financially, as was sugar.

Outer Islands

If it is the relative position of sugar that ought to be borne in mind when contemplating the progress of plantations in Java, it is necessary as well to consider the position of Java's plantations in relation to that of others in the Outer Islands. For even during the years when sugar was booming in Java but was still unable to outpace the growth of such plantations as tea, tobacco, and rubber in that island, there was an expansion of plantation land and plantation productive capacity outside Java that threatened in the long run to overtake (and in fact in the aberrant year of 1936 did overtake) that principal producer (see Table 7.13). This Outer Island boom was fuelled in particular by the spread of tobacco, rubber, tea,

TABLE 7.13 Value of Agricultural Exports from Indonesia and of Estate Exports from Java/Madura and the Other Islands (million guilders)

Year	Agricultural Exports Indonesia	Estate Exports	
		Java/Madura	Other Islands
1894	154	116	21
1898	153	115	23
1902	183	123	23
1906	212	148	21
1910	282	187	18
1913	419	231	88
1917	513	339	89
1921	817	516	133
1924	1,179	675	205
1927	1,292	604	284
1930	833	404	170
1933	306	115	66
1936	362	112	117
1939	495	187	122

Source: C.E.I. Vol. 1, Table 2, pp. 38-9

coffee, and coconut plantations. Growth occurred in a number of places in the archipelago, including parts of Borneo, Sulawesi, and South Sumatra, but the major site for plantation activity outside Java was the East Coast of Sumatra, which changed from an almost endless jungle in the 1860s to one of the world's premier estate sites in the 1920s.[9]

East Sumatra. The *Cultuurgebied,* or Estate Region, in East Sumatra was built upon three main factors. First was the fact that the land in certain sections of the Malay states of Deli, Serdang, and Langkat was capable, under the right conditions, of producing the finest and most expensive wrapper-leaf tobacco in the world—almost four times the price of Cuban tobacco and more than four times the price of Java tobacco in 1938 (van de Waal 1959, p.38). Second was the ability of Western firms to sign long-term pacts with local rulers that guaranteed access to and control over wide stretches of land for long periods, regardless of the interests of the local people.[10] And the third was the system that brought in tied labour, first from China and then from Java, to do the plantation work,which autochthonous people shunned. On that foundation, the Deli tobacco plantation industry managed to erect an infrastructure of administrative and financial services, of urban amenities, of shipping facilities, and of transportation networks that served to attract the attention of firms interested in establishing plantations in other crops. When the elevated terrain outside the main tobacco regions was found to be quite suitable for tree and bush crops, and when arrangements for land and labour similar to those enjoyed by the tobacco companies proved possible in other Malay states and in the territory of the Simelungan Batak, a startling expansion of East Sumatra's plantation economy began in the early decades of this century. First rubber, then tea and oil palm and fibre plantations spread out over thousands of hectares of previously little-used land (Table 7.14). Over 300 separate plantations hired more than half a million labourers to produce goods for the export market (Thee 1977, p.41). From their centre around Medan, East Sumatran plantations by the 1920s stretched out in almost unbroken swathes running 100 kilometres northeast to the border with Aceh, 100 kilometres south to the hills behind Pematang Siantar, and over 200 kilometres southeast to the highlands around Rantau Prapat in Asahan (Pelzer 1978, Map X). The region's roads ran out of Medan, through the central tobacco zone, and on into areas where upland crops occupied the land as far as the eye could see. Under the aegis of the colonial administration, Western firms had been given almost a free hand in their expansion, and they used that opportunity to transform an entire area into an estate region that even the Great Depression could not humble (Table 7.15).

Because rubber came to be the chief export of the East Sumatran plantations, as of plantations elsewhere outside Java, the setbacks suffered by rubber during the Great Depression did have effects in the regions. (Deli tobacco, a

TABLE 7.14 Major Plantation Crops on the East Coast of Sumatra

Year	Tobacco (bales)	Rubber (ha)	Rubber (tons)	Palm Oil (ha)	Palm Oil (tons)	Tea (ha)	Tea (tons)
1865	189						
1870	2,868						
1875	15,355						
1880	64,965						
1885	124,911						
1890	236,323						
1895	204,719						
1900	223,731						
1905	225,369	1,337					
1910	234,133	29,471					
1915	323,911	103,112				3,273	805
1920	145,507	150,156	37,277	8,462	1,719	10,099	5,667
1925	213,956	188,875	52,168	29,402	6,905	12,835	8,010
1930	211,137	273,094	71,786	61,229	48,015	21,273	10,461

Source: Thee (1977, pp. 9, 14, 30, 32)

TABLE 7.15 East Coast of Sumatra: Number of Plantations and Estate Area under Cultivation in 1938

Crop	Plantations	Area (ha)
Rubber	207	260,184
Palm Oil	35	56,595
Tea	16	21,891
Coconuts	9	5,581
Gambir	1	1,225
Cacao	1	77
Vezel	5	10,000
Tobacco	46	112,000[a]
Gutta Percha	2	180
Total	322	468,000

[a] Only 14,000 ha were actually under production in 1938; since plantation land was cultivated only once every eight years, the amount of land given for tobacco plantations is 8 x 14,000 ha.

Source: van de Waal (1959, p. 36)

luxury good, did somewhat better.) Still, a scheme worked out through the government to restrict rubber output managed to keep most of the rubber plantations in business. Compared to the paring experienced by the sugar industry is Java, they survived fairly well, and were able to come back onto the market impressively in the late 1930s when demand increased again as a result of the lead-up to the war.

This brief overview of the growth of the plantation industry in Indonesia between 1830 and 1940 provides a broad outline of when, where, and under what circumstances the development of plantations for certain crops took place. Those developments, however, did not take place in a vacuum, and in order for this overview to serve most usefully as a contribution to economic history, it must be supplemented by information on how those plantations interacted with the colonial government and with the Indonesian population. A full treatment of those subjects would constitute a long-term project on its own, but a number of important points on each can be made here.

Plantations and Government

The relationship between the government and the plantation industry in Indonesia was an elemental one, vital to both of those institutions. This is evident in the fact that the political economy division of the period 1830-1940 (which is in fact a political/plantation economy division) into the years of the Cultivation System (1830-1870), the Liberal Era (1870-1900), the Ethical Policy (1900-1930), and the Depression (1930-1940) is the one used not only in the analysis here but in the analysis presented in almost every text dealing with Indonesian history as well.

Under the Cultivation System, the Indonesian government actually took the leading role in the plantation economy, sponsoring and demanding the large-scale production of export crops. This production not only provided funds for the government officially, it also provided extra personal funds for government officials in the form of the percentages to which they were entitled. While this made the administration doubly interested in the official cultivation programs, the government was also supportive of private efforts where those were legal: it supported the government-contracting sugar millers quite handsomely (Furnivall 1944, pp.141-43), and it also shepherded other entrepreneurs, many of whom would have been either retired officials or else relatives and acquaintances of active officials. It is also undoubtedly from this period that *perintah halus,* or friendly persuasion, began to be extended by government officials on behalf of planters facing land or labour problems.

During the Liberal period, the active role of government in plantation production declined considerably, but despite its supposed *laissez-faire* stance, the government did not simply stay on the sidelines during the years between 1870 and the end of the century (Day 1904, chs. 10 and 11). It still had important interests in coffee and quinine production, it went out of its way to ensure that assistance was provided to the sugar industry in its adjustment to free-enterprise conditions, and it took a leading role in providing the road, rail, and port facilities that helped to increase the fitness and attractiveness of the plantation industry for investors. It also provided support for various producers, but especially coffee producers, in their continuing struggle to combat the pests and diseases that hampered production. What is more, it is possible in this period to link up the expansion of Dutch control in the islands outside Java with the needs and desires of private entrepreneurs, while within Java the powers conferred on the government by the Agrarian Law of 1870 to dispose of unused lands were certainly used in a manner to benefit pioneers or firms hoping to establish plantations.

If the purpose of the Ethical Policy was to help to cut back on the careless and unrestrained abuses connected with the free-enterprise system, the growth of the plantation network between 1900 and 1930 shows that the key element in that free-enterprise system was not itself held back. There were limitations imposed: proposed sugar plantations had to go through fine screening before they could be opened; a labour inspectorate was established; minimum amounts were set for land rentals to Europeans; and steps began to be taken towards the elimination of penal-sanction systems of indentured labour on plantations outside Java. But the fiscal nexus between government and plantations, a nexus which had weakened with the withering of the Cultivation System, was growing tighter again: for its expanding services, government was increasingly more dependent on taxes levied on profits and incomes—sources associated with the plantation sector—and increasingly less dependent on land taxes and poll taxes; by 1926, it was estimated that Indonesians were providing only 30 per cent of government revenue, down from some 70 per cent twenty years earlier (O'Malley 1977, p.52, n.26). The financial power and the influence of planters in Indonesia and of planting companies and retired planters in the Netherlands was something which few administrators in the government bureaucracy could have afforded to forget when matters dealing with plantation interest crossed their desks.

The Great Depression helped to clarify just how tightly the interest of plantations and government in Indonesia were bound. As the collapse in world markets for almost all agricultural products threw industry after industry into crisis, the Indonesian government not only found its revenues shrinking alarmingly, it also found the previously haughty planters' groups turning to it for succour. In those circumstances, the government took whatever stop-gap measures seemed useful, countenancing worker dismissals and reductions in wages even when they involved breaking contracts, and assisting planters in reaching inexpensive agreements and accommodation with Indonesian land-holders over leased land that was no longer wanted. Even more indicative, however, was the way in which the government involved itself in licensing and restriction schemes and in international agreements in order to preserve what it could of the goose that had for over a century been laying ever larger golden eggs.[11] The government's salvage operation during the Depression was reasonably successful for most of the plantation crops, though it helped to drive the plantations even more tightly into the industry-wide groups and syndicates which they had been forming for some decades. But the way in which the operation was performed, often at cost to Indonesians involved, could have left little doubt in the minds of many people in Java, Sumatra, and Borneo that plantations and government were, and perhaps always had been, a single force.

Plantations and People

The interrelationships between Indonesians and plantation economy have engendered discussion, producing varying levels of heat and light, for over a century and a half. The big question of exactly how the plantation economy affected the folk economy in different places, at different times, and over the long run can hardly be answered fully in the final paragraphs of this paper, but attention can still be focused on a few important items connected with that larger question.

With regard to the monetization of the economy, there can be no question that plantations played an important part. Monetization on some scale undoubtedly preceded the plantation era, but the regular disbursement of cash to all levels of society (though not in equal amounts) was something new with the Cultivation System and something normal and widespread in the years thereafter. In 1930, almost 530,000 Indonesians were employed by the sugar industry (though many of them were only seasonal workers) and over 820,000 were employed by the other plantations (*Volkstelling* 1930, Vol.5, p.104).

The plantations were important in shaping the way that many of the traditional elites behaved in the years after 1830. In the Vorstenlanden and in East Sumatra, the rulers were able to maintain (or to adopt) a style of splendour because of the money they gained from plantations for use of lands which the rulers could claim as rightfully belonging to them. On the other hand, the leading *priyayi* in Dutch-ruled Java prospered sufficiently through their percentage payments under the Cultivation System that they forwent the option of gaining or retaining control of land, thus locking the door on the possibility of any landed gentry class in Java. The disappearance of many of the plantation-connected traditional elites in independent Indonesia suggests, however, that though the financial benefits of dealing with planters could be substantial in the short run, the long-term effects of the elites/estates relationship were not as beneficial as they seemed at the time.

The plantation networks interacted with popular agriculture in numerous and complex ways, and the long-standing debate on the rice/sugar system ought not to be the only word on the subject. Tobacco on Sumatra's East Coast was intercropped with rice and corn in an elongated system that has been mapped out (Pelzer 1978, chs 4 and 5), but in Central and East Java it was also rotated with rice in ways that are as yet understudied as far as their local economic and social ramifications are concerned (Beets 1949; Jaeggi 1949; Broersma 1913, pp.16-48). Some crops which started as plantation specialties squeezed over the estate boundaries and became important sources of cash for smallholders. This was true especially for tea in Java, but the great success story was that of rubber in the Outer Islands. There, smallholders collectively came into a position where for total production capacity they could, by the 1930s, challenge the great rubber plantations (*C.E.I.*, Vol.1, Tables 8 and 10). Kapok and coconut products, on the other hand, were largely smallholder industries that managed to attract plantation interest and investment. Coffee moved through an entirely different cycle—from the status of smallholder crop in the eighteenth century, through its Cultivation System history to large plantations, and finally, by the late 1930s, back to the stage where smallholders' exports (though this time from the Outer Islands, mainly Sulawesi) were once again important (*C.E.I.*, Vol.1, Table 12). Such crops as cassava and maize were raised and processed on plantations during the years that they were spreading as popular foodstuffs in Java. And one of the more important aspects of the sugar plantation system was that, except for isolated pockets, it precluded the development of any important smallholders' cane industry, and choked off experimentation involving the raising of cane on dry, instead of irrigated, fields.[12]

Plantations could create new jobs and even new categories of jobs for Indonesians. Such jobs as carters for the sugar plantations, shed-builders for the tobacco plantations, clearers of terrain for the hill plantations, and providers of packing materials for all the plantations could come and go over time. Something more important, because it was more enduring, was the fact that it was possible in plantation employment for a person of no background or education to gain security and to rise in pay and position by dint of effort and of acquired skill—in short, to make a career of it. The attractiveness of that option for many in Java should not be underestimated.

Whatever the interplay between plantation and people in such things as monetization, elite maintenance, agriculture, population mobility, and jobs, in the long run the plantations came to be seen by many Indonesians as symbols of oppression and of unwarranted and flaunted privilege. With their cold-hearted efficiency, their instinctive reliance on the letter of the law when it was on their side and on the flexibility of the law when it was not, and their insistence on holding onto wide expanses of land even as that land was becoming scarce for farmers, the plantations had not engendered much good will for themselves in their own neighbourhoods. Once the colonial government lost control of the local communities surrounding those plantations, the other factors considered above ceased to be of much importance: no matter how bright their past and how clear their potential, the future of the plantations grew clouded with the passing of the colonial state with which they were identified.

Notes

1. There is a great amount of literature on the Cultivation System and on the workings of the sugar industry under it. The most frequently cited of the older works are Day (1904) and Furnivall (1944). Most recent works, which have helped to change the focus, are van Niel(1964c, 1969, 1972), Fasseur (1975), Elson (1979), and Fernando (1982a).
2. Fasseur (1975), Chapters V and X, covers the politics and implications of this in some detail.
3. The impact of the 1930s depression on the money economy can be seen from the drop in total payments (wages, rent, and other categories) paid by the sugar industry to indigenous society from a figure of *f*128.6 million in 1929 to *f*10.9 million in 1936 (Helsdingen 1941, p.516).
4. For various of these aspects of the sugar industry, told from a less than critical point of view at the height of sugar's success, see Tichelaar (1927), van der Mandere (1928), and Sibinga Mulder (1929). For more thoughtful contemporary considerations, see Tio (1923) and Gimbrère (1928).
5. Forced coffee cultivation was also a fact of life in West Sumatra from 1847 to 1908. See Young's contribution to this volume and Dobbin (1983, ch.7) for insightful looks at the economic and social meaning of the policy there.
6. Indigo continued to be grown with some success in Yogyakarta, where the rights and the wishes of the people were a far less significant factor, until the turn of the century (O'Malley 1977, p.171, p.204 [fn.19-21]).
7. From the 1880s onwards, these two areas regularly produced together more than two-thirds of the value accruing to Java tobacco (Beets 1949, p.416).
8. Some idea of these can be obtained from the data gathered in Appendix V of *Koloniaal Verslag* 1926.
9. The classic ode to the area's growth is in fact called *From Jungle to Estate Region* (Volker 1928).
10. In two recently published works, Karl Pelzer examined in detail the nature and significance of the land pacts signed between traditional rulers and plantation firms in East Sumatra (Pelzer 1978; 1982).
11. See Boeke (1946, pp.39-84) for a detailed explanation of this and Creutzberg (1974, pp.xi-xiv) for further views on the subject. Creutzberg (1974, pp.616-750) contains important official documents relating to the topic of restrictions.

12. Deinum (1948, pp.405-18) treats the smallholders' cane industry as a whole. Van der Kolff (1925) presents much material on it as it was practiced in the Tulungagung region.

CHAPTER EIGHT

Peasants and Coffee Cultivation in Cirebon Residency, 1800-1900

M. R. Fernando and William J. O'Malley

Socioeconomic change in rural Java in the nineteenth and early twentieth centuries was greatly influenced by colonial economic policies, particularly those oriented toward the production of export crops for the world market. The received view (Day 1904; Furnivall 1944) is that Javanese peasants were passive victims of the evolving plantation economy, and this perspective has continued in more recent theorizing on social change in colonial Java (Geertz 1963; White 1973; Alexander and Alexander 1979; Boomgaard 1981). The historical evidence, however, has begun to show that the growth of commercial agriculture after 1830 had a stimulating effect on the rural economy, with commercialization leading to improved standards of living for the majority of the rural population, at least through the middle decades of the nineteenth century (Van Niel 1972 and 1981; Elson 1979; Knight 1982a; Fernando 1982a). The reason for this discrepancy between the views of theorizers and those of historians can be traced largely to a misunderstanding of the way in which large numbers of peasants were absorbed into the process of cultivation, and to a failure to appreciate the importance of coffee production in nineteenth-century Java. This essay will focus on precisely those problems.[1]

Much of the latter-day discussion of socioeconomic change in colonial Java is centred on an examination of the allegedly disastrous impact which the sugar industry had on indigenous society. This is because researchers have had to come to grips with the Geertzian hypothesis that, with their freedom of economic activity circumscribed by the way in which the colonial sugar industry exploited their land and labour, peasants in Java had to spread the available economic resources as widely as possible, a process eventually paving the way to "agricultural involution" and "shared poverty" (Geertz 1963).

A basic assumption in Geertz's argument is that from its inception in the early nineteenth century, the sugar industry had a tremendous influence on rural society, much like the influence which the industry was observed to have in parts of Java in the 1920s when it reached its apogee. Historical materials, however, indicate that up until the last decades of the nineteenth century, the sugar industry did not occupy a notably prominent place in the plantation economy of Java. The area planted under sugar cane, for instance, remained less than 3 per cent of all arable land until 1895; even thereafter it occupied no more than 4 per cent of all arable land in Java. Furthermore, no more than 13 per cent of all agricultural households were ever employed by the sugar industry in Java. And while the cultivation of sugar cane does appear to have had a considerable impact on rural social organization in those areas where that cultivation was important, the sugar industry did not prevail everywhere in Java and the intensity of its operation also varied from one region to another.

Coffee cultivation, on the other hand, spread over much wider stretches of Java and employed as many as 50 per cent of all agricultural households until well into the late nineteenth century. The ecological conditions required for coffee cultivation were different from those for sugar. Until it ceased to be a major export crop early in this century, the production of coffee was left almost entirely in the hands of indigenous people, thus leading to repercussions quite different from those connected with the sugar industry in Java. The archetype of socioeconomic change in Java envisaged by Geertz and then widely adopted by other scholars does not fully take into account the impact of coffee production. Partly for that reason, the social history connected with coffee cultivation has received very little attention in recent studies of rural Java. It is time to begin to fill in that social history, and in examining the effects of coffee cultivation in Cirebon Residency—an area on the north coast of Java where sugar was an important crop but coffee was more important even—it should be possible to see the difference that coffee made and to start to re-evaluate our understanding of the processes of change in colonial Javanese society.

Coffee cultivation was introduced into Java by the Dutch East India Company in the last decade of the seventeenth century. It became widespread in the island, particularly in western Java, in the 1720s when coffee proved to be a lucrative product of the European market.[2] The Priangan region and a considerable area in Cirebon, especially in the highland sections over 1,000 metres above sea level, became major sites for coffee cultivation in the early decades of the eighteenth century. At that time Cirebon was still ruled by an independent sultanate, but it gradually came under the direct control of the Dutch who manipulated internal conflicts to serve their political interests in the region. The more the Dutch found out about the economic resources of Cirebon, the more they became interested in the potential income they could derive from it, chiefly, they thought, from the production of commercial commodities.

The Cirebon realm with which the Dutch were dealing in the late seventeenth century was divided into areas assigned by the Sultan to members of his nobility. Under these regents, the population was organized into *cacah,* which were households made up of a core family together with its dependent relatives and attendants. In the lowland region of Cirebon, these *cacah* lived in small settlements within easy distance from the residence of their regent, but in the wide highlands the *cacah* appear to have been far more mobile and far less controlled. There they were free to move and frequently did, changing their location every few years as they searched for new land for swidden agriculture (Fernando 1982a, pp.25-31; pp.54-55).

Dutch commercial and political interests began to alter this way of life, and coffee was a major factor in the alteration. At first, the Dutch simply offered to pay the Cirebon nobility for any coffee delivered to the Company. The price was apparently attractive enough to encourage some regents to have their *cacah* begin to lay out coffee plantations in Cirebon's southern highlands, but as late as 1713, the amount of coffee sold to the V.O.C. in Cirebon amounted to only some 150 kg (de Haan 1911, pp.493-95). As Dutch control grew stronger and the demand for coffee on European markets continued to expand, cultivation was taken far more seriously. The regents slid into a position where they had to please the Dutch in order to make their own positions secure, and they also began to need higher incomes to maintain their increasingly extravagant lifestyles. The approval of the Europeans and the funds for supporting the regents' lavish establishments could both be gained through coffee deliveries, and in the 1720s, there was a dramatic expansion of coffee cultivation on the slopes of Mt. Ciremai and Mt. Sawal, as the *cacah* hastened to comply with the demands of their masters for increased yields. In 1730, coffee production in Cirebon had reached 375,000 kg, and it stayed at impressively high levels through the remainder of the century (de Haan 1911, p.511). Within the coffee-growing regions, however, the major effect of this extraordinary production was a social rather than a strictly economic one. In economic terms, there had been a massive transfer of land and labour into coffee production. But this did not have the transforming effect that it might have had, because the regents took less and less interest in coffee cultivation when the Dutch unpredictably reduced purchase prices in order to attempt to balance production and market conditions, while the *cacah,* who received no cash recompense from the regents for their coffee-raising efforts, also became indifferent to the cultivation.[3] In social terms, however, the need to produce coffee in such quantities helped to bring together various *cacah* and compelled them to establish more settled communities, working both coffee plantations and permanent fields—either dry *tegalan* or terraced wet-rice *sawah*—for subsistence crops in Cirebon's hinterland (Fernando 1982a, p.44; pp.52-54).

The first fifteen years of the nineteenth century were not happy ones for the coffee cultivators in Cirebon. The Napoleonic wars posed problems for the coffee trade in Europe and Asia, and when the British arrived in 1812, they found coffee warehouses bulging with undisposable beans. Under the influences of liberal economic views, the British then attempted to reform the entire system of coffee production. Using what they considered to be the government's claim to all land, the British leased out the right to the coffee gardens to the Cirebon regents. The regents were then free to have coffee raised on the land and to sell that coffee. In turn, they were to use part of the proceeds to pay the cost of the leases and the land tax for the areas under cultivation.[4] In theory, this was to give the regents a greater stake in the success of the coffee plantation: the greater the production, the higher their return. In practice, things did not work out so well. The government turned out to be the only purchaser of coffee, and it kept its prices at a very low level.[5] The cost of leases and land tax, however, was high, and, caught in the resultant squeeze, the regents began to neglect or to abandon their leases. The coffee gardens, as a consequence, were let to go to grass and shrubs.[6]

When the Dutch returned, they saw that there was no future in this way of handling affairs. Guided by their own determination to raise a class of "virile yeomen" on the land in Java, the Dutch administration removed the regents from the coffee picture in Cirebon. They turned the rights to leases of the gardens over to those who were now to be the key men in coffee production, the village heads in the coffee areas.[7]

Under this new scheme, villagers would raise and process the coffee, and their village heads would be responsible for the financial side of things. The village heads had either to turn a portion (usually a third to a half) of the yields to the government or to pay an equivalent amount of cash as land rent on the gardens. They were thus free to sell at least some of their coffee to private merchants if they chose. From the government's point of view, this had the advantage of abolishing compulsory cultivation in favour of peasant enterprise. From the point of view of the leading villagers, the new scheme could work to put cash, and power, in their hands in a way that had never previously been possible. From the point of view of common villagers, the scheme promised little that was new, except additional work.

The results of this "freeing" of coffee cultivation were highly impressive. By 1823, the four coffee-growing regions of Cirebon, the Regencies of Kuningan, Majalanka, Cirebon, and Galuh, possessed some four and a half million coffee bushes, producing some 650,000 kg of coffee.[8] Just as impressive as the results of free coffee production, however, was the way in which Cirebon's rural society was being shaped by the pressures generated by the new system.

Under free cultivation, the village heads were the crucial element in coffee production, and they used their new wealth and power to establish themselves firmly on top of the local social pyramid. What is more, they used their influence to distribute coffee gardens to selected members of the *sikep* class, those villagers who had full-fledged rights to cultivable land. The *sikeps* were responsible for the planting and maintaining of the coffee bushes, but they themselves did not do the work. That was the task of *wuwungs* (married, non-landholding peasants) and *bujangs* (landless bachelors), who earned their livelihood as tenants and agricultural labourers. These groupings had already existed in Cirebon villages before the implementation of free coffee cultivation, but the divorcing of the regents from a major economic endeavour, the entrusting of the supervision of the system to village heads, and the distribution of cash from the top down caused a strengthening of the position of village elites that was unprecedented. Common villagers, who faced increased burdens not only in raising the coffee bushes but in processing and transporting the expanded yields as well, occasionally protested that they were receiving no rewards for their efforts. But during the decade and a half that free cultivation was in force, their position became more obviously inferior in the coffee-growing areas of Cirebon.[9]

The Cultivation System, as it came to work in Cirebon's coffee-growing areas, did not so much transform the free cultivation system as intensify it. Du Bus de Gesignies in the late 1820s had recommended that the government make coffee a monopoly crop, not least because he believed that free traders buying up coffee beans in rural areas were most responsible for exploiting the peasants. In 1832, coffee was brought within the Cultivation System. Thereafter, all the crop had to be sold to the government at a price of *f*25 per *picul*. Of the *f*25, two-fifths was deducted as land-rent, another *f*3 was taken out to meet transportation costs and only the remaining *f*12 per *picul* was actually paid out to those who delivered the coffee to government warehouses.[10]

Under this new scheme, the village heads and other influential *sikeps* were able to maintain their important positions in production. As had been the case with free cultivation, they were the ones who designated the areas to be brought under coffee, they organized the required labour, they supervised the planting, tending, plucking, and processing, and they ultimately took charge of delivering the coffee and distributing the money thus earned. But the interest of village leaders in seeing that the new system worked was now shared by the supra-village elites, for regional administrators stood to gain as well through the premium payments they were to receive from the Cultivation System, payments whose size depended on the amount of produce delivered to the government by those in their charge.[11] With both the village leaders and the local *priyayi* standing to benefit financially from the System, involvement in it and production under it were almost bound to increase. The first few years after its introduction, indeed, saw substantial gains for Cirebon coffee: the baseline of only some 16,000 households working in coffee in 1835-1836 had risen to an average of 22,000 households between 1840 and 1845, while production moved upward from an annual average of 22,700 *piculs* of coffee in the period 1835-1839 to a figure of 39,400 *piculs* in the years 1840-1844 (Figures 8.1 and 8.2).

The areas responsible for these coffee gains under the Cultivation System were not spread evenly throughout Cirebon Residency. There were smaller

FIGURE 8.1 Number of Agricultural Households engaged in Coffee Cultivation ('000)

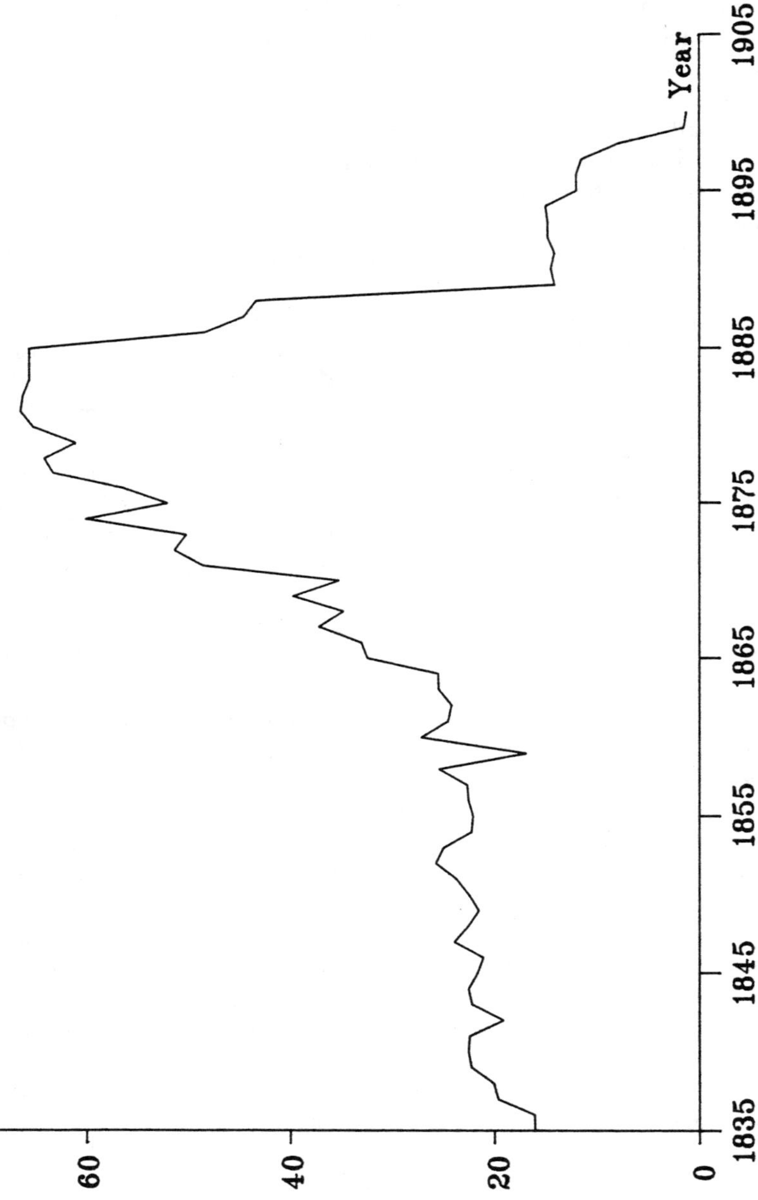

Source: Kultuur Verslag 1834–1851; Koloniaal Verslag 1852–1905.

FIGURE 8.2 Per Centage of Coffee-Cultivating Households of all Agricultural Households engaged in Cultivation of Commercial Crops

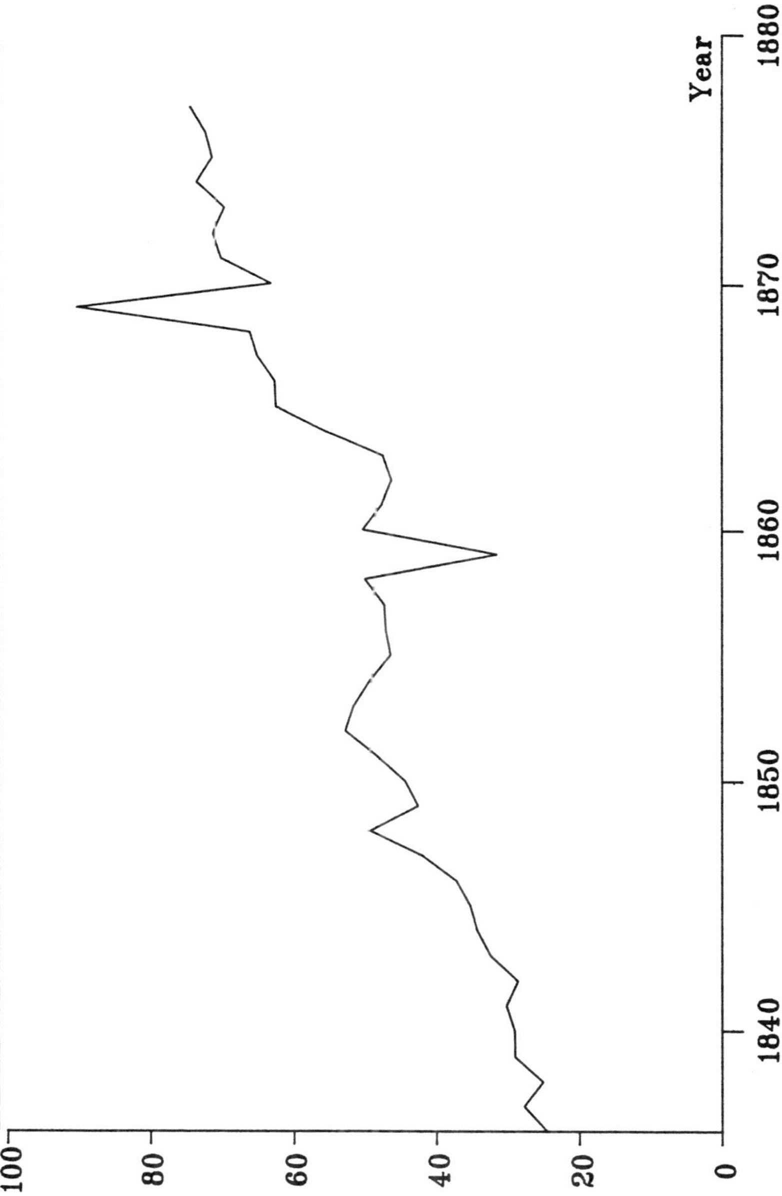

Source: Kultuur Verslag 1834-1851; Koloniaal Verslag 1852-1885.

coffee-growing areas in Majalanka and Cirebon Regencies, but the truly important sites of coffee cultivation were on Mt. Ciremai and Mt. Sawal in the southern regencies of Kuningan and Galuh. In the north, sugar and other crops were grown for government export, but the south was coffee country, and both the ecology and the society there were conducive to coffee production.

In Kuningan and Galuh, the landscape was dominated not by the wide *sawah* stretches of the coastal plains but by the forested slopes of the interior. Here, in the middle of the nineteenth century, less than a quarter of the land was under cultivation and a major portion of the farming was done on *tegalan,* or unirrigated fields. Rural communities lived in isolated villages scattered over wide areas, communications were poor, and, in comparison with the more advanced northern areas, the agricultural sector was still rather undiversified. This meant that there were great expanses of favourable hillside and mountainous terrain onto which coffee bushes could spread and that the money from increased coffee production would be a most welcome addition in a comparatively simple economy (Fernando 1982a, Maps 1, 3 and 5).

The labour needed to raise the coffee was not too difficult to mobilize. As a legacy of the earlier *cacah* system, households in the hilly stretches of Cirebon were still large units, with the important land-owning farmers, or *sikeps,* accepting responsibility for and exercising influence over landless labourers who lived with them. Though it was nominally only the *sikeps* who were responsible for raising crops for the government, they were in a position to see that much of the physical labour required by the Cultivation System came from those dependent on them.

As had been the case with coffee growing under some of the earlier systems, this land and this labour came together easily to boost coffee production in Cirebon's mountainous regions during the early decades of the Cultivation System, a time when large plantations were laid out in the highlands, stretching up to almost 1,000 metres above sea level on all sides of Mt. Ciremai and Mt. Sawal. The work that went into establishing and tending these plantations was organized in a way already familiar in Cirebon. Village officials gathered together a workforce from among the less well-off villagers and led it up the slopes, often tens of kilometres from the village. The initial preparation was begun in May and was finished in July. The forest was cut down and the fallen vegetation was set on fire. The ashes were then spread and mixed with the soil, which was turned over with hoes. On steeper slopes, terraces had to be created. Once this work was done, the cleared area was fenced to keep out wild animals. Sometimes all of the preparatory work might be shared by farmers from a number of villages, but as the rainy season approached, planters from different villages began to work on their own once more. As soon as the first rains fell, in October or

November, seedlings were planted in holes that had been dug earlier, and the first stage of establishing a coffee garden was completed.

The first stage often required villagers to spend months away from their homes, but even after it was finished the ordeal was not over. In their first three years, the young coffee plants needed to have the ground around them weeded and turned over once a month, and for this purpose some of the planters and their families had to live close to the plantation, often in temporary huts. When the coffee finally began to ripen on the mature bushes, the entire workforce would again be assembled and would move out to the plantation site once more. These workers had to stay there for the whole harvesting season, since the coffee beans did not all ripen simultaneously and the picking had to be done continuously—plucking the ripe beans without damaging the younger, still maturing ones. After the completion of the harvesting, the beans were transported back to the villages, where they were stripped of their outer shells and dried. The finished beans were finally taken to the local district town and turned in at the government storehouse in exchange for cash.[12]

The amount of money flowing into Cirebon from the sale of coffee to the government varied greatly from year to year, depending on the size of the harvest and other factors. It is possible, however, to say that on the whole those amounts were substantial. Between 1835 and 1844, official figures show that households involved in raising coffee earned on average almost *f*17 per year for their efforts. After 1844, the Dutch felt the low world market prices for Java coffee compelled them to lower the base price they paid to cultivators from *f*25 per *picul* to *f*21.67. From 1845 until the early 1850s, coffee-raising households were returned only *f*12.06, on average, for their produce each year. Though the world market price recovered in the 1850s, it wasn't until 1859 that alterations were made in the amounts paid to producers; after that year, in accordance with stipulations in the new constitutional statutes of 1854, the amounts paid for beans were to be determined by the market price for such beans in Batavia. The deductions for the land rent and for the costs of transportation were still continued, however, and the returns to households averaged only *f*11 each year in the 1860s (Figure 8.3).[13] These were substantial sums of money for the time, and the totals became more significant when it is realized that the number of households involved in raising coffee increased in each of these periods. But though calculations can be made now to determine the average amount returned to each family involved, the most important social fact connected with government coffee cultivation in Cirebon was that the money acquired from the sale of coffee was not distributed evenly at the time. Instead, the distribution process was controlled by the leading *sikep* families, who retained a disproportionately large amount of the money.

In the coffee-growing regions of Cirebon, differentiation had already existed among the peasantry before the Cultivation System was instituted, but the

FIGURE 8.3 Amount of Coffee Delivered to the Government (hundreds of tonnes)

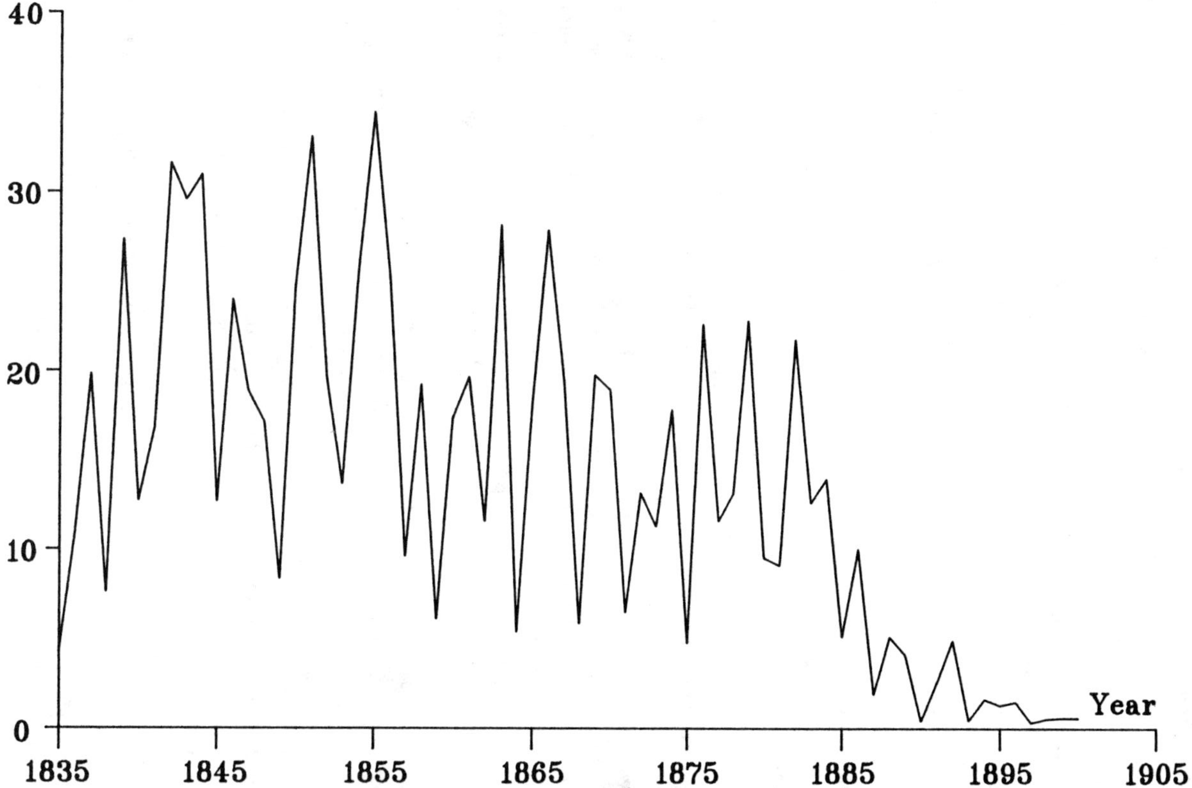

Source: Kultuur Verslag 1834–1851; Koloniaal Verslag 1852–1905

way in which the System worked helped to strengthen still further the position of those at the top of the village hierarchy. The Dutch were neither eager nor able to supervise cultivation, so unless there was outrageous failings, the business of raising and delivering coffee remained under the control of the *priyayi* and the leading villagers. The *priyayi* in Cirebon had already grown distant from the agricultural aspects of rural life even before 1830, and, like the Dutch, they were willing to sit back and reap the rewards of the System without bothering themselves greatly about actually directing it. This left the village officials and other leading *sikeps,* men who controlled the *balai desa,* or village meetings, in charge of the System on the ground, and in the coffee areas these people used their favoured positions to enhance their economic, social, and political status.

Economically, the leading *sikeps* benefited disproportionately in a number of ways. Controlling the exchange of coffee beans for cash at the government warehouses, they saw to it that as little as possible of the money coming to the community passed out of their hands to those who had actually done most of the work of producing the coffee. Later on, some of the *sikeps* were even appointed as official supervisors of the coffee gardens, and for the work—which they were doing anyway and which they already found rewarding—they received fixed monthly salaries. While in other stretches in Cirebon and elsewhere in Java, it became necessary early in the Cultivation System period for villages to include previously landless peasants among those who were to get shares in village land in order to expand the pool of people subject to the demands of the System, in the coffee regions this tendency was much less pronounced.

Socially, those who ran the *balai desa* also made advances during the years of the Cultivation System. They began to establish better connections with the indigenous supra-village officials and to mix more easily with the Chinese. In addition, they were able to distance themselves somewhat from the lower segments of village society, a distancing given concrete form in many instances by the ability of important *sikeps* to make the pilgrimage to Mecca and thenceforth distinguish themselves by the title *haji.*

Politically, the leading *sikeps* took advantage of the general lack of concern with village affairs on the part both of the *priyayi* and of the European administration to consolidate their control of village institutions. As long as the hill villages continued to produce large coffee crops, the outside authorities did not bother themselves at all with village affairs. This situation left the village officials to preside unchecked over village government and to ensure that those who succeeded them in their positions came from their own groups in village society.[14]

For some thirty years, this System worked reasonably well. The administration received coffee in amounts which, if they fluctuated widely from year to year, still on average were impressive (Figure 8.4). Supra-village officials received regular payments. And though the money was far from evenly distributed, the peasantry received impressive sums of cash for the coffee they raised. But by the 1860s a number of problems had begun to appear within the System in Cirebon, and the forced cultivation of coffee began a downhill slide that was to last until the turn of the century.

The root of the difficulty was closely connected with the very reasons why the coffee-raising effort had met with early success. In the 1830s, and even before, the suitable lands along the slopes of Mt. Ciremai and Mt. Sawal had been filled with coffee gardens, first close to villages and then farther and farther away. By the 1860s, however, those plantations had begun to drop off in production as the bushes in them reached an advanced age. What is more, the soil had been depleted to the point where it was no longer possible simply to cut down older bushes and replace them with new substitutes. So the best coffee lands were turned into *tegalan* used for raising other crops, while the labour gangs had to travel still greater distances to fields which were higher and also less suitable for the establishment of new gardens. As a result, over the 1860s and 1870s, the industry in Cirebon faced three trends that together contributed to an unhealthy situation.

First, the number of households involved in coffee cultivation grew noticeably larger, from an average of some 24,500 a year in the late 1850s to 36,200 in the late 1860s to 61,250 households per year in the late 1870s (Figures 8.1 and 8.2). Second, production failed to keep pace with labour inputs, rising on average only some 20 per cent from the late 1850s to the late 1860s and then declining again in the late 1870s (Figure 8.3). And third, the payments to the populace, though they were now tied to the world market price for coffee instead of being arbitrarily fixed, did not rise appreciably after the late 1850s, and thus the average return to the households involved in raising coffee declined considerably (Figure 8.4).

The colonial government was aware of the signs of stagnation in Cirebon's coffee zones, and in the mid-1870s steps to alleviate this potentially worrisome state of affairs were taken. Imitating reforms that had proven moderately successful in the Priangan highlands in the early 1870s, officials moved to concentrate Cirebon's coffee plantations closer to the villages and to ensure that new trees were planted to replace those which were going out of production. These reform measures, however, were only half-heartedly enforced by an administration that was highly skeptical of their ability to spur the coffee industry forward. The measures also were long-term, and by the 1880s they were rendered largely irrelevant by the outbreak of a coffee disease which threatened to end coffee production on the Cirebon slopes once and for all.

FIGURE 8.4 Crop Payment per Household (guilders)

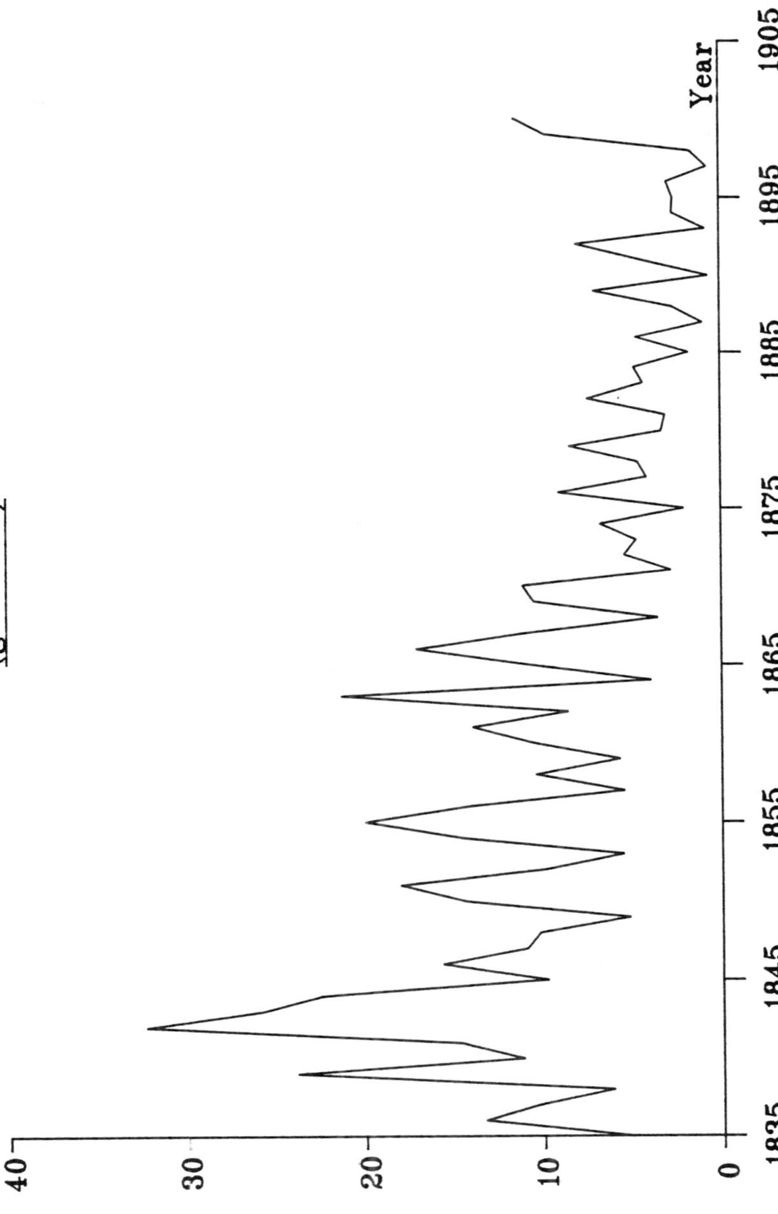

Source: Kultuur Verslag 1834-1851; Koloniaal Verslag 1852-1905.

Hemilia vestatrix appeared in Java in 1879, but, since it had been known in earlier times, the colonial government did not take it very seriously at the start. Within two years, however, its devastating results were felt throughout the island's coffee regions, and Cirebon was one of the areas hardest hit. The authorities attempted to halt the spread of the disease and to limit its effects by urging the peasants to work the land more thoroughly, to use appropriate fertilizers, and to improve the drainage of the plantations. These steps, however, were not enough to counter the *vestatrix* plague, and by the middle of the 1880s, when *vestatrix* disappeared from western Java, the damage in Cirebon had been done: production, which had averaged almost 28,400 *piculs* per year in the late 1870s, had fallen off to less than 9,000 *piculs* per year in the late 1880s, while in 1889, only some 14,000 households were still involved in coffee production, less than one-quarter the number earlier in the decade.

There were official attempts to renew enforced coffee cultivation in Cirebon late in the century, but the effort required to begin again almost from scratch proved too much for both the administration and the people. In 1893, proposals were made simply to drop coffee production for compulsory delivery in the Residency. In 1905, the once unthinkable idea had become a reality, and the government's connection with coffee production in upland Cirebon was severed.

Over the course of the nineteenth century, the influence of coffee on Cirebon's southern hinterlands was extremely strong. Following directions from Batavia, but under the control of local people, coffee production had helped greatly to shape village life in the Regencies of Galuh and Kuningan. After a number of experiments in the early decades of the century—experiments based upon different readings of older patterns of production and control—the responsibility for raising coffee and for guiding the production efforts had come to rest after 1817 with the leading members of village society. The position of these important *sikeps* and village officials was further bolstered after 1832 when they found themselves part of the major economic effort of the Dutch colonial government under the Cultivation System. In the half century between the institution of the System in the coffee-growing regions and the death blow dealt it by the *vestatrix* disease, production surged forward and then began to falter. But despite this long-term trend, and despite temporary fluctuations in coffee's fortunes, the village leaders in southern Cirebon were able, as the chief organizers of labour and distributors of crop payments, to use the whole period to put greater social distance between themselves and the growing and more settled populations over whom they presided. Differentiation was already a fact of life in rural communities in these regions long before the Cultivation System with its increased emphasis on coffee production, but here the freedom of action accorded to, and the cash incomes accruing to, leading villagers meant further polarization rather than social compression during the years the System was in force.

Notes

1. This brief discussion of coffee cultivation and its impact on rural society in the Cirebon region is based on information in Fernando 1982a. Further documentation and analysis can be found in that work.
2. For information on the early history of coffee cultivation in Java, see S. de Graaf *et al.* (1918, pp.385-99) and N.P. van der Berg (1879).
3. The V.O.C. coffee-cultivation policy is discussed by Glaman (1958, pp.183-211).
4. 'Algemeen Verslag aan Kommissarissen-Generaal over de Residentie Cheribon op 1816', Collectie J.C. Baud 26, Algemeen Rijksarchief, The Hague (hereafter ARADH).
5. In 1816, the Resident of Cirebon remarked that the purchase price of coffee was only 3 *stuivers* a point; at the same time, rice in Batavia was selling for *f* 4.00 per *picul*. This meant that coffee was priced at some *f*0.25 per kg, only four times the price of an equivalent amount of rice. See letter Servatius to Governor-General, 30-9-1816-19, Arsip Daerah (hereafter AD), Cirebon 63.2, Arsip Nasional Republik Indonesia Jakarta (hereafter ANRIJ) and "Prijs der rijst op Batavia," Collectie Baud 251, ARADH.
6. Letter Servatius to the Governor-General, 30-9-1816-19; 'Algemeen Verslag aan Kommissarissen-Generaal ... 1816'.
7. Algemeen Verslag aan de Kommissarissen-Generaal ... 1816'; the new regulations of coffee cultivation were promulgated by *Staatsblad* (hereafter *Stb.*) 1817, No. 55 and *Stb.* 1818, No. 15. For a discussion of this policy, see van der Kemp (1916, pp.123-72). On the ideological background of the liberal policy of the restored Dutch regime in Java, see Van Soest (1869, pp.117-47), and Burger (1939, pp.92-93).
8. 'Statistiek van Java en Madoera: Residentie Cheribon', Archief Ministerie van Kolonien (hereafter AMK) 3048, ARADH.
9. The account of the effects of the new policy is based on information in 'Rapport van den Resident van Cheribon over den Staat der koffij kultuur in deze Residentie zoo also deselve bevonden ... voor het Dienstjaar 1821', AD, Cirebon 29.5, ANRIJ; 'Algemeen Verslag aan Kommissarissen-Generaal ... 1816'.
10. On Du Bus's proposals made following an inquiry into the coffee cultivation, see Van Deventer (1866, Vol. 2, pp.494-99). The initial resolution of 30-1-1832-1 (*Stb.* 1832, No. 15) to bring coffee cultivation under the aegis of the Cultivation System was elaborated by the resolution of 3-2-1833-1 (*Stb.* 1833, No. 7. This measure led the way to a prolonged debate between Van den Bosch and his articulate liberal opponent, P. Merkus; the proceedings of this debate can be found in Van Deventer (1866, Vol. 2, pp.502-48).
11. On the cultivation premium payment under the Cultivation System in general, see Reinsma (1980).

12. The preceding paragraphs are based on information in the following documents: 'Verslag van de gehouden Inspectie der Kultures in de Residentie Cheribon over het jaar 1834', Collectie Baud 457; Letter Landre to the Governor-General, 20-8-1835-1333, Collectie Baud 452; and 'Aantooning betreffende de Koffijcultuur in de Residentie Cheribon, bijlage van het Algemeen Verslag der Uitkomsten van het Onderzoek betreffende de Koffijcultuur op Java', AMK, Verbaal 24-11-1871-32, ARADH. This last document is part of a report resulting from an inquiry into the state of coffee cultivation made in the mid-1860s. The general report and a series of local reports were published in the proceedings of the lower chamber of the Dutch parliament during 1869-1872. On the inquiry and the debate over its findings, see Goedhart (1948, pp.55-65).
13. In 1843, the Governor-General Merkus took measures to reduce the price paid for coffee; from 1844 onwards, the actual amount of money cultivators received was reduced from *f*12 to *f*10 a *picul* (Van Deventer 1866, Vol. 2, pp.188-89; Fasseur 1975, p.43). The legislation to adjust the purchasing price in accordance with the market price of coffee in Batavia was published in *Stb.* 1859, No. 57.
14. These aspects are discussed at length in Fernando 1982a, Chapters 2 and 3.

CHAPTER NINE

Government and the Emerging Rubber Industries in Indonesia and Malaya, 1900-40

Colin Barlow and John Drabble

> The rapid development of the tropical world began in the last quarter of the nineteenth century, in response to cheap transportation and the industrialisation of Europe and North America. (Lewis 1970)

This rapid development was based upon the production of primary commodities as industrial inputs, among which rubber was one of the most significant. Commercial planting of rubber began in the 1890s, and by 1940 the total world area under rubber amounted to some 3.6 million hectares. Indonesia and Malaya[1] were by far the foremost producers, each with around 1.4 million hectares (Table 9.1). Prior to World War II the rubber industries of these countries became their largest single contributor to export earnings (Table 9.2); this development had widespread effects on their economies and brought changes to their ethnic composition. Involved as producers were European corporate investors, migrant Asians, and indigenous farmers operating a very wide range of holding sizes. In 1940, 46 per cent of the planted area in Indonesia belonged to estates and 54 per cent native holdings, while in Malaya estates comprised 60 per cent and smallholdings 40 per cent.[2]

The two colonial governments became increasingly involved in the affairs of the industries. It is thus instructive to compare selected aspects of their roles and assess the relative importance of government to rubber development in the two countries.

The Historical Pattern

The events surrounding the introduction of *Hevea Brasiliensis* from South America to South and Southeast Asia in the late nineteenth century are well documented (Drabble 1973; Voon 1976). Rapid and sustained development began in Indonesia and Malaya at the turn of the century, with the latter country in the lead in terms of planted area (Table 9.1).

In Indonesia, rubber-growing on estates (or plantations) followed the example of well-established export crops (notably sugar and tobacco). It quickly

TABLE 9.1 Planted Area and Production of Rubber, Indonesia and Malaya, 1900-40

	Indonesia						Malaya					
	Area ('000 ha)						Area ('000 ha)					
	Java	Outer Islands										
Year	Estates	Estates	Smallh.	Total	Production ('000 tons)	%[b]	Estates	Smallh.	Total	Production[a] ('000 tons)	%[b]	%[c]
1900	-	-	-	-	-	-	2	-	2	-	n.a.	100
1905	n.a.	1	-	1	-	100	19	-	19	-	n.a.	100
1910	64[d]	40	6	110	3[e]	n.a.	166	53[f]	219	6	n.a.	67
1915	109	131[g]	24	264	16	n.a.	335	187[f]	522	72	n.a.	82
1920	157	195	109	461	79	87	559	324	883	177	n.a.	69
1925	181	235	466	882	192	55	599	395	994	213	n.a.	53
1930	229	344	729	1,302	246	63	763	483	1,246	456	52	65
1935	230	365	n.a.	595[h]	287	52	816	471	1,287	379	64	57
1940	241	385	731[i]	1,357	546	52	843	547	1,390	554	61	50

a Production was generally 2-3% more than net exports
b Percentage which estate production forms of combined estate and smallholding production
c Percentage which Malayan production forms of combined Malayan and Indonesian production
d Included about 15,000 ha of Ficus (as opposed to Hevea), which then gradually declined in area over the years
e "Wet" rubber
f Assuming that 80% of the "Asian" area (Figart 1925) was estates, and the balance smallholdings
g Area in 1914 (1915 area not avaliable)
h Excluding smallholding area
i Including 16,400 ha of smallholdings in Java

Sources: Indonesia smallholder area, 1910 and 1915: Figart (1925)
Indonesia smallholder area, 1925 and 1930: Whitford (1931)
Other Indonesian data: C.E.I. Vol. 1, Table 10
Malayan data: Malaya (1932-41); Figart (1925)

TABLE 9.2 Value of Exports from Indonesia and Malaya, 1912/13-1937

Items	Indonesia						Malaya					
	1913		1925		1937		1912		1925		1937	
	M.f.	%	M.f.	%	M.f.	%	M.S.d.	%	M.S.d.	%	M.S.d.	%
Rubber	24	4	582	32	321	32	28	8	763	59	489	54
Petroleum	113	17	173	10	165	17	-		-		-	
Tin Ore	37	6	94	5	84	8	107	29	175	14	190	21
Coconut products	55	8	102	6	63	6	17	5	35	3	31	3
Sugar	157	23	370	20	50	5	-		-		-	
Tea	22	3	74	4	49	5	-		-		-	
Tobacco	92	14	111	6	41	4	-		-		-	
Palm oil products	-		-		25	3	-		-		7	1
Coffee	23	3	68	4	25	3	-		-		-	
Other	148	22	227	13	165	17	208	58	317	24	189	21
Total	671	100	1,801	100	990	100	360	100	1,290	100	906	100
(in US$)[a]	242		648		356		180		645		453	

M.f. = million florins
M.S.d. = million Straits dollar
[a] At concurrent exchange rate

Source: Allen and Donnithorne (1954)

assumed a corporate pattern of organisation, attracting capital and managerial personnel. There was also a transfer of resources with existing plantations changing over to rubber. Two main centres of plantation activity developed; one on the East Coast of Sumatra where rubber became the impetus for renewed economic expansion following the tobacco crisis of the 1880s (Schadee 1918; Thee 1977), the other in Java. The estates were relatively large organisations, with hierarchically structured management and labour forces, producing a uniform commodity through a central processing factory. The export of rubber, and its sale on world markets, were effected through a network of agents and produce brokers.

The smallholder rubber industry in Indonesia was established somewhat later, getting well under way in the boom years from 1909 to 1912 (Table 9.1), when London rubber prices averaged between 8 and 9 shillings per pound (Figure 9.1). This was a spectacular case of spread effects, in which a basically simple technology with a high promising final return could be readily and cheaply fitted into a traditional agricultural system; it was therefore taken up very quickly. The key element of the technology, the rubber seed, was easily obtainable from the estates. Smallholder rubber in Indonesia was confined almost entirely to the Outer Islands where rubber seeds were planted, together with rice or other subsistence crops, at the beginning of the normal swidden cycle, following clearing of jungle or secondary growth.[3] Thus in contrast to the heavy initial expenditure incurred by monocultural estates in clearing, planting, constructing roads and buildings, etc., the initial outlay for smallholders was minimal. After two to three years the rubber trees shaded out other crops, and they could be left virtually untended for eight to ten years until tappable. The resultant 'slab' rubber had a high moisture content and impurities, but was readily saleable through the Chinese rural trading network which made available ample consumer goods in return. Peasants planted mainly along rivers and the few existent roads, and much of their land under rubber was well away from estates. The primary sites were in what are now the provinces of Jambi and South Sumatra, with smaller areas in North Sumatra and Riau (Table 9.3). The other principal location was in South and East Dutch Borneo (now Kalimantan). Land, covered by virgin jungle, was freely available in all these places. Even after taking up rubber planting, the farm families generally continued to produce some subsistence crops.

Prior to the introduction of rubber, the Malayan economy had experienced far less agricultural development than that of Indonesia. Chinese proprietary planters (pepper, tapioca and gambier) had predominated until the 1880s and 1890s, when European pioneers (also proprietary planters) took up sugar and coffee cultivation. The crops and cropping methods of the Chinese planters, however, caused progressively more soil exhaustion. This was accompanied,

Figure 9.1 Average Annual Spot Prices (Buyers') of RSSI[a] in London, 1900-40

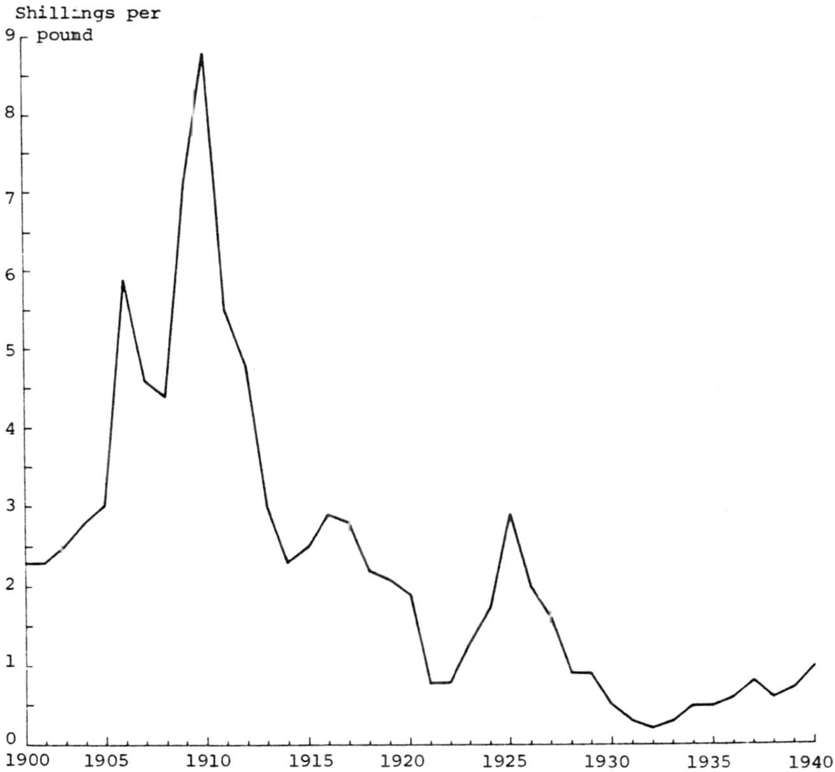

[a] Average rubber prices only before 1906

Source: Agalawatta, Rubber Research Institute of Ceylon, private communication.

TABLE 9.3 Extent and Production of Rubber on Estates and Smallholdings, Indonesia, 1922

Region	Estates		Smallholdings		
	Area ('000 ha)	Production ('000 tons)	Trees (million)	Area[a] ('000 ha)	Production[b] ('000 tons)
Java	164	29	-	-	-
Sumatra					
East Coast)	153	40	2.4	5	1
Tapanuli)[c]	7	2	1.8	4	-
Aceh	15	1	-		-
Riau	14	1	4.0	8	2
Lampung	9	1			-
Palembang[d]	2	-	7.3	15	1
Westcoast[e]	1	-	-	-	-
Jambi	-	-	21.2	43	10
Subtotal	201	45	36.7	75	14
Borneo[f]	-	-	15.7	32	12
Total	365	74	52.4	107	26

a Calculated from quoted numbers of trees by estimating 494 trees per hectare
b Some smallholding production is thought to have been included with that of estates
c Now North Sumatra Province
d Now South Sumatra Province; figures include Bangka
e Now West Sumatra Province
f Now Kalimantan

Source: Figart (1925)

after 1894, by a slump in coffee prices and the onset of plant disease. These difficulties prompted a widespread move to estate rubber growing from the early 1900s (Jackson 1968). Ample supplies of seed were available from the Singapore Botanical Gardens, where the crucial breakthroughs in tapping techniques had already been made (Drabble 1973). The first decade of the twentieth century saw a rapid development of rubber estates in which pioneer European planters, with limited personal capital resources, sold out to freshly-floated public companies, many with capital in sterling and registered in the United Kingdom.[4] Chinese interests also developed estates, but for the most part preferred to keep to their customary ownership forms of family or private partnerships. They often financed their new enterprises by switching profits from existing businesses (mines, shops, etc.), although some borrowing from moneylenders (usually Chettiars) also occurred.

The smallholder rubber sector in Malaya was not far behind the estate sector in its growth, especially after 1910 (Table 9.1). Chinese and Malays (the latter including many migrants from Indonesia) were the main participants, responding again to the promise of good cash incomes from high rubber prices and also to the possibility of selling their planted areas to estates, which were often willing to pay large sums to acquire small parcels to expand their operations. The fact that the lands of estates and smallholdings were intermingled in most regions improved the farming practices of the latter through force of example. The common links which Chinese smallholders often had with commercial activities doubtless helped produce a higher degree of specialisation and technical sophistication compared to the Indonesia peasant plantings. Many blocks in Malaya were devoted entirely to rubber plantings, without subsistence intercrops, and trees reached tappable size in five to six years. The product was mainly processed into unsmoked sheet with a low moisture content and few impurities (Barlow 1978). Rubber cultivation in Malaya was widespread although largely concentrated on the western side of the peninsula (Table 9.4).

While rubber prices declined again following the 1909-1912 boom (Figure 9.1), substantial planting continued in both Indonesia and Malaya. Companies had made a heavy commitment of funds at the time of flotation, and they wished to extend their revenue earning area in order to reduce the average capital cost per hectare and to pay attractive dividends. At the same time, smallholders were coming to view rubber as a year-round source of income far superior in its regularity and magnitude to the income received from traditional annual crops (van Gelderen 1961; Drabble and Drake 1974).

The war period from 1914 to 1919 saw further substantial plantings as rubber prices revived due to strengthened American demand. Since Holland remained neutral, there were no war constraints on the industry in Indonesia. However, in Malaya the export of strategic raw materials, including rubber, was

TABLE 9.4 Extent and Production of Rubber on Estates and Smallholdings, Malaya, 1921

	Area ('000 ha)			Net exports[a] ('000tons)
	Estates	Smallholdings	Total	
Federated Malay States[b]	310	190	500	94
Unfederated Malay States[c]	137	132[e]	269	30
Straits Settlements[d]	81	51	132	34
Total	528	373	901	158

a Exports do not necessarily all come from within the region indicated
b Perak, Selangor, Negri Sembilan, and Pahang
c Johore, Kedah, Trengganu, Kelantan, and Perlis
d Singapore, Penang, Province Wellesley and the Dindings (Sebarang Prai), and Malacca
e Including 14,000 hectares not distinguished in the original statistics, but thought to be largely smallholdings since located in Kelantan and Perlis

Source: Figart (1925) quoting area figures from the 1921 Malayan census

subject to metropolitan government licensing, and companies with capital in sterling were unable to make fresh share issues. This factor is likely to have restrained estate expansion in Malaya. After a brief post-war boom, the Western industrial economies plunged into a depression (1920-22), and rubber prices fell to around 7 pence per pound in 1921 (Figure 9.1). The principal problem here was that extensive plantings from earlier booms were reaching maturity at a time of falling demand, with surplus stocks piling up on world markets.

In an attempt to increase the price and in the absence of Dutch agreement, official restriction of exports from Malaya and other parts of the British Empire (known as the Stevenson scheme) operated for six years until October 1928. Market price levels improved up to 1925, when a buying panic due to an inflexibility in the scheme forced average prices up to 3 shillings per pound. In both Indonesia and Malaya this led to a planting boom, an outstanding feature of which was the very large area planted by smallholders in Sumatra and Kalimantan (Table 9.1; Whitford 1931). Rubber prices declined in the late 1920s, and it became evident that Malaya's preeminent position in the industry was being progressively eroded by the Indonesia. The British government accordingly withdrew restriction at the end of 1928.

The decade of the 1920s witnessed the end of major additions to the planted area in both countries. The industry had by then reached the broad ownership structure and regional distribution which would obtain for the rest of the period treated here, and well into the post-independence era (Tables 9.3 and 9.4). In both countries, European ownership predominated in the estate sector, with indigenous farmers dominant in the smallholder sector. In Indonesia, the Chinese had a relatively small ownership stake in plantation rubber, amounting to only 11 per cent of the value of all estate agricultural land in 1921 (Cator 1936). The reasons for this are discussed below. There were virtually no Chinese smallholders, and the comparatively few Javanese in this sector were mainly autonomous migrants to Sumatra. In Malaya, on the other hand, the Chinese were the principal owners of smaller estates (mostly in the 40-200 hectares range), and very possibly of most smallholdings between 10 and 40 hectares.

The growth of the industry virtually ceased in the 1930s, when the Great Depression (1929-32) brought even worse problems of excess productive capacity than had occurred in the early 1920s. The average London price fell from ten pence per pound in 1929 to an all-time low of just over 2 pence in 1932 (Bauer 1948, p.42). In Indonesia the aggregate value of rubber exports dropped from 587 million guilders in 1925 to 34 million guilders in 1932 (C.K.S. 161, Table 2) and in Malaya it slumped even more. Following long negotiations, the International Rubber Regulation Agreement came into operation from mid-1934, cutting back the output of all natural rubber producing countries in South and Southeast Asia. The agreement operated initially up to 1938, and was then renewed for a further five years to 1943, though it was interrupted by the outbreak of war with Japan (McFadyean 1944).

Attitudes Towards Development

As noted, the rubber industry became very significant to the economies of both Indonesia and Malaya; it was of greater and more general importance to the latter, but was also central to the economy of the Sumatran East Coast. While this significance bore directly on those producing the crop, it also affected overall commercial activity through an associated demand for ancillary services (transport, finance, produce dealers etc.). Rubber price fluctuations thus became of major consequence. The depressions, particularly those of 1920-22 and 1929-32, saw stocks of rubber building up, both in Asia and in the industrialised countries. The low prices quickly restricted cash-flow which led, in turn, to such problems as reduced trade and difficulties (especially among smallholders) in maintaining debt repayments. The boom periods, on the other hand, had marked beneficial effects. Aggregate export earnings shot up, with concomitant increases in personal incomes, government revenues, and improved trading conditions.[5]

On balance, rubber growing was well-regarded by the colonial governments of Indonesia and Malayan, which in the late nineteenth and early twentieth century were strongly motivated by the basic colonial objective of creating favourable commercial opportunities, especially where these benefited metropolitan interests. The official view on how to achieve this was relatively simplistic, growing out of the assumption that what was needed for "development" was primarily the exploitation of the country's natural resources by large-scale capitalistic enterprises. Almost by definition, these were of European and metropolitan origin. What Geertz (1963) has termed the "politico-economic device" of the corporate estate or plantation system was taken as the principal model, superior not only in marshalling capital and other requirements from overseas, but also in enabling the efficient application of scientific cultivation and marketing techniques.

The rapid growth of an estate sector in which only the soil had a "purely indigenous character" (van Gelderen 1961, p.120), where "the capital, the managers, and their assistants are European, and the labourers are migrants," occurred in differing historical situations in the two countries. In Indonesia during the nineteenth century, the Dutch had switched from the extraction of export commodities by coercive policies (the Culture System, 1830-70) to more *laissez-faire* approaches (the Liberal Policy, 1870-1900). In each case there had been a large initial boost to export earnings, but the growth rate had tapered off after a decade or so, with evidence that proportionate economic benefits were not filtering through to the peasantry. Rubber began to be taken up by estate interests at more or less the same time as government implemented yet another policy change, namely the Ethical Policy (1900-42) which aimed at countering the trend of "diminishing welfare" among the indigenous population, notably in Java. As a result of this policy Chinese investors throughout the Indies were subjected to various official constraints both on their land ownership and on their freedom of movement in rural areas. Thus as Williams (1952) notes, "the Chinese and their funds gravitated toward economic activities in the main concerned with the exchange rather than the production of goods." Government also facilitated the acquisition of labour for plantations on the East Coast of Sumatra and made some provision for early rubber research.

As we have seen, the entry of the indigenous Indonesian population into the industry as smallholders owed little or nothing to government policies, and in fact occurred almost entirely outside Java where Dutch administration was neither as strong nor as deeply entrenched as in Java. In Malaya, economic policy was broadly *laissez-faire*, and when the rubber boom commenced in the early 1900s, both European and Chinese investors were able to secure land readily. Government did directly facilitate the importation of Indian workers for European estates, however, while the Chinese organised their own recruitment network. The government also expanded the infrastructure of roads, railways and ports, and in 1905 it established a Department of Agriculture to conduct research and assist estate managers with technical advice (Drabble 1973).

As with Indonesian smallholders, the involvement of Malays in small-farm rubber growing occurred without active government support or encouragement. Rather, the reverse was the case. A basic rationale which the British offered for their rule was the position of "trusteeship" for Malays, whom they considered more suited to traditional economic pursuits, such as rice growing, rather than to producing commercial crops like rubber. When increasing numbers of Malays took to rubber cultivation, in many cases with a view to planting land and later selling it to non-indigenous interests, there was official concern that this loss of "ancestral" areas would deprive Malays of their only real asset. Various measures, including legislation, were taken to discourage Malay rubber-planting activities and to direct attention back towards food crop cultivation.

For both governments the post-war depression (1920-22) posed the dilemma of whether to restrict the volume of exports, in an attempt to raise world prices, or to stay clear and allow the market forces to operate in a "survival of the fittest" contest with Indonesia and Malaya as the main protagonists (Drabble 1981). The government of Malaya, and its metropolitan superior in Britain, were swayed to some degree by the arguments of corporate interests that rubber was now too vital to the economy to be abandoned to such a struggle, and accordingly they implemented the Stevenson Scheme (1922-28). The Dutch declined to participate in this scheme, but after the Great Depression (1929-32) they agreed to sign the International Rubber Regulation Agreement (1934-42). Both governments had by then come full circle from their initial development stance (as far as estates were concerned) to a position which Rudner (1981) has characterised as "custodial." This attempted to preserve the *status quo*, and particularly to check the further expansion of the smallholder sector (Bauer 1948, pp.214-15).

Comparative Experiences

In comparing the role of government in Indonesia and Malaya, it is helpful to focus on certain crucial policy areas where major similarities and differences between the two countries can be examined in more detail.

Land. The easy availability of land on favourable terms was vital to estate development in both countries (Voon 1976). In Java the substantial "wastelands," to which neither private persons nor local communities had established property rights, came under government jurisdiction through the Agrarian Law of 1870. These lands were made available largely to European estate enterprises under long leases at charges amounting to one to two per cent of total development costs (Aken 1923). On the East Coast, agricultural concessions were secured with government approval directly from local rulers under similar but slightly more expensive and less uniform conditions (Pelzer 1978, p.78). In Malaya the colonial government alienated large blocks of estates on very long term leases, at charges of three to four per cent. In both colonies, the land administration appears to have facilitated speedy processing, and to have permitted extensive alienation when demand was high.

The colonies were not so similar in respect of smallholder rubber development. In Java almost no smallholder rubber emerged, for the unused "wastelands" were in practice reserved for estate enterprises. On the East Coast, the demands of local European planters for more land were largely conceded by the government with the result that smallholdings were confined to the unwanted "fringes" of estate cultivation (Pelzer 1978, p.88). Continuing resentment and sporadic unrest were generated by "the half century of injustice" resulting from such policies (van Vollenhoven 1932, pp.83-90). The great majority of smallholding development took place in regions of East Sumatra well away from the estates, and in other parts of Sumatra and Kalimantan where serious estate expansion was not envisaged (Table 9.3). In these areas the customary system of effective occupancy and use as the basis of land tenure was applied; this made planting possible for all indigenous peoples prepared to put in the necessary effort. The Chinese, however, were not permitted to develop land in this way.

In Malaya, in contrast, the land administration provided specifically for the indigenous population, who could hold blocks of less than four hectares under a heritable and saleable title, also usable as a security for loans. Land rents were low, although somewhat higher than those applicable to estates. These titles were taken up by both Malays and Chinese, and were a major element in smallholder land ownership. While numerous cases of discrimination against intending rubber smallholders certainly existed, and have been well documented by Lim (1977), the intertwining pattern of estate and smallholding lands outside the earliest plantation areas in modern Malaysia shows that this discrimination was minor compared with that in Indonesia.

A further distinguishing element in the Malayan situation was the government "trusteeship" role. This led to "no rubber" conditions being specified in some titles, and later to the Malay Reservations Enactment (1913) which set aside certain areas as reserves where Malays could hold land, and where charges were fixed differentially to favour crops other than rubber. While this legislation was largely successful in preserving the designated lands for Malays, it did not prevent them from planting highly profitable rubber. Accordingly, they came to own about half the rubber smallholdings, but considerably less than half the rubber smallholding area (Malaya 1954). The balance was mainly held by Chinese.

In Indonesia, and especially in Sumatra, land was easy to obtain until the early 1930s, when new planting was banned under the conditions of the International Rubber Regulation Agreement. In Malaya all alienation of land for rubber was prohibited in 1930, although estates in particular were able to continue rubber establishment for somewhat longer in unplanted reserves.

Labour. The availability of labour was also basic to successful development, for rubber is one of the more labour-intensive perennial crops. The labour requirements of estates were swelled in the early years by their grossly inefficient utilization of labour, a result of both the primitive technology then extant and the frequent need to duplicate labour forces to allow for losses through malaria (Barlow and Jayasuriya 1984). While estates in Java could secure their labour from the impoverished local populations, those in Sumatra and Malaya had to import workers from outside, since indigenous locals would not work on plantations. These locals derived a better living from their land-extensive agriculture than they would have from estate wages, and they certainly enjoyed much freer lifestyles. Later when they began producing rubber themselves, their cash returns were also far higher than estate wages. The estate labour imported to the East Coast came first from China and then increasingly from cheaper sources in Java. Malayan estates relied heavily on migrants from India, and to a lesser extent on Chinese and Javanese workers.

The rubber estates in Java faced little official intervention in labour recruitment, except in prohibiting any form of contract labour. Wages were set freely by negotiation, with most labour resident in nearby villages off the estates, and often engaged in supplementary activities on its own lands. This paralleled the situation in other Javanese plantation enterprises, and reflected an earlier policy of allowing small farmers to operate freely in their own sphere, as well as to take advantage of relevant commercial opportunities.

Both on the East Coast of Sumatra and in Malaya, however, government intervention was considerable. On the East Coast, the notorious "penal sanction system" of indentured labour remained predominant until the early 1930s. This involved severe punishment of workers who violated their contracts and caused such a storm of protest in Holland in the early 1900s that the colonial government was forced to regulate working conditions (Figart 1925; Thee 1977). In 1907 a Labour Inspectorate was set up, but although it achieved progressive improvement, conditions still remained primitive. The unsatisfactory nature of recruitment by individual companies, where the "crimping" of labour before fulfillment of contract was quite common, led to government supervision of the recruiting process and to the formation of the Java Immigration Bureau (1912) to coordinate recruitment and further improve worker conditions. The Bureau also helped arrange repatriation of many workers during the depressed conditions of the 1920s. It is significant, however, that government did not abolish either the indenture system or the penal sanction, for fear that this might severely reduce the availability of labour. Thus Thee (1977) argued that without the indenture system East Coast rubber development would have been impossible, since it could not have drawn on an adequate supply of voluntary immigrants. Such "free" workers formed only about five per cent of the total up to the early 1920s.

In Malaya, the Tamils recruited to estates from the British-administered area of South India were largely secured by special recruiters or "Kanganis" in an official Indian Immigration Committee system. This operated successfully from 1908 and was organized in a similar fashion to the Java Immigration Bureau. Unlike the latter, however, it landed immigrants in Malaya "free of all debt." The indenture system had been dominant in earlier years when it was used especially to obtain workers for the unpleasant conditions on the sugar plantations. It had been entirely abolished in 1910 as a result of metropolitan pressures. A considerable number of free immigrants came to Malaya under their own arrangements. The real wages and conditions of Malayan plantation workers were much better than those of their counterparts in Java (Netherlands East Indies 1941; Parmer 1960), and far above those of the "cheap" indentured labour on the East Coast. Yet the general conditions of plantation labour remained poor, and various official welfare provisions were made from an early stage.

It is noteworthy that some Javanese estate workers chose to stay on East Coast plantations as free labourers after serving their indentures, and that growing numbers became locally domiciled; subsequently their children also joined the estate work force (Hugo 1980). Indeed, such families sometimes moved into smallholding cultivation, especially after the retrenchments of the Great Depression when they were offered land near plantations. Such smallholders were influential in improving rubber management. Similar trends occurred in Malaya where the Chinese, who always preferred their own independent settlements outside estates, moved into smallholdings in large numbers. Autonomous migrants, particularly from Java, also entered both the Outer Islands and Malaya to open up smallholdings, and they were especially important in facilitating expansion in the boom period (Tunku Shamsul Bahrin 1965).

Infrastructures. Access to markets was naturally essential for all rubber producers and a major factor in the location of planting in Sumatra and Malaya. In Java, where communications were generally much better, location was determined more by other features, including the availability of wasteland and character of the soil. Some earlier rubber plantations on the East Coast were situated near rivers navigable to the sea, but the extension by a private company of the Deli railway system, originally established to serve the tobacco plantations, provided an important artery to the ports (Schadee 1918). The 200-kilometre belt of rubber planted along this line is evident today. Most early roads were built by plantation companies, and apart from the main North-South highway, little new construction was effected by government until the late 1920s. Substantial expenditures were thus incurred by the East Coast developers on infrastructures, but they were subsequently rewarded by excellent returns. In contrast to the estates, the great majority of Outer Islands smallholdings had no means of access except by navigable rivers, which therefore determined their location, a situation which persists to the present.

In Malaya, both estates and smallholdings were situated along roads and railways, which were first established to serve the tin mines. Later they were extended by government into what became, by 1910, was a well-spread network throughout the western areas (Ooi 1963). Official action in the development of infrastructure was thus far more direct and important in Malaya than in Indonesia. While this work was facilitated by higher tax revenues from tin, and later from rubber, during the period to 1915, it also reveals a more positive approach on the part of the British colonial government to promoting development.

Technology. Both governments placed early emphasis on improving rubber technology following the introduction of seeds, but they promoted this development in rather different ways. In Indonesia attempts were made from the 1890s through the *Cultuurtuin* at the Buitenzorg (now Bogor) Botanic Gardens to improve yield capacity through importing further South American material and selecting better yielding trees as seed sources. In 1916 the first commercially applicable method of "bud grafting" or vegetative propagation was developed and, by directly doubling the previous feasible yield, this still remains the biggest single advance ever made in rubber production technology. These highly important but limited government efforts were increasingly complemented after 1910 by private company research. Beginning in 1916 two major "cooperative" experimental groups were financed by the corporate plantations, and coordinated under one body with government representation.[6] The experimental groups had excellent rapport and contact with their sponsoring companies and estates, and the high quality and commercial applicability of their work has been documented by Dijkman (1951). There was, however, almost no interaction with the small-holder sector, except through a very small extension service organised by government in the mid-1930s.

In Malaya, the early development of tapping techniques and then of processing technology through the government-sponsored Botanic Gardens in Singapore was a major spur to the early establishment of commercial plantations (Wycherley 1959), but there was far less stress on improving yield capacity than in Indonesia. This difference continued after most rubber research passed to a new Federated Malay States Agricultural Department in 1905. Several private European estate groups also funded their own research organisations, which worked on "commercial" applications as opposed to what many planters regarded as the unduly experimental activities of the Department. Indeed, advances in the all-important area of plant breeding were essentially left to private groups, and especially to one particular planter who enthusiastically followed up the work at Buitenzorg (Gough 1927). In general, and apart from its vigorous start, the quality and applicability of rubber research in Malaya was well below that in Indonesia, and work was further slowed by the absence of many scientists during the First World War. Although most officially and privately sponsored work was combined after 1926 in the Rubber Research Institute of Malaya, which was financed through a special rubber export tax, this seems to have made relatively little impact up to 1940 (Rubber Research Institute of Malaya 1931-41). Yet while Bauer (1948, p.276) also criticised the work of the Institute for its extensive preoccupation with estates, a substantial smallholders' advisory staff assisted by village demonstrators was at least in place by 1940 (Rubber Research Institute of Malaya 1950).

From the late 1920's new developments in technology were increasingly adopted by estates in both countries. By 1940, thirty-six per cent of the estate area in Indonesia had been planted with new budded rubbers, and about half this area was just commencing production (McFadyean 1944). In Malaya, twenty per cent of the estate area was under such trees. These very different national figures are good guides to the relative innovation achieved. On the other hand only one or two per cent of smallholdings in each country were under the newly bred varieties; these were mainly in large parcels and resulted from special circumstances. The productive techniques of smallholders nonetheless improved over time, most notably in areas close to estates in North Sumatra and Western Malaya.

Regulation. We have already seen that regulating rubber supply so as to increase its price emerged as quite an early concern, but it was practiced more by the British than by the Dutch. The Stevenson scheme imposed output quotas on Malaya and Ceylon, which contributed about seventy per cent of world production in 1921 (Rowe 1931; Whittlesey 1931). The scheme also received voluntary support from British estates in Indonesia.

There were several reasons why Indonesian government did not participate in the Stevenson arrangements. One was the prevailing official belief in *laissez-faire*, which was shared by many Dutch plantation companies. In addition, there was hesitancy over imposing restrictions on vast tracts of smallholder plantings, both in the absence of tenure records and in the face of growing political opposition to the colonial authorities. Neither of these considerations was important in Malaya, where smallholding output quotas were actually set at an unfairly low level in relation to previous production (Lim 1977). It is also pertinent that rubber was of greater overall significance to the Malayan than to the Indonesian economy, so that short-term dislocations from low rubber prices posed a far more serious threat.

In the event, Indonesia benefited greatly from the general British output restriction, and when demand recovered in the mid-1920s (Figure 9.1), the Dutch colony was able to take up the slack with large increases in production and planted area. The smallholdings of the Outer Islands were particularly stimulated, and increased about sevenfold in extent between 1920 and 1930 (Table 9.1). For several years during the Stevenson scheme, output from Indonesia approached the (restricted) output of Malaya (Table 9.5), and by 1928 the share of the British producing areas had declined to fifty-six per cent of world production.

The Great Depression (1929-32) and the dramatic associated decline in prices helped to change the previous Dutch attitude towards restriction. It now became apparent to both officialdom and planters that production capacity was already too high, that it would be further increased when earlier plantings came to maturity, and that continued expansion could cause worse problems. In this context the smallholder sector, with its obviously low production costs, could be seen as a major competitive threat to the estates, especially when regarded *en masse* in its unknown real capacity. In fact, the smallholders with their low fixed costs and alternative food producing activities were able to reduce production during the depression much more than the East Coast estates with their high overheads (Table 9.5). For the latter, labour costs were difficult to reduce since,

TABLE 9.5 Rubber Production in Indonesia and Malaya, 1922-33

('000 tons)

	Indonesia			Malaya
	East Coast			
Year	Estates[a]	Smallholdings[a]	Total[b]	Total
1922	n.a.	n.a.	89	216
1923	n.a.	n.a.	118	187
1924	n.a.	n.a.	147	155
1925	55	15	192	213
1926	55	14	202	291
1927	62	17	231	246
1928	68	19	232	304
1929	72	22	263	464
1930	72	16	246	456
1931	84	16	261	439
1932	82	9	215	422
1933	88	21	287	465

[a]Rubber "exports" rather than production.

[b]Including the production of all Indonesian estates and smallholdings (i.e. also taking in those of Java).

Sources: Eastcoast data: Thee (1977)
Indonesian total: C.E.I. Vol. 1, Table 10
Malayan data: Malaya (1932-41)

although workers were expensive to retain, they were also expensive to repatriate (Thee 1977).

Despite some recovery in price, the Dutch metropolitan authorities finally agreed to enter the International Rubber Regulation Agreement. This restricted output to agreed national quotas, banned further new planting except for a short period in 1939-40, and severely limited replanting in an arrangement which covered about ninety-eight per cent of all world production capacity (McFadyean 1944). While an impossibly low quota for Indonesian smallholdings was subsequently revised upwards, there is no doubt that the heavy *ad valorem* tax required to depress smallholding output to even the revised quota level severely penalized this sector in relation to the estates (Bauer 1948). The ban on new planting also stopped the smallholders' previous low-cost expansion of planted area, which was to have been their means of generating future income. Although estate production was not reduced so significantly, the virtual freezing of output by individual quotas tended to preserve the relative position of high and low cost producers, and to discourage technical progress. The Agreement also encouraged early synthetic rubber production in industrial countries.

In Malaya, the basic perspective of using control to deal with over-capacity still remained after the Stevenson scheme, especially with the massive burgeoning of Indonesian smallholdings. There was also concern over the rising area of local smallholdings, and this was heightened by perception of the tradeoff between producing rubber and food (Whitford 1931). With the Depression, the government's attitude that rubber plantings were now sufficient was reflected in its 1930 ban on further land alienation to rubber. At the metropolitan level, British interests were active in encouraging the still reluctant Dutch to enter the International Agreement. When restriction finally began, the production of local smallholdings was again under-assessed in relation to that of estates (Bauer 1948, pp.209-13; Lim 1977). The much longer period of restriction in Malaya delayed economic adjustment more severely than in Indonesia, and partly explained the lower rate of technical progress on estates.

Taxation. Further differences between the colonial governments appeared in taxation policies. In Indonesia the major tax on rubber producers until the 1930s was on plantation company profits. Although this tax was only around ten per cent, it was obviously regarded as heavy both in comparison to the general levels of company taxation prevailing at the time and in relation to other rubber-producing countries (Figart 1925). There were also small taxes associated with the acquisition of land rights by plantations. On the other hand, the large potential revenue from smallholder rubber was not exploited until the mid 1930s, for no export duty was imposed until then. Land taxes on smallholdings were impracticable, owing to the absence of cadastral surveys. In the 1930s, faced with even more severe financial problems, the government imposed a general *ad valorem* rubber export tax of five per cent. For the three years of the International Rubber Regulation Agreement, 1934-1936, a further "special tax" ranging up to fifty per cent of the average rubber price in the producing areas was also levied on smallholder production, in the vain attempt to cut it to the official quota (Bauer 1948, p.113). Despite this extraordinarily high assessment and the large revenues which accrued, little or no public expenditure was directed back towards the smallholder sector.

In Malaya, a 2.5-3.0 per cent export duty was levied on all rubber from the outset. Together with land premia and rents collected from rubber growers, this constituted a growing source of government revenue. Profit taxes were never imposed on rubber companies in Malaya, although the "sterling" estate companies were subject to them in the United Kingdom. The colonial government of Malaya appears to have been in a sound budgetary position up to the First World War, and despite later difficulties no further taxes were levied apart from a small cess to cover the costs of the new research facilities at the Rubber Research Institute of Malaya. While the much closer administrative control over Malayan smallholdings meant that taxation was never needed as a method of output control, few public expenditures were specifically directed towards this sector except in setting up the fledgling extension service in the late 1930s.

Conclusions

The emergence of the Indonesia and Malayan rubber industries was a major international economic development, in which the governments of both countries played important but differing roles. A striking feature of both industries was the emergence of two sectors—corporate estates and family smallholdings.

From the early 1900s, both governments approached rubber development with a pronounced bias towards corporate plantations as the mode of advance. Although the Indonesian government appeared far more attached to a *laissez-faire* approach to the industry, it nonetheless acted positively both to control and to facilitate plantation development, notably in the acquisition of land and labour and in generating appropriate technologies. It also favoured specifically European enterprises, and limited what might otherwise have been a much larger Chinese involvement. In the slump of the 1930s, government acted strongly albeit reluctantly in the International Rubber Regulation Agreement to control rubber output, especially from the smallholding sector where its action could be seen as discriminatory and a "custodial" attempt to preserve the *status quo*. In general, however, the Indonesian authorities completely ignored rubber smallholdings until the 1930s except insofar as they connived at efforts to keep them out of the plantations' way. They were neither assisted nor taxed, and the discrimination of the late 1930s may be seen largely as an act of desperation in face of unexpected output increases.

The government in Malaya was far more interventionist. With greater financial resources than its Indonesian counterpart, it moved vigorously to support rubber estate development, establishing relevant infrastructures itself and conducting most research in its own institutions. It also acted much sooner to control output, in an approach supported by the private corporate developers. The Malayan government again gave little positive assistance to rubber smallholders, but taxed them from the outset, and substantially underassessed their outputs during restriction. It nonetheless followed a land allocation and tenure system which had significant effects in establishing a mix of estates and smallholdings in most regions. In its "trusteeship" tradition it made special provision for Malay farmers, while attempting to discourage them from rubber cultivation. In Indonesia, despite the Ethical Policy, no such measures seem to have been considered in respect of Outer Islands farmers.

The policies of both governments seem to have benefitted estates through the early support measures, which were especially important in Malaya, but to have had adverse long term consequences through the "custodial" aspects of restriction. The earlier Malayan restriction of the 1920s caused much profitable expansion and technical progress to be sacrificed to the benefit of unencumbered producers of Indonesia. In addition, the Malayan policy of developing research under government auspices was less successful then the more direct private enterprise method used in Indonesia.

The extent to which government policies influenced the economic outcome for smallholders is less clear. The policies in Indonesia certainly accentuated the distinctness of the two emerging sectors, where the East Coast estates in particular formed a modern dynamic and technologically-advanced corporate plantation enclave. Thee (1977) has indicated the plantations' extensive overseas remittances of earnings and the absence of linkages with other local industrial activities. This enclave contrasted with the indigenous smallholdings which were located well away from the estates, and were adapting the potential of the new rubber seeds to their own relative resource endowments and traditional agriculture. Such separation was not nearly so marked in Malaya. There the land and tax policies of government, as well as the joint involvement of many small farmers in estates and other non-subsistence activities, were added to the advantage of a smaller geographical area in promoting linkages between the sectors and with the wider national economy.

It can nonetheless be asked whether the separating policies of the Indonesian government, and its lack of other supports, really disadvantaged the smallholdings as much as is sometimes suggested. The basic technology introduced by estates was soon transmitted to smallholdings, which right up to 1940 achieved average yields per hectare as high as, if not higher than, those of estates with much lower development costs. The Outer Islands rubber smallholdings expanded rapidly over time, and continued to do so again once restrictions were removed after the Second World War had ended. In the situation of the 1930s, the smallholdings in both the Indonesia and Malaya were still highly competitive with estates, as Bauer (1948) convincingly demonstrates. Thus, although the "cleavage" between the "foreign capitalist" and "primitive traditional" worlds suggested by Boeke (1953) certainly existed in the Indonesian rubber industry, Boeke was incorrect in suggesting that smallholdings were static, as Geertz and many others have also pointed out.

The key to this argument is partly in the underlying technology, which in the period to 1940 mainly comprised unselected rubber seedling materials easily adaptable to smallholding conditions and without economies of scale in production. Once modern high-yielding trees were introduced, however, complementary capital inputs and high managerial expertise were needed, and the position changed radically. At this stage the managerial hierarchy of large-scale estates, and their access to capital, began to have important advantages. The Indonesian estates, and to a lesser extent those in Malaya, had begun their move into high-yielding technology by 1940, but the economic effects of this were still barely perceptible.

Yet looking back from the situation of the 1980s, the perspective is different. The economic effects of new technologies on the estates of both countries, and Malayan smallholdings, have been important. On Indonesian smallholdings, whose remoteness has made it impossible for them to adjust independently and rendered government help very expensive, their effects have been negligible (Barlow and Muharminto 1982). It is a moot political question as to whether independent rubber smallholdings in Indonesia have any future role at all (Mubyarto 1983). In contrast, better adjustment has already been achieved in the smallholding sector of the more integrated Malayan economy, although significantly less in Malay reservation areas where change has been held at bay by the old 1913 tenure restrictions. While colonial governments alone were by no means wholly responsible for the dichotomy, their actions and inactions have made the rubber development problems of the present even more difficult.

Notes

1. The Malay Peninsula during this period was divided into the Straits Settlements (S.S.), Federated Malay States (F.M.S.), and the Unfederated Malay States (U.M.S.), collectively referred to as "British Malaya" or "Malaya." The latter term is used in this chapter.

2. In Indonesia, the dividing line between estates and "native" rubber holdings was drawn on legal grounds; estates had legal status as incorporated enterprises. In Malaya, estates were units above 40 hectares of planted rubber, and smallholdings those below this figure. Both "native" holdings and smallholdings were generally from one to five hectares, and were based on single farm families.
3. The swidden system in the Outer Islands was a form of shifting cultivation, in which the jungle was cleared and planted with rice. This was then succeeded by other crops over a two three year period, until land fertility was exhausted. Farmers then moved to another area and only returned to the same site after a long interval.
4. Between 1903 and 1912 about 260 sterling capital companies were floated to operate in Malaya (Drabble 1973).
5. A crude estimate of Gross National Income for the Federated Malay States shows a rise in the value of rubber exports from Straits $265 million in 1924 to $518 million in 1926 (Federated Malay States 1932).
6. One, under the General Association of Rubber Planters of the Sumatran East Coast (AVROS), was centred in Medan. The other, under the General Agricultural Syndicate (ALS), dealt with Java and the remaining areas, and was centred at Buitenzorg (Bogor).

CHAPTER TEN

The Evolution of Fiscal Policy and the Role of Government in the Colonial Economy

Anne Booth

Introduction

The aim of this chapter is to examine the economic impact of government on the economy of colonial Indonesia in the nineteenth and twentieth centuries, up to 1940. We begin with a brief survey of developments until 1903, when an act was passed in the Netherlands which clearly separated the finances of the home government from those of the colony. We then examine in greater detail developments in the first four decades of the twentieth century, looking at the evolution and impact of tax, expenditure and debt policy, as well as the wider issue of the growth of government intervention in the economy. We conclude with a comparison of the Indonesian experience with that of other colonial territories.

Colonial Fiscal Policy in the Nineteenth Century

In a survey of the Dutch colonial fiscal system published in 1900, Day divided the nineteenth century into three periods (Day 1900). The first of these, from 1800 to around 1830, was "a period of experimentation" but the experiments, most notably the British attempt to establish a uniform system of land taxation based on individual assessment, failed (Bastin 1954). After the termination of the British interregnum, the colony went through a period of "badly organised" financial administration, and by 1829 the accumulated government deficits came to 38 million guilders, rather more than twice the level of imports in that year (*C.E.I.* Vol.2, p.17). Most of the government expenditure at this time was for military purposes, although some military projects, such as road construction, could have had an important impact on the civilian economy.

In the second period, coinciding with the culture system, experimentation gave way to systematic exploitation, the main purpose of which was to secure as large a fiscal surplus as possible for remittance to the Netherlands. The indigenous cultivators were forced to grow specified products which were then taken by government agents and sold in the European market, the cultivators receiving little by way of payment. Day comments:

> Thanks to favouring conditions in the market, especially the rise in the price of coffee, the government secured a return much in excess of the costs of economic and political administration... . Expenditures, on the other hand, especially on items like education and the administration of justice, were reduced to a point that menaced the permanent welfare of the people. (Day 1900, p.77)

In terms of modern national income accounting, the balance of payments surplus (the difference between exports and imports) must equal the government surplus (the difference between government revenue and expenditure) plus the difference between private savings and investment:

$$(X - M) = (T - G) + (S - I)$$

In fact when we look at the data on the balance of commodity trade for Java between 1834 and 1875, and compare it with the fiscal balance (total revenues less total expenditures) we note that in most years the balance of commodity trade was much larger (Figure 10.1). It was only at the height of the cultivation system, in the late 1850s, when the fiscal surplus was around 40 per cent of exports, that the two moved close together. Of course, the balance of trade is only a rough approximation to X – M in that it ignores "invisible" outflows including transport and other costs of exporting, and remitted profits. To the extent that these items were negligible, the fact that the balance of commodity trade was larger than the fiscal balance over such a long period indicates that there must have been a substantial accumulation of private savings in Indonesia. It is much more plausible to argue that remitted profits on private account were far from negligible and probably accounted for most of the difference between the two balances.

Given the data deficiencies, macroeconomic accounting exercises for this era of Indonesia's colonial history will probably not prove very enlightening. We can, however, note that the evidence summarized in Figure 10.1 does suggest that not all the "drain" from Java which took place between 1835 and 1875 (during this forty-year period the budget balance was only once negative) was due to the government. Indeed, the data assembled by Creutzberg for the period 1846 to 1875 indicate that not all the net revenue accruing to government from the sale of products was in fact remitted home as a fiscal surplus (*C.E.I.* Vol.2, Tables 2 and 3). From the mid-1850s onwards the revenue surplus from sale of products considerably exceeded the overall fiscal surplus (Figure 10.2). Much of the revenue was spent in the colony, mainly on general administration and defence.

FIGURE 10.1 Commodity Trade Balance and Fiscal Balance, 1834–1873

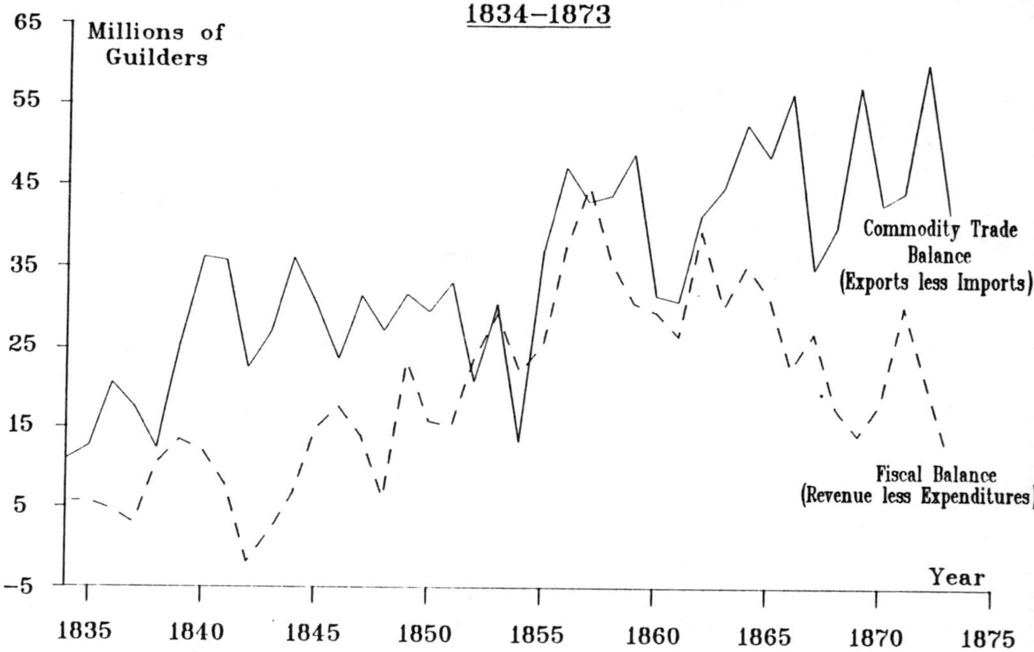

Sources: Fiscal balance: C.E.I. Vol. 2, Tables 2 and 3
Commodity trade: C.K.S. 160

FIGURE 10.2 Net Revenue Surplus and Fiscal Balance, 1846–1873

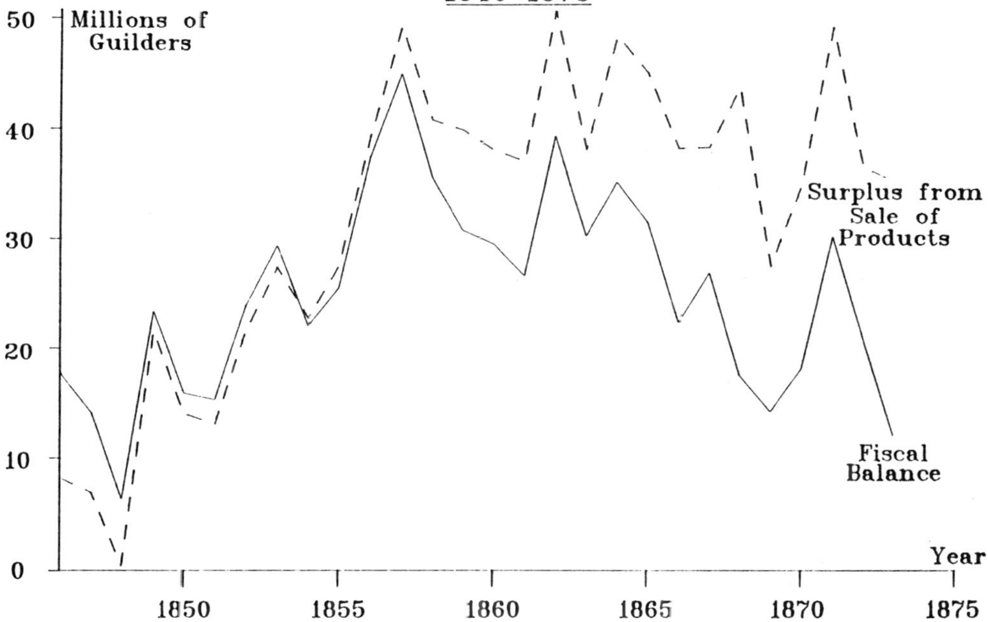

Source: Fiscal balance: C.E.I. Vol. 2, Tables 2 and 3
Net revenue surplus: C.E.I. Vol. 2, Table 3

Throughout the period of the Cultivation System, gross revenue from sale of products accounted for between 50 and 60 per cent of total revenues; the balance came from monopolies (salt and opium), the land tax, and export and import taxes. The land tax (*landrente*) was the most important single tax, although it never accounted for more than 12 per cent of total revenues, on average, in any decade (Table 10.1). At the height of the system, total expenditures amounted to only 70 per cent of gross receipts, although in the decade from 1866 to 1875 this figure jumped to 85 per cent, at least partly because of increased military expenditures (Table 10.1).

Because such a high proportion of total government revenue during the cultivation period was derived from products sold in the Netherlands, and because most of the government expenditure was made in the colony rather than in the Netherlands, the overall budgetary surpluses during the period between 1835 and 1875 were accompanied by large budgetary deficits within the colony. By the mid-1870s, these deficits were running at about 20 per cent of commodity exports; if we assume that commodity exports were about 15 per cent of national income by this time, then the domestic budgetary deficit was in the vicinity of three per cent of national income. A domestic deficit of this magnitude must have had some impact on domestic liquidity. The available evidence does indeed indicate a threefold increase in the value of coins and notes in circulation in the period from 1855/9 to 1875/9 (*C.E.I.* Vol.6, p.62). The inflationary impact of such an expansion in the domestic monetary base would depend in turn on the real growth rate of the economy and the rate of growth of monetization. Either or both could well have been rapid during this period.[1]

Day regards the outbreak of the Aceh War in 1873 as the major factor in bringing to an end the long era of colonial fiscal surpluses. However, the size of the overall budget surplus was already diminishing perceptibly in the late 1860s; this was due in part at least to a growth in non-military expenditures, particularly expenditures on so-called "utilities." As Creutzberg points out:

> Initially the utilities comprised only monopolies, and revenue from the cultivation on high authority. Postal services and the Government Printing Office were until 1867 still included under General Administration. After the introduction of the *Indische Comptabiliteitswet* (Public Accounts Act) the number of utilities increased; the railways, mining industry, and government agricultural estates then played a big role. (*C.E.I.* Vol.2, p.52)

These trends became more evident in the last three decades of the century when expenditures on what we would today consider "development" activities—in particular infrastructure and education—showed marked increases as a percentage of the total (Table 10.2), as did expenditures on pensions, the bulk of which were paid in the Netherlands. There was a steep decline in the proportion

TABLE 10.1 Revenue and Expenditure Components as a Percentage of Total Revenues

	1846-55	1856-65	1866-75
Land Tax	12	9	11
Trade Taxes	8	7	6
Revenue from Sale of Products	52	60	49
Revenue from Monopolies	15	15	15
Total Expenditures	75	70	85
Expenditure on Navy and Defence	17	19	26

Source: C.E.I. Vol. 2, Table 3.

TABLE 10.2 Percentage Breakdown of Budgetary Expenditures, 1871-95 (Budget Estimates)

	1871	1881	1895
Justice	4.2	4.4	4.9
Finance	7.8	8.9	11.7
Tax Collection	3.1	3.1	2.8
Pensions etc	3.6	4.4	7.6
Interior	45.3	32.0	22.9
Administration	7.3	6.4	9.2
Crops	30.1	19.7	6.0
Education	1.7	2.4	3.4
European	0.7	1.0	1.7
Native	0.3	0.8	1.0
Medical	0.8	1.3	1.6
Mines and Industry	4.6	4.2	6.1
Public Works	8.5	17.1	20.4
Railways	0.7	6.8	8.1
War	19.2	22.0	21.5
Navy	7.9	7.7	6.0
Interest	-	-	1.4
Total	100.0	100.0	100.0

Source: van den Berg (1895, Appendix D)

TABLE 10.3 Percentage Breakdown of Revenues, 1871-95

(Budget Estimates

	1871	1881	1895
Taxes	24.6	28.2	42.2
Landrente[a]	13.9	14.1	16.3
Customs and Excise	5.4	6.4	12.3
Tax on Trade and Professions:			
Natives	0.9	1.8	2.2
European	-	0.4	0.7
Head Tax on Natives	-	-	2.3
Government Monopolies	15.8	17.2	20.8
Opium	10.5	12.5	14.0
SALT	5.3	4.7	6.8
Sale of Government Produce	55.6	48.5	22.9
Coffee	32.9	38.2	16.3
Sugar	16.2	6.6	0.3
Quinine	-	0.1	0.1
Tin	6.3	3.5	5.0
Coal	0.1	0.1	1.2
Railways	"	1.7	7.6
Other Revenues	4.0	4.4	6.5
Total	100.0	100.0	100.0

[a]Including land and house tax

Source: van den Berg (1895, Appendix C)

of expenditures devoted to the cultivation and selling of export crops, in turn reflecting the decline in the proportion of revenues derived from this source (Table 10.3). By 1895 revenues from taxation amounted to over 40 per cent of total revenues, although the proportion of government expenditure devoted to tax collection appears to have fallen slightly. Certainly, taxes were a much "cheaper" source of government revenue, in terms of collection costs, than revenues from sale of produce.

Between 1876 and 1899 the budget was in surplus in only six years; in order to finance the deficits, loans were contracted by the Department of Colonies from the Netherlands Department of Finance. As the century closed these loans grew considerably; in 1898 a law was passed in the Netherlands authorising a loan of 57.8 million guilders, a sum equal to almost 40 per cent of budgetary expenditures in that year. Interest and debt repayment charges in 1900 amounted to 4.3 million guilders, about three per cent of budgetary expenditures (Day 1900, pp.97-98).

Day has claimed that the changes in colonial fiscal policy which occurred between 1870 and 1900 amounted to "nothing less than a revolution" (Day 1904, p.388); while this might seem something of an exaggeration, there can be no doubt that public expenditures in Indonesia did show substantial real growth in the period from 1870 to 1900 (Figure 10.3). But it should also be noted that most of this real growth took place in the 1870s and early 1880s; after 1885 real levels of *domestic* expenditures, in particular, showed some decline, recovering again only in the late 1890s. Indeed, when we survey the growth in real public expenditures (both total and domestic) in the period 1848 to 1913, it is possible to detect four phases. From 1848 to 1866 there was little sustained growth; from 1867 through to 1885 there was sustained growth with some fluctuations; from 1886 to 1894 there was some decline, while in the period from 1896 to 1913 real levels of public expenditure almost doubled. We return to the causes of these fluctuations in real government expenditures, and their consequences, in the final section of the chapter.

Developments in the Twentieth Century

The last four decades of Dutch colonial rule in Indonesia were marked by a number of changes in revenue and expenditure policies, in debt policy and, more broadly, in the role of government in the economy. These changes were accompanied by a number of innovations in government accounting procedures, which make direct comparison of twentieth century data with those from earlier decades difficult. We have already referred to the 1903 Act which "clearly separated the finances of the Kingdom in Europe and the Netherlands Indies by withdrawing provisions relating to the transfer of Netherlands Indies' remit-

FIGURE 10.3 Growth of Real Government Expenditures, 1848–1913[a]

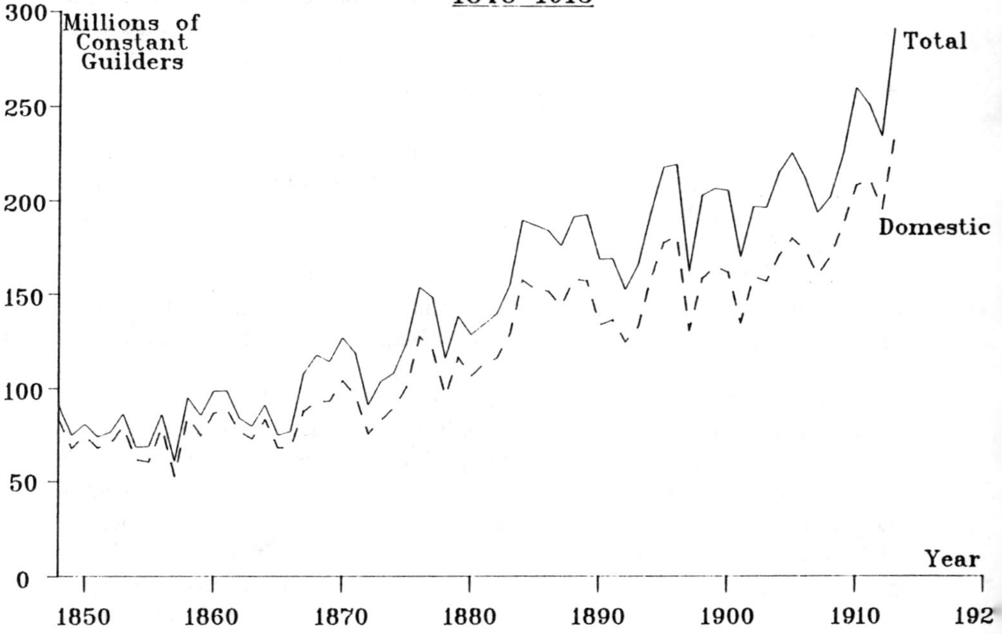

[a] The rice price index (C.E.I., Vol. 4, Table 1) has been used as a deflator to produce the real expenditure series.

Source: C.E.I. Vol. 2, Tables 3 and 4

tances to the Kingdom in Europe" (Creutzberg 1972, p.xxi). A second change involved the distinction, first introduced in 1907, between ordinary and extraordinary government expenditures; the former were meant to refer to routine government activities while the latter were expenditures on durable assets. This distinction changed over time, with the result that the data are not comparable without some adjustments (*C.E.I.* Vol.2, pp.32ff).

A third change seriously affecting the comparability of the public accounts in the inter-war years stemmed from the introduction of the *Indische Bedrijvenwet* in 1927. This was a set of accounting rules applied from 1930 onwards to a number of public utilities and government enterprises. As a result of these rules, total revenues and expenditures of utilities and enterprises were no longer listed separately in the government accounts but netted out, with only the surplus or deficit being included. Even before the introduction of these rules, in the early 1920s, the official yearbooks began to give summaries of "net" revenues and expenses defined as the revenues from sale of products and monopolies net of all expenses incurred in these operations. The effect of this change was to increase the apparent proportion of all government revenues accruing from taxation (*C.E.I.* Vol.2, p.29).

A further problem concerns the increase in both the number and the financial responsibilities of local government. Creutzberg has pointed out that after 1905 the financial transactions of the lower levels of government should be added to those of the centre to ensure comparability with earlier years. In addition, the finances of the so-called principalities, both in Java and elsewhere, were given separately from those of the directly-governed territories. As this was always the case it does not affect comparability over time, but it does mean that the published data do not have complete national coverage. As both the local authorities and the principalities entered on a period of financial expansion in the 1920s, the central government statistics became over time "less and less representative of the revenue and expenditure of the government in general" (*C.E.I.* Vol.2, p.60).

The official yearbooks for the 1920s and 1930s give an "historical survey" of central government revenues and expenditures back to the mid-1860s; the data for the nineteenth century were adjusted upwards to include expenditures on all fixed assets so that the series is comparable over time. However, as Creutzberg has pointed out, this series does tend to exaggerate the size of both revenues and expenditures because of the double-entry book-keeping methods used. Creutzberg has produced a set of amended estimates which endeavour to show trends in the size of the public sector between 1900 and 1939, where public sector transactions are defined as all financial flows between government instrumentalities and third parties (*C.E.I.* Vol.2, p.29ff. and p.60ff.).

Creutzberg's amended series indicates a marked jump in the money value of both central government revenues and expenditures in the period between 1913 and 1921, although that was in part due to the wartime and post-war spurt of inflation (Figure 10.4). During the 1920s and early 1930s, the level of prices in Indonesia continually fell; while the index of government revenue and expenditures also fell, the rate of decline was not as steep, implying that their real values grew. By 1939, when the retail price index was back at 1913 levels, the revenue index had gained 72 per cent and the expenditure index 96 per cent (Figure 10.4).

From 1921 onwards, we can use Polak's national income estimates to examine both revenue and expenditure growth in relation to growth of national income. As a proportion of national income, government expenditure reached a peak of almost 25 per cent in 1933, and then declined to about 19 per cent by the end of the decade. The gap between revenue and expenditure also reached a peak in 1933, when it was almost eight per cent of national income (Figure 10.5). Tax revenues as a proportion of all government revenues rose steadily throughout the period, although they equalled only about 50 per cent of central government expenditures by the end of the 1930s (*C.E.I.* Vol.2 Table 4).

The data assembled by Creutzberg thus suggest a substantial increase in the real value of both government expenditures and revenues in the period from 1913 to 1940, a growth in tax revenues as a proportion of total revenues, and a growth in the size of the budget deficit, especially in the 1930s. Used in conjunction with Polak's national income data, they also suggest that government expenditure reached a peak of 25 per cent of national income in 1933, apparently a much higher percentage than prevailed in, for example, India, at the same time. We turn now to examine in more detail trends in revenue and expenditure patterns, and debt policy, before attempting a comparison of colonial Indonesian fiscal policies with those of other parts of colonial Asia.

Revenue Policy. We saw in the previous section that the proportion of government revenues accruing from taxation rose during the last three decades of the nineteenth century (Table 10.3). Creutzberg's adjusted series for the first four decades of the twentieth century shows a continual growth in the proportion of tax revenues to total revenues, from 38 per cent in 1900 to 63 per cent in 1939. By the late 1930s tax revenues equalled about 10 per cent of national income (Figure 10.5). This increase in the relative importance of tax to total revenues at the expense of revenues from monopolies and sale of products, was accompanied by a change in the composition of tax revenues. The share contributed by *landrente* (the tax on agricultural land owned by the indigenous population) and the capitation tax fell, while that contributed by excises and income tax rose (Table 10.4).

FIGURE 10.4 Index of Expenditures, Revenues and Prices, 1913–1939

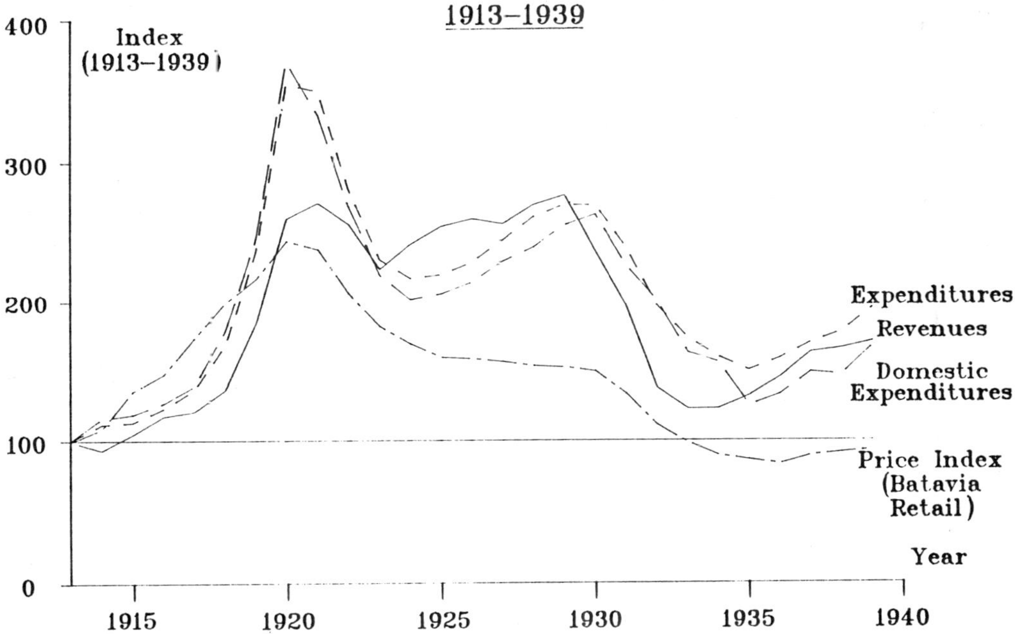

Sources: C.E.I. Vol. 2, Table 3
Retail price index: C.K.S. 146, p.41

FIGURE 10.5 Revenues, Expenditure and Taxes as a Percentage of National Income, 1921–39

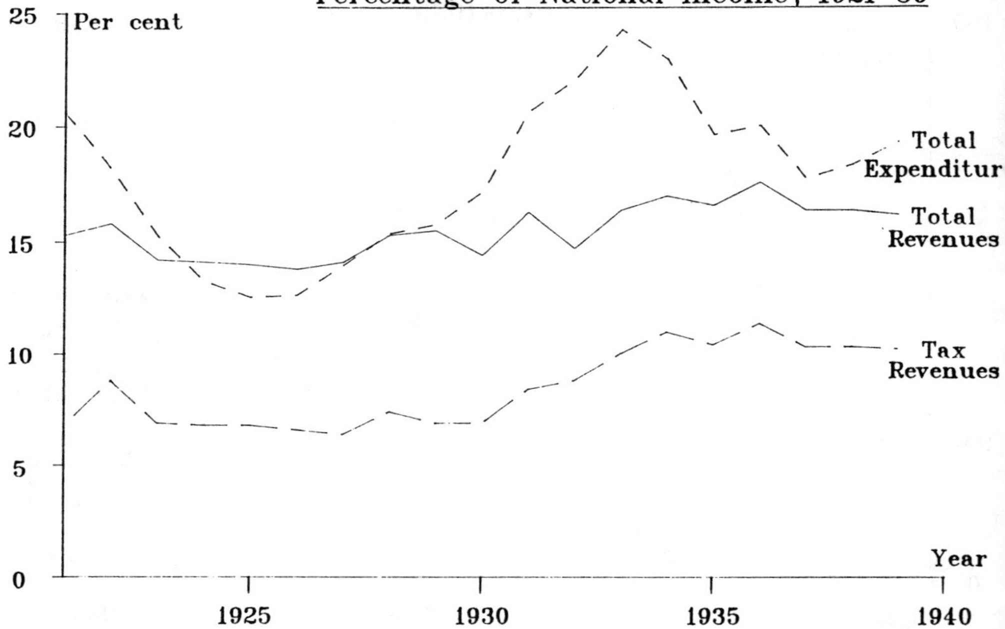

Sources: C.E.I. Vol. 2, Table 3
C.E.I. Vol. 5, p.70

TABLE 10.4 Percentage Breakdown of Tax Revenues, 1912/16 and 1936/40

	1912/16	1936/40
Import Duties)	25.2	17.9
Export Taxes)		11.6
Excises	11.1	21.9
Income Tax	21.8	
Personal	n.a.	18.9
Corporate	n.a.	11.7
Verponding[a]	3.0	1.7
Stamp Duties	3.5	2.7
Slaughter Taxes	2.4	1.5
Landrente[b]	20.4	7.7
Capitation Taxes	5.9	-
Personal Taxes	1.6	1.3
Other	5.1	3.1
Total	100.0	100.0

[a]Urban property tax
[b]Rural land tax

Sources: Jaarcijfers (1921, pp.114-5); Central Bureau of Statistics (1941, Table 194)

TABLE 10.5 Percentage Breakdown of Budgetary Expenditures, 1905-21

	1905	1913	1921[a]
Justice	4.5	3.2	2.3
Finance	17.5	19.6	17.0
Pensions	8.3	5.6	4.7
Interior	20.1	12.2	9.8
Administration	7.9	3.8	1.8
Crops	4.0	"	"
Education	3.7	4.1	3.5
European	2.0	1.7	n.a.
Native	1.1	1.9	n.a.
Medical	1.7	1.9	1.7
Mines/Industry	7.5	3.4	2.5
Public Works[b]	18.5	37.7	39.2
Railways	8.9	11.3	16.4
War Department	21.7	12.3	11.5
Navy Department	5.6	5.6	4.4
Other	"	"	8.1
Total	100.0	100.0	100.0

[a]Provisional figures.
[b]Includes expenditures on roads, bridges, public buildings, irrigation works, and government enterprises including railways and post and telegraphs.

Source: *Jaarcijfers*, various issues.

The issue of the burden of taxation and other government imposts such as corvée labour on the indigenous population was of great concern to colonial authorities during the last four decades of Dutch rule, and several enquiries were carried out. At first sight it might appear that the changes which took place in the composition of revenues, and in particular the trend towards income and excise taxes and away from land and capitation taxes, would have made the overall tax burden more equitable since the former fell on the relatively better-off members of both the indigenous and non-indigenous populations. For example, excises were mainly on goods such as petroleum, matches, processed tobacco, and sugar which were consumed largely by the urban middle classes, and the rural elites. However, it should also be noted that, although revenues from the native land tax fell, both absolutely and as a proportion of total revenue, indigenous incomes were falling even faster in the early 1930s, with the result that the burden of taxation on indigenous incomes increased during the depression years.[2]

Expenditure Trends. We have already drawn attention to the changes which took place in the allocation of government expenditures between 1871 and 1895 (Table 10.2); further important changes took place in the first two decades of the twentieth century. Broadly these changes involved declines in the percentage share of total government expenditure taken by administration (including expenditures on the procurement of crops which had accounted for almost one third of the budget in 1871 and which had become negligible by 1921), by military expenditures, and a very marked increase in the share of public works (Table 10.5). Public works expenditures included expenditures on buildings, roads, bridges, irrigation works, port facilities, and government enterprises, of which the railways and post and telegraph facilities were the most important. The railways alone accounted for 16 per cent of all government expenditure by 1921.[3]

Not only were there important changes in the composition of government expenditures during the first two decades of this century, but also expenditures as a whole rose rapidly in real terms. The amended Creutzberg series shows a doubling in nominal expenditures between 1900 and 1913; in real terms (deflated by the rice price index), expenditures rose by about 41 per cent or 4.6 per cent per annum (Figure 10.3). After 1913 we can compare the growth in government expenditures with the Batavia retail price index; it is clear that the expenditure growth which occurred between 1913 and 1918 was more than offset by rising prices but after that expenditure growth outstripped the rise in the price index (Figure 10.4). We have already noted that, while the Batavia retail price index was back at 1913 levels by the late 1930s, the index of government expenditures was almost twice that of 1913. However, the index of domestic government expenditures (i.e. expenditures made within the colony) was only 68 per cent above 1913 levels in 1939, because of the increasing share of external expenditures in the total.

How can we explain the growth in real public expenditures which occurred during the period 1900-1940 in Indonesia, and especially the growth which occurred in the first two decades of the century? First, we should note that the period from 1900 to 1913 was almost certainly one of quite rapidly rising income. According to the estimates published by Zimmerman, which in turn were based on unpublished work of Egbert de Vries, per capita income in real terms rose at over two per cent per annum during this period (Zimmerman 1962). If population was growing at 1.5 per cent per annum, then real national income must have been growing at about 3.5 per cent per annum. Even so, real growth in public expenditure of almost five per cent per annum implies some increase in the ratio of government expenditure to national income over the period.

The second factor involved in the growth of public expenditures during this period was the implementation of the "ethical policy," with its emphasis on improving indigenous living standards through more systematic provision of education and infrastructure. This emphasis was undoubtedly one reason for the increase in the proportion of government expenditure devoted to public works.[4] At the same time it seems likely that changes in government policy priorities could not have led to rapidly rising real levels of government expenditure in the absence of faster rates of overall growth, which were in turn due to more buoyant demand conditions in world markets for Indonesia's leading exports. To some extent growth in real levels of expenditure were the consequence of growth in real revenues, which were in turn due to faster rates of growth of real output. We explore this issue further in the concluding section.

Government expenditure continued to grow in real terms in the inter-war period; however, as a proportion of national income it fell in the mid-1920s, and rose in the 1930s (Figure 10.5). Because of the changes in government accounting procedures already alluded to, it is difficult to produce figures on the expenditure breakdown after 1921 which are comparable to those given in Table 10.5. The amended series of public expenditures prepared by Creutzberg for the period 1900-40 shows that extraordinary or capital expenditures fell rapidly, as a proportion of total expenditures, through the 1920s, and all but disappeared after 1932. By the end of the 1930s, expenditures on the navy and defence had risen to over 30 per cent of the total, only slightly lower than the percentage in 1900 (Figure 10.6).

Overall, the share of government in total expenditure on the creation of fixed assets in the economy up to 1940 was quite minor. Creutzberg has produced a series for the period 1910-39, which indicates that the government share reached a maximum of 25 per cent in 1921, and thereafter fell quite rapidly (*C.E.I.* Vol.3, Table 1 & Graph 1). Although Creutzberg's data may understate the

FIGURE 10.6 Defence, Debt Service and Extraordinary Expenditures as a Percentage of Total Expenditures, 1900–1940

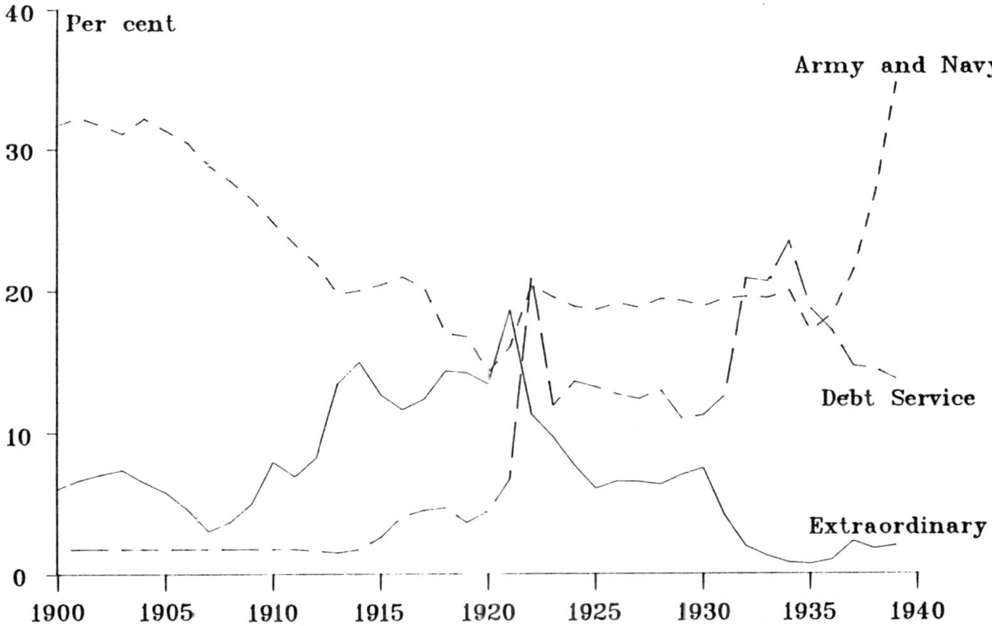

Source: C.E.I. Vol. 2, Table 4

role of public sector capital formation, the point that most capital formation in the colonial economy was carried out in the private corporate sector seems indisputable.

Budgetary Deficits and Debt Policy. We have already noted how the persistent budgetary deficits of the last decades of the nineteenth century necessitated loans from the Netherlands Department of Finance to the Department of the Colonies. A major aim of the legislation separating the financial administration of Indonesia from the Netherlands was to enable the colony to negotiate loans on its own account, although any loans thus concluded still had to be approved by the States-General in the Netherlands. In fact, the improvement in the colony's economic performance between 1900 and the outbreak of the First World War meant that revenue performance exceeded expectations, while the conclusion of the war in Aceh led to a decline in defence expenditures as a percentage of total expenditures. Although the overall budget balance was positive in only four years, the deficits were not very large in relation to total revenues and it was not until 1915 that new loans were contracted by the Indies government using the powers granted them in 1905 (*C.E.I.* Vol.2, Table 6).

Between 1915 and 1923 sixteen public loans were raised by the colonial government. The first of these were issued by a consortium of Amsterdam bankers, but as successive flotations in the Netherlands were undersubscribed, further loans were raised in both New York and London. Between 1923 and 1929 no new loans were raised, although the colonial government took advantage of lower interest rates prevailing on world capital markets over this period to convert some existing loans. As the size of the overall budget deficit grew again in the 1930s, further loans were negotiated. Although in nominal terms these loans were no larger than those negotiated during and immediately after the First World War, the declining price level meant that the real value of both principal and debt servicing charges increased substantially.

From 1921 onwards, we can use Polak's data to trace the growth of the overall budget deficit, public sector borrowing and debt charges in relation to changes in national income. In 1921 the overall deficit amounted to about five per cent of national income; at that time the accumulated public debt was roughly 23 per cent of national income and debt service charges (interest and repayment) amounted to 1.4 per cent of national income and 5.7 per cent of commodity exports (Table 10.6). As the decade of the 1920s progressed, the overall budget deficit fell and by 1925 had turned into a slight surplus; the total debt outstanding as a proportion of national income also fell after reaching a peak in 1923. As the depression worsened in the 1930s, the budget deficit grew rapidly in relation to national income; the resulting borrowing led to an increase in both public debt outstanding and debt servicing in relation to national income.

It is difficult to ascertain from the available evidence exactly what proportion of the total public debt was held in Indonesia, and what proportion was held abroad. Creutzberg has emphasised the lack of a developed money and capital market in Indonesia before the Second World War and the tendency of both private and public enterprises to turn to foreign sources for their capital requirements:

> There are ostensible exceptions to this general picture. Thus subscriptions to a few Netherlands Indian loans were invited simultaneously in the Netherlands and in Indonesia. After the First World War, substantial sums were subscribed in Indonesia... . But the large sums were only subscribed as conditions gave rise, e.g. a temporary fluctuation in exchange rates or the need to have short-term funds readily available... a portion of Netherlands Indian paper was held in portfolio in Indonesia, e.g. by pension funds, life insurance companies and savings banks, for covering their obligations in Indonesia. In addition, securities were purchased for the investment of private savings, although in so far as these were held by individual savers they were repatriated with their owners. (*C.E.I.* Vol.3, p.31)

An important point about the overall budget deficit in the twentieth century was that, in the great majority of years, it was primarily a foreign deficit. This meant that while foreign expenditures greatly exceeded foreign earnings, domestic expenditures either exceeded domestic revenues by a much smaller amount, or were indeed less than domestic revenues. Thus we observe that for the period 1928-39 the overall budget was in continual deficit, but the domestic budget was only in deficit in 1932-34, and the domestic deficit was a much smaller proportion

TABLE 10.6 Trends in the Budget Surplus/Deficit and Debt Changes in Relation to National Income, 1921-39

	As a Percentage of National Income				Debt Service Charges as a Percentage of Exports
	Domestic Deficit/ Surplus	Overall Deficit/ Surplus	Accumulated Public Debt	Debt Service Charges	
1921	-1.1	-5.4	22.8	1.4	5.7
1922	1.3	-2.4	26.3	3.8	15.0
1923	2.2	-1.1	29.8	1.8	5.8
1924	3.9	0.9	26.2	1.8	5.5
1925	4.2	1.4	23.2	1.7	4.6
1926	3.4	1.1	20.9	1.6	7.8
1927	3.2	0.1	20.8	1.7	5.3
1928	3.1	-0.1	20.5	2.0	6.2
1929	2.4	-0.3	20.7	1.7	5.8
1930	0.6	-2.8	25.6	1.9	7.4
1931	0.4	-4.3	39.6	2.6	10.7
1932	-3.4	-7.2	55.1	4.6	19.6
1933	-2.3	-7.8	73.5	5.1	20.0
1934	-1.5	-6.0	75.0	5.4	19.8
1935	2.2	-3.1	67.8	3.7	16.2
1936	2.9	-2.5	62.4	3.5	12.6
1937	2.8	-1.3	49.1	2.6	7.2
1938	3.8	-1.9	48.6	2.7	10.6
1939	1.7	-3.3	46.8	2.7	10.0

Sources: C.E.I. Vol. 2, Tables 4 and 7 ; C.E.I. Vol. 5, p.70

of national income (Table 10.6). This difference was due mainly to the growth of domestic revenues on the one hand and foreign expenditures (first for imports and then for debt servicing) on the other.

Thus the macroeconomic impact of budgetary policy in the twentieth century, and particularly during the depression period, was exactly the opposite of budgetary policy during the Cultivation System. Then the overall budget surplus had been very large, but this was entirely due to the excess of foreign earnings over foreign expenditures, the domestic budget being in almost continual deficit during the entire period. This domestic deficit was certainly an important factor in the rapid growth of the money supply which took place in the middle decades of the nineteenth century. In the twentieth century, by contrast, the overall budgetary deficit, which in some years exceeded five per cent of national income, was accompanied by either a domestic surplus or a much smaller domestic deficit. The rapid growth of foreign borrowing was thus largely used to finance the foreign deficit, and the impact of the budget on domestic liquidity for most of the period was contractionary.

Government Regulation of the Economy. A common theme among many foreign accounts of the government and economy of Indonesia in the early twentieth century was the very high quality of the Dutch administrators. Numerous commentators praised their professional competence, integrity, and devotion to duty. However, some of the more perceptive, or outspoken, of these commentators also referred to the "administrative tyranny" implicit in the "incredible meddling by officials in the private affairs of the natives," meddling which appeared to extend to virtually every facet of social and economic life. Bousquet made a comparison between the French, Dutch, and British colonial administrations in Asia and Africa.

> In India officialdom concerns itself as little as possible with the personal affairs of the natives; in the Indies it meddles in everything. The French administration in North Africa stands between these two, but it definitely has more in common with the liberal spirit of the British... . The Dutch administration considers the native to be a child and meddles with the pettiest trifles in native life. (Bousquet 1940, pp.51-52)

The depression of the 1930s led to a marked increase in government expenditures and revenues as a proportion of national income, and also to a growth in government intervention in most aspects of economic activity. Boeke discusses in detail the regulation of exports necessitated by the shrinkage of world markets and the growth of protectionism, and the regulation of imports both to encourage domestic industries and to protect imports from favoured countries against those from Japan. He also traces the growth of government interference in the market for basic foodstuffs, especially rice, and in domestic industries, especially textiles (Boeke 1953, Ch.23).[5] Much of this intervention had several objectives, as the following description of textile licensing in the 1930s by a senior official in the Department of Economic Affairs makes clear:

> In order to keep the market open for domestic textiles, a system of import quotas was set up in such a manner that there would always be a market for domestic production. In addition the factories were legally bound to a licensing system. These licenses indicated the productive capacity of the factory, stated in numbers of mechanical or hand looms, while stipulations could be added concerning the types of goods to be manufactured, the wages to be paid, etc. In this way it was possible to guard against exhausting price wars, against a cartellization of the large factories to the detriment of the smaller ones, against a socially unwarrantable division of incomes, etc. In short, the far-reaching intervention of the Government in industrial affairs fostered healthy industrial development, beneficial for all concerned. (Sitsen 1940)

As Higgins has pointed out, it was this approach to industrial regulation, already clearly articulated in the 1930s, which the post-war government of independent Indonesia inherited (Higgins 1968, Ch. 31).

Comparisons with other Countries

Having traced the development of the government sector from the early nineteenth century through to 1940, we turn now to comparisons with other countries. In posing the question how large was the government sector in Indonesia compared to, say, British India, or Thailand, we must recall that, in the pre-war period, government accounting procedures were by no means standardised, and care is needed in making cross-country comparisons. Comparisons of the ratio of government revenues and expenditures to national income suffer from lack of comparability of the government data as well as from the fact that national income accounting techniques were in their infancy during this period. They were frequently neither very accurate in themselves, nor comparable across time and space. Thus all the comparisons presented here can be considered at best roughly indicative of broad patterns and trends. More detailed research is needed before accurate international comparisons can be made.

We begin with an examination of ratios of government revenues and expenditures to national income as an indication of the size of the government sector in selected countries in the period 1900-41. Over the twenty-year period which is covered by Polak's series on national income, the ratio of government expenditure to national income fell and then rose again, while the ratio of tax revenues to national income rose steadily (Figure 10.5). Of the other colonial countries for which reasonable fiscal and national income data are available, it would appear that the revenue-income ratio was higher in Egypt, at least by the late 1930s, about the same in Burma and Japan, but much lower in British India (Table 10.7). Similarly government expenditure as a percentage of national income was substantially higher in Indonesia than in India in the 1920s, and even higher than in the USA; however it was lower than in Egypt, and much lower than Germany or the United Kingdom (Table 10.8).

When we examine the more disaggregated data on expenditures as a percentage of national income, it is noteworthy that Indonesia was spending about the same percentage as India on defence, rather more on administration, debt service and social services (mainly health and education), and very much more on "economic services," including capital works (Table 10.8). Indeed, Indonesia was spending a larger percentage of national income on economic services in 1929 than Japan a decade earlier, although the overall percentage of government expenditure to national income was slightly lower.

Turning from composition of expenditures to composition of revenues, Indonesian tax structure appears to have exhibited the same broad changes in the first four decades of the twentieth century as those which occurred in other parts of Asia (Table 10.9). The proportion of total government revenues accruing from land taxes fell, and the proportion accruing from taxes on foreign trade and incomes, and specific excises, rose. Like most other countries in the region, Indonesia derived a large share of total revenues from non-tax sources, such as government monopolies and charges for publicly provided services, including utilities and education. The surprising features of the Indonesian tax structure by the end of the 1930s were the rather low proportion of revenues derived from taxes on foreign trade, and the rather high proportion derived from taxes on personal and corporate incomes. The proportion of total government revenues derived from foreign trade taxes was lower than in India, although Indonesia was the more open economy.[6] On the other hand, Indonesia was deriving a higher proportion of its total revenues from income taxes than any other country, higher even than Japan in the first decade of the century.

The last aspect of fiscal policy in which it is possible to make international comparisons concerns the scale of government borrowing. If we assume, as seems not unreasonable, that all the loans negotiated by the colonial government in Indonesia in the twentieth century ultimately constituted foreign liabilities, then we can compare Indonesian public debt outstanding both as a proportion of exports, and as a proportion of national income, with data on foreign public debt outstanding for other countries which were major borrowers during the period. By the late 1930s, total foreign public debt outstanding was about 47 per cent of national income in Indonesia, a figure roughly equal to Egypt and substantially higher than in Argentina, Canada, India, or Thailand. Only Australia had a significantly larger ratio. The greater openness of the Indonesian economy,

TABLE 10.7 Revenues as a Percentage of National Income: Indonesia and Selected Comparisons

	Tax Revenues	Total Government Revenues
Japan		
1885	10	11
1900	10	12
1921	11	15
India		
1901-2	6	8
1921-2	5	6
1941-2	7	10
Burma		
1901-2	n.a.	15
1921-2	n.a.	12
1941-2	n.a.	18
Indonesia		
1921	7	15
1930	8	16
1939	10	16
Egypt		
1938-9	17	21

Sources: Japan: Ohkawa and Shinohara (1979, pp.251-2, pp.376-7). India: Dharma Kumar (1983, Table 12.6). Burma: Revenue data - Shein, Thant and Sein (1969, Appendix 2); National Income data - Aye Hlaing (1964, p.143). Indonesia: Revenue data - C.E.I. Vol. 2, Table 4; National Income data - C.E.I. Vol. 5, p.70. Egypt: Mead (1967, Appendix Tables I-A-1 & VI-E-1).

TABLE 10.8 Categories of Expenditure as a Percentage of GDP: Indonesia and Selected Comparisons

Country and Year	Administration, Law and Order	Defence	Public Debt Servicing	Social Services	Economic[a] Services	Total
Indonesia (1929)	3	3	2	2	5	16
India (1920-1)	2	3	1	1	1	8
Japan (1921)	7[b]	6	1	1	2	17
Egypt (1930-9)	8	1	2	4	8	25
Germany (1929)	4	4	1	19	3	31
United Kingdom (1929)	2	3	7	9	3	24
U.S.A. (1927)	1	1	1	3	3	12

[a]Includes public works

[b]Government consumption expenditures less current military expenditures

Sources: Indonesia: Expenditure data - C.E.I. Vol. 2, Table 4 and Statistisch Jaaroverzicht (1929, pp.448-63); National Income data - C.E.I. Vol. 5, p.70. India: Dharma Kumar (1983, Tables 12.6 & 12.8). Egypt: Mead (1967, Appendix Tables I-A-1 & VI-E-2). Japan: Ohkawa and Shinohara (1979, pp.251-2, 370-4). Germany, United Kingdom and U.S.A.: Musgrave (1969, pp.94-5).

TABLE 10.9 Percentage Breakdown of Government Revenues: Indonesia and Selected Comparisons

<table>
<tr><th></th><th>Land Revenue</th><th>Taxes on Foreign Trade</th><th>Excises</th><th>Income Taxes</th><th>Other Taxes</th><th>Non-tax Revenues</th><th>Total</th></tr>
<tr><td>Indonesia</td><td></td><td></td><td></td><td></td><td></td><td></td><td></td></tr>
<tr><td>1900</td><td>12</td><td>8</td><td>5</td><td>3</td><td>10</td><td>62</td><td>100</td></tr>
<tr><td>1939</td><td>5</td><td>17</td><td>14</td><td>21</td><td>6</td><td>37</td><td>100</td></tr>
<tr><td>India</td><td></td><td></td><td></td><td></td><td></td><td></td><td></td></tr>
<tr><td>1900-1</td><td>37</td><td>6</td><td>7</td><td>2</td><td>18</td><td>30</td><td>100</td></tr>
<tr><td>1940-1</td><td>13</td><td>19</td><td>11</td><td>13</td><td>13</td><td>31</td><td>100</td></tr>
<tr><td>Burma[a]</td><td></td><td></td><td></td><td></td><td></td><td></td><td></td></tr>
<tr><td>1900</td><td>42</td><td>13</td><td>7</td><td>1</td><td>14</td><td>23</td><td>100</td></tr>
<tr><td>1930</td><td>29</td><td>31</td><td>8</td><td>-</td><td>15</td><td>17</td><td>100</td></tr>
<tr><td>Japan</td><td></td><td></td><td></td><td></td><td></td><td></td><td></td></tr>
<tr><td>1879-83</td><td>64</td><td colspan="2">18</td><td>8[b]</td><td>4</td><td>5</td><td>100</td></tr>
<tr><td>1909-11</td><td>15</td><td colspan="2">22</td><td>15[b]</td><td>8</td><td>40</td><td>100</td></tr>
<tr><td>Egypt</td><td></td><td></td><td></td><td></td><td></td><td></td><td></td></tr>
<tr><td>1900</td><td>42</td><td colspan="2">23</td><td>-</td><td colspan="2">35</td><td>100</td></tr>
<tr><td>1939-40</td><td>13</td><td>36</td><td>11</td><td>7</td><td>3</td><td>30</td><td>100</td></tr>
<tr><td>Thailand</td><td></td><td></td><td></td><td></td><td></td><td></td><td></td></tr>
<tr><td>1905</td><td>8</td><td>11</td><td>8</td><td>8[c]</td><td>20</td><td>45</td><td>100</td></tr>
<tr><td>1938</td><td>6</td><td>30</td><td>6</td><td>8[c]</td><td>1</td><td>49</td><td>100</td></tr>
</table>

a Data refer to 10 year averages ending in the years shown
b Includes residence and inheritance taxes
c Includes capitation taxes

Sources: Indonesia: Central Bureau of Statistics (1941, Table 194) and C.E.I. Vol. 2, Table 4. India: Dharma Kumar (1983, Tables 12.6 & 12.7). Burma: Shein, Thant and Sein (1969, p.11). Japan: Oshima (1965, p.359). Egypt: Mead (1967, Appendix Table VI-E-1) and United Nations (1950, Table 3). Thailand: Ingram (1971, p. 185).

TABLE 10.10 Public Foreign Debt Outstanding as a Percentage of National Income and Exports: Indonesia and Selected Comparisons

	Debt Outstanding as a Percentage of:			
	National Income		Exports[a]	
	Early 1920s	Late 1930s	Early 1920s	Late 1930s
Indonesia	23	47	79	174
Argentina	n.a.	10	37	77
Canada	10	14	54	85
Australia	54	70	288	397
India	14	21	128	208
Japan	9	5	71	46
Egypt	n.a.	48	159	263
Thailand	n.a.	7	68	28

[a]Merchandise exports

Sources: Total debt for Indonesia taken from C.E.I. Vol. 2, Table 7; for all other countries data on foreign public debt taken from United Nations (1948). National income and export data are derived from the following sources: Argentina: Diaz Alejandro (1970, pp.398 & 475). Australia: Butlin (1962) and official yearbooks, various issues. India: Dharma Kumar (1983, Tables 12.6 & 12.7) and Chaudhuri (1983, p.839). Japan: Ohkawa and Shinohara (1979, p.253) and Key (1971, Appendix Table 1). Egypt: Mead (1967, Appendix Table I-A-1 & V-A-4). Thailand: Ingram (1971, pp.146 & 332-5).

compared with countries such as India or Egypt, meant that the ratio of debt to exports was rather higher in both these countries than in Indonesia, although Australia's ratio was still the highest (Table 10.10).

The remarkably high level of public borrowing abroad on the part of countries of recent settlement such as Australia is reflected in the very large share of the public sector in total capital formation. We noted earlier that, according to the series compiled by Creutzberg, the government share in total expenditure on fixed assets reached a peak of about 25 per cent in 1921, and declined thereafter. These data may be compared with the series produced by Butlin, Barnard and Pincus for Australia which shows that the public sector share of gross domestic capital formation never fell below 40 per cent between 1910 and 1939, and was frequently well over 50 per cent (Butlin, Barnard and Pincus (1982), Tables 2.1 & 2.3).

Had the major colonies of Asia, including Indonesia, been able to borrow abroad on the scale undertaken by Australia in the early years of this century, they would have emerged into independence with a much stronger infrastructural base. In the Indonesian case, roads, railways, and irrigation projects could have been constructed outside Java on a scale sufficient to greatly accelerate the economic development of Kalimantan, Southern and Central Sumatra, and Sulawesi. Instead, these regions remained backward and relatively under-developed, and their populations developed resentments against the colonial government which were transferred to the Javanese-dominated government of independent Indonesia. The scene was set for the bitter separatist struggles of the 1950s.

On the other hand it must be conceded that even if Indonesia had not been a colony in the early years of this century, it might not have chosen to borrow heavily abroad to invest in productive infrastructure. Here the case of Thailand is particularly instructive. The maintenance of independence from imperialist domination was the over-riding preoccupation of the Thai monarchy and indigenous elite. Therefore the Thai government borrowed very little abroad in the pre-1940 era, and chose to concentrate scarce domestic investment resources on railways and defence infrastructure rather than on irrigation and agricultural research (Feeny 1982a). This retarded the growth of both agriculture and industry, leaving Thailand with a larger undeveloped economy by the outbreak of the Second World War.

Conclusions

In tracing the evolution of the role of government in the Indonesian economy from the onset of the cultivation period to 1940, we can discern five distinct eras. The first, from the 1830s to the mid-1860s, was a period when real government expenditures and revenues were quite stable, when revenues were largely derived from sale of products and expenditures largely devoted to the extraction of these products, and when the overall budget was in continual surplus. This surplus took the form of a surplus of foreign receipts (from sale of products in Europe) over foreign expenditures and was paid directly into the Dutch exchequer.

A second period, from the late 1860s through to the mid-1880s was characterised by rising real expenditures, and a significant change in the composition of these expenditures away from administration (especially the extraction and sale of crops) and towards public works. There was also an appreciable increase in expenditure on defence. Revenues continued to be heavily reliant on the government opium and salt monopolies, and on sale of products. During the latter part of this period the overall budget balance became negative.

The third period, from the mid-1880s to the end of the century, was one of quite severe recession in the world and the Indonesian economy. During this period, real government expenditures were stable or falling; the composition of expenditures continued to shift away from administration and towards public works, particularly railways. There was a marked fall in the share of revenues accruing from sale of products which in turn reflected the severe problems facing both coffee and sugar producers in this period. The share of taxes, especially foreign trade taxes, in total revenues grew. The overall budget continued in deficit, necessitating substantial borrowing.

The fourth period lasted from the turn of the century to 1921, and was characterised by a fairly steady growth in real levels of government expenditure, with some deviation from trend in the war years, 1914-18. This was a period of substantial real growth in the economy, but it would appear that government expenditures grew even more rapidly than income. The composition of expenditures further changed in favour of public works, while revenues became more dominated by tax receipts, to the exclusion of monopolies and sales of products.

After 1921, government expenditures fell in both money and real terms, increased again after 1925, only to fall again in the early 1930s. The fall after 1930 was relatively slight, given the magnitude of the recession, and both domestic and total real expenditures were well above 1913 levels by the end of the 1930s. However, the share of expenditures devoted to capital works appears to have fallen over the entire period 1921-39, and particularly sharply after 1930.

By the late 1930s defence was again claiming over 25 per cent of all expenditures, with the bulk of the remainder going on debt servicing and general administration.

What determined these fluctuations in the level of government activity over the century from the 1830s to the 1930s? One influential argument in the literature of colonial economic development is that government expenditures were primarily determined by revenues which in turn, in a undeveloped open economy, were mainly a function of export earnings. According to this view, to the extent that colonial governments were concerned with providing infrastructure at all, such provision was directed entirely to the export sector. Thus, models have been developed (e.g. Birnberg and Resnick 1975) where export earnings are seen as a function of government expenditure and in turn generate revenues (mainly, although not entirely, through trade taxes). These revenues in turn generate further government expenditures leading to further exports and so on.

A major implication of this model of colonial development is that revenues and expenditures will be closely correlated with exports, although the "best fit" would involve some lags. When a partial adjustment model, of the type used by Leff (1982, pp.119-21) on Brazilian data, is applied to the Indonesian data for 1840 to 1913, the short and long-run elasticities of both revenue and expenditure growth with respect to exports are found to be rather lower than in the case of Brazil during the nineteenth century.[7] For the twentieth century, comparisons can be made with a number of countries for which Birnberg and Resnick (1975) have supplied data; it would appear that the long-run elasticities of both revenue and expenditure with respect to exports are around unity in most cases.

The rather low long-run elasticities of both expenditure and revenues with respect to exports during the nineteenth century in Indonesia would suggest that factors other than export fluctuations were important in determining trends in both government revenues and expenditures. It would appear that both were influenced by deliberate actions of government, taken in response to changing perceptions of national priorities. One such change occurred after 1870 when the cultivation system was gradually abandoned in favour of more liberal economic policies and it was no longer necessary to devote a substantial proportion of government expenditure to the extraction and sale of products. A further reorientation of priorities occurred with the outbreak of war in Aceh, when there was an obvious need to spend more on defence. With the implementation of the Ethical Policy in the twentieth century, the government embarked on a much more ambitious programme of public investment than had hitherto been attempted, necessitating after 1915, foreign borrowing on a substantial scale.

These successive policy changes meant that both the purpose and the instruments of government intervention in the Indonesian economy changed substantially in the hundred years up to 1940. During the Cultivation System, the purpose of intervention was to secure as large a quantity of crops as possible for sale overseas, in order to maximise the contribution of the colony to the exchequer of the Netherlands. All other aims of policy were subordinated to this end. In the last three decades of the nineteenth century national integration was one major policy goal; this led to growing expenditures on "integrative infrastructure." Another important policy goal was rapid growth of production, primarily for export on private, rather than government, account. This also required infrastructure investment which in turn required a far more efficient system of revenue raising than that which had prevailed under the Cultivation System.

In the twentieth century, when native welfare became a major concern of policy, the instruments of government intervention in the economy were diversified to include a number of measures designed to regulate prices of basic commodities, and to protect certain sectors of the economy, such as handicrafts, from import competition. Although in the twentieth century, and particularly after 1913, it would appear that both government revenues and expenditures were more influenced by earnings from commodity exports than was the case in earlier periods, there is substantial evidence that expenditures were not simply a function of current revenues, whose fluctuations were in turn largely determined by fluctuations in export earnings. In the early 1920s and again in the 1930s, government made substantial use of overseas loans to maintain real levels of expenditure in the face of declining revenues, although the composition of expenditures shifted away from economic infrastructure, and back towards general administration and defence.

Almost certainly the government was a much more important economic actor in late colonial Indonesia than it was in British India, or indeed in many other colonial territories. Furthermore it is at least arguable that the aim of fiscal policy in Indonesia in the late nineteenth and twentieth centuries was more consciously "developmental" than in many other parts of the colonial world. But in spite of both the rhetoric and the accomplishments of the half century up to 1930, the total achievement was disappointing, as influential scholars and administrators were forced to acknowledge even before the onset of the depression of the 1930s. The disillusion was expressed by Boeke in a lecture given in 1927:

> The attempt made over the past fifty years and more to pursue a welfare policy with the help of administrative authority has failed—failed not in the sense that nothing has happened, nothing has been accomplished, (all too much has been accomplished, only to disappear again without a trace), but in the sense that, at least on Java, developments have brought native society as a whole no closer to the ideal of a well-integrated, highly differential society capable of fulfilling its economic function on its own strength. (Boeke 1961,

p.296)

What additional policy measures would have been necessary to have achieved the kind of society Boeke envisaged here? With the wisdom of hindsight we can say that far more should have been done in the fields of education, agricultural extension, irrigation, transport infrastructure (especially outside Java), and credit. This is not to say that these areas were neglected by colonial administrators. Rather, what was accomplished proved inadequate, even though by the beginning of the third decade of the twentieth century government spending amounted to almost 20 per cent of national income. If government had wanted to do more in these crucial areas of development policy, it would have had to reduce expenditures elsewhere (for example on salaries and perquisites of civil servants), raise more revenues through taxation or from non-tax sources, or borrow more heavily abroad. None of these options would have been considered feasible by a colonial administration already under attack from business and right-wing political quarters in the Netherlands for its excessively spendthrift "welfare" policies.

Notes

1. No domestic price index is available before 1913. The best available proxy is an index based on rice prices (see *C.E.I.* Vol.4,Table 1).

2. For a more detailed discussion of the burden of taxation on the indigenous and European populations in the late colonial period see Booth (1980).

3. In 1915 the total length of track (train and tram) open for traffic in the entire country was 5216 km. This jumped to 7120 km by 1925 and 7425 km by 1930. It fell marginally in the 1930s, especially in Java.

4. The proportion devoted to education did not in fact change very markedly, although expenditure on "native" education rose.

5. For further discussion of the growth of government intervention in the rice market see *C.E.I.* (Vol.4, p.21ff.)

6. Trade taxes amounted to roughly 11 per cent of commodity exports and imports in India in 1940; the comparable figure for Indonesia was only six per cent.

7. A partial adjustment model fitted to the Indonesian data for 1840 to 1913 yielded long-run elasticities of revenue and expenditure with respect to exports of 0.52 and 0.64 respectively. Leff's analysis of the Brazilian data yielded elasticities of 1.08 and 1.04.

Sources for Figures

Figure 10.1 Fiscal balance: C.E.I., Vol 2, Tables 2 and 3 Commodity Trade: C.K.S. 160

Figure 10.2 Fiscal balance: C.E.I. Vol 2, Tables 2 and 3 Net revenue surplus: C.E.I., Vol 2, Table 3

Figure 10.3 C.E.I., Vol 2, Tables 3 and 4

Figure 10.4 C.E.I., Vol 2, Table 3 Retail price index: C.K.S. 146, p.41

Figure 10.5 C.E.I., Vol 2, Table 3 C.E.I., Vol 5, p.70

Figure 10.6 C.E.I., Vol 2, Table 4

CHAPTER ELEVEN

Between the Java Bank and the Chinese Moneylender: Banking and Credit in Colonial Indonesia

Jan T.M. Van Laanen

Introduction

In spite of the availability of much statistical data and several important archives, the monetary history of colonial Indonesia remains largely unexplored.[1] Yet, like that of many other former colonies, it offers a variety of interesting and exciting themes. Among the most promising, the following deserve special mention:

1. The monetisation ratio, that is, the proportion of the total of goods and services that is monetised, in the sense of being paid for by the purchaser. The monetisation ration is one of the most important characteristics of the level and course of economic development (Goldsmith 1969; Chandravarkar 1980).
2. The market-system, in particular the development of the indigenous peasant market *(pasar)* versus the export market, and the role of Chinese middlemen.
3. The efficacy of the price-mechanism that operated in the Western and in the indigenous economic systems respectively. This mechanism makes it possible, for example, to analyse the impact of money supply on the general level of economic activity.
4. The international value of the Netherlands-Indian guilder (the monetary unit) and the impact of the frequent intervention of the monetary authorities.
5. The partial re-writing of the history of the large commercial banks, such as the Java Bank (*De Javasche Bank*) and the Netherlands-Indian Trading Society (*Nederlandsche Handel-Maatschappij*), and indigenous forms of credit, by making use of unexplored archives.[2]
6. The interdisciplinary analysis of the non-economic consequences of the penetration of money.
7. The construction of time-series of relevant monetary variables to obtain a quantitative picture of Indonesian economic history.

Some progress has been made with the last item, culminating in the publication of the sixth volume of the *Changing Economy in Indonesia* series. This chapter will treat the development of both Western banking and indigenous credit systems during the nineteenth and early twentieth centuries in a general economic and monetary context. However, before embarking on this theme some general comments about the economic structure of colonial Indonesia, and its influence on the use of money, are in order.

Money in a Colonial Economy

Two principal sectors were distinguishable within the colonial economy of Indonesia throughout the nineteenth and the first part of the twentieth centuries: the traditional agrarian sector on the one hand and the relatively advanced, export-oriented, Western sector on the other.[3] To put the role of money (and the credit and banking system) in such an economy in a proper perspective, a brief outline of the two sectors is presented below with the help of the classification given by Dalton (1967, pp.264-66). Dalton makes a clear distinction between primitive (or subsistence) economies and peasant (market-dominated) economies. Primitive economies are further subdivided between marketless economies and economies with peripheral markets only. In marketless communities, land and labour are not transacted by purchase and sale but are allocated on the basis of kinship rights or tribal affiliation. There are no formal market places where goods are bought and sold. Livelihood does not depend on production for sale. The transactional modes to allocate resources and labour as well as produced items and services are reciprocity (gift-giving between kin and friends) and redistribution (obligatory payments to political authority which uses the receipts to provide community services). In economies with peripheral markets only, market places exist in which a narrow range of product is bought and sold, either with some money-stuff used as a medium of (commercial) exchange, or via moneyless market exchange (barter). Land and labour are not bought and sold, and most people do not derive the bulk of their income from market sales. In peasant economies a large proportion of all exchanges of land and labour as well as goods and services are transacted by market purchase and sale, and most people depend upon the market sale of labour or products for livelihood. Peasant economies differ from primitive economies in that peasant producers depend upon production for sale. Both peasant and primitive communities differ from large-scale, nationally integrated economies on two counts: modern technology is largely absent, and traditional social organisation and culture practices are largely retained.

This classification, applied to colonial Indonesia, leads to the following characterisation. On the one hand, the indigenous sector of the economy was devoted to satisfying the subsistence needs of the small producer and his immediate environment. The distinguishing characteristics of this sector included a low level of labour productivity and, concomitantly, severely limited disposable incomes, especially on Java; the lack of private cash savings; a low rate of technical progress over time; an overwhelming share of the primary sector in total value added; a trade system almost exclusively in the hands of the Chinese; and the absence of a strong Indonesian entrepreneurial class. Economic aspects of life were inextricably interwoven with religion, ethics and *adat*-law. This meant that individual freedom to do business was subject to constraints according the rules of the production organisation (village, clan) to which an individual belonged.

In this economy, which in many respects belonged to Dalton's "primitive economy with peripheral markets only," the indigenous market (*pasar*), nonetheless, was of much more than marginal significance, even in the nineteenth century. The *pasar* showed fundamental differences with Western capitalistic markets. During the colonial period, it was characterised by:

(a) a "sliding" price system. Usually, prices were the outcome of time-consuming haggling between seller and buyer. When the *pasar* closed, sellers were much more compliant than early in the morning;
(b) the importance of monetary transactions, although pure barter still existed;
(c) limited trading hours; in Javanese villages trade in the *pasar* was usually conducted only once a week (of five days);
(d) a sharply fluctuating supply, from day to day and from *pasar* to *pasar*. Therefore—and this even held true for villages in close proximity to each other—large price differences could exist; also most transactions were extremely small and traded merchandise was not bulky, storable, and portable;
(e) a lack of own working capital. Frequently, money borrowed in the morning from Chinese middlemen was paid back (at a high interest rate) late in the afternoon;
(f) a high dependency on labour-intensive techniques, local knowledge and individual initiative.

Although the exchange of goods and services via the *pasar* gradually reached a prominent position in colonial Indonesian society, even to the extent that in relatively industrialised areas peasants became seasonally dependent on monetary income, reciprocity and redistribution, the two transactional modes of primitive society, remained important and in many remote corners of the archipelago even dominant.[4] Examples of reciprocity included all kinds of mutual help (*gotong royong*), the exchange of gifts (sometimes in anticipation of future rights, as in the case of dowry), and labour in exchange of a harvest-share, while well-known forms of redistribution included levies and taxation in kind by local authorities. The twentieth century, however, showed a decline in reciprocity and redistribution, although there was no question of a continuous, irrevocable development.

It is obvious from this that the indigenous sector was only monetised to a limited extent. A large part of economic life remained outside the monetary system, and consisted of production for own consumption, levies and payments in kind, mutual help, etc. Precise data on all these items are not available, and it is noticeable that leading contemporary writers tend to hold rather different views on the monetisation ratio of the indigenous economy. However, in spite of numerous problems of comparability, both geographically as well as chronologically, it seems that in normal years 50 per cent of the staple crops were sold for money.[5] The money used by the Indonesian population was usually of a special nature. It did not serve concurrently as a means of exchange, a unit of account and a store of value (all-purpose money). Only one or two of these functions were relevant at the same time (limited-purpose money).

Paper money, issued by the Java Bank in large denominations, was hardly used. Silver coins such as the silver *rijksdaalders* (*f*2.50) and guilders were often hoarded or melted down into ornaments. Small change such as the silver *kwartje* (*f*0.25) and *dubbeltje* (*f*0.10) and the copper *stuiver, gobang, cent* and *halve cent* (*f*0.05, 0.025, 0.01 and 0.005 respectively), were used as the means of indigenous commercial exchange *par excellence*. However, Western money was by no means essential. Goods that were widely accepted by the population, such as a *gantang* (half a coconut) of rice, salt, or *kerbau* (the Indonesian buffalo), often served as a substitute for money in all kinds of barter transactions, in particular in periods of money-scarcity.

The enterprises run by non-indigenous members of the population which acquired their value-added primarily through the export of agricultural raw materials or minerals (petroleum, tin) belonged to what may be termed the *Western sector*. This sector may be regarded as a frontier post of Western-oriented trade and industry, operating at the periphery of modern capitalism. If the indigenous sector was, to an important extent, dominated by fluctuations in harvests, the price of export goods on the world market was decisive in determining the economic well-being of the Western sector. Production techniques in use were far more capital-intensive than in the indigenous sector and, above all in the sugar industry, required the importation of an appreciable quantity of capital goods. In order to acquire the necessary finance, when this could not be derived from operating surpluses and depreciation, use was made of the services of specialised commercial banks. Labour productivity ultimately made it possible for incomes within the Western sector to exceed those in the indigenous sector by, minimally, a factor of fifty (Polak 1943, p.65).

The course of foreign commerce, to a large measure determined by the presence of this Western sector, exhibited conspicuous similarities with commerce in most other tropical-colonial agrarian economies. The trade balance almost always showed a large surplus which, in part, flowed out of the country in the form of profits and interest.[6] In the Western sector, the markets—wholesale import and export trade and urban retail trade—were a very strong integrative force (Van Gelderen 1927, pp.145-48). They should be seen as intersections of demand and supply in an abstract sense, instead of places where buyer and seller met physically, as was the case in the indigenous economy. The market principle was the dominating transactional mode, and especially reciprocity but also redistribution were of limited significance only. Self-interest (profit maximisation) was consequently pursued in this fully monetised sector. The money used (banknotes issued by the Java Bank, token coins such as rixdollars and guilders, and also small change) simultaneously served as a means of payment, a unit of account and a store of value.

Even from this short sketch of colonial economic life, it is evident that the role of money was entirely different in the Western and the indigenous economic sectors. It is therefore not surprising that their respective banking and credit systems were utterly dissimilar. We now turn to examine these in more detail.

A Brief History of the Western Banking System

Major Institutions. Among the major banks operating in colonial Indonesia, the most important were the Java Bank, which was the bank of issue, the Netherlands-Indian Trading Society (usually known by its Dutch initials, NHM), the Netherlands-Indian Commercial Bank (NIHB) and the Netherlands-Indian Escompto Company (NIEM). The so-called Agricultural Banks (*Cultuur banken*) were distinguished from the commercial banks in that they concentrated on credit extension to the large-scale agricultural sector.[7] The minor importance of their borrowing operations raises the question of whether some of the agricultural banks should be regarded as banks at all. The Amsterdam Trading Association (*Handelsvereeniging Amsterdam* or HVA), for example, furnished agricultural enterprises almost exclusively with fixed capital, and thus exploited its own undertakings. If this type of agricultural banking is disregarded, it leaves only the Colonial Bank (*Koloniale Bank*), the Principalities Agricultural Company (*Cultuurmaatschappij der Vorstenlanden*), and the "mixed" NIHB and the NHM. Since this survey aims only at a description of banking business proper, that is, the extension of short- to medium-term commercial credit, the Colonial Bank and the Principalities Agricultural Company (which was of limited size only), both mainly concerned with commission business, should also be left out of consideration. In fact, the NHM and the Netherlands-Indian Agricultural Company (*Nederlandsch-Indische Landbouw Maatschappij*), the latter founded by the NIHB, often accounted for more than 50 per cent of total agricultural banking business.

Absence of a properly developed money market. One of the most characteristic features of the economic structure of colonial Indonesia was the foreign ownership of the large-scale, export-oriented enterprises (Table 11.1). Taken together with the commercial enterprises of the colonial government (in 1940 these were valued at 1.25 billion guilders), 80 per cent of the capital value in business could be regarded as being in Dutch hands. The powerful expansion of Western enterprises, especially after 1900, was financed only to a small extent by capital that was almost completely bound to the territory of Indonesia. This capital supply consisted of the following categories:

1. Capital tied to the country by virtue of the nationality of its owner, i.e. Chinese, Arabs and sometimes also well-to-do Indonesians. This capital was usually invested in real estate or stocks, but also in *desa*—credit extension (the purchase of rice and commodity trade by the Chinese).
2. Assets supplied by Europeans, mainly in the form of securities, bank deposits, and life insurance premiums. These types generally ran parallel with the length of residence in Indonesia.
3. The capital of funds managed by enterprises whose headquarters and shareholders were in Indonesia (a small minority). Financial reserves of this kind, which were accumulated out of undistributed operating surpluses, were invested in securities and bank deposits.

TABLE 11.1 Foreign Private Investment in Indonesia by Country of Origin, 1922 and 1940 (million guilders)

	Sugar		Other agricultural estates		Oil and others		Total	
	1922	1940	1922	1940	1922	1940	1922	1940
Netherlands	322	420	545	1,074	1,290	1,160	2,157	2,654
Britain	-	-	245	200	55	260	300	460
USA	-	-	28	100	7	195	35	295
Others	3	-	127	150	18	100	148	250
Total	325	420	945	1,524	1,370	1,715	2,640	3,659

Source: C.E.I. Vol. 3, p. 25

Apart from these relatively small financial resources, in normal years of profitable production considerable amounts of liquid assets (profits and depreciation) came out of the production process of enterprises with their headquarters outside Indonesia such as the Batavian Petroleum Company, the HVA and the Royal Packetboat Company (*Koninklijke Pakketvaart Maatschappij* or KMP). These assets were destined to flow back abroad within a short time. Therefore they could be invested in Indonesia only on a short-term basis. However it frequently happened that there was insufficient short-term demand for such financial surpluses, and the banks were forced to transmit them abroad.

But generally most foreign enterprises chose themselves to keep their surpluses in foreign financial centres. For example, the Batavian Petroleum Company's export of petroleum products was, of course, included in the official export data, but in fact most was sold abroad and the revenues went directly into the company's bank accounts in the Netherlands, and were only remitted back to the colony if needed for further investment. The inevitable result of such practices was that the banks within the colony had only very limited financial resources at their disposal, and it was virtually impossible for a local money market to develop.[8] Neither could the Java Bank implement an autonomous monetary policy, even if it had wanted to.

"It is clear," wrote a high-ranking Java Bank official in March 1948, "that this situation can change only as the economic development of the country in horizontal and vertical direction—especially through industrialisation—will have progressed considerably and in the course of this progress the formation of Indonesian capital will have set in; for it is exclusively these factors which may lay the foundations for an Indonesian money and capital market, viz. a considerably increased demand for short-term money for a differentiated and integrated system of production inside Indonesia and a supply of capital by Indonesian depositors. This process will," this official concludes, "probably yet take several decades."[9]

The Java Bank. Extensive sources are available on the history of the Java Bank (*De Javasche Bank*), a private banking institution set up under Order in Council No. 28 of 1827 (see in particular De Bree 1928, and Van Laanen 1983). Initially, the main aspect of the Java Bank's operations consisted of discounting, chiefly of promissory notes issued by the purchasers of imported goods to the order of their importers. Until the 1850s, the Bank remained the only private institution providing credit to traders who were subject to the provisions of the Cultivation System. While certain trading houses extended credit to agricultural enterprises during this period, they generally did so not with their own capital but by passing on credit obtained from the Java Bank (Gimbrère 1928).

During the first few years of its existence, the issue of banknotes (the Java Bank's own credit instrument) was not tied to a fixed limit. No provisions whatever were made with regard to the amount of coin and bullion to be kept in reserve as a guarantee for the convertibility of the note-circulation. Gradually, the credit and loan operations were extended to an unreasonable degree. In 1839, it became evident that the Java Bank was almost insolvent, no longer able to exchange the notes held by the public for silver or gold.

A transitional arrangement was introduced in 1846, and then an amendment to its charter in 1848 brought the inevitable reaction to the excessive liberty the Java Bank had enjoyed. A limit was imposed on the quantity of notes issued by the Bank. The introduction of this limit came at rather an unfortunate time, since this period also witnessed the decline of the Cultivation System, which was coupled with an increased demand for private credit. The period of restrictive measures lasted until 1875, when a system of proportional cover was introduced. In 1875, the cover ratio was set at 40 per cent of the Bank's direct liabilities; between August 1914 and June 1928 this ratio was lowered to 20 per cent. Between 1854 and 1875, the Java Bank had to adjust its operations to the available gold and silver balance, and the demand for credit was adjusted to these more limited possibilities by jacking up the discount rate. The net result was a regrettable (as far as the Java Bank was concerned) reduction in its commercial scope.

During the 1860s, however, the substantial export of specie to British India led to a temporary credit expansion since bills were discounted in order to obtain the silver money required for arbitrage (*C.E.I.*, vol.6, para.4.5). Attracted by profit opportunities, a sizeable amount of bank capital flowed into the country before 1875 for investment purposes. As far as the extension of credit to private individuals was concerned, the Java Bank steadily lost ground to new, more specialised banking institutions. The Bank decided to enter into competition with these commercial banks in a number of areas. It was not just a matter of promissory notes being placed increasingly with these banks; competition was also becoming more intense in the direct financing of commodity trade, that is, loans on security. In the case of merchandise credit, for example, the percentage advanced and the quality of the security played an even larger role than in the discounting of promissory notes. One of the consequences of the uncertain behaviour of the world market for tropical producers at this time was that merchandise loans or securities tended to be much more sensitive to the percentage advanced than to the discount rate, which was the Java Bank's main instrument.

Nevertheless, the scale of the Bank's operations gradually shrank between 1860 and 1890. Declining dividends (the shareholders' interest) and the increasing need to be able to intervene actively in international money transactions compelled the Bank to change track around 1890. In 1891, the Java Bank became empowered to negotiate bills of exchange drawn on London and Amsterdam by means of an agency especially set up for the purpose in Amsterdam. Table 11.2 illustrates the significance of the resultant gold-exchange system, under which the value of the colonial guilder was in fact maintained through the medium of negotiating foreign bills. It may be seen that the average rates of exchange remained almost continually within the gold points (99.25-100.75 for bills drawn on the Netherlands), excluding disruptive external factors such as wars. Furthermore, the official discount rate was virtually steady over a long period, while at the same time due attention was paid to a full-bodied and high percentage cover for fiduciary money.

A number of authors have drawn attention to the great importance of the Java Bank as the central banking institution of colonial Indonesia. But the Bank's activities certainly did not measure up to the standard definition of a central bank: an institution on which private banks can fall back in order to bolster their liquidity, which acts as the Alpha and Omega of the flow of funds, and to which a certain responsibility for the money and credit system as a whole may be ascribed by virtue of the special position it occupies. As has been explained, this has to do with the fact that in colonial Indonesia there was (if one excludes the relatively modest markets for call money and subscriptions to treasury paper) a lack of any independent money and capital market. In many cases the Java Bank simply administered transfers from the Netherlands monetary sphere to that in Indonesia and was, as such, no more than an intermediary in the flow of funds. Between the commercial banks and the Java Bank there existed a credit relationship in the form of (re-)lending on merchandise and securities as well as (re-)discounting of treasury paper and promissory notes, although the size of these operations cannot be determined from the published data. Despite this relationship, however, the Bank was unable to control effectively the domestic monetary system with the limited instruments at its command (i.e., discount policy). The Java Bank did not, therefore, act fully as a banker's bank, nor as a lender of last resort. In retrospect, the Java Bank might best be depicted as a private bank which:

(a) by means of the periodic extensions to its Charter by the colonial government of Indonesia, possessed the exclusive right to issue notes (although its notes did not become legal tender until 1914);
(b) clearly behaved like a commercial bank, notably by participating in the direct financing of trade (and agricultural enterprises), especially during periods of economic depression;
(c) last but not least, carried out some of the functions restricted to a central bank, like the stabilisation of both the domestic value (purchasing power) as well as the external value (exchange rate) of the Indonesian guilder.

TABLE 11.2 Consequences of DJB's Gold Exchange Policy, 1891-1939

Year	Gold as a % of demand liabilities[a]	Gold and gold bills as a % of demand liabilities[a]	Official discount rate[b]	Exchange rate Batavia on Amsterdam[c]
1891-1896	9.9	18.0	4.77	100.76
1895	10.4	16.9	5.37	100.75
1897-1902	17.5	26.8	4.83	101.31
1900	17.9	27.0	4.50	101.06
1903-1908	16.2	25.1	5.02	99.96[d]
1905	15.9	27.6	5.00	100.38
1909-1914	21.6	33.0	3.50	99.91
1910	11.3	25.7	3.50	100.13
1915-1920	40.2	47.9	3.50	99.52
1915	22.1	26.2	3.50	98.75
1920	43.1	46.2	3.50	97.38
1921-1926	46.6	52.9	3.83	98.68
1925	41.8	48.0	4.50	100.25
1927-1932	44.9	53.9	4.42	100.25
1930	44.0	54.2	4.65	100.44
1933-1938	45.5	46.5	3.75	99.88
1935	53.8	54.2	3.83	99.81
1939	45.8	52.3	3.00	99.63

[a]As at 31 March

[b]Averages for financial years, i.e. 1891=1891/1892, etc.

[c]Averages for calendar years

[d]Up to 1903: bank bills, six months after date. Thereafter: telegraphic transfers

Sources: De Bree (1928, Annexes) and Verslag van den President van De Javasche Bank en van den Raad van Commissarissen over het ... boekjaar [Report of the President of the Java Bank and of the Board of Directors for the Financial Year ...]: various reports.

Other Dutch Commercial Banks

Until the 1850s, the Java Bank remained virtually the sole banking institution that met the requirements for short-term credit of the private trading sector. The dominant field of activity for the NHM, after its establishment in 1824, consisted of export consignments of the colonial government's products; at that time its credit extension to private individuals was still unimportant. The Government was forced to compensate for the shortfall in private bank credit and to provide funds to enterprises involved in the processing of export crops produced under the regulations of the Cultivation System (principally sugarcane).

The situation began to change when agricultural products were once again auctioned in Java and the Government's share in commodity trade began to decline. The NHM began to extend consignment credits to private planters on a somewhat larger scale, in competition with the old trading houses which were also witnessing a revitalisation at this time. When, from the 1860s onwards, the system of forced deliveries wound down, the Government ceased to act as a provider of credit. Up to 1883, however, the NHM stayed out of banking business proper. In 1883, so-called giros (repayable on demand) and deposits, loans and advances appeared in the balance sheet for the first time (Verrijn Stuart 1923, pp.99-100). Apart from the Java Bank, whose operational scope was severely circumscribed at that time, banking business in a strict sense was conducted initially only by the NIEM, which was set up in 1857. This bank, with limited capital stock, confined its early activities to Batavia.

In these circumstances, the overall demand for credit needed to rise only slightly to exceed the maximum available supply. Something of this kind happened 1862. The sharp rise in interest rates drew new bank capital to Indonesia. The following year saw the establishment in rapid succession of the NIHB, the Rotterdam Bank, the International Credit and Trading Association of Rotterdam (*Internatio*) and an agency of the Chartered Bank of India, Australia, and China. It soon turned out, however, that the actual demand for credit had been grossly over-estimated. The resultant structural over-capacity obliged the banks to enter into business with agricultural enterprises, many of which had a marked need for long-term credit. With the exception of the NIEM, whose shareholders were apparently content to accept lower profits, most of the new banks threw themselves into this long-term business with youthful enthusiasm, extending large-scale credits, mainly to sugar companies.

Although the Rotterdam Bank disposed of its interests in Indonesia to the Chartered Bank of India, Australia, and China in 1873 and the *Internatio* severely curtailed its activities, this did not result in the necessary degree of caution among the remaining banks. Their rashness becomes understandable in the light of the considerable improvement in the psychological climate that followed upon the introduction of the Sugar Act and the Agrarian Regulations of 1870. With this legislation the Government substantially widened the scope of investment possibilities for private enterprises. Moreover, at that time a wave of mechanisation, notably in sugar production, led to increased requirements for financing.

A period of relative prosperity set in, lasting until 1883. Meanwhile, a practice persisted that can only be described as risky in the extreme, namely the encashment of bills of exchange by banks in Indonesia which were drawn on their head office. These transactions came to be referred to as "pig on pork" drawings. When, partly in response to the overproduction of beet sugar in Europe, the price of sugar on the world market fell sharply in 1883 and 1884, the receipts from auctioned sugar did not suffice to pay the bills (which were normally drawn in Indonesia six months in advance) at their maturity date. A number of banks which had frozen an excessive proportion of their funds in long-term loans in the agricultural sector were suddenly faced with bankruptcy. This threat was intensified when it turned out that "pig on pork" paper was practically unsalable.

The Java Bank and the NHM (which was able to absorb the blow because of its size and because its agricultural interests were at that time still limited) did their utmost to meet the needs of the trading sector. Their support was not enough. The banking system as a whole was faced with a loss of no less than 40 million guilders. Rescue operations were conducted by banks in the Netherlands. In the first place, the NIHB's agricultural interests were removed and transferred to a new agricultural bank, the Netherlands-Indian Agricultural Company (NILM). Financial assistance was also extended to the Colonial Bank, which had been established two years after the HVA in 1881, while *Dorrepaal en Co.* transferred its agricultural interests to the Principalities Agricultural Company. Thus, with the exception of the Java Bank, the NHM, and the NIEM, the banking system in Indonesia was thoroughly reformed. A fundamental reorganisation also took place in relations with the trading and agricultural sectors. In all, 27 million Netherlands guilders in bank capital was transferred to Indonesia.

The crisis of 1884 enforced a clear distinction between general banking business, that is, the provision of short- to medium-term credit, and the so-called agricultural banking business, which was concerned with long-term loans (often in the form of holdings in agricultural enterprises). With the exception of the NHM, which was to retain its "mixed" character and, to a lesser extent, the NIHB, the remaining banks gradually divested themselves of their direct agricultural interests. As far as possible, all long-term undertakings, mortgages and the like were shortened or called in. The banks switched to the provision of working capital (in the sense of operating capital) to commercial enterprises. Resources obtained also became largely liquid. Various new banks emerged, which specialised in financing agricultural enterprises. Because these banks placed their capital permanently at the disposal of agricultural estates, it would no longer be apt to describe them as credit-intermediaries but rather as agricultural holding companies. The HVA and the NILM are outstanding examples of this genre. By contrast, the NHM and the *Internatio* owned hardly any enterprises. The Colonial Bank and the Principalities Agricultural Company were agricultural banks from the outset. Table 11.3 gives an impression of the scale of operations of enterprises owned by the agricultural banks in 1933.

TABLE 11.3 Relative Share of Production of Enterprises Owned by Agricultural Banks in Total Production[a] or Total Exports[b], Indonesia, 1933

Enterprises owned by	Sugar	Coffee	Tea	Rubber
NHM	25	9	7	7.5
NILM	6	0.4	0.6	0.3
Internatio	4	5	2	1
HVA	12	x	x	x
Koloniale Bank	6	13	4	0.4
Cultuurmij. der Vorstenlanden	6	-	-	-
Total	61	27.4	13.6	9.2

a Sugar
b Coffee, tea, rubber
x unknown
\- negligible

Source: Verrijn Stuart (1923, p.205)

During the reconstruction phase after 1884, the foundations were laid out for the almost uninterrupted growth of the commercial banking system. There was a particularly marked expansion in the activities of the NIEM, which was one of the few "pure" general banks (meaning in this context a bank not having direct agricultural interests). In contrast to the NHM and the NIHB, the NIEM's operations were confined to Indonesia.

Indigenous Credit

A clear distinction has to be drawn between Western commercial banking described above, on the one hand, and indigenous credit (both unorganised rural credit as well as government-organised credit), on the other. The commercial banks were not geared to providing an adequate system of credit serving the needs of indigenous agriculture. Their contact with the village community, given the latter's slender capital resources, remained extremely limited. In addition, the banks posed a considerable psychological barrier to potential indigenous clients. The history of indigenous credit (in which money is involved) is closely connected with such factors as shifts in individual preferences, the penetration of a money economy, the prevalence of barter and the extent of *gotong royong*.

As a consequence of the gradual penetration of money, increasingly large segments of the indigenous community were periodically borrowing money. Money income and expenditure were highly seasonal in nature, and did not coincide. This was particularly true of regions in which the cultivation of *palawija* (mainly maize, cassava, sweet potatoes, groundnuts, and soy beans) had not yet led to a greater proliferation of money incomes. Budget surveys revealed that, after the provision of basic living requirements and the payment of taxes, very little money was left over for building up reserves or for capital formation.[10] In so far as there were any savings they were in kind, in the form of land, cattle, trinkets and also rice. Disruption of the uncertain budgetary equilibrium by small fluctuations in money income was an ever-present threat. In such cases, credit afforded the only way out. The main sources of obtaining necessary additional funds for agricultural purposes, the provision of basic living requirements, payment of taxes, redemption of debts, etc., were:

(a) mutual lending and borrowing among the Indonesians themselves;
(b) negotiating loans with private money-lenders;
(c) using credit facilities created by the Government.

The Unorganised Supply of Credit. Mutual credit extension among the Indonesian populace or "native credit" as Fruin (1931) called it, was closely connected with the *gotong rojong* principle. This type of credit was non-commercial by its very nature. Especially where barter still prevailed, it probably was the main source of meeting budgetary shortfalls. Negotiating loans with commercial money-lenders, generally of Chinese origin, was the other main "unorganised" type of rural credit. An important source of credit for the small cultivator was that offered by merchants, who bought up the farm produce for export or domestic distribution. By offering payment in advance these traders secured the crop at a discount. The so-called *ijon* system or advance on the green crop, was very common.

The non-European traders all over the countryside were mostly of Chinese origin. Often they were shopkeepers as well as buyers of produce. They supplied the farmer with all sorts of goods on credit against his future crop. In this connection, the *"mindering Chinees"* (instalment Chinese) also deserves mention. The *"mindering Chinees"* derived his name from his professional habit of going round the villages and market places collecting his interest and payments on principal a few *centen* or *duiten* at a time. He mostly lent out only tiny sums to a fairly numerous clientele, consisting chiefly of small traders, street hawkers and farmers' wives, who traded in the *pasar* and along the streets. The *"mindering Chinees"* himself borrowed his working capital from the more well-to-do of his own countrymen.

The major drawback to these types of lending was the exceptionally high rate of interest. On the demand side, this was caused by:

1. urgent necessity from time to time;
2. the marked tendency to under-estimate future needs and commitments; and
3. in more general terms, the community's lack of familiarity with monetary matters. Factors on the supply side included the high cost associated with small-scale credit and the rather risky nature of the collateral.

It frequently happened that a certain amount of money was lent for a six-month period against an undertaking to repay twice that amount. In the case of default, the principal sum was generally recovered from the security held. Despite the lenience usually displayed by lenders, this could, in the long term, entail the loss by the borrower of his major source of income, namely his land or the yield from his field or home garden. After 1900, there were only sporadic instances of peonage.

In the first few years after the proclamation in the Netherlands of the "ethical colonial policy" by Queen Wilhelmina in the Queen's Speech of 1901, a number of investigations were conducted into economic conditions at the local level, as a result of which a better understanding was gained of the needs of the Indonesian community. At the same time, interest grew in government circles in providing credit on "reasonable" terms.

People's Credit System (Volkskredietwezen). The basis for a centrally-organised credit system serving the interests of the indigenous community was laid by a civil servant and agricultural specialist, De Wolff van Westerrode. His noteworthy experiments with the Purwakarta Savings and Agricultural Bank led to his being commissioned by the Government to carry out a survey in 1900 into the prospects for establishing people's banks in Indonesia. In 1904, the People's Credit System became an official responsibility. From its inception, the main objectives of this system were:

1. the provision of cheap credit to the indigenous community, on condition that the expenses were to be kept to a minimum;

2. the encouragement of greater productive activity among the indigenous community by tapping idle production potential. Because of the lack of relevant data, the Government assumed for a considerable time that the indigenous community did indeed possess considerable "idle" capital in the form of cash and precious metals.

Initially, the district or regency banks (*volksbanken*) were set up, with a good deal of official financial support. These banks extended loans on a somewhat larger scale, often to individuals outside the *desa* framework, such as *priyayi*, European settlers in areas which had been opened up recently, and the urban community. They were later to provide support for the first local cash credit institutions. The *volksbanken* gradually attracted funds from these institutions, as well as from Europeans (in the form of deposits).

In general, the provision of credit by the *volksbanken* was not of a sufficiently specialised nature to reach the average villager. In villages where the cultivation of rice provided the basic means of support, and where the money economy was still at a rudimentary stage, it was thought more suitable to build on existing forms of credit in kind. To this end, so-called *desalumbung* (rice credit-banks) were set up in Java, with a rice capital deposited by the local community. In this way credit was to be extended from the villager's own resources. Wage labour, trade and small-scale industry existed in most regions of Java. Barter began to give way to a money economy, although this was by no means a continuous process, and there were substantial regional variations. Some government officials placed the use of money at *desa* level in perspective by referring to it as the halfpenny-housekeeping (*halvecentenhuishouding*).

The *lumbungs* were soon unable to meet the increasing (at least in an absolute sense) requirement for credit in the form of currency, even though, as mentioned above, these banks gradually began lending money as well as rice. Small *desabanken* (village banks) were established at the local level as early as 1904, which lent money for short periods and in small amounts. Initially, their number grew less quickly than the number of *lumbungs*, indicating that a cautious approach was adopted by the authorities, particularly in Java. Outside Java, and especially on the west coast of Sumatra, the People's Credit System was introduced in regions where money was already more commonly used as a result of smallholder export production. In 1912, the *volksbanken*, which had hitherto operated independently, were brought under the Central Fund for the People's Credit System (*Centrale Kas voor het Volkskredietwezen*). This Fund extended assistance to *desabanken* in temporary difficulty, and also supervised the extension of credit by the banks under its aegis as well as the municipal credit institutions. All the *volksbanken* (with the exception of those in North Sulawesi), together with the Central Fund, were brought under the General People's Credit Bank (*Algemeene Volkskredietbank* or AVB) in 1934.

The growth of the People's Credit System is shown in Table 11.4. In this table, the paid credit lent by the *desalumbungs* was converted into money terms by using the rice prices prevailing at that time.[11] The total provides little indication of the average amounts that were outstanding, for the sources consulted do not provide information on the duration of the loans. Nevertheless, the rapid growth until the depression years of 1929-1935 is apparent.

TABLE 11.4 Extension of Credit by the People's Credit System in Indonesia, 1905-1940 (million guilders)

	Volksbanken	Desabanken	Desalumbungs	Govt. Pawnshop Service	Total
1905[a]	0.82[b]	-	-	2.96	-
1910	7.38	-	-	23.49	-
1915	21.68	7.67	-	75.90	-
1920	39.36	8.78	31.41[c]	136.52	216.07[d]
1923	43.24	21.71	17.95	150.52	233.42
1925	52.38	33.77	19.60	166.25	272.00
1928	68.30	45.99	19.49	181.46	315.24
1930	72.44	44.39	20.20	194.14	331.17
1933	17.45	17.49	8.32	78.12	121.38
1935	17.40	14.79	8.25	67.52	107.96
1938	26.66	20.71	9.17	85.31	141.85
1940	28.80	23.43	9.16	88.19	149.58

[a] Financial year

[b] Incomplete

[c] 1921

[d] Estimate

Source: C.E.I. Vol. 6, Tables 6 and 7

An indication of the effect of the People's Credit System on the general level of prosperity may be obtained by comparing the savings and deposits which the indigenous community lodged at the various financial institutions with the credits they took up (Table 11.5). The Government Pawnshop Service was included for this purpose because a large proportion of the Indonesian population did not save in cash. The sums from the Pawnshop Service reflect these types of saving to a large extent. During the entire period up to 1940, "voluntary" savings by the indigenous community (i.e., excluding savings accrued by representative bodies) were insufficient to meet the demand for credit. It remained necessary to bring in funds from outside, although on a declining scale.

TABLE 11.5 Savings and Borrowings[a] by the Indigenous Community in Indonesia, 1915-1940

(million guilders, as at 31 December)

	Savings (1)	Borrowings incl. Pawnshop Service (2)	As (2) excl. Pawnshop Service (3)	(1) as % of (2) (4)	(1) as % of (3) (5)
1915	4.32[b]	41.02	20.53	10.5	21.0
1920	8.94	68.86	33.73	13.0	26.5
1923	9.71	97.54	44.88	10.0	21.6
1925	10.46	102.06	50.32	10.2	20.8
1928	13.97	126.19	66.66	11.1	21.0
1930	16.50	138.61	70.86	11.9	23.3
1933	14.29	65.70	34.72	21.8	41.2
1935	13.88[c]	51.31	25.23	27.1	55.0
1938	18.38[c]	65.39	32.39	28.1	56.7
1940	13.39[c]	67.41	34.15	19.9	39.2

[a] For the sake of convenience it was assumed that under the People's Credit System and the Pawnshop Service all credits were extended to the indigenous community

[b] Incomplete

[c] Estimate

Source: As for Table 11.4

Finally, Table 11.6 provides a rough indication of the rates of interest charged under the People's Credit System. The sources referred to in this table provide detailed information on variations in the interest rates charged, which depended on initial expenses and the loan period, as well as on the causes of the declining interest rates over time.

TABLE 11.6 The People's Credit System: Estimated Rates of Interest, 1905-37 (annual percentage rates)[a]

	Volksbanken		Desabanken		Desalumbungs
	1	2	1	2	1
1905-1913	12-18	-	24-45	-	-
1913-1926	13-19	9-17	40-60	0-33	30-60
1929-1937	8-15	8-15	30-40	20-30	25-30

1 = Java & Madura
2 = Other Islands

[a]Converted on the basis of the average loan period

Sources: Cramer (1929, pp.64-5, 111-2, 162-3, 183 & 213) and Sumitro (1943, pp.55-9, 88-91, 111-3, 127-30, 141-3, & 165-6)

Government Pawnshop Service (Gouvernements Panhuisdienst). At first sight the conversion of commodities into money and vice versa, which forms the customary business of pawnshops, would appear to have little in common with the types of credit tied to private individuals as described above. If, however, pawn-credit is regarded as "deferred" money income, which one could only obtain by pawning the surplus that had been accumulated previously in the form of goods, it may then be seen that the individual credit-worthiness was determined by the volume of savings in kind, i.e. by the relative level of prosperity. This subjective element in the provision of loans by the pawnshop services clearly illustrates the credit nature of this type of business. The first pawnshop was set up along European lines in Batavia as early as 1746, while Governor-General Van Imhoff was in office, largely through the agency of the Dutch East India Company (V.O.C.). The pawnshop was dissolved during the British Interregnum in 1811. Under Raffles, licences were initially allocated to private individuals, especially Chinese, but increasing abuse led to their replacement by a leasing system as early as 1814, in which there was a much greater degree of direct involvement by the authorities. With the exception of the period between 1870 and 1880, when licensing was reintroduced, pawnshops continued to be leased to individuals. This system, too, was increasingly abused. In response the Government decided in 1900 to conduct a survey into the scope for improvement, under the direction of De Wolff van Westerrode. On the basis of the recommendations made, the leasing system was replaced by government monopoly. Direct control by the Government came into force throughout Java and Madura in 1904.

Initially, particular efforts were made to eliminate all sorts of undesirable lending practices that operated to the detriment of the community, such as excessive lending rates, manipulated auctions, and inadequate care of pawned commodities. In this manner, the confidence of broad sections of the community was gradually won. By 1916, government pawnshops were established throughout Java and Madura, with the exception of the Principalities, where the licensing system, being a princely prerogative, remained in force. The pawnshop monopoly was not extended outside Java until 1921.

In contrast to Europe, credit obtained from a pawnshop in Indonesia should not be regarded as a final act of resistance in the struggle against poverty. Instead, pawn credit (as was also the case with the People's Credit System) fulfilled a requirement for cash that did not necessarily stem for dire necessity. Savings generally took the form of commodities, and at any given moment, these commodities could be converted into money at the pawnshop or, conversely, money could be converted into commodities. In this way it was possible to link up with the traditional types of saving, which in turn facilitated the monetisation of the indigenous community.

There were a number of differences between the pawnshop service and the People's Credit System. The most significant of these was the non-personal nature of pawnshop credit. Unlike the People's Credit System, individuals could not fall into arrears with a pawnshop; if the term of the commodity pawned expired or the commodity was unredeemed, and was not used as collateral for further loans, it was automatically disposed of at auction. Later, it might possibly be repurchased by the original owner. Even so, the consequences of excessive borrowings or a sudden economic downturn on the indigenous community were substantial, as is illustrated by Table 11.7 for the depression years of 1929-1933.

However, it is also clear from the table that, even in 1932-33, the amounts lent by the pawnshops exceeded redemptions, at least during the *paceklik* period, before the main harvest. It should, however, be noted that considerable inroads were made during this time into the amount of gold hoarded by the population. The rates of interest remained notably stable and were not exceptionally high, when the enormous administrative expenses connected with the small loans are taken into account (Table 11.8).

TABLE 11.7 Net Income[a] of the Indigenous Community from Official Credit, 1929-1934 (million guilders)

	Government Credit Banks		Pawnshops	
	May to October	November to April	May to October	November to April
1929-1930	+0.2	+5.5	+5.4	+17.8
1930-1931	-3.4	-0.5	+0.6	+11.6
1931-1932	-6.3	-3.3	+2.6	+7.5
1932-1933	-7.0	-3.0	-1.2	+2.4
1933-1934	-3.5	-	-2.0	-

[a] Balance of borrowings and redemptions

Source: de Stoppelaar (1934, p. 533)

TABLE 11.8 The Pawnshop Service: Rates of Interest, 1901-1940 (annual percentage rates)

	Loans extended, in guilders				
	0-0.50	0.50-25	25-50	50-75	75-100
1901-1919	72	72	60	48	36
1920-1924	(0-10) 48	(10-30) 36	(30-50) 16	(50) 12	
1924-1940	72	72	60	48	36

Source: Verslag betreffende den Gouvernements Pandhuisdienst [Report of the Government Pawnshop Service], 1902-38. Batavia, 1903-39.

Concluding Remarks

This chapter has presented a brief outline of Western banking and indigenous credit systems in Indonesia in the nineteenth and early twentieth centuries. Much more detailed research remains to be done. The substantial archives of the Java Bank in Jakarta and the NHM in the Dutch State Archives in the Hague could be drawn on for more detailed histories of particular banks and financial institutions, for research into the history of indigenous types of credit, and also for enquiries on many specific topics. Among these could be mentioned issues such as: did Western banking facilitate or hamper the monetisation of the indigenous economy? What were the reasons for the conflicts between the Netherlands Central Bank and the Java Bank in the early 1920s? What was the influence of such outstanding personalities as N.P. Van den Berg and G. Vissering on the development of banking in Indonesia? Hopefully, scholars in the near future will address these and other questions and throw more light on an important area of colonial economic history.

Notes

1. Usable introductory sources written by contemporary economists are rare. Among the most important are Van der Berg (1907), Verrijn Stuart (1923), Vissering (1920), and de Jong (1946). English-language introductions to the colonial monetary and financial system are even rarer. The most useful are Van den Berg (1895), Spalding (1918), Java Bank (n.d.), and Wardhana (1971). Furnivall (1934a, 1934b) discusses both the official and unofficial credit sources available in the 1930s.
2. In 1981 and 1982, under the supervision of the *Bank Indonesia* the author was involved in a project which opened up the archives of *De Javasche Bank*, the central bank and one of the largest commercial banks in colonial Indonesia. More than 800 metres of archive materials were critically examined, resulting in an inventory guide of some 5,500 files and maps.
3. Foreign Asiatics, mainly Chinese, are here subsumed under the Western sector.
4. For further discussion of the significance of the *pasar* economy, see van Gelderen (1927, pp.42-75).
5. Estimates of the ratio of money transactions to total transactions of about 0.5 are given in Gonggrijp (1938); Huender and Meyer Ranneft (1926, p.9); Polak (1943); and de Vries (1931, p.290 ff.).
6. For a discussion of the colonial "drain" see Berkhuysen (1948), Boeke (1942, pp.131-93) and Golay (1976).
7. For an excellent description of the role of the agricultural banks see Helfferich (1914).
8. According to *De Indische Financier*, May 8 and 12, 1923, Nos. 59 and 60, "Eene geldmarkt in Indië?" (A Money Market in Netherlands India?), the average

capacity of the colonial Indonesian money market should be put at little more than 50 million guilders.

9. Quote from *Notities omtrent de vereischten waaraan de door de Vereenigde Staaten van Indonesië te octrooieren circulatiebank en de regeling van het geldwezen van dat gebied zal moeten voldoen* [Some Considerations on a new Central Bank for the United States of Indonesia and the Regulation of the Money System], *Archive of De Javasche Bank*, No. 127, p.65 (March 1948).
10. For details of the most important budget studies, see Boeke (1926), Van Deventer (1904), and Huender and Meyer Ranneft (1926).
11. *CEI*, vol.4, pp.45-46.

CHAPTER TWELVE

Foreign Trade and Domestic Development in the Colonial Economy

Anne Booth

The Impact of Trade on Growth and Development: The Debate

During the nineteenth century, accelerated economic growth in the countries of Europe, North America, and Australasia went hand in hand with a dramatic expansion in world trade, so that commerce between nations came to be known in the economic literature as the "engine of growth." Many parts of the tropical world also shared in this expansion of trade but their economies did not undergo the kind of transformation that characterised the countries of the now developed world. In his recent study of Thai agricultural development, Feeny (1982a, p.1) has posed the basic problem of Thai economic history thus:

> In the Thai case, the economy responded vigorously to the opportunities which international trade created. In the period from 1857 to 1941, rice exports in metric tons increased more than twenty-fold, and Thailand became a major rice exporter. Yet living standards advanced very little. Why did this considerable expansion in trade not lead to more impressive growth?

The same question can, and has, been asked about many of the tropical colonies in Asia and elsewhere (see, for example, Sundrum and Aye Hlaing 1961, p.8). It is obviously a question of crucial relevance to Indonesia in the nineteenth and twentieth centuries and this chapter seeks to provide at least some provisional answers. We begin with a brief summary of the debate on trade and development, before examining the Indonesian experience in detail.

That the static neo-classical theory of international trade based on the Heckscher-Ohlin model is ill-suited to explaining the dynamic relationship between trade and growth has been acknowledged by many writers. For example, Krueger (1980, p.288) has argued that "there are many static propositions but few useful theorems about the effects of alternative trade policies on growth." Similarly Sodersten (1970, p.188) in his well-known textbook has pointed out that "static theory has little to say" on the relationship between trade and longer run economic development. The classical economists, in particular Smith and Mill, stressed that countries could reap dynamic gains from trade for several different reasons. First, the process of opening up an economy to trade allows hitherto unutilised resources to be brought into productive use; this is the so-called vent-for-surplus argument. In stressing this argument, Mill in particular argued that the division of labour inherent in more specialised production for an extended market would in turn induce innovations and improvements in the production processes (Mill, as quoted in Meier, 1975, p.429). In addition Mill thought that trade would introduce a range of new goods which in turn would serve as inducements for greater effort on the part of the hitherto under-employed labour force.

The classics also argued that trade encourages growth not just in the export sector but in the rest of the economy, "through the educational effects of exposure to foreign competition and foreign ways of doing things" (Johnson 1977, p.427). This part of the classical message has been echoed by Lockwood (1954, p.320 ff.) who spoke of trade as a "highway of learning" in the context of Japan, bearing the skills of the industrial West to Meiji Japan, and by Haberler (1959, p.705) who spoke of trade as "the most important vehicle for the transmission of technological know-how."

The vent-for-surplus argument was revived by Myint in a well-known paper in which he argued that it had proved the best explanator of the process of "opening up" to trade which many tropical countries underwent in the nineteenth century (Myint 1971, Ch. 5). This process made use of the idle land and labour found in many parts of the tropical world to produce both agricultural output and minerals for export. The production processes were characterised by fairly simple technology which was, in many cases, replicated by the local populations on their own land. Myint (1971, pp. 113, 124) concludes:

> Thus instead of a process of economic growth based on continuous improvements in skills, more productive recombinations of factors and increasing returns, the nineteenth-century expansion of international trade in the underdeveloped countries seems to approximate to a simpler process based on constant returns and fairly rigid combinations of factors...it must be admitted that, in contrast to the tremendous stimulus to further economic development enjoyed by the advanced countries, international trade seems to have had very little "educative effect" on the people of the backward countries except in the development of new wants.

Elsewhere, Myint (1973, p.39) has argued that, while the indigenous populations of many tropical countries were able to benefit from the market opportunities which trade presented, they were less able to reap the potential technological benefits. In this respect, their experience must be sharply distinguished from that of Japan, and more recently, other rapidly industrialising countries such as Korea and Hong Kong. It is this experience which has given rise to a new spate of empirical work on the connection between trade and growth. However, where this work is based on statistical correlations, it is vulnerable to the kind of criticisms made by Kleiman (1980). Probably the most rigorous treatment of the relationship between trade and growth is that given in Cornwall (1977, chs. 9 and 10). In his exposition, it is manufacturing which is the engine of growth, and there is a cumulative growth process based on a "virtuous circle" resulting from manufactured exports. But Cornwall also stresses that the same cumulative process could be triggered by domestic production of manufactures, what he termed "homespun growth."

Among contemporary writers on economic development, several different explanations have been given for the failure of trade to lead to economic transformation through rapid technological change in many parts of the tropical world. One school of thought emphasizes the failure of both colonial and post-colonial governments to make efficient use of the initial profits accruing to them from participation in international trade. Hirschman (1977, p.72 ff.) has pointed to the importance of what he terms "fiscal linkages" in determining the longer run impact of trade on growth. These linkages depend crucially on the extent to which the export sector is taxed on the one hand, and the productivity of government expenditures on the other. Several country studies, including those of Feeny (1982a) for Thailand and Leff (1982) for Brazil, have argued that the tendency of governments to spend their revenues on administration and military-related infrastructure, rather than on productive projects, meant that such fiscal linkages were weak during most of the nineteenth century.

Colonial governments have also been blamed for failing to encourage the emergence of a domestic entrepreneurial class which could utilise gains from trade to develop manufacturing and service industries. Lewis (1970, p.43) argues that "when one has been through all the other factors, one is left with lack of entrepreneurship as the most powerful explanation of failure to make significant progress in manufacturing." He points out that most colonial governments did little to create the kind of atmosphere in which domestic entrepreneurship would flourish, and some were quite hostile to whatever local industry did emerge, especially when it threatened foreign interests. When foreign capital showed little interest in providing certain services, such as retail trade, colonial governments tended to favour migrant aliens. Such policies, pursued over long periods, tended to plant "an inferiority complex, with either genetic or cultural overtones; or at least a propensity for destructive criticism, rather than for constructive initiatives" (Lewis 1976b, p.151)

Lewis (1969, p.25) has also criticised governments, both colonial and post-colonial, for their almost complete neglect of research on yield-raising technologies in the foodcrop sector. "For the last eighty years, the tropical countries have put practically all their agricultural research and extension funds and effort into trying to raise the productivity of export crops...and virtually no effort into food productivity." He stresses that in many cases the gains from cashcrop productivity growth were almost entirely lost through declining terms of trade, whereas increases in food productivity in the tropical countries, by increasing the opportunity cost of labour, may actually have lead to an improvement in world prices for tropical export staples (Lewis 1969, pp.17-22; 1978, pp.14-20).

A further school of thought, associated with the work of Baldwin (1956), stresses not so much the world price as the nature of the production function of the export staple in determining the extent to which trade leads to a dynamic process of structural transformation through accelerated technological change. This notion is also implicit in Hirschman's linkage concept, which he considers to exist whenever an ongoing economic activity gives rise to a new one (Hirschman, 1977, p.81). If a particular staple or set of staples is associated with a richer constellation of linkages than others, then economies specialising in these staples will develop more rapidly. But as Hanson (1980, pp.46-50) has argued, this theory is unable to deal with the fact that the growth performance of economies producing the same staples has often been rather different, owing to the role of government or private entrepreneurs.

In contrast to arguments stressing the role of government, private entrepreneurship, or the nature of particular export staples, economists of more radical persuasion have tended to stress those aspects of international trade which may actually make trading nations poorer than they would have been under conditions of autarky. Hymer and Resnick (1971, p.487) have argued that, even in the case where colonial governments invested the gains from trade in economic infrastructure, it was primarily intended to encourage further export production, often at the expense of domestic production. This in turn could lead to a process of immiserising growth, in the case where more production depressed world prices, thus leading to a severe deterioration in the country's terms of trade. Other writers have stressed the measures used by colonial governments to force the production of export crops at the expense of foodcrops, leading to increased indebtedness and, in extreme cases, to famine and a severe decline in indigenous living standards.

The radical critics of the impact of trade on primary exporting countries also stress the very large export surpluses which some of the major colonies accumulated during the late nineteenth and early twentieth centuries (see, for example, Frank 1976). These export surpluses were, to some extent, balanced by deficits on invisible trade, but critics such as Frank argue that in many cases, most of the export surplus was remitted in one form or another, usually in the form of profits. Frank's arguments have in turn been challenged by other students of colonial trade (see, for example, Latham 1978, and Hanson 1980, pp.121-28). We will examine them in the Indonesian context below.

Many of these arguments concerning trade and growth can be illustrated by considering the effects of an export enclave on the rest of the economy. In the extreme case of a pure enclave, there are no linkages with the rest of the domestic economy, but only with the rest of the world. Capital and labour are imported from abroad and combined with hitherto idle land to produce exports, and the profits are again remitted abroad. Gross domestic production (GDP) for the country as a whole goes up by the amount of the value added in the export sector, although the rise in gross national income will be less because of the remitted profits. The indigenous sector of the economy will be untouched by development in the enclave sector, except in so far as it reduces potential for further growth by exhausting non-renewable resources. In this case, the contribution of trade to the overall rate of GDP growth in the economy as a whole is equal to the growth in volume of exports multiplied by the ratio of exports to total income in the initial period. But the contribution to growth of national income would be lower.

A much more realistic case is that of the export enclave which generates substantial linkages with the rest of the economy. The flows are of several kinds (Lewis 1976a, pp.26-27). First, there are payments for factors drawn from the indigenous economy into the export enclave, principally land and labour. Second, there are payments for other inputs which the enclave "imports" from the rest of the economy, such as raw materials, food, and various services. Third, there are the taxes and other levies paid by the enclave to the indigenous government. Then there are the technology transfers in the form of new production skills passed from the enclave to the rest of the economy. To quote Lewis (1976a, p.27), the enclave " serves as an example of the productivity of new techniques, institutions, and methods of organization." As in the pure enclave model, capital, and possibly labour, are imported from the rest of the world. output from the enclave is exported, and profits remitted. However not all the export earnings are remitted in the form of profits; some are now used to finance imports to the rest of the economy, demand for which has been stimulated by increased cash incomes from the enclave sector.

There are several costs to set against these benefits. The factors of production drawn from the indigenous sector have an opportunity cost in terms of production foregone in that sector. In the extreme case where these factors are coerced into employment in the enclave (corveé labour or the compulsory leasing of land), it must be assumed that net benefits are negative. In addition, products produced by the enclave, or imports financed by the foreign exchange it earns, may compete with and ultimately destroy traditional products of the domestic economy. The enclave may also give rise to economic, social, and geographical polarisation, attracting the most gifted members of the domestic economy, and thus draining it of talent and enterprise (Lewis 1976a, p.29).

Over time, these various flows can be expected to have second and subsequent round effects on both the enclave and the rest of the economy. The flow of technology from the enclave will lead to the establishment of a parallel indigenous sector producing export crops using less capital-intensive production techniques than the foreign sector with ready access to imported capital. The impact of this indigenous, small-scale export sector on the rest of the domestic economy will in turn depend on the use its producers make of the profits from export production. If they are largely spent on consumption of imported goods, or remitted abroad, then their ultimate impact will be little different from that of the foreign producers operating in the enclave. But if the profits are reinvested in the domestic economy, and if the indigenous producers learn entrepreneurial skills which they can then apply in other sectors, the multiplier effect could be considerable.

The writers who have stressed the beneficial impact of trade on development, such as Myint, emphasize the opportunities which trade offers the indigenous economy to use its factors more productively, learn at least some new skills, and thus earn higher incomes than were possible in the pre-trade situation. Critics such as Lewis, while not denying the potential benefits offered by trade, tend to stress those factors which have made the actual benefits far less than they could have been. More radical critics emphasize those factors which can make the sum of all the flows into and out of the indigenous sector negative. We turn now to discuss these arguments in more detail in the Indonesian case.

The Indonesian Experience: Growth of Trade

The island world of Southeast Asia had been involved in maritime trade for many centuries before the advent of Europeans in the sixteenth century. Traders from China, India, Arabia, and mainland Southeast Asia were all drawn by the archipelago's forest and seafood products, gold, and spices. From the fourteenth century onwards, the production of cashcrops began in earnest, with pepper being cultivated in Northern Sumatra, and cloves in Banda and Maluku (Reid 1980b, p.236). Other cashcrops, such as coffee and tobacco, were rapidly taken up when European traders created or expanded a market. Large and flourishing port cities established themselves in Aceh, Banten, and Makassar, while several of the cities along Java's north coast were also important trading centres by the sixteenth century (Reid 1980, Table 1).

In the seventeenth and eighteenth centuries the archipelago's international and inter-regional trade came increasingly under European (especially Dutch) control, and was organised in their interests. Reid (1984) has discussed several factors which made Indonesia at this time vulnerable to Western intrusion;

Table 12.1 Growth in Volume and Price of Export Production, 1830-1910

Year[a]	Index (1)[b] of Prices	Index (1)[b] of Quantities	Index (2)[c] of Prices	Index (2)[c] of Quantities
1830	71	15		
1835	90	32		
1840	93	58		
1845	78	70		
1850	78	72		
1855	92	86		
1860	107	88		
1865	112	89	109	95
1870	100	100	100	100
1875			136	123
1880			105	148
1885			85	199
1890			90	207
1895			84	215
1900			66	266
1905			60	329
1910			78	403

Annual Average Rates of Growth of Output[d]

1827-40	14.2
1840-73	2.0
1871-84	5.5
1885-94	0.3
1895-1913	4.2 (6.2)[e]

a Five year averages, centered on the years shown.

b Divisia indexes of quantities and prices, calculated from the SHAZAM package. Data refer to exports of indigo, coffee, rice, sugar, and tin. Prices are unit export values.

c Divisia indexes of quantities and prices, calculated from the SHAZAM package. Data refer to production of copra, coffee, sugar, tobacco and tea.

d Calculated by fitting an exponential function to the annual index data.

e Figure in brackets refers to growth in smallholder production of copra, coffee, tea and tobacco.

Sources: Index (1): C.K.S. 160
Index (2): Output data: C.E.I. Vol 1, Table 5.
Price data: C.K.S., 166.
Smallholder production: C.E.I., Vol.1, Tables 8,12,13,14

certainly the various indigenous kingdoms were no military match for the larger ships and superior weapons of the Europeans. In 1669 the V.O.C. destroyed Makassar, and in 1684 Banten was taken. Although exports of coffee, pepper, spices, indigo, sugar, and rice all continued to grow through the V.O.C. period, it would seem that in most cases the gains from trade accrued largely to company officials and the indigenous ruling elites.

A sustained growth in exports from Indonesia began again in the nineteenth century, with the implementation of the Cultivation System in Java. Like many other tropical colonies, Indonesia became increasingly involved in international trade in the last century of colonial rule. Both the improvement in shipping consequent upon the opening of the Suez Canal, and the emergence of new export staples, first in Java and then in Sumatra and Kalimantan, drew many millions of Indonesians into increasing dependence on the world economy for their livelihood, either as employees of foreign estates or as smallholder producers of export products.

Reasonably comprehensive data on Java's international and inter-regional trade are available from the 1820s; corresponding data for all of Indonesia are available from 1874. These data have been discussed by several scholars and the broad trends indicated by them can be summarized as follows.[1] During the 1830s, after the establishment of the Cultivation System, exports grew very rapidly in volume and value terms. To some extent, this growth may be a statistical artifact due to under-reporting of exports in the early years of the System; even so, the data indicate that export volume grew by more than 14 per cent per annum in the years from 1827 to 1840 (Table 12.1). But in the 1840s the growth rate slackened off considerably and was almost zero in the second half of the decade. Export volume growth never regained the momentum of the 1830s; the average for the entire period 1840-1870 was only about 2 per cent per annum (Table 12.1; see also Caldwell 1964, p.75). During these three decades, coffee and sugar were the major staples and between them accounted for about 60 per cent of total export earnings (Table 12.2; see also O'Malley, this volume).

The process of economic liberalisation which began in the 1870s together with the opening of the Suez Canal led to a considerable acceleration in the rate of growth of export volume compared with the previous three decades (Table 12.1). There was also a sharp decline in the percentage of exports accruing from government procurement as a result of the demise of the consignment system (Caldwell 1964, p.76). However the production spurt proved short-lived and, from the mid-1880s to the mid-1890s, the volume of production of the five major export crops scarcely grew at all (Table 12.1). Moreover the slump in world prices which occurred during the 1880s was particularly severe for tropical products, and Indonesia's net barter terms of trade almost certainly declined.[2] Prices in fact continued to deteriorate until the end of the century, and the index of of the income terms of trade showed little growth between 1876 and 1890 (Figure 12.1).

TABLE 12.2 Percentage Breakdown of Exports from Java by Commodity, 1830-70

	Indigo	Coffee	Rice	Sugar	Tobacco	Tin	Other
1830	..	29	2	10	..	5	54
1835	3	40	5	16	..	4	32
1840	8	47	2	18	3	4	18
1845	7	30	1	30	2	6	24
1850	7	32	3	28	1	8	21
1855	4	38	6	24	1	5	22
1860	3	27	4	29	1	7	29
1865	4	29	2	28	2	7	28
1870	3	32	1	27	3	6	28

a Export earnings from crops indicated as a percentage of total exports, both international and inter-regional.

Source: C.K.S. Mededeeling No. 160

These data make it clear that the nineteenth century was not a golden era of rapid export growth in Indonesia. The initial rapid growth in exports from Java during the 1830s was short-lived, and for the rest of the century export growth was often slow and always erratic. The comparative data provided by Hanson (1980, p.28) show that in fact Indonesia's growth rate of per capita exports in US$ terms was rather lower than the mean for a sample of twenty-two countries in Asia, Africa, and the Americas between 1860 and 1900.[3] The reasons for this poor performance were partly connected with trends in international markets for Indonesia's staple crops, especially sugar and coffee, but they also lay with domestic policies, which we discuss in greater detail below.

With the turn of the century, the fortunes of Indonesia's export economy began to improve. The quantity index of the five major export commodities grew at about four per cent per annum over the period 1895-1913; in the 1920s, the pace of growth quickened, and the quantity index grew at over eight per cent per annum (Table 12.3). These years saw substantial export diversification in four important directions. First, the commodity composition of exports changed with the traditional staples tea, coffee, and sugar all declining in relative importance and new staples rubber, palm oil, and petroleum products growing. Second, Java

FIGURE 12.1 Index of Income Terms of Trade, 1874–1938
(1913 = 100)

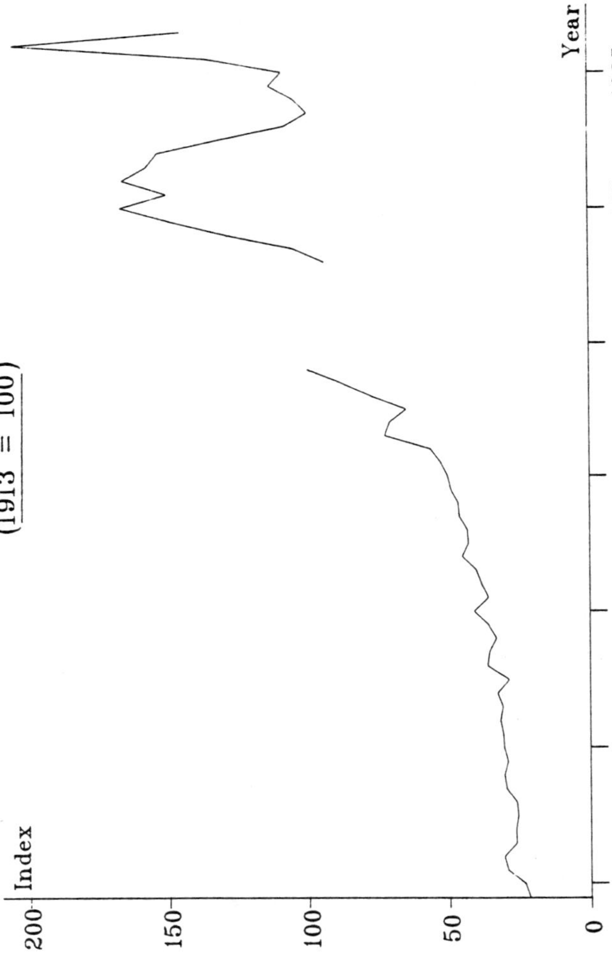

Source: Value of exports from C.K.S. 161, deflated by the index of prices of manufactures, as given in Lewis (1952).

Table 12.3 Indexes of Export Output and Prices. 1920-40
(1920 = 100)

Year	Quantity: All Output[a]	Quantity: Smallholders[b]	Prices: All Output[a]	Prices: Smallholders[b]
1920	100	100	100	100
1921	105	108	45	64
1922	114	113	41	65
1923	121	129	51	87
1924	136	163	50	100
1925	158	199	57	116
1926	156	203	52	116
1927	177	224	45	122
1928	201	253	36	113
1929	207	254	33	111
1930	200	221	24	94
1931	197	225	16	65
1932	191	231	14	57
1933	160	233	13	54
1934	162	284	15	58
1935	149	261	14	54
1936	162	268	18	65
1937	218	322	23	84
1938	185	271	17	60
1939	201	295	19	66
1940	201	295	19	66
Annual Average Growth Rates of Production				
1920-30	8.3	10.6		
1931-40	2.1	4.2		

a Production of tea, coffee, sugar, copra tobacco, palm oil, petroleum, tin, and rubber.

b Smallholder production of tea, coffee, copra, tobacco and rubber.

Source: Production data: C.E.I. Vol ´, except for petroleum and tin, which were obtained from C.K.S. 167, pp. 4-5.

TABLE 12.4 Percentage Import and Export Shares of Major Trading Partners: 1875-1935

		1875	1895	1905	1915	1925	1935
Europe	X	75	54	42	42	32	38
	M	62	50	54	54	48	36
Holland	X	64	37	31	27	15	21
	M	47	33	33	29	20	13
America	X	8	7	4	5	14	15
	M	2	2	2	4	7	8
Asia	X	12	32	43	42	50	35
	M	35	47	43	41	42	52
Singapore	X	11	18	20	16	27	18
	M	24	31	24	17	15	11
Japan	X	-	-	4	2	5	5
	M	-	-	1	8	11	30
Australia	X	4	1	1	4	2	5
	M	1	1	1	1	3	3
Africa	X	"	7	10	4	1	3
	M	-	-	-	-	-	1
Sabang etc	X	-	-	-	-	1	4
	M	-	-	-	-	-	1

Source: C.K.S. 161

lost its dominant position until, by 1925, the Outer Islands were producing over 50 per cent of all agricultural exports. Third, associated with the rise of new export staples outside Java was the rise of the smallholder producer. After 1895, smallholder production of export crops grew more rapidly than estate production (Tables 12.1 and 12.3). Whereas in 1894, 90 per cent of agricultural export commodities were produced by estates, this figure had fallen to 63 per cent by 1925; outside Java, smallholders were producing about 60 per cent of all agricultural exports (C.E.I.,Vol.1 Table 2). Fourth, there was a dramatic change in the direction of export trade. Even before the increase in export volume in the 1890s, the importance of Europe (and Holland in particular) in Indonesia's export trade had begun to decline (Table 12.4). By the early years of this century, Holland was receiving less than one third of Indonesia's exports, and Asia, including Singapore, over 40 per cent. By 1925 these percentages were 15 and 50 respectively. On the import side, Japan was increasing her penetration of the Indonesian market, especially after the First World War.[4]

In common with the other major trading nations, Indonesia suffered a sharp contraction in volume and value of exports in the early 1930s. Some staples, especially sugar, were more badly hit than others, such as rubber and petroleum. The income terms of trade, which had grown almost continually between 1893 and 1925 suffered a severe decline between 1927 and 1933 (Figure 12.1). The purchasing power of Indonesia's export earnings in 1932 was only 60 per cent of what it had been in 1925, although there was a marked recovery in the later 1930s. On balance, the smallholder producers were less adversely affected by the depression than the large estates, experiencing a less dramatic downturn in output volume in the early 1930s, and making a more rapid recovery in the latter part of the decade. This was partly because the prices of the major smallholder staples did not deteriorate nearly as rapidly as the aggregate price index of all export commodities (Table 12.5), which in turn reflected the steep decline in the price of

Table 12.5 Index of Net Barter Terms of Trade: Indonesia and Selected Comparisons, 1913-38

	1913	1920	1925	1929	1933	1936	1938
Indonesia	100	99	100	66	49	73	56
Ceylon	100	35	70	49	48	74	69
Egypt	100	119	164	134	102	117	n.a
India	100	53	99	95	82	89	n.a
Nigeria	100	39	38	42	33	43	n.a
Philippines	100	100	97	89	86	92	65
Taiwan	100	108	78	74	76	77	n.a
Thailand	100	71	118	121	91	133	n.a
World Indexes							
Prebisch	100	n.a	84	84	67	72	70
League of Nations	100	n.a	90	86	65	74	73
Lewis	100	n.a	94	89	67	77	75
United Nations	100	n.a	98	91	61	76	68

Sources: Data from all countries except Indonesia taken from Birnberg and Resnick (1975, Appendices). World Indexes from Spraos (1980), p.111. Indonesian index constructed from the import price index given in C.K.S. 146, pp. 1-2, and Central Bureau of Statistics (1941, p.116). The export price index is as shown in Table 12.3.

two important non-smallholder staples, sugar and petroleum. However, smallholders increased their share of production even of those staples where they competed with the large estates, such as rubber and coffee, which suggests that the smaller production units using less capital-intensive cultivation techniques were better able to withstand the troubled economic environment of the 1930s than the large estates.

From 1900 onwards, it is possible to compare the growth in Indonesia's export volume with the data compiled by Birnberg and Resnick (1975) for India, the Philippines, Thailand, and Sri Lanka (Figure 12.2). Indonesia performed very favourably in comparison with these other countries, especially after 1913. Only the Philippines had a comparable volume growth in the 1920s and 1930s. While it is true that the use of 1913 prices favours the rubber-exporting countries (rubber prices were very high in 1913, and thus a high weight is given to the fastest growing export commodity), there seems little doubt that Indonesia's export volume growth after the First World War was very rapid by international standards.

On the other hand, Indonesia's commodity terms of trade declined sharply from 1925 onwards, even compared with the average experience of all primary exporting countries (Table 12.5). The weighted index of export prices was about the same in 1929 as it had been in 1913, although the import price index had increased by 50 per cent. This decline was so steep in the early 1930s that the income terms of trade also declined, although they recovered somewhat in the latter part of the decade (Figure 12.1).

The Indonesian Experience: Growth of Output and Income

For most of the period 1830-1940, detailed national product and income estimates are not available. De Vries has provided some estimates of per capita real income growth, which suggest almost a doubling between 1860 and 1929 (Zimmerman 1962, p.53). This implies an average annual growth of about one per cent per annum, which seems on the high side, given that living standards at the end of the colonial era were still very modest, and that Scheltema's data indicate little change in per capita rice consumption in the century or so up to 1930 (Scheltema 1936, Table 2). More recent estimates prepared by Van Laanen (1984) using data on the growth of real money supply suggest that real per capita income growth could not have exceeded 0.5 per cent per annum.

What seems certain is that export growth must have been more rapid than income growth in the entire period up to 1940. The national income data assembled by Polak (C.E.I., Vol.5) indicate that the ratio of exports to income rose to 36% by 1925 (Figure 12.3), whereas it is unlikely to have been more than 10 per cent in 1830. An important question thus becomes, to what extent was the

FIGURE 12.2 Index of Export Volume Growth, 1900–1938 (1913 = 100)

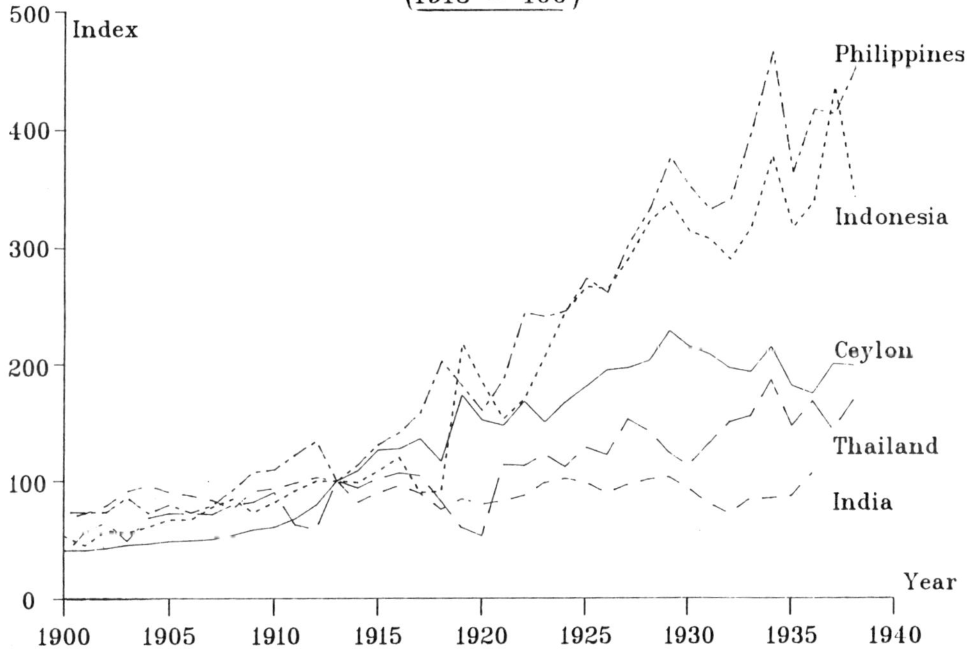

Sources: All export volume data except Indonesia from Birnberg and Resnick (1975). The Indonesian index was constructed from quantities exported of sugar, tea, quinine, palm oil, coffee, tobacco, copra, and rubber, weighted by 1913 wholesale prices, taken from C.K.S. 146, Table IV.

FIGURE 12.3 Exports as a Percentage of National Income, 1921–1939

Sources: Exports: Central Bureau of Statistics (1941, p.71)
National Income: C.E.I. Vol. 5, Table 15.1

export growth which occurred at the expense of growth in domestic production? In order to explore this further we need to examine, in particular, the available evidence on foodcrop production.

We begin with Java in the period 1830-1870. The export quantity index already presented in Table 12.1 can be compared with an index of rice production growth, and sugar production growth. From 1860 onwards, we can also construct an index of real growth in the money supply, which gives us a further clue to trends in real output growth in the monetised sector. Unfortunately, the rice production data are too fragmentary before 1840 to allow us to form accurate estimates of the impact of the dramatic export growth in the 1830s on food production, although it seems almost certain that the demands that the Cultivation System made on the indigenous labour force must have had some adverse effect on food crop production during the system's initial phase (see the chapters by Boomgaard, Elson, and Van Niel, this volume). The data from the 1840s suggest rice production grew at about one per cent per annum during this decade, while sugar output grew at almost six per cent per annum; it was the decline in coffee exports which was responsible for the negative growth in export volume (Table 12.6). Of the major export crops, it was sugar which directly competed with rice for land; there can be little doubt that the rapid rise of sugar cultivation in Java in the 1830s and 1840s slowed down foodcrop growth and was at least partly responsible for the famines of the 1840s (Fernando 1980; Elson 1984).

During the 1850s and 1860s the situation changed considerably. Rice production growth accelerated markedly, and sugar production growth declined.[5] Although rice exports also increased during the 1850s, and there is little evidence that per capita consumption of rice rose—Scheltema's data indicate little change in per capita rice availability during this period—other indicators suggest some improvement in per capita living standards in these two decades. For example, the real value of imports grew at about two per cent per annum between 1850 and 1873 (Table 12.6). In addition, the money supply data indicate an annual real growth of over five per cent per annum from 1850 to 1873. If, following Leff (1982, p.30), we assume that some decline in velocity must have occurred, then the growth of incomes in the monetised sector would have been lower, but still possibly of the order of three per cent per annum, suggesting some improvement in per capita income.[6]

In the period from 1870 to 1940 we have export data for the whole of Indonesia, although the data on foodcrop production are still available for Java only. Until 1885, rice production continued to exceed probable population growth in Java in spite of an accelerated growth in sugar production (Table 12.7). Scheltema's data indicate a marked rise in per capita rice availability during the 1870s, partly because of rising production, but partly also because net exports turned to net imports in Java during this decade. But after 1885, the rate of growth

Table 12.6 Annual Average Rates of Growth[a] of Rice Production, Exports, Imports, Government Expenditures and Money Supply, 1827-1913

	Rice Production[b]	Real Value of Government Expenditures[c]	Real Money Supply[c]	Real Value of Imports[d]	Export Volume Growth[e]
1827-40	n.a.	n.a.	n.a.	5.0	14.2
1841-50	1.1	n.a.	n.a.	1.4	1.1
1851-73	2.8 (2.2)	2.2	5.6	2.0	1.3
1874-85	1.8 (1.9)	3.7	4.5	5.5	5.9
1886-1900	0.8 (0.8)	1.4	0.8	3.0	2.1
1901-13	2.7 (1.7)	3.2	4.0	6.0	4.4

a Derived by fitting an exponential function to the annual data for the years indicated.

b Data refer to Java and Madura only. Figure in brackets refer to the growth in harvested area (planted area for 1851-73).

c Nominal data deflated by a simple average of the rice price index, export price index and the Sauerbeck index, as reported in Van Laanen (1984).

d Up to 1873, data refer to Java only; thereafter data cover all Indonesia. The nominal data were deflated by the Sauerbeck index of U.K. wholesale prices.

e For details on the construction of the index of export volume, see Tables 12.1 and 12.3.

Sources: Rice data; Koloniaal Verslag and Jaarcijfers, various years.
Imports: C.K.S. 160 and 161
Money Supply: Van Laanen (1984).
Sauerbeck index of U.K. wholesale prices: Journal of the (Royal) Statistical Society, various issues from 1886 onwards

in rice production fell sharply as did growth in real money supply. The reasons for the poor rice performance in Java in the latter 1880s and 1890s are not immediately obvious, although poor weather is alleged to have played a part (Creutzberg 1972, p.xxxi).

If uncertainty exists about what was happening to per capita incomes of indigenous Indonesians in the closing decades of the nineteenth century, there seems little doubt that a marked improvement occurred in most indicators of income and welfare in the decade or so preceding the First World War. Rice production accelerated and per capita rice availability increased from 100 kg per capita in 1905 to 117 kg per capita in 1915 (Scheltema 1936, Table 2). The acceleration in rice production was at least in part due to increased expenditures on public works, which we discuss further below. Export volume growth also accelerated, particularly from the smallholder sector outside Java. Indonesia's

TABLE 12.7 Area of Irrigated Riceland (Sawah), Harvested Area of Wetland Paddy (Padi Sawah), and Harvested Area of Sugar, 1885-1940 ('000 hectares: five-year averages)

Year	Sawah Area (a)	Harvested Area of Padi Sawah (b)	Harvested Area of Sugar (c)	(c) as a percentage of (b) (d)
1886-1890	1955	1939	53	2.7
1891-1895	1966	1965	79	4.0
1896-1900	2060	2077	102	4.9
1901-1905	2072	2109	132	6.3
1906-1910	2137	2285	144	6.3
1911-1915	2354	2505	175	7.0
1916-1920	2995	2806	153	5.5
1921-1925	3163	2886	166	5.8
1926-1930	3246	3050	191	6.3
1931-1935	3298	3279	103	3.1
1936-1940	3365	3580	78	2.2

[a]After 1916 data include the native states

Sources: Sawah area: Jaarcijfers and Statistisch Jaaroverzicht, various issues
Harvested area of sugar: Jaarcijfers and C.E.I. Vol. 1, Table 7

income terms of trade also improved (Figure 12.1), and real money stock grew at over four per cent per annum (Table 12.6).

Export volume, the income terms of trade, and real money supply all continued to grow rapidly in the period from 1916 to 1930. But it appears that in this period much of the export growth occurred outside Java, although sugar production accelerated to over five per cent per annum (Table 12.7). However both rice production and total foodcrop production in Java grew at rates which scarcely exceeded population growth. In the 1930s, by contrast, although export volume grew far more slowly, and sugar production actually declined, foodcrop production accelerated to almost three percent per annum, or over one per cent in per capita terms.

The data in Table 12.7 would lead one to guess that in Java indigenous income growth was faster in the depression decade of the 1930s than in the boom times of the 1920s, while the reverse was true in the export retions outside Java. Polak's data on real income growth by region and ethnic group support this hypothesis (C.E.I., Vol.5, Table 16.4). Whereas in the decade from 1921 to 1929 real indigenous income in Java grew by 2.1 per cent per annum, in the period between 1929 and 1939 it grew by 2.5 per cent per annum. Comparable figures for the Outer Islands were 3.2 per cent and 1.8 per cent respectively.

The Indonesian Experience: The Impact of Trade on Growth and Development

Having reviewed the evidence on growth of exports, output, and income in Indonesia in the nineteenth and early twentieth centuries, we now look at the links between them. Three separate questions need to be addressed. First, we need to examine to what extent the growth which took place was due to trade. Second, we ask to what extent the indigenous economy was able to reap the potential benefits from trade. Last, we try to establish whether there were any periods in Indonesian economic history between 1830 and 1940 when economic growth would have been faster without participation, or with less participation, in world trade. In answering these questions, it is helpful to divide the period 1830-1940 into a number of sub-periods and examine Java and the Outer Islands separately.

1830-1849. In the first two decades of the Cultivation System in Java, export growth was at first rapid, although it tapered off in the 1840s. Foodcrop growth was slow, at least partly because of the demands for labour which the system made on the local populations (Elson, this volume, gives details on these). Some of this labour was unpaid corvée; even where payments were made for labour and land, in most cases they were insufficient to compensate the owners for the income foregone. This is particularly the case if we assume that leisure had some value to the indigenous labour force, many of whom were far from idle before the system began. During most of the 1830s and 1840s, the export surplus (exports of goods and precious metals less imports) fluctuated between 40 and 60 per cent of total exports (Figure 12.4), implying a large outflow of funds on both government and private account (see also Figure 10.1). Most of the profits from sale of crops were in fact retained in Holland and entered the Dutch budget. Government expenditures within the colony were minimal and mainly administrative. Technology transfers were virtually zero. Over these two decades it would appear that the net benefits derived from trade by the domestic economy were probably negative.

Obviously, this need not have been the case. Had more positive incentives been given to the indigenous population to develop new land for the production of sugar, coffee, tobacco, and tea, the rate of growth of exports may still have been considerable, without as much harmful effect on foodcrop production. Some regions of Java could have specialised in export production and imported their food either from other parts of Indonesia or from abroad. And if the profits

FIGURE 12.4 Export Surpluses as a Percentage of Exports, 1834–1940

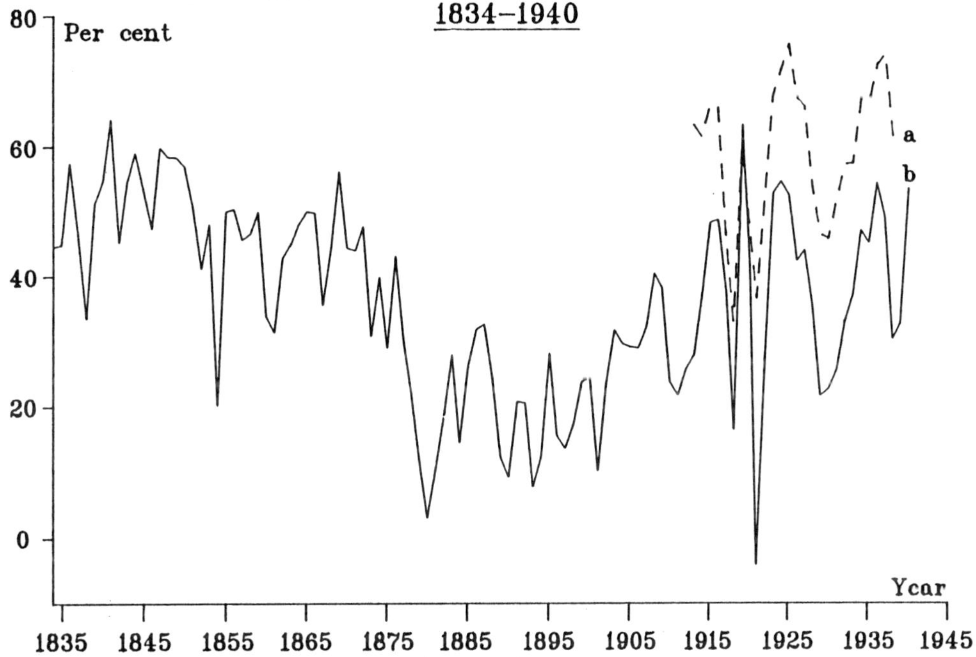

[a] Sumatra: East Coast (1913–38)

[b] Java (1834–73); Indonesia (1874–1940)

Sources: Export Surplus: C.K.S. 160 and 161, and Central Bureau of Statistics (1941, p.71)
Data for Sumatra taken from Thee (1977, p.57)

from sale of crops in Holland had been used for infrastructural development in Java, the productive capacity of the domestic economy could have been rapidly expanded. Here was a case where a colonial government failed to permit a colony to secure full benefit, indeed any benefit at all, from participation in trade.

1850-1885. Some change did occur in Java over the next three decades. To begin with, total export growth slowed down and rice production grew more rapidly, mainly because of the rapid opening up of new lands (Table 12.6). By the end of the 1860s, the overall budget surplus was diminishing rapidly in size, at least partly as a result of accelerated expenditures within the colony (Figure 10.1). In the decade from 1874, real government expenditures grew at almost four per cent per annum, and much of this increase was used for public works (Table 10.2). The export surplus, although still substantial, was on average slightly less as a percentage of exports than in the 1830s and 1840s. In addition, payments to the indigenous population for labour and other inputs increased after 1860, especially for coffee (O'Malley, this volume, Table 7.9). These payments, together with increased government expenditures in the domestic economy, at least partially compensated for compulsory use of inputs at payments less than their opportunity cost.

1885-1899. The last two decades of the nineteenth century present more problems in that it is not at all clear to what extent the slowdown which occurred in rice production in Java can be attributed to growth in export crops. Certainly harvested area of sugar grew more rapidly than harvested area of rice, in percentage terms, during the last fifteen years of the nineteenth century, while the reverse had been true of the previous fifteen years (Table 12.6). This might suggest that sugar was competing increasingly with foodcrops for land, and especially for irrigated *sawah*, in the closing years of the century. However, given that the harvested area of sugar was so small relative to that of rice, it is unlikely that this effect was very important for Java as a whole. Exactly why the expansion of *sawah* area slowed down in this period is not clear, although it is possible that changing government policies towards the settlement of new lands were involved. On balance it is likely that a combination of poor weather, a slowing down in the rate of migration to new lands, and more aggressive competition from the large estates all contributed to the poor performance of the rice sector in Java during the period between 1885 and 1900. The slowdown in export growth in the last fifteen years of the century was also reflected in a decline in growth of public expenditure, which would have reduced employment opportunities, and almost certainly contributed to a slower pace of growth in the non-export sectors of the economy.

Outside Java the experience was rather different. The last decade of the nineteenth century saw the beginnings of the massive expansion of smallholder exports which was to accelerate rapidly after 1900. At this stage technology transfer was obviously limited; the fastest growing export crop up to 1913 was copra which was almost entirely a smallholder crop, and appears to have benefited little from technology transfers from the large estate sector. There was little coercion involved in its cultivation and, to the extent that foodcrop or other types of indigenous production suffered as a result of its cultivation, this must have reflected a conscious decision on the part of individual producers that copra cultivation was the best use of their resources.

The last fifteen years of the nineteenth century also saw considerable change in the magnitude of the drain from the colony through the export surplus. The export surplus as a percentage of total exports dropped markedly (Figure 12.4) until in some years it was below ten percent. Given that the balance of invisible trade must have been negative, it is even possible that the overall balance of payments was in deficit and financed by capital inflows. Most of these were in fact on government account to finance the increasingly frequent and large government deficits.

1900-1913. As we have already noted, the period from the late 1890s to 1913 was one of considerable output growth on all fronts. Export volume growth accelerated, especially from the smallholder sector, and the income terms of trade improved (Figure 12.1). In addition, rice production in Java began to grow more rapidly, in spite of continued expansion in sugar hectarage and production. Most of this expansion was due to expansion of *sawah* area, as neither the cropping ratio nor yields changed perceptibly in the period up to 1913. Probably the most significant change which occurred after 1900 was in the role of the government sector in promoting rapid development of economic infrastructure. Real government expenditures grew at more than three per cent per annum, which could well have been faster than the growth of real income. In addition, expenditures on public works increased relative to total expenditures (Table 10.5). This, combined with the increased payments to the indigenous workers by the sugar estates in Java and the rapid growth of the plantation labour force in East Sumatra, meant that the net total of flows between the export enclave and the domestic economy on the one hand, and the domestic economy and the rest of the world on the other favoured the domestic economy to a greater extent than previously. This is not to deny that the benefits from trade to the domestic economy could have been even larger, had there been no coercive renting of *sawah* in Java by the sugar companies, and had more of the profits from the estates been retained for productive investment in the domestic economy. (The export surplus in fact increased somewhat relative to total exports compared with 1880-1900). But on balance, this was a period in Indonesian history when, in the words of Kindleberger (1962, p.211), the demand was right abroad and the supply was right at home, and participation in trade led to a higher rate of growth in the domestic economy than would have occurred with less or no involvement in foreign trade.

1919-1939. After the First World War it seems that a sharp disparity emerged between the economic fortunes of the indigenous economy in Java and the export areas of the Outer Islands. We have already noted that indigenous incomes grew more rapidly outside Java in the 1920s; this seems to have been due to the slowdown in food production in Java and the increase in smallholder export production, particularly of rubber, outside Java. On Java the scope for further extension of land, and particularly *sawah*, tapered off during the 1920s; as population pressed more heavily on the available land, the forced renting of *sawah* to the sugar companies became more burdensome. Although the sugar industry did make substantial payments to indigenous workers in addition to rentals (Pelzer 1945, p.256; O'Malley, this volume, Table 7.8), there can be little doubt that it was wasteful in the extreme to use well irrigated *sawah* for a crop which needed controlled water supply only for the first few months of growth (Alexander and Alexander 1978, p.210). If the sugar industry had been forced to pay the full economic rent for the *sawah* they used, they would have used less well irrigated land, possibly outside Java, and the cost to the indigenous foodcrop sector in terms of production foregone would have been much lower. By the 1920s Java was probably losing its comparative advantage in a land-intensive crop such as sugar, and should have been devoting its resources to labour-intensive, land-saving crops, and of course to manufactures. That this did not happen was due in part to important vested interests within the colonial power structure.

The history of the sugar industry in Java from the 1870s through to the 1930s well illustrates the argument of Lewis, quoted above, that the gains from technological progress in cashcrop agriculture were largely lost through deteriorating terms of trade. Between the 1870s and the 1930s sugar yields more than trebled in Java, mainly because of the successful development and dissemination of high yielding varieties (Evenson and Kislev 1975, ch.3). But the value of output per hectare in terms of manufactured goods, after rising dramatically between the first and second decades of the century, fell again after 1925, so that by the late 1930s it was about what it had been in the 1880s (Booth 1988, Table 6.14).

Outside Java the story was very different. Smallholder cashcrop production grew rapidly, with practically no assistance at all from government or the large estate sector. Land and labour were in elastic supply, and the availability of consumer imports provided the incentive for subsistence farmers to grow cashcrops for the export market (Thee 1977, p.17ff). To begin with, the indigenous population also played a leading role in processing and marketing export crops, although for rubber in particular, Chinese traders with better access to capital began to assume prominence as output volume grew (Thomas and Panglaykim 1976, p.141).

The experience of Java in the Great Depression of the 1930s again differed markedly from that of the Outer Islands. Attention has already been drawn to the marked acceleration in foodcrop production which occurred in Java during the 1930s. This was due in part to the dramatic collapse of the sugar industry, although the decline in harvested area of sugar of about 100,000 hectares between the latter part of the 1920s and between 1936 and 1940 hardly accounts for the increase of over 500,000 hectares in harvested area of paddy (Table 12.7), even allowing for the fact that two or perhaps even three rice crops could be grown on a hectare of land previously used for one crop of sugar. It would appear that the heavy irrigation expenditures in Java during the 1920s (Van der Meulen 1940, pp.148-50) were, by the 1930s, yielding substantial benefits in terms of expanded double-cropping, which in turn permitted the more rapid expansion of rice and other foodcrops.

While the depression of the 1930s brought some relief to Java from the export "hypertrophy" or forced growth of the previous fifteen years, the Outer Islands suffered a slowdown in economic growth. Smallholder producers proved more resilient than the large estates (Table 12.3) and indigenous real incomes outside Java continued to rise, albeit at a lower rate than in the 1920s. Obviously, the severe drop in the income terms of trade which occurred in the early 1930s implied a reduced capacity to import, although this was counteracted to some extent by a sharp decline in remittances abroad (C.E.I., Vol.5, Table 14.1).

Overall, however, the 1920s and 1930s saw a marked rise in the export surplus as a percentage of total exports, compared with the period between 1875 and 1913 (Figure 12.4). From 1921 onwards, we have more comprehensive balance of payments and national income data, and we can make a more informed judgement about the magnitude of the flows involved. In 1925 the export surplus reached 19 per cent of national income as computed by Polak. Although debt servicing charges and other "invisible" payments accounted for some of this surplus, the bulk was taken up by remittances of individuals and corporations (C.E.I., Vol.5, Annex 2). Although the surplus dropped relative to national income during 1929/32, it rose again towards the end of the 1930s (Figure 12.5).

An important aspect of the export surplus phenomenon as it developed in Indonesia in the inter-war period concerned its regional incidence. In the major export-producing areas outside Java, the ratio of the export surplus to exports was even larger than for the country as a whole. Thus regions such as North Sumatra experienced a double drain, to Java on the one hand, and to the rest of the world on the other. This is well brought out in the data provided by Thee (1977, p.57), which are included in Figure 12.4. Through the entire period from 1913 to 1940,

FIGURE 12.5 Export Surpluses as a Percentage of National Income, 1921–1939

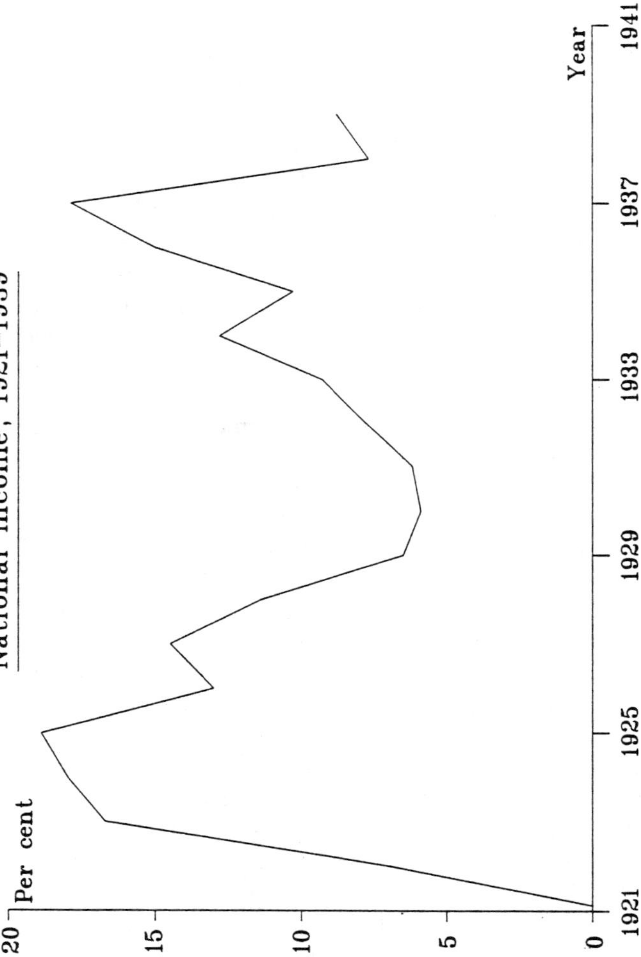

Sources: Export surplus: as for Figure 12.4
National Income: as for Figure 12.3

the export surplus from Sumatra's east coast was much larger than for the country as a whole.

Conclusions

We now return to the question posed at the outset: why did growing involvement in international trade not lead to more rapid economic transformation of the Indonesian economy in the period from 1830 to 1940? It is clear from the preceding discussion that most of the contributions to the debate on trade and growth which were discussed in the first section are relevant to at least some aspects of the Indonesian experience. In the 1830s, the gains from trade were largely drained off to the Netherlands; what remained in the colony was spent on routine administration and defence rather than on public infrastructure. For much of the rest of the century, export volume growth was too slow to have had a significant effect on income; as Leff (1982, p.91) argues in the case of Brazil, the engine was both too small and too slow-moving to make much impact. The point can be illustrated with a simple numerical example; if export volume was growing by less than two per cent per annum between 1860 and 1900 and exports were only about 10 per cent of total output in 1860, then the direct contribution of exports to growth of total output would have been only about 0.2 per cent per annum.

There was a real chance for Indonesia to embark on a process of sustained growth after the turn of the century; by this time exports probably accounted for 15 or 20 per cent of national output, and were growing at over four per cent per annum. In the two decades before the outbreak of the First World War, the government made a more determined effort to harness some of the gains from trade for productive infrastructure development; as Lewis (1970, p.44) has commented, if the momentum built up in many parts of the tropical world in these years had continued, many countries would be unrecognizable today. Even after 1918, the growth momentum was maintained outside Java, but too little was done with balanced infrastructural development and the great potential of Sumatra, Kalimantan, and Sulawesi remained largely untouched at the termination of Dutch rule. In addition the drain of remitted profits, which was substantial for the last three decades of colonial rule, meant that much of the net gains from trade were not available for investment within the colony.

How did the Indonesian experience compare with other colonial territories? We have seen that in the twentieth century Indonesia's export volume growth was quite rapid in comparison with other Asian countries (Figure 12.2). In addition, her exports were more diversified than those of many other colonies, although this was mainly due to her size. Hanson (1980, p.40) has shown that in 1900 the Hirschman concentration index of exports was lower for Indonesia than for any other Third World country except China and India. Only 29 per cent of total export earnings came from her major staple, compared with 60 per cent for Brazil, 50 per cent for the Philippines, and 78 per cent for Egypt.

On the other hand, the drain from Indonesia in terms of remitted profits and other outward capital flows was very large by contemporary standards. The export and fiscal surpluses from Java during the period of the Culture System had few parallels elsewhere in the colonial world, but the foreign drain did not stop with the end of the budget surpluses in the 1870s. Maddison (this volume, Table 14.1) has shown that the ratio of exports to imports was higher in Indonesia than in many other Asian countries in the period from 1913 to 1938.[7] He has argued that this reflects the "double drain" on both Dutch and Chinese accounts. In addition, the export surplus to national income ratio was almost certainly higher for Indonesia than for many other colonies; Maddison argues that the "unrequited" export surplus was only 1.5 per cent of Indian national income in the 1930s, compared to 13.4 per cent for Indonesia (Hanson 1980, p.127). Had more of these funds been retained in the colony for investment in productive infrastructure and in education, Indonesia's economic position at independence could have been very different.

Notes

1. See in particular Caldwell (1964) and Van Leeuwen (1970).
2. The weighted price index of coffee and sugar prices (weighted by 1870 export volumes) fell from 125 in 1875 to 77 in 1885, although it recovered in the 1890s to the level of the 1870s. Deflated by the manufactures price index of Lewis, the weighted index moved as follows:

1870	94
1875	113
1880	110
1885	86
1890	119
1895	124

3. A detailed account of Japan's penetration of Indonesian markets in the inter-war years is given in Van Gelderen (1939, ch.2). Indonesia was not alone in this experience; for an account of Japanese penetration of the Indian market, see Chaudhuri (1983, pp.865-69).
4. The data on rice production are still controversial for this period, and further research is necessary before we can form an accurate picture of rates of growth. But it does seem probable that there was an acceleration in production growth compared with the 1840s. Certainly there were no serious famines during these decades.
5. Hanson (1980 p.28). One explanation for Indonesia's poor performance during the last decades of the nineteenth century is that she remained on the gold

standard, while most of the major Asian countries were on the silver standard (c.f. Nugent 1973). But this approach fails to explain why Indonesia did so well in comparative terms in the twentieth century, while still staying on the gold standard.

6. Van Laanen (1984) discusses likely movements in velocity in Indonesia between 1850 and 1940. He reports a "surprisingly rapid growth between 1850 and 1885" in real money stock and real income.
7. An interesting case is that of Burma, where according to the data assembled by Aye Hlaing (1964, p.110 ff.), the export surplus was almost 30 per cent of net domestic product in the late 1930s. It is probably no accident that the two Southeast Asian countries which experienced the largest export surpluses during the 1930s were the two which Myint (1971, ch.12) called the most "inward-looking" during the 1960s. For further discussion of the colonial and post-colonial drain in Southeast Asia see especially Golay (1976).

CHAPTER THIRTEEN

Interisland Trade, Economic Integration, and the Emergence of the National Economy

Howard W. Dick

Introduction

Economic integration has been almost a non-issue in Indonesian economic history. Perhaps the only writer to devote any attention to it, and then only as part of a very broad survey, was Paauw (1963). He observed, with masterful understatement, that "integration of separate island economies into a national whole was not a major objective of colonial policy" (Paauw 1963, p.157). At the same time, he recognised that a pattern of regional specialisation and trade was beginning to emerge by the late colonial period, although at the time of the Japanese invasion it was still "embryonic" (Paauw 1963, p.163). This chapter does not challenge these broad conclusions. But from the perspective of the very long term, there is an important problem that must be explained. The "dichotomy" between Java and the Outer Islands did not emerge, as Paauw argued, in the first three decades of the twentieth century. Nor even, as Geertz (1963) argued, did it emerge after 1830 with the introduction to Java of the Cultivation System. The dichotomy already existed by the end of the first millennium, and on the eve of the European intrusion there was an impressive degree of regional specialisation and trade. Why then did the economy of the archipelago fragment during the colonial period, while the underlying dichotomy sharpened to the point of caricature? Moreover, why was it only in the last decade of Dutch colonial rule that the logic of resource endowments at last began to manifest itself in patterns of specialisation and trade?

This chapter argues that the emergence of the national economy can be divided broadly into three phases. Before the arrival of the Europeans there was, of course, no Indonesian nation. The archipelago was politically fragmented but tied through trade to the wider international economy, production for which was facilitated by a good deal of intra-regional specialisation. Brought to Asia on a tide of emerging nationalism, the Europeans proceeded to impose a narrow bilateralism on the region.

By the nineteenth century most of Southeast Asia had been divided quite arbitrarily into British, Dutch, Spanish, and French spheres of influence. Between 1816, when Britain returned Java to the Dutch at the end of the Napoleonic War, and the outbreak of World War I in 1914, the geographical entity which was to become Indonesia acquired political form as a colony of the Netherlands. Except by definition, however, there was no colonial economy, but merely separate fragments contained within the political boundaries. Integration of the country as an economic system, which is the third phase, did not really begin until the 1930s, when it was first encouraged by deliberately protectionist measures.

The chapter begins with a review of the impact of Dutch colonialism upon the economic integration of the archipelago. An examination of interisland trade statistics (which first became available in 1915) precedes an attempt to understand why such obvious differences in inter-regional comparative advantage had so little influence upon the level and composition of interisland trade until the 1930s.

The Colonial Impact on the Java-Outer Islands Dichotomy

Those writers who maintain that the dichotomy in resource endowments and population between Java and the Outer Islands is a phenomenon of the late colonial period are afflicted by a serious historical myopia. The dichotomy existed already at the end of the first millennium and was a constant factor in the pre-colonial history of the archipelago.[1] Java, or rather what is now East and Central Java, was the main "rice bowl" of the archipelago. Its fertile river valleys and sophisticated irrigation systems supported Indianised court civilisations with a high population density. The rest of the archipelago (including West Java) was almost entirely jungle, with scattered population groups engaged in shifting agriculture and a few fishing villages on the coast. Perhaps no economic development would have occurred if the sea route between India and China had not passed through the narrow Straits of Malacca. To serve this trade, the great entrepôt of Srivijaya arose in the seventh century near the site of contemporary Palembang. On the basis of naval control of the Straits of Malacca, it established a supremacy which lasted for about 600 years. Early in the fifteenth century, after some hiatus, its heritage passed to Malacca on the other side of the Strait.

Both Srivijaya and Malacca were primarily entrepôts and produced almost nothing themselves for international trade. Indeed, they had almost no hinterland and, even for their own subsistence, produced little besides coconuts and fish. Rice, salt, and such items as onions and garlic were obtained through trade—mainly from Java. As Malacca had become one of the largest cities in the world by the end of the fifteenth century (Reid 1980), this provisioning trade was absolutely essential. Yet the economic integration of Java and the Outer Islands went much further than this. Pepper would not have been grown in the western part of the archipelago had there been no rice and salt to exchange; the same is true for the spices of the Moluccas, where rice had supplanted sago as the staple food. Java also produced cotton textiles for these export-producing regions.[2]

By the sixteenth century the archipelago thus displayed a marked degree of specialisation according to comparative advantage. Moreover, the quantities involved were not insignificant. About 6,000 tons of pepper were exported from the archipelago in 1600, compared with 20,000 to 30,000 tons in the late 1920s, and about 3,000 tons of spices.[3] Approximately 30,000 tons of rice seem to have been shipped from Java; about one third went to the Moluccas and the balance to Malacca and the pepper-growing districts of Sumatra (Van Leur 1955, p.210). The Javanese dominated all this trade. Malacca was the great entrepôt—the stapling point where Chinese, Indians, and traders from all over Southeast Asia mingled. But Java was the pivot on which the whole system turned—and it was indeed a system.

Its internationalism was a notable feature of Southeast Asian trade in the pre-colonial period. Traders of all nationalities and religions were welcome as long as they paid the ruler's tolls and obeyed the local laws. In some ports, rulers exercised certain rights of pre-emption, but, in general, the regime seems to have approached free trade. The rationale for this freedom from regulation was that if a ruler became too restrictive, traders would simply take their business elsewhere. It was therefore not in the power of individual rulers to nationalise or monopolise the trade, even though, from time to time, there were wars between rival rulers attempting to shift the flow of trade. In European history, perhaps the closest parallel is the period of the Hanse, although in this case the member cities formed a league and attempted to limit the trade of non-members.

Just as the Hanseatic system was unable to withstand the intrusion of the Dutch and the English, the internationalism of trade in Southeast Asia was disrupted by the intrusion of the Europeans. The Portuguese destroyed the prosperity of Malacca when they captured it in 1511. However, in time, they were absorbed into the existing pattern of trade because they lacked the naval strength to enforce their claims to a monopoly of the spice trade. The Dutch, however, were both more efficient and more ruthless in pursuit of the same objective. In 1604 they captured the island of Ambon from the Portuguese, and subsequently endeavoured to concentrate there the cultivation of cloves, systematically destroying trees growing elsewhere. In 1621 they seized the nutmeg-producing Banda Islands, killed or carried off most of the population, and instituted production with minifundia and slave labour. After further struggles, the Dutch also gained control of the spice islands of the North Moluccas and blockaded the pepper port of Banten in West Java until it was brought to terms. With the capture of Makassar in 1669, which had been the last stronghold of free trade in the archipelago. Dutch supremacy was complete. This achievement was not, however, entirely through Dutch efforts. In the course of consolidating the new Javanese kingdom of Mataram, Sultan Agung had captured and laid waste the port cities of North Java (Demak in 1604 and Surabaya in 1625) which had blossomed after the fall of Malacca to the Portuguese (Burger 1956, p.7). He failed only narrowly to capture Batavia from the Dutch in 1629. His successor, Amangkurat I, introduced a royal monopoly of the rice trade in 1651, and ordered the closure of the North Javanese ports between 1655 and 1657, and again in 1660 (Pigeaud and de Graaf 1976, pp.59-63). All these measures effectively ruined Javanese shipping and trade and drove the survivors to Makassar, before its trade was in turn curtailed by the Dutch.

The rapid growth of Southeast Asian trade during the sixteenth century under the stimulus of European demand for spices therefore came to an end in the seventeenth century. But trade did not merely stagnate; it greatly contracted.

> The conquest of the spice islands by the Dutch East India Company put a stop to a complete branch of traditional trade and thus disorganised the whole of it.
>
> (Van Leur 1955, p.122).

Spices and pepper had been the main items which Europe sought from Southeast Asia. First the Portuguese and later the Dutch attempted to monopolise their trade. The Dutch sought a monopoly partly to shut out their European rivals and partly to gain control over the prices, that is to "buy cheap and sell dear." But as long as there was competition from the Javanese, the Dutch could hardly persuade the producers to sell below the market price. Hence there was a need to capture the spice islands. The destruction of the Javanese trading cities and restriction of the rice trade by the rulers of Mataram was of great assistance because spices and pepper were grown in order to obtain rice, salt, cloth, etc. The combined effect of the Dutch monopoly and the decline of the rice trade was therefore to abort the cash crop revolution which had gathered pace since about the twelfth century. Henceforth, if spices and pepper were to be grown at all, they were to be grown under duress. The consequence was that the sophisticated commercial system collapsed and the archipelago reverted to virtual self-sufficiency. The enforcement of a national monopoly of the spice trade resulted not in the diversion of trade but in its destruction. Consequently, the trade of the archipelago was far more backward in 1800 than it had been in 1600. And, in the end, even the Dutch were worse off, for the East India Company itself went bankrupt in 1797.

In the course of the eighteenth century, after impoverishing the Outer Islands and earning little profit from the spice trade, the Company began to develop the export potential of Java, hitherto little more than a stapling point for the spice trade. It was found that coffee grew well in the Priangan district of West Java.[4] Delivery quotas were imposed upon the local regents. Tonnages became significant only by the end of the century and too late to save the Company from bankruptcy, but the system was retained. In 1830 it became, with some modifications, the basis for the Cultivation System, which attempted to develop export crops in a systematic way. Coffee remained the main crop, together with sugar and indigo, but there were many other experiments. Several points deserve to be noted. This was the first time that Java had been a significant export producer for other than inter-regional trade. Apart from modest tonnages of pepper from West Java, its commercial role until the Dutch invasion had been mainly in provisioning the export-producing areas of the Outer Islands. In addition, the Dutch used the Cultivation System to forge a tighter economic nexus between Java and the Netherlands. Although some sugar was exported to markets in Asia, under the Consignment System the *Nederlandsche Handel Maatschappij* (NHM), was given the monopoly of the shipment of export crops, which had to be carried in Dutch-flag ships. Thirdly, the Outer Islands, as the term itself implies, became increasingly a periphery, claimed within the Dutch sphere of political influence but virtually ignored in terms of commercial interests. In 1837 the Dutch presence was, in fact, confined to only fifteen ports (Earl 1971, p.310n).

The outcome of Dutch preoccupation with Java was that, after the foundation of Singapore in 1819, the trade of the Outer Islands became focused increasingly upon that colony.[5] Filling a vacuum that had existed since the fall of Malacca in 1511, Singapore became not only a magnet attracting much existing trade within the archipelago but also a catalyst, reviving the tempo of trade. The Dutch viewed this growth in trade with misgiving. Singapore was considered a Trojan horse for British economic penetration, which had begun already during the British occupation of Java from 1811 to 1816. The Dutch therefore tried in various ways to restrict British trade via Singapore. Although the Anglo-Dutch treaty of 1824 specified that the differential tariff could be no more than 100 per cent, it was not until the tariff revision of 1837 that this was actually achieved. Despite strong protests from Singapore, a new and much lower tariff was introduced in 1866 with rates of only 6 and 10 per cent and differential tariffs on few goods, among which were textiles (Wong 1960, p.48). These tariffs could not be enforced in areas where there was no direct Dutch control.[6] Under the 1824 treaty, the spheres of Dutch and British influence were defined, but it was not until the mid-1830s that the Dutch began to advance in Sumatra, and then only in fits and starts. In 1871, after long negotiation, the Treaty of Sumatra was signed giving Straits merchants equal rights with Dutch subjects in Dutch-controlled territories in Sumatra (Wong 1960, p.60). Another way in which the Dutch tried to restrict the trade of Singapore was through the opening of rival free ports: Riau (1829), Pontianak and Sambas (1834), Sukadana (1837), Makassar (1847),

Menado (1848), and Ambon, Banda and Ternate (1852) (Wong 1978, p.58). These free ports did not so much divert trade from Singapore as become "advance posts." Dutch policy may have slowed Singapore's commercial penetration of the Outer Islands somewhat, but the process was irresistible. Stimulated by the lower tariff of 1866, economic liberalisation in Dutch Indonesia, and the development of regular steamship services between 1870 and 1890, Singapore's recorded trade with the surrounding region increased a further threefold (Wong 1978, p.66). Its trade was also expanding with the whole of Southeast Asia, from Burma to Indo-China and the Southern Philippines. While Southeast Asia had been carved up politically into colonial spheres of influence, the old internationalism still held sway commercially. Singapore emerged as a worthy heir to Malacca.

The 1890s marked the turning point in Indonesian commerce, not only because the ending of the twenty-year-long Acehnese War released military resources for the consolidation of Dutch influence in the Outer Islands, but also because measures were taken to reduce the commercial dependence on Singapore. The loss of the trade via Singapore by the Dutch shipping lines, S.M. Nederland (SMN) and Rotterdam Lloyd (RL), led them to cooperate in 1888 in the formation of the *Koninklijke Pakketvaart Maatschappij* (KPM), which lobbied intensively to win the new interisland mail contract, effective from 1891.[7] The British-owned firm, the Netherlands Indies S.N. Co., which had held the contract since 1866, was accused of neglecting services between the Outer Islands and Java and concentrating upon services to Singapore. This was hardly fair. The NISN was not responsible for the pattern of trade which had emerged. Nevertheless, and notwithstanding that its tender per mile was considerably higher, the KPM was successful. From the outset the Dutch company set about undermining the British and Chinese lines trading out of Singapore. Apart from a variety of predatory tactics, the main device was the "through bill of lading," whereby the KPM as first carrier would tranship in another Dutch colonial port to either the SMN or RL at a through rate as low or lower than shipment via Singapore. Commercially the KPM's strategy was most successful. Its control of a network of routes over the entire archipelago gave it a great deal of leverage in cutting rates against competitors in some trades, while making good its losses from others. The company was assisted by the military conquest of the Outer Islands and, at the same time, hindered by the primitive facilities in most Indonesian ports. Tanjung Priok (constructed as a new deepwater port for Jakarta in the late 1880s) was the only port with proper wharves; other ports had to rely on jetties or lighterage. The situation in North Sumatra, which had become the main exporting region in the Outer Islands, was quite appalling. The carriage of export commodities by small ships for transshipment in Singapore therefore continued to be the most attractive option.

The consolidation of Dutch control over the transshipment trade of the Outer Islands awaited massive investment in the infrastructure of modern deepsea ports. In 1911, two Dutch engineers presented a report on the development of ocean harbours at Belawan (North Sumatra), Tanjung Priok, Semarang, Surabaya, and Makassar. These five ports were to be the nodes for the trade of the empire, with the KPM accumulating goods from the outports and transshipping there to the ocean lines. Belawan would serve North Sumatra; Tanjung Priok, the southern part of Sumatra and West Borneo; Surabaya, besides the sugar trade of East Java, South and East Borneo and Nusa Tenggara; and Makassar the rest of the *Groote Oost*. A free port on Sabang Island off the northern tip of Aceh was developed by a private company, but this never grew into much more than a coaling station and post office. Such an ambitious program took a decade to complete, but the facilities were in full operation by 1920/21. The KPM and the "through bills of lading" could then work as intended to channel the trade of the Outer Islands through Dutch ports. Singapore was not entirely eclipsed but its sphere of influence contracted greatly. This was most noticeable in the eastern part of the archipelago. After about 1920, ships from Singapore sailed no further east than Banjarmasin and Surabaya. Increasingly the trade in rice from Burma, Thailand, and Indo-China and sugar from Java was shipped directly to and from Indonesian ports. Nevertheless, Singapore remained the main port for the western part of the archipelago, except perhaps for North Sumatra and Aceh which fell more in the sphere of Penang. The primary reason was Singapore's stranglehold of the rubber trade, especially of the smallholder product. Yet it was no longer the case that Singapore pre-empted Dutch control over the economies of the Outer Islands, for that control was firmly established. Rather, Dutch interests (including the KPM) were now prepared to accept Singapore's role as an extra-territorial port of the colony and to strive for the largest possible share in its trade for themselves. Nevertheless, the fact that by the 1920s most of the export-import trade of the Outer Islands was under Dutch control did not mean that any significant economic integration had been achieved or that there was yet a "national" economy in any substantive sense.

Interisland Trade Data: 1915-1939

If economic history begins with the availability of data, then the history of interisland trade does not begin until 1915. Nevertheless, it does not greatly matter that statistics on interisland trade were published only towards the end of the colonial period. It is perhaps no coincidence that the "pacification" of the Outer Islands, that is, the political integration of colonial Indonesia, was completed in the same year. Even if a longer series of data were available, it would be maddeningly incomplete for the period up to the First World War. More to the point, are the figures of any use even after 1915? Until 1923, unfortunately, the answer is "not much." For the first eight years there are figures for imports from the Outer Islands (as a group) to Java and for exports from Java to the Outer Islands (as a group). Under imports were listed fourteen items by value, while under exports were listed fourteen items by quantity.

Figures for the years after 1923 are more useful. First, the Outer Islands were disaggregated into Sumatra, Borneo, Celebes, Moluccas, and Nusa Tenggara (after 1934 these last three categories are combined as the *Groote Oost*). It should be noted, however, that the figures still refer only to trade between the Outer Islands and Java, not between the Outer Islands, or to intra-island trade. Second, after 1923 interisland exports from Java to the Outer Islands are presented in value as well as volume, although it is not until 1934 that the import figures are also presented in quantity terms. Third, the total value of interisland exports and imports is presented, which makes it possible to relate the individual items to the whole. Unfortunately, however, there are never any totals given by tonnage. The figures were apparently compiled from the customs document known as the AVI (*aangifte van inlading* or declaration of cargo) which was obligatory for interisland trade, the justification evidently being to control the transshipment of smuggled imports—probably a necessary measure while parts of the Outer Islands still exercised a degree of commercial independence. The justification appears later to have become the collection of interisland trade statistics. Some goods shipped to and from remote places (for example by *prahu* to and from Madura), may have continued to evade the statistical net, but in the main ports, the coverage must have been complete. There seems to have been no incentive at that time to underdeclare, as there was after Independence. One important category of interisland cargo did not enter the reckoning, namely cargo transshipped on "through bills of lading" which was counted as foreign export or import. In other words, the figures refer only to "local" (*lokaal*) cargo, notwithstanding that some of it would later be transshipped for export on separate bills of lading. The distinction between *lokaal* and *through cargo* was therefore in practice rather arbitrary.

Tables 13.1 to 13.3 present the data, such as they are, for the years 1915 (the first year for which figures are available), 1920 (the peak of the post-World War I boom), 1929 (the eve of the Great Depression) and 1939 (the last year for which figures are available). The value of exports from Java to the Outer Islands (Table 13.1) shows that between 1915 and 1929 (and especially between 1920 and 1929), there was extremely rapid growth in the shipment of cigars and cigarettes and of cars and car parts, with much slower growth in the case of (net) petroleum products (mainly kerosene), sugar, and textiles. The behaviour of iron and steel goods, however, is quite different, growing more rapidly than any other item over the period 1915 to 1920 but halving over the subsequent decade. This effect may be explained by temporary natural protection during, and just after, the First World War. The surprise is, perhaps, that trade in textiles did not increase more rapidly. In interpreting all of these figures, however, it needs to be borne in mind that the price level as measured by the cost of living index for Indonesians fell by about 25 per cent from 1921 to 1929, and a further 56 per cent between 1929 and 1939 (C.E.I., Vol.5, Table 16.2). The effect is therefore to magnify the growth (or reduce the decline) during the 1920s, while converting the substantial decline in most items between 1929 and 1939 into modest gains or, at worst, stagnation. Thus the apparent decline of 20 per cent in textile trade is converted into a real growth of about 60 per cent. In real terms there is a marked decline only in the case of cars and car parts. The net rice trade shows a remarkable eightfold growth, reflecting the government's policy of promoting self-sufficiency.

TABLE 13.1 Interisland Trade in Selected Items by Value (million guilders)

Java/Outer Islands	1915	1920	1929	1939	'000 tons
Textiles	11.7	20.1	26.8	21.6	9.3
Cigars & cigarettes	0.5	2.1	24.4	20.2	8.4
Groceries	2.1	5.1	5.3	4.0	n.a.
Cars & parts	0.7	3.2	14.1	5.1	n.a.
Iron & steel goods	2.4	17.8	8.8	5.4	n.a.
Sugar	3.5	6.4	13.1	6.3	125.0
Rice	3.3	11.5	4.4	12.4	194.7
Petroleum products	1.0	1.3	4.4	6.0	n.a.
Other	n.a.	n.a.	73.6	56.7	n.a.
Total	n.a.	n.a.	167.4	137.6	n.a.

Source: *Statistisch Jaaroverzicht* (1922-1940)

TABLE 13.2 Interisland Trade in Selected Items by Value (million guilders)

Java/Outer Islands	1920	1929	1939
Coal	3.7	5.8	3.6
Petroleum products	6.8	4.8	3.9
Cement	n.a.	1.3	1.0
Copra	12.4	3.5	3.1
Coffee	4.6	10.0	3.0
Rattan	0.6	2.0	0.2
Tin	23.7	38.4	23.4
Fish	1.5	4.3	3.9
Rice	0.9	1.7	1.1
Gambir	1.9	3.1	2.0
Pepper	8.4	15.3	0.6
Other	n.a.	44.7	27.8
Total	n.a.	134.9	73.6

Source: As for Table 13.1

TABLE 13.3 Interisland Trade in Selected Items by Tonnage

('000 tons)

Outer Islands/Java	1915	1920	1929	1939
Coal	n.a.	175.0	547.0	562.0
Petroleum products	8.4	80.6	154.2	262.4
Cement	3.0	71.0	278.0	553.9
Copra	10.7	33.7	16.2	63.4
Coffee	11.7	13.8	12.6	21.0
Rattan	2.9	3.8	2.0	15.8
Tin	-	10.3	15.1	13.8
Fish	n.a.	17.6	31.6	43.9

Source: As for Table 13.1

In the case of trade between the Outer Islands and Java, Table 13.2 shows a modest increase in most export commodities, the majority of which would later have been transshipped as exports on separate bills of lading. These goods came mainly from areas which did not receive direct calls by deepsea ships. Thus, there was a substantial trade in pepper and coffee from Lampung to Jakarta, in tin ore from Bangka and Billiton to Jakarta, in rattan and damar from Borneo to Jakarta (West Borneo) and Surabaya (South and East Borneo), and in coffee from Nusa Tenggara to Surabaya. It is therefore doubtful whether these goods, except for relatively small quantities of coffee and rattan used for domestic consumption in Java, should be counted as genuine interisland trade at all. Copra is a rather different case. During World War I, the loss of processing facilities in Germany and increasing difficulties in shipment led to a boom in coconut oil production in Java. After 1920 the European mills were again buying copra and, deprived of their natural protection, the mills in Java lost most of their export markets (Kamerling 1979). The decline in the interisland copra trade during the 1920s is therefore readily explicable and represents a decline in genuine interisland trade. Of the non-export items, the main growth during the 1920s is in coal, with a more modest growth in cement (from Padang in West Sumatra). There is also a steady growth in the fish trade, mainly from the Chinese fishing port of Bagansi-api-api, but also from Borneo.

The growth in shipments from the Outer Islands to Java is much clearer from the tonnage statistics, which have the great virtue of abstracting from price movements (Table 13.3). It can be seen that by 1929 the tonnage figures are dominated by coal, cement, and petroleum products. Over the next decade there is little growth in the coal trade but a doubling in the tonnage of cement and an 80 per cent increase in the volume of petroleum products. There is also a fourfold increase in the copra trade to a tonnage almost double that in 1920, this revival being in part attributable to a revival of coconut oil and soap production in Java. It is interesting to compare the tonnage figures from the Outer Islands to Java with those from Java to the Outer Islands for the year 1939 (Table 13.1). Although the figures are incomplete, it is clear that in terms of tonnage, the trade is dominated by rice (almost 200,000 tons gross) and sugar (125,000 tons). The tonnages of textiles and cigarettes are fairly minor.

These interisland trade figures are usefully supplemented by some volume figures of cargoes carried by the KPM (Table 13.4). Since the company had a near monopoly of the interisland trade, the figures can be taken as a fair indication of its magnitude in terms of total volume, something which cannot be determined from the government statistics. Unfortunately the KPM figures are not altogether comparable. First, except for coal, the unit of measurement is not the ton but the last, a unit somewhat like the "manifest ton" which has the annoying characteristic of varying according to the commodity concerned.[8] One is therefore, in effect, adding up different units. Second, the KPM figures include all intra-island and interisland trade, not merely that between the Outer Islands and Java but between the Outer Islands themselves and also with Singapore and Penang, which from the commercial point of view were regarded as interisland ports. Despite these problems, the figures do offer some insights. Given that the last is usually rather larger than a ton, it is clear that in terms of tonnage, interisland trade was dominated by coal. If coal is excluded, however, it appears that there was little growth in cargoes on government account over the entire period 1920 to 1937.[9] In the case of private (non-coal) interisland cargo, there was also virtual stagnation over the entire period. Although no detailed breakdown is available as a series, it may be noted that the main items by tonnage were sugar, rice, cement, petroleum products (mainly cased kerosene), and copra. The only category to show any marked growth between 1920 and 1929 was through shipment (*doorvoer*), reflecting the diversion of cargo away from Singapore to the five new Indonesian ports and a growing preference for shipment on a single bill of lading rather than separate *lokaal* and *deepsea* bills of lading.

Therefore what stands out most clearly from the KPM figures is that, aside from the transshipment of export cargoes on through bills of lading, there was little growth in the tonnage of the interisland trade either during the 1920s or over the whole period 1920 to 1937. What Paauw (1963) saw as a modest growth in interisland trade during the 1930s appears to have been a restoration to the level prevailing in 1929. Yet, with the possible exception of coal, even in 1929 the level

TABLE 13.4 Cargoes Carried by KPM
('000 lasts)

	1920	1929	1937
Private[a]	966	1095	1056
Local[b]	79	615	598
Government[a]	118	111	129
Coal[c]	555	785	690
Total	1718	2606	2473

[a]Excludes coal
[b]Includes Singapore and Penang but excludes other foreign lines
[c]Includes own bunker coal
Source: KPM, Annual Reports

of interisland trade was not significantly above what it had been in 1920. The rate of growth in private *lokaal* cargo carried by the KPM increased just 13 per cent over the decade, an annual rate of growth of about 1.5 per cent per annum. This is a little less surprising in view of Polak's estimates of national income, which suggest that in nominal terms national income showed almost no growth between 1921 and 1929 (C.E.I., Vol.5, Table 15.1). Real growth was about three per cent per annum, so interisland trade seems to have increased at barely half the rate of real national income. If coal is included, and one heroically adds the tonnage of coal to the total number of lasts, then the rate of growth of the total is virtually the same as the real rate of growth of national income over the period 1921 to 1929. This is in marked contrast to the situation after 1969 when interisland trade has tended to grow faster than the real rate of growth of national income. In short, there is little evidence during the 1920s of a shift towards regional specialisation and interisland trade.

Even during the 1930s the trend towards increasing economic integration is not clear cut. Broek (1942) pointed out that between 1929 and 1939 the ratio of the value of trade between Java and the Outer Islands to the value of foreign trade increased from 12 to 17 per cent. Table 13.5 reconstructs these figures. It can be seen that the value of trade between Java and the Outer Islands fell less rapidly than the value of all foreign trade, that is, by a third instead of about half. The picture is complicated, however, by reference to tonnage figures. Tonnage of imports fell by 40 per cent, whereas the tonnage of exports actually rose by almost 20 per cent. On balance the tonnage of foreign trade therefore rose by a modest five per cent. Unfortunately we do not have similar aggregate tonnage figures for interisland trade, although the above KPM figures suggest that there was almost no change over the decade. If tonnage is taken as the criterion, it would therefore appear that there was no overall improvement in the degree of economic integration even during the 1930s. Nevertheless, there were some important changes in the structure of interisland trade, especially in the case of textiles and of rice. Some comment is warranted on each.

TABLE 13.5 Interisland and Foreign Trade by Value and Tonnage

	1929	1939	% change
Value	(million guilders)		
Interisland			
Java/Outer Is.	174.9	137.6	-21.3
Outer Is./Java	134.9	73.6	-45.4
Total	309.8	211.2	-31.8
Foreign			
Imports	1,072.1	472.4	-55.9
Exports	1,446.2	746.3	-48.4
Total	2,518.3	1,218.7	-51.6
Ratio (%)	12.3	17.3	
Tonnage	('000 tons)		
Foreign			
Imports	3,389	2,064	-39.1
Exports	10,185	12,103	+18.8
Total	13,574	14,167	+ 4.4

Source: As for Table 13.1

During the 1930s, increased protection and government promotion of import substitution resulted in an unprecedented boom in industrial production, but from a very small base. In terms of employment the greatest expansion was in the weaving industry which, by 1939, excluding cottage industry, employed 70,000 workers.[10] Of these, about half worked in registered industrial establishments and constituted a quarter of the total employment of that sector of manufacturing (Broek 1942, p.82). The number of improved handlooms (ATBM) increased from 500 in 1930 to 35,000 in 1940, while the number of improved mechanical looms increased over the same period from 40 to 6,600. Nevertheless, by 1939 Indonesia still produced only one seventh of total consumption of woven goods (Broek 1942, p.83). There seems to have been also a less spectacular growth in the output of *batik sarongs*, of which in 1939 about one quarter of the output was sold in the Outer Islands (Broek 1942, p.85). This, however, was a well-established trade and not something that became important in the 1930s. The apparent real growth of about 60 per cent in interisland trade in textiles between 1929 and 1939 is therefore highly significant, but at the end of the decade Indonesia still produced only 5 per cent of its requirements (Van Oorschot 1956, p.49). Unfortunately the figures are not sufficiently disaggregated to reveal the extent to which there was growth in interisland trade of other manufactures, except perhaps for cigarettes. Clearly there was a trend in this direction, but Paauw seems justified in describing the pattern of specialisation at the end of the decade as "embryonic."

In terms of both value and tonnage, the most spectacular growth in interisland trade during the 1930s was in the rice trade from Java to the Outer Islands. Java had long maintained an export surplus with the Outer Islands, but by the 1920s rice supplies of the main export-producing regions were drawn predominantly from Burma, Thailand, and Indo-China (Table 13.6). Indeed, the KPM maintained direct lines with all of those countries, backloading with large tonnages of Javanese sugar. Although, based on harvests, there were considerable year-to-year fluctuations in the proportion of net exports from Java to the Outer Islands to imports to Indonesia, there was no discernible trend during the 1920s. Leaving aside the years 1919 and 1920 when imports were unusually low, the proportion of 3.1 per cent in 1918 and of 2.5 per cent in 1921 was of the same order as that of 2.8 per cent in 1929 (Table 13.6). By 1939, however, the proportion had leapt to a remarkable 71 per cent. In 1940, after a good harvest, net imports fell to a minimal 31,600 tons and Indonesia was, to all intents, self-sufficient. This was a noteworthy achievement, which was attributable partly to the release of land from the cultivation of export crops (most notably sugar) and partly to government measures to restrict imports and promote rice production and interisland trade.[11] Thus, although it is true that during the 1930s there was increasing specialisation between Java and the Outer Islands in terms of labour-intensive and resource-intensive industries, it is not valid to equate this distinction as one between manufacturing and primary production. In terms of value, the growth in interisland trade was biased towards manufacturing, but in terms of volume it was heavily biased towards primary products.

TABLE 13.6 Foreign and Interisland Trade in Rice
('000 tons)

	1914	1921	1929	1939	1940
Interisland					
From Java/Madura	36.6	31.5	30.1	197.1	102.0
To Java/Madura	12.8	12.5	9.8	15.8	27.8
Net outflow	23.8	19.0	20.3	181.3	74.2
Foreign					
Imports	471.2	764.3	735.2	278.3	108.7
Exports	51.9	2.4	12.3	21.7	77.1
Net inflow	419.3	761.9	722.9	256.6	31.6
Net Interisland outflow as % of imports	5.1	2.5	2.8	65.1	68.3

Source: C.E.I. Vol.4, Table 6

Some comment should be made about factor flows, or at least about labour. In a simple economic model, it might be supposed that differences in the availability of employment and in real wages would be overcome by migration from Java to the Outer Islands. Some migration did occur, but the rate at the best of times was only a small fraction of the annual population growth of Java and Madura. Figures are available for the two main flows of emigrants, namely of indentured labour and of transmigrants. Table 13.7 shows that in the prosperous period of 1919 and 1920 and the mid-1920s, there was a net flow of between 40,000 and 50,000 indentured Javanese coolies per annum to work on the plantations and in the mines of the Outer Islands. These joined a pool of more than 100,000 Javanese coolies who were already there and had been re-engaged. It may be noted that in the late 1920s there was a net annual inflow of between 10,000 and 15,000 indentured Chinese coolies, who (allowing for re-engagements) constituted between a fifth and a quarter of the total industrial work force of about a quarter million (Table 13.3).[12] In the 1930s net emigration from Java ceased, and by the mid-1930s about 100,000 coolies had been repatriated to Java (Table 13.7). In 1937, after abolition of the old coolie ordinance, there was again a large net outflow of 55,000, but in the next two years this fell back to only about 10,000. Meanwhile there was a remarkable revival of the official transmigration (i.e. resettlement) program, which had virtually lapsed in the 1920s. In 1939 the net outflow of transmigrants was an unprecedented 40,000 (Table 13.9). Taking the net outflow from Java of transmigrants and free labourers together, however, the total was still only 50,000, which was not 10 per cent of the annual population increase for Java in that year.[13] It cannot be maintained that the low level of trade between Java and the Outer Islands was compensated for by factor flows.

TABLE 13.7 Flow of Indentured Labour to and from Java

Year	From Java	To Java	Net Loss/Gain to Java
1919	69,126	17,485	-51,641
1920	57,923	20,597	-37,326
1921	38,465	44,167	+ 5,702
1922	13,980	35,191	+21,211
1923	21,545	24,750	+ 3,205
1924	38,044	19,786	-18,258
1925	63,900	17,777	-46,123
1926	75,346	23,534	-51,812
1927	67,510	26,035	-41,475
1928	58,963	32,708	-26,255
1929	77,662	37,800	-39,862
1930	29,350	47,923	+18,573
1931	3,005	42,805	+39,800
1932	1,119	38,471	+37,352
1933	5,507	14,792	+ 9,285
1934	4,953	9,963	+ 5,010
1935	3,025	6,922	+ 3,897
1936	4,222	4,455	+ 233
1937[a]	65,750	10,392	-55,358
1938[a]	23,334	11,755	-11,579
1939[a]	25,347	15,396	- 9,951

[a]Under new ordinance of 1/11/36 includes free labourers

Source: As for Table 13.1

TABLE 13.8 Indentured Labour Drought In and Re-engaged

Year	Chinese			Javanese			Total	Per cent Javanese
	New	Re-engaged	Total	New	Re-engaged	Total		
1926	11,954	51,276	63,230	74,884	126,291	201,175	264,405	76.1
1927	15,927	44,779	60,706	65,689	121,237	186,926	247,632	75.5
1928	11,240	38,499	49,739	56,120	143,536	199,656	249,395	80.1
1929	15,236	33,999	49,235	70,612	158,932	229,544	278,779	82.3
1930	7,944	43,397	51,341	33,793	146,686	180,479	231,820	77.9

Source: As for Table 13.1

TABLE 13.9 Net Outflows From Java of Labourers and Transmigrants

Year	Labourers (Net)	Transmigrants (Net)	Total
1937	55,358	13,356	68,714
1938	11,579	29,932	41,511
1939	9,951	39,402	49,353

Source: As for Table 13.1

Some Simple Economic Analysis

The (static) theory of comparative advantage does not concern itself with internal trade because it assumes that resource endowments within a country are homogeneous. This is because it is assumed in turn that differential factor rewards will be eliminated by the mobility of both capital and labour. It is accepted by definition that although there are barriers to factor (labour) mobility between countries, such barriers do not exist within countries. Regional real income disparities are therefore merely an adjustment problem. This approach may be somewhat valid in western countries, but it certainly does not fit the situation of colonial Indonesia. While capital was mobile, labour was not. The flows of labour from Java/Madura to the Outer Islands in the form of indentured labour, spontaneous migration, and officially-sponsored transmigration were insignificant compared with the flows that would have been necessary to eliminate real wage differentials. The "comparative advantage of Indonesia" was therefore ambiguous, and there was scope for both international and internal specialisation. It does not follow, however, that internal specialisation could manifest itself to any marked degree in the absence of protection. In other words, the goods in which Java would have a comparative advantage in supplying to the Outer Islands might well be goods which, in the absence of some form of protection, could more cheaply be imported. It is therefore necessary to consider first the nature of the colonial "open economy."

Colonial Indonesia had a classic export economy on a very large scale. In 1925, at the peak of interwar prosperity, the ratio of exports to domestic product was estimated at the extraordinarily high figure of 36 per cent (Paauw 1963, p.183). By 1929 the ratio had fallen somewhat to about 30 per cent and, by the end of the 1930s, after the dislocation of the Depression, it had fallen further to 25 per cent. Even this, however, was still a very high figure. Yet, granted that Indonesia was an "export economy," it would be more accurate to describe it as an "export/import economy." This was epitomised by the powerful role of the "Big Five" trading houses, and was very apparent at the village level where export commodities were bartered directly for import items by Chinese middlemen. The great concern in the 1930s with Japanese penetration was not that it harmed exports, but that it redirected the source of imports and undermined the "efficient import mechanism" (Boeke 1946, p.30). Indonesia was therefore an "open economy" on both the export and the import side, and its institutions were adapted accordingly.

The effort, which culminated in the 1920s, to divert the export/import trade of the Outer Islands away from Singapore and Penang to transshipment via the main ports of Indonesia had little to do with comparative advantage and economic integration. Its main purpose and effect were to ensure that, by transshipment through Indonesian ports, the services of Dutch (rather than British) shipping, warehouses, banking, and insurance were utilised. The very device used to gain control of transshipment, namely the through bill of lading, ensured that transshipment precluded further processing or even sorting and grading. This clearly differentiated transshipment via Indonesian ports from shipment via Singapore, which fulfilled a genuine entrepôt function and, in the rubber trade at least, continued to do so. In this regard the transshipment system of the interwar period was not so very different from the old Consignment System of the *Nederlandsche Handel Maatschappij* during the period of the Cultivation System.[14]

The efficiency of interisland shipping therefore facilitated transshipment rather than local production. In the nineteenth century there would have been some substance in the argument that poor shipping services between Java and the Outer Islands were an obstacle to economic integration. Although most parts of the archipelago under Dutch control had some scheduled steamer mail service from Java under government contract, the main cargo lines were between the Outer Islands and Singapore. The KPM was called into existence to take over the contract mail services from the beginning of 1891 with the primary aim of redressing this imbalance. By the interwar years, virtually every port of any commercial significance received a regular scheduled service by KPM steamer from Java, which was the hub of the KPM system. Singapore continued to be a major port for the west of the archipelago but there were no direct steamer services from Singapore any further east than Surabaya and Banjarmasin (South Borneo). Virtually the entire trade of the East was directed by KPM steamer through Makassar and Surabaya. The KPM services were as frequent as the trade justified and reliable, while the rates charged do not seem to have been excessive. By the interwar years the ports of Indonesia were also efficient, even if many smaller ports still relied heavily on lighterage (but so did Singapore and Hong Kong). It is therefore difficult to point to deficiencies in (sea) transport infrastructure. The point is, however, that rather than opening the markets of the Outer Islands to the production of Java, the efficient sea transport services made possible the economic transshipment of imported goods, thereby pre-empting those markets.

The export/import economy did not mean that economic integration between Java and the Outer Islands was impossible, but its scope was severely constrained. During the 1920s there was some development in two main areas, namely energy resources and consumer goods. In the case of energy resources, Indonesia was in the fortunate position of being self-sufficient in both coal and oil. Coal was produced only in the Outer Islands and shipped to Java in large quantities. The development during the First World War of the Bukit Asem mine near Palembang in addition to existing mines in West Sumatra and Borneo (South and East) enabled Indonesia to meet its own rising demands, with a small export surplus for shipment mainly to Singapore and Hong Kong. Oil was produced not only in Sumatra and East Borneo but also in Central and East Java, where there was a large refinery near Surabaya. During the interwar years the cross trade in petroleum products between Java and the Outer Islands moved increasingly in favour of Java. Most of the output, however, was exported. The abundance of coal and oil produced few forward linkages with other sectors. The one notable exception was the cement factory adjacent to the Ombilin coal mine at Padang in West Sumatra—the output was shipped mainly to Java. Otherwise, the development of energy resources merely confirmed Indonesia's status as an exporter of raw materials.

In the case of consumer goods, the 1920s saw some examples of import substitution. This was most noticeable in the case of two new consumer products—cigarettes and cars. Cigarettes gained worldwide popularity during the First World War. At the end of the war a handicraft industry sprang up around Kudus producing the unique *kretek* cigarettes for "native" consumption (Boeke 1946, pp.126-27). This was followed in 1925 by the establishment of a large factory by the British American Tobacco Company (BAT) to produce machine-rolled white (western) cigarettes. Some time later, Faroka also set up a plant. As mentioned above, both products were shipped in growing quantities to the Outer Islands; the growth in production and trade were sustained during the 1930s. The automobile was also a new product. Few were found in Indonesia before the First World War, but afterwards, with the reduction in price made possible by mass production, they became increasingly popular. General Motors set up an assembly plant at Tanjung Priok, the port of Jakarta, in 1926, and from there shipped to the Outer Islands. There was also some development of local production in food and beverages (including beer and soft drinks). A common factor behind this modest expansion of import-substitution, except perhaps in the case of *kretek* cigarettes, was the rapid growth of the European population, which between 1920 and 1930 grew about 40 per cent to almost a quarter of a million (Central Bureau of Statistics 1941, p.5). This still constituted only 0.4 per cent of the total population, but in terms of purchasing power it was very much more important. Products such as automobiles (assembled) and bottled drinks obviously bore a high transport cost which favoured local assembly. In other cases such as white cigarettes, the local availability of raw materials such as tobacco may have been a factor. If the Depression had not intervened in 1929, it is conceivable that some further import substitution would have occurred along these lines. Nevertheless, it is hard to imagine any substantial and sustained industrial expansion without some protectionist measures. The backwardness of the textile industry seems to be a good indication of this. So also was the short-lived burst of industrial expansion during the First World War.

The First World War provided a strong boost to industrial development in Indonesia because of the big increase in the level of natural protection. Freight rates rose from the beginning of the war and, with the seizure of neutral Dutch ships by Britain and the United States in 1917 and 1918, the country was effectively isolated. One industry to benefit greatly was engineering. Before the war it had been of modest size, serving mainly the sugar industry, railways, and local shipping. Its rapid growth under wartime conditions was reflected in the interisland trade figures for 1915 and 1921 (iron and steel goods).

The coconut oil industry is a somewhat different case. The nucleus of a modern industry supplying the domestic market had existed before the war, whereas the war provided the opportunity to expand into export markets, initially in the Netherlands (which had lost its usual supplies from Germany) and then in the United States. Expansion was so rapid that by 1920 the installed capacity, including some plants still under construction, was sufficient to absorb more than the entire country's copra production (Kamerling 1979, pp.110-11). Of this capacity, about three-quarters was in Java and one-quarter in the Outer Islands. After the economic downturn of 1920, however, both industries went into decline. The decline of the coconut oil industry was the more spectacular. The export market was entirely lost and the firms which survived were forced to try to compete with the many Chinese mills which had sprung up to cater for the once despised local market. The decline of the engineering industry was less marked. In the case of marine engineering there was even some expansion in the production of steel-hulled lighters and small motor vessels, although the latter were not produced in any significant number until the 1920s. Nevertheless, there is validity to the general conclusions that the extraordinary boost to Indonesian manufacturing from the First World War was not translated into sustained expansion, and that much of the ground was lost during the 1920s. The significance of the episode is that it showed that capital and entrepreneurship were not lacking for local production, given some protection from normal import competition and from foreign export processing. In the absence of another war, further economic integration seemed to await government intervention. Ironically it was the Depression of the 1930s that made this possible.

Because it involved first and foremost a collapse of world trade, the Depression was a disaster for the export/import economy of Indonesia. *Laissez-faire* was clearly no longer a viable policy, as other countries, including Britain, were hastening to introduce protectionist measures. Yet the impact of the crisis on Indonesia was worsened because the Dutch guilder, to which the currency was tied, was not devalued until 1935. The problem for the colonial government was therefore to develop industries to absorb the displaced labour and arrest the fall in living standards, especially of the Indonesian population. Because there was little to hope for from the export sector, whether agriculture or mining, the government was forced to consider import substitution. This shift in policy became somewhat easier because of Japan's success in the early 1930s in capturing markets for textiles and light consumer goods formerly served by the Netherlands and other European countries. The Japanese share of the value of all Indonesian imports increased from about 10 per cent in 1929 to 31 per cent in 1933 in the trough of the Depression (Van Oorschot 1956, p.44). The share of textile imports was as high as 60 per cent (Broek 1942). In the beginning, the commercial invasion of Japan was welcomed because cheaper imports from this source helped to bring down the domestic price level and cushion the fall in real income of the Indonesian population. As the invasion progressed, however, the Dutch began to grieve not so much at the loss of markets as at the threat to the European-dominated distribution system in Indonesia (Boeke 1946, pp.29-30). The introduction in 1933 and 1934 of an elaborate regulatory system of import quotas, distribution licenses, and industry licensing (*bedrijfs-reglementering*) therefore seems to have been favoured with a wide measure of consensus.

As economic recovery became apparent in the mid-1930s, there began to emerge some difference of opinion between those who saw the protectionist measures as temporary and those who looked upon them as the start of a "New Economic Policy." The debate was conducted in terms of "economic cooperation" between Indonesia and the Netherlands. The conservatives wished to restore the export/import economy and feared that protectionist measures would raise the cost level. This "cheap labour" point of view was represented by the Rutgers commission of 1936:

> As Indonesia as an exporter of agricultural products must produce as cheaply as possible for the world market, protectionist measures to assist Indonesian industry with the consequent rise of the price level were thought by the Commission to be most undesirable. (Van Oorschot 1956, p.50)

At the same time, the Commission was not opposed to taking advantage of the low wages in Indonesia to develop the production of cheaper goods which would not compete with more valuable goods manufactured in the Netherlands. Two years later the Van Mook Commission took a more liberal viewpoint which gave greater weight to Indonesian interests; it was no doubt significant that Van Mook was the Director of Economic Affairs in Indonesia whereas Rutgers was a member of the Privy Council in the Netherlands. The Van Mook Commission argued that the industrialisation of Indonesia ought not be constrained by the need to provide a market for the industries of the Netherlands but rather that the Netherlands ought to adapt its economy accordingly and compensate by investing in industrial development in Indonesia (Van Oorschot 1956, pp.54-56). In other words, the government of Indonesia ought to be able to protect its emerging industries not only against import competition from Japan[15] but also against imports from the Netherlands.

The articulation by the Van Mook Commission of an Indonesian economic interest not necessarily coinciding with that of the Netherlands, at least in the short-run, represented a significant step. It reflected an underlying change in the nature of the Indonesian government which came about in response to the Great Depression. Despite the Ethical Policy, the government had remained, until the beginning of the 1930s, a colonial administration concerned primarily with *rust en orde* (peace and order) and with providing the infrastructure required by an efficient export economy, which was essentially an engineering task. The crisis measures of 1933 and 1934 involved a greatly extended role for this administration in the detailed regulation of a wide range of industries. One result was a dramatic increase in the size and importance of the Department of Economic Affairs, which by the late 1930s was probably the major department. In the process, the colonial administration became a real government to all intents and purposes, a role it was forced to assume after the invasion of the Netherlands in 1930. The young and enthusiastic civil servants of the 1930s may not have appreciated it at the time, but they were in fact laying the foundations of the Indonesian state, notwithstanding the simultaneous repression of the nationalistic movement.[16] They also helped to set the scene for the bitter conflicts of the late 1940s by ensuring that the issue would not be whether or not there would be an Indonesian nation, but rather who would control it.

Conclusion

That genuine economic integration between Java and the Outer Islands began to emerge in the 1930s reflected not some logical next stage in colonial economic development but rather the breakdown of the old colonial order. The Depression of the 1930s was a great crisis of internationalism. For more than a century, the growth of world trade had been a means of reconciling the internationalism of capitalism with the nationalism of the European powers. Colonialism had been a dependent nationalism imposed upon the rest of the world in order to strengthen the position of the European powers in world trade. The collapse of trade brought about pressures towards autarchy not only in Europe but also in the colonies. In response to the crisis, the colonial administration in Indonesia began to play something of the role of a national government in economic management and, by restricting international trade, facilitated economic integration between Java and the Outer Islands. This could not have occurred in the absence of a significant measure of self-government. Authors such as Boeke, who wrote in the late 1930s about the economic prospects for the colony, no doubt like the Director of Economic Affairs, Van Mook, seem to have envisaged the achievement of some kind of a multiracial society with a self-governing dominion status under Dutch tutelage. That possibility was destroyed by the Japanese occupation. The tragedy was that enlightened people on the Dutch side took so long to recognise it. Nevertheless, the new state of Indonesia[17] took over the economic nationalism of the 1930s and many of the economic policies. Had it not been for the colonial experience there would, of course, have been no Indonesian state. That was perhaps the fundamental inheritance.

Notes

1. The material on trade in the pre-colonial and early colonial archipelago is drawn mainly from Meilink-Roelofsz (1962), Van Leur (1955) and Wolters (1967).
2. However, as Reid (1984) points out, by the seventeenth century, Java was not the main source of textiles shipped to the Outer Islands.
3. These figures are taken from Van Leur (1955) and C.E.I., vol.1.
4. An outline of the establishment of coffee cultivation can be found in C.E.I., vol.1, Table 12.
5. The material for this paragraph has been drawn from Wong Lin Ken (1960 and 1978).
6. The rate on textiles was 10 per cent on Dutch goods and 20 per cent on foreign goods, reduced in 1869 to 16 per cent. This was to protect the Dutch textile industry which had been built up after the secession of Belgium.
7. On the KPM and interisland shipping, see Dick (1977, Ch.2).
8. A last equals 2 tons of sugar, 1.8 tons of rubber and 1.2 tons of copra.

9. The conclusion would not be greatly modified if account was taken of the fact that in the mid-1920s the colonial government began carrying its own salt from Madura to the Outer Islands (mainly to the fishing centre of Bagansi-api-api) on its own account.
10. There was no spinning capacity until 1939.
11. Boeke (1946, pp.112-16) contains a good summary of rice policy in the 1930s. See also C.E.I., Vol.4.
12. Indentured labour constituted only part of Chinese migration to Indonesia. Unfortunately no figures are available for the 1920s but in the late 1930s the excess of arrivals over departures was 34,180 (1937), 21,901 (1938) and 7,779 (1939).
13. In 1938 the Central Bureau of Statistics estimated the population of Java and Madura at 46 million with a rate of growth of 1.5 per cent per annum (Boeke 1946, p.147). This would mean an annual population increase of about 700,000.
14. Until the 1850s the export commodities of Java could not even be sold in Java.
15. Restrictions on Japanese imports were as much directed towards reserving the Indonesian market for Dutch goods as encouraging local industrialisation.
16. Boeke (1946, pp.34-38) was one who did seem to realise this.
17. Anderson (1983) argues that after the hiatus of the Sukarno period, the modern Indonesian state is now being restructured in a way that harks back to the late colonial period.

CHAPTER FOURTEEN

Dutch Colonialism in Indonesia: A Comparative Perspective

Angus Maddison

This chapter is concerned mainly with the situation in Indonesia in the 1930s, and concentrates on a comparison with other colonial regimes, particularly in Asia. It considers (a) the scale of foreign presence which colonialism introduced into Indonesia; (b) the payments "drain"; (c) the impact of the 1930s' depression and the policy response it induced from the colonial authorities.

According to the 1930 Population Census, there were 240,000 Europeans living in Indonesia, roughly 0.4 per cent of the total population and 3.1 per cent of the population of the Netherlands. Of these, 20,700 were Dutch officials or Dutch military personnel, 63,600 were working in plantations as professionals, traders, etc., and 156,400 were family dependents. On average for the period 1921 to 1939, this group received 10.6 per cent of Indonesian net domestic product at factor cost. In addition, five per cent of national income in Indonesia accrued to non-residents (mainly Dutch) and to government entrepreneurship.

Over the period 1921 to 1939, Indonesian NDP (net domestic product at factor cost) averaged 82 per cent of Dutch NDP at current prices. As the incomes earned by the Dutch in Indonesia equalled 15.6 per cent of Indonesian NDP, these same incomes represented an "augmentation" of income claims by metropolitan citizens of 12.8 per cent. The actual amount remitted to the Netherlands was less than this as the Dutch in Indonesia used some of their income for consumption and for asset accumulation in the colony. Between 1921 and 1939, total Dutch income from abroad from all sources averaged 9.4 per cent of Dutch NDP; the bulk of this came from Indonesia. There seems to be general agreement that remittances from Indonesia amounted to about 8 percent of Dutch NDP in this period, or nearly 10 per cent of Indonesian NDP. In addition there were remittances from Indonesia to some other countries, with around 0.5 per cent of Indonesia NDP going to China.[1]

In the 1930s, the Dutch style of colonial rule could be described as "free trade imperialism" based more or less on the British model. In 1870 the Dutch had discarded the notorious Cultivation System which involved close bilateral ties with the metropole, compulsory levies of specific crops, or compulsory labour service with the proceeds remitted directly as tribute to the Dutch state (following more or less the early Spanish model in Latin America). The new policy was more acceptable to liberal opinion at home, more respectable internationally, led to more efficient resource allocation, and was also more profitable, if one considers the degree to which the two systems "augmented" Dutch NDP.[2]

A striking feature of colonialism in Indonesia is that the Dutch presence encouraged the growth of the Chinese community and that of other Asiatics (Indians and Arabs), although these foreign Asiatic groups were present (in a somewhat smaller proportion) before the Dutch and still remain in Indonesia. In 1930 there were 1,233,000 Chinese in Indonesia, 71,000 Arabs, and 45,000 other Asiatics, amounting to 2.22 per cent of the total population. On average for the period from 1921 to 1939, this group had 8.35 per cent of national income. The Chinese were not so unambiguously a product of colonialism as the Dutch, but they did retain strong contacts with their ancestral home and seem to have remitted about 6 per cent of their income to China.[3]

In India, the British presence was relatively much smaller, more heavily concentrated on government pursuits, with a smaller resident dependency rate, which indicated a lower proportion of permanent residents than in Indonesia. In 1931 there were 168,000 British living in India, amounting to 0.05 per cent of the population or about one eighth the size of the foreign proportion of the population in Indonesia (Table 14.1).

About 60,000 of the British were in the army and police and 4,000 in civil government. Only 26,000 British were engaged in private sector activities (0.008 per cent of population compared with 0.15 per cent for the corresponding group in Indonesia). According to my estimates, the British share of income of all kinds in India was around five per cent in the 1930s, only about a third of the Dutch (resident and non-resident) share in Indonesia. There were only 78,000 British family dependents in India, a dependency ratio of 87 per cent, whereas the Dutch had a 185 per cent dependency ratio. It should also be noted that 71 per cent of the Europeans living in Indonesia in 1930 were born there (Hugo 1980, p. 119), whereas 60 per cent of the Europeans in India were born in the U.K.[4]

In the years between 1921 and 1939, Indian net domestic product at current prices averaged 66.7 per cent of that in the United Kingdom. As British incomes in India were five per cent of Indian domestic product, we can see that the British in India "augmented" British incomes by 3.3 per cent. About 1.5 per cent of Indian product was actually transferred to the U.K., and this transferred part therefore augmented U.K. domestic product by about one per cent.[5]

It is clear therefore that the "drain" from India, which Indian nationalists assailed as the major burden of colonial rule, was not as big as it was from Indonesia. This was partly due to a difference in colonial policy, but it also reflected a difference in economic potential. India was a land of ancient

TABLE 14.1 The Dimensions of Foreign Presence Under Colonialism

	"Europeans", metropolitan nationals, and those of assimilated status [a]	Percentage of total population
Dutch Colony		
Indonesia (1930)	240,162	0.40
British Colonies		
Burma (1931)	34,000	0.23
Ceylon (1929)	7,500	0.15
India (1931)	168,134	0.05
Malaya (1931) (inc. Singapore)	33,811	0.77
Everybody's Colony		
China (1921)	267,000	0.06
French Colony		
Indochina (1937)	42,345	0.18
Japanese Colonies		
Korea (1930-35)	573,000	2.62
Taiwan (1930)	228,000	4.96
U.S. Colony		
Philippines (1939)	36,000	0.15

[a] Includes Eurasians in Indonesia (134,000); in Malaya (16,043); and in Indochina (approx. 14,000). The Philippines figure includes 10,500 Japanese, but excludes U.S. military personnel and 200,000 Hispano-Filipino mestizos.

Sources: Burma - Aye Hlaing (1964); the figure refers to foreign races other than Indian and Chinese. Ceylon - Snodgrass (1966, pp. 60 & 306). China - Feuerwerker (1976, pp. 17-18); excludes some Russian and Japanese and all of the Korean population of Manchuria but includes 26,000 foreign military and police personnel. India - Hutton (1933). Indochina - Robequain (1944). Indonesia - Central Bureau of Statistics (1941). Korea - Sang-Chul Suh (1978, p. 115). Malaya - Vlieland (1932). Philippines - Robequain (1948). Taiwan - Kuznets (1979, p. 18).

settlement, with a smaller potential vent for surplus than Indonesia or other British colonies such as Burma, Ceylon, and Malaya.

In British Malaya where the economy was even more export-oriented than in Indonesia, the proportionate colonial commercial presence was bigger than in Indonesia; the "European" population was 0.4 per cent of the total in 1931 and Eurasians with assimilated status formed another 0.37 per cent. In Burma, Europeans and assimilated were just half the Indonesian proportion and in Ceylon they were somewhat less than half (Table 14.1). In all these colonies, the British encouraged the growth of ethnic minorities. In Malaya, the nature of the Chinese role was similar to that of the Chinese in Indonesia, but in Burma and Ceylon the ethnic minorities were Indian and were used largely as labourers in plantations. All three of these British colonies were vent-for-surplus countries in Myint's sense (Myint 1958), relying on plantation and smallholder agriculture to provide a high export ratio.

I have less evidence to compare Dutch with French colonialism in the 1930s, but the French presence in Indochina was relatively smaller than that of the Dutch in Indonesia (0.18 per cent of the population). I suspect that the commercial element was a smaller proportion than in Indonesia and the dependency ratio a good deal higher than in India, because the French established good secondary schools in their colonies, whereas British colonials got subsidies to ship their children to boarding schools in England.

In Japanese colonies, the colonial involvement was much bigger than in Indonesia. In Korea, the Japanese population was 573,000 in the period from 1930 to 1935, or 2.6 per cent of the total. This community had been there for centuries, although when Korea was annexed in 1910, the Japanese numbered only 172,000, so most of the Japanese there in the years between 1930 and 1935 were recent settlers. Japanese colonialism involved much stronger bilateral ties with Korea than those between the Dutch and Indonesia, whose exports went to world markets. The Japanese were innovative landlords spreading new techniques in agriculture. They occupied skilled jobs in the rapidly growing Korean industry in which Japan had invested heavily. In 1935, 52,000 Japanese worked in administration and the professions in Korea. In Taiwan, the Japanese conquest (1895) was earlier than in Korea, and development efforts were more heavily concentrated in agriculture, particularly sugar. There was, in fact, a higher proportion of Japanese settlers in Taiwan than in Korea (about five per cent of the population).

Japanese colonialism was more developmental than that of other countries because it involved a greater effort to transfer and develop technology, higher physical investment, and better development of local education and human capital. Unlike most of Asia, Korea actually seems to have enjoyed a significant net inflow of Japanese capital as it had a trade deficit, whereas almost all the other colonies ran trade surpluses.

U.S. colonialism in the Philippines dated from the Spanish American war and was less exploitative than Dutch rule in Indonesia, with a smaller trade drain, and a bigger educational effort. The American presence in the Philippines (8,700) was proportionately as light as that of the British in India, but Americans were outnumbered by other foreign settlers, particularly by Japanese.

China, which was not the colony of any particular power, had been forced to cede territorial sovereignty to many foreign powers in the treaty ports. This foreign presence was relatively small by Asian standards and of about the same order of magnitude as the British presence in India. The peacetime economy of China was much less affected by the colonial presence than that of other Asian countries, and the ratio of foreign trade to GDP was very low. Because of large remittances to China by emigrant Chinese communities, and because the foreign powers in China often spent more there on colonial-type purchases than they raised in local revenue, China ran a persistent trade deficit.

In default of complete balance of payments data for most of the countries, one crude clue to the size of the payments burden or "drain" involved in colonial rule is the size of the commodity trade balance. It is quite clear that in the period when the Asian countries were colonies, most of them had substantial export surpluses, and that since independence most of them have been able to run deficits. Trade accounts provide only a partial indicator of the balance of payments situation because part of the trade surplus was offset by service imports, or imports of precious metals.

In the period between 1913 and 1938, the proportionate trade surplus of Indonesia was high, with exports (f.o.b.) exceeding imports (c.i.f.) by an average of 75 per cent (Table 14.2). This is more than that of any of the other Asian country and reflects the drain to the Netherlands on Dutch account (residents' home remittances, remittances to non-residential commercial interests, and government transfers) and much smaller remittances on Chinese account. In the period between 1870 and 1912, the drain from Indonesia was smaller, but in the period between 1840 and 1869 of the Cultivation System and primitive tribute, it was substantially higher.

In interpreting Table 14.2 it should be kept in mind that the ratio of trade to GDP varied a good deal between countries. For example, the average trade ratio in Indonesia was four times as high as in India (Table 14.3). If we combine this information with that in Table 14.2, it suggests that the unrequited export surplus was 2 per cent of Indian national income and 12.4 percent of that of Indonesia, and therefore is a rough confirmation of our more direct estimates above.[6] In all the other Asian countries (with the probable exception of Burma[7]) the drain as measured in this proxy fashion was smaller than in Indonesia in the years from

TABLE 14.2 Average Ratio of Exports (f.o.b.) to Imports (c.i.f.)

	1840-69	1870-1912	1913-38	1950-59	1960-73
Developing Countries					
Indonesia	244.7	145.4[a]	175.0	139.1	112.2
Argentina	n.a.	107.2	124.5	92.6	112.4
Brazil	97.9	126.3	127.0	100.6	97.8
Ceylon	86.0	96.4	122.8	109.1	97.8
China	n.a.	106.8	79.0	94.6	109.2
Egypt	155.3[b]	153.8	107.3	79.7	80.0
India	172.5	148.0	133.4	79.6	71.9
Indochina	n.a.	101.3[c]	122.9	26.8	13.7[d]
Korea	n.a.	47.5[e]	85.1	7.7[f]	34.1
Malaya	n.a.	n.a.	115.7	140.1	118.0
Mexico	n.a.	109.6[g]	131.6	78.0	67.8
Philippines	n.a.	118.3[h]	118.6	86.0	93.7
Thailand	n.a.	139.2	134.4	86.7	72.7
Average	n.a.	116.7	121.3	86.2	83.2
Developed Countries					
France	107.1	86.4	70.7[j]	94.5	95.6
Germany	n.a.	85.6[i]	98.9[j]	107.5	114.9
Japan	n.a.	83.8	95.7	75.1	97.1
Netherlands	78.4[k]	80.1	70.1	83.2	88.8
U.K.	74.4	68.6	62.3	82.0	85.4
U.S.A.	92.3	125.2	140.0	136.4	118.7
Average	n.a.	88.3	89.6	96.5	100.1

a Excludes 1875
b 1850-1869
c 1883-1912
d Excludes 1973; from 1955 the figures refer to South Vietnam
e 1886-1912
f Excludes 1950 and 1951
g 1881-1889 and 1892-1910
h 1885-1912
i 1880-1912
j Excludes 1914-1919
k 1846-1869

Sources: 1950 onwards from United Nations, Yearbooks of International Trade Statistics, except for China which is from Chinese Economy Post-Mao (1978, p. 733). Earlier years for Developing Countries: Argentina - 1870-1910 from Ferns (1960, pp. 492-3); 1911-38 from Diaz Alejandro (1970, pp.461, 475-6). Brazil - 1840-1938 from I.B.G.E. (1960, p.84). China - from Hsiao Liang-lin (1974, pp. 268-9) adjusted to a c.i.f./f.o.b. basis, and excluding re-exports (pp. 22-4). Mexico - 1881-1910 from Comercio Exterior (1960, p. 175); 1913-38 from La Economica Mexicana (1966, pp. 243-4). 1913-38 imports adjusted upwards by 47.4% for undercounting of border trade; this is an average adjustment factor apparently applied by the Bank of Mexico in revaluing 1950-53 imports for this purpose. The previous figures for 1950-53 are in 50 Años de Revolucion (1963, p. 140). Thailand - 1870-1938 from Ingram (1971, pp. 333-4); includes trade in precious metals. Other Developing Countries from Mitchell (1982). Developed Countries: Earlier years for France, Germany, Netherlands and the U.K. 1913-38 from Mitchell (1975); U.K. - 1840-1913 from Imlah (1958, pp. 95-8) with re-exports excluded from imports. Japan - from Ohkawa and Shinohara (1979, pp. 332-5). U.S.A. - from Historical Statistics Vol.2 (1975, pp. 884-6).

TABLE 14.3 Ratio of Merchandise Exports to GDP at Current Prices

	1929	1938	1950	1960	1973	1982
Developing Countries						
Indonesia	29.0	23.4	7.7	13.5	19.7	31.1
Argentina	26.7	14.1	8.7	8.8	8.1	7.2
Brazil	15.4	13.5	7.7	5.2	7.6	7.7
China	n.a.	2.1	3.0	n.a.	2.0	n.a.
Egypt	n.a.	14.8	18.9	13.3	11.6	9.8
India	7.8	5.9	6.5	4.2	3.8	4.3
Korea	19.0	24.2	0.0	0.9	24.5	31.8
Malaya	n.a.	46.0	63.0	49.4	42.3	46.5
Mexico	12.4	12.2	9.1	6.3	5.0	8.1
Philippines	n.a.	20.0	9.5	8.0	16.9	12.5
Thailand	n.a.	19.0	18.4	16.0	14.7	n.a.
Average	n.a.	17.7	13.9	12.6	14.2	n.a.
Developed Countries						
France	14.0	6.9	10.6	11.2	14.3	17.0
Germany	15.3	5.6	8.5	15.7	19.4	26.7
Japan	16.0	14.9	7.8	9.4	9.0	13.0
Netherlands	29.4	18.4	28.6	36.1	39.8	48.3
U.K.	15.5	8.4	16.7	13.9	17.1	20.5
U.S.A.	5.0	3.6	3.6	4.0	5.3	6.9
Average	15.9	9.6	12.6	15.1	17.5	22.1

[a] 1951 [b] 1928-9 [c] 1933 [d] 1977 [e] 1981

Sources: Developing Countries for pre-war years: Indonesia - C.E.I., Vol. 2 and Polak (1943); GDP in 1951 from Muljatno (1960). Argentina - Diaz Alejandro (1970, pp. 14, 406, 461, 479). Brazil - Exports divided by current price GDP from Contador and Haddad (1975). China - in 1933 Hsiao Liang-lin (1974, p. 280) and Liu and Yeh (1965, p. 66); post-war years years: An Economic Profile, Vol. 1 (1967, pp. 73 & 125), Chinese Economy Post-Mao (1978, pp. 231 & 733) and World Bank data. Egypt - Hansen and Marzouk (1965, p. 174). India - Cambridge Economic History of India. Korea - Exports from Mitchell (1982); GDP from Sang-Chul Suh (1978). Malaya, Philippines and Thailand in 1938 from Paauw (1963); Malayan GDP in 1950 and 1960 from Lim Chong-Yah (1967, p. 317). Mexico - GDP in current pesos from Fitzgerald (1984). Post-war years generally from U.N. Yearbooks of International Trade Statistics and World Bank (1980). Developed Countries: Sources given given in Maddison (1983).

TABLE 14.4 Indonesian Balance of Payments 1929–38[a] (million guilders)

Year	Merchandise Exports (1)	Exports of Precious Metals (2)	Capital Inflow (3)	Merchandise Imports (4)	Imports of Precious Metals (5)	Profits & Dividends Remitted (6)	Net Outflow on Government Account (7)	Interest (8)	Net Outflow for Other Services (9)	Capital Outflow (10)	Unexplained Items (11)
1929	1,500	5	59	1,165	14	250	67	79	113	103	+ 227
1930	1,198	5	180	933	3	189	57	81	111	80	+ 71
1931	756	54	103	600	3	64	51	89	75	58	+ 27
1932	548	52	180	385	0	35	96	85	49	55	- 65
1933	474	52	129	330	0	21	79	89	40	71	- 25
1934	506	55	151	291	0	20	55	90	36	170	- 50
1935	476	69	16	277	1	28	45	80	34	43	- 53
1936	598	37	12	293	9	49	42	76	32	108	- 38
1937	993	22	25	508	47	89	64	68	31	102	- 131
1938	690	22	29	492	10	167	51	53	32	74	+ 138
Average 1930-38	693	41	92	457	8	74	60	79	49	85	- 14

[a]Columns 1, 2, and 3 are credit items, columns 4 to 10 are all debit items, column 11 is a net item marked with a plus sign when it was in credit and with a minus sign when in deficit.

Source: C.E.I. Vol. 5

TABLE 14.5 Items in India's Balance of Payments 1929-38[a] (million rupees)

Year	Merchandise Exports	Exports of Precious Metals	Service Receipts	Capital Inflow	Merchandise Imports	Imports of Precious Metals	Profits Remitted	Net Outflow on Government Account	Interest	Other Service Payments	Capital Outflow
1929-30	3,613.4	15.7	201.1	78.4	2,694.4	277.7	29.3	74.1	524.9	419.4	32.8
1930-31	2,578.5	24.3	389.1	437.1	1,892.6	269.1	30.0	199.9	443.8	357.7	33.5
1931-32	1,819.0	629.1	153.6	161.3	1,403.5	74.1	29.6	247.0	424.5	295.2	230.4
1932-33	1,538.6	679.2	156.9	189.9	1,459.1	31.2	29.2	257.5	425.4	338.1	144.7
1933-34	1,713.4	591.9	154.6	302.6	1,295.7	20.8	28.3	452.8	458.5	293.7	189.9
1934-35	1,757.3	577.3	145.7	44.9	1,486.4	52.2	28.6	306.4	449.6	318.4	40.0
1935-36	1,860.3	418.8	147.6	171.5	1,520.2	56.6	30.5	+ 62.2	480.4	317.0	223.2
1936-37	2,262.5	300.0	154.5	77.1	1,405.4	156.8	30.1	169.3	507.6	359.8	251.2
1937-38	2,254.7	183.2	157.1	55.1	1,775.2	40.2	29.3	148.9	506.0	364.4	92.2
1938-39	2,032.3	147.0	151.6	11.5	1,532.2	22.4	26.9	159.9	478.8	347.4	76.0
Average 1930-38	1,979.6	394.5	179.0	161.2	1,530.0	80.4	29.2	208.8	463.8	332.4	142.7

[a] Fiscal years beginning 1st April

Source: Banerji (1963, pp. 27, 90, 115, 137 & 195)

1913 to 1938. However, the trade deficit overstates the payments drain for reasons already mentioned. A more accurate picture is given by the complete balance of payments data for Indonesia and India (Tables 14.4 and 14.5).

It is sometimes suggested that the apparent drain simply represents a normal and legitimate return on foreign investment in the colony, or on the entrepreneurship and skills furnished by the foreign settlers and administrators. It is true that there was a substantial foreign-owned capital stock in Indonesia, and it was bigger in per capita terms than in any other Asian country except Korea and Malaya (Table 14.6). However, in colonial situations such as in Indonesia, where there had been a consistent and substantial trade surplus for 300 years, it is clear there was never any net transfer of funds from the metropole, and that the foreign claims on Indonesia arose basically from reinvested earnings of the colonialists.[8]

TABLE 14.6 Per Capita Net Foreign Capital Position of Developing Countries in 1938 (Portfolio and Direct Investments)

	Foreign Obligations ($ million)	Foreign Assets ($ million)	Population ('000)	Net Obligations Per Capita ($)
Indonesia	2,378	7	68,409	35
Burma	200	0	15,800	13
Ceylon	125	0	5,826	21
China (inc. Manchuria)	2,557	770	528,000	3
India	3,644	203	308,230	11
Indochina	391	0	23,000	17
Korea[a]	1,718	0	23,434	73
Malaya	696	1	4,235	164
Philippines	307	28	15,814	18
Taiwan	201	0	6,493	31
Thailand	200	0	14,755	14

[a] 1941

Sources: Foreign obligations for all countries except India and Korea from Lewis (1948, pp. 321-41). India - Gurtoo (1961, p. 69). Korea - Sang-Chul Suh (1978, p. 129).

Similarly, some of the earnings of foreigners derived not from the intrinsic worth of their entrepreneurial, administrative, and technical skills, but rather because they operated in a milieu which favoured them over the indigenous population who had little access to education or on-the-job methods of acquiring highly paid skills. The political system, too, systematically favoured expatriates. They had the dominant voice in the limited parliamentary body, and the higher levels of bureaucracy, which took orders from The Hague, were entirely Dutch. The banking, shipping, and insurance network was mainly in the hands of the Dutch, and so was estate management. Provision for indigenous education was weak, and the upper echelons of the old indigenous elite functioned mainly as instruments of the Dutch bureaucracy. Local entrepreneurs were almost entirely Chinese, not Indonesian. Colonialism skewed the "human capital" situation against the locals.

On the other hand, it is only fair to note that the Indonesian trade balance continued to be positive after independence, presumably because of the continuance of substantial Chinese remittances, and the heavy dependence on expatriate skills and foreign capital.

Apart from the drain and the handicap in developing indigenous human capital, the colonial tie also meant that Indonesia did not have autonomous macroeconomic policy weapons, as policy was dictated by the metropolitan conception of Dutch interests. In the 1920s, this may not have been too harmful to Indonesia. Nationalists would have preferred tariff freedom to protect infant industry and provide revenue, but it is doubtful that this would have done much to improve welfare and growth in that period.

In the 1920s, the Dutch kept Indonesia out of the Stevenson scheme which the British devised to stabilise rubber prices, and this benefited Indonesia whose share of world markets grew. However, after 1929, one can argue that Dutch conjunctural policy damaged Indonesia.[9] In the first place, the Dutch stayed in the gold bloc until 1936, long after British and U.S. devaluations; both the Dutch and the Indies guilder thus appreciated substantially against most major currencies during the 1930s (Table 14.7).

This was not sensible from a metropolitan viewpoint, but in Indonesia, which was competing on world markets with identical exports to those of neighbouring countries, it imposed deflationary hardships which could have been mitigated by simultaneous devaluation along with sterling. The Japanese sensibly devalued by more than the British, which is one reason their exports did so well in the 1930s. In fact, Indonesian exports did not fall as much in volume as those of neighbouring countries because Dutch deflationary policy pushed prices and wages down very substantially.

TABLE 14.7 Exchange Depreciation of Other Currencies Against the NEI Guilder

Year	Malaya	India	Japan	U.K.	U.S.A.
1929	100.0	100.0	100.0	100.0	100.0
1930	99.3	98.9	106.0	99.8	99.6
1931	93.6	93.4	106.0	93.3	100.0
1932	73.0	73.6	62.1	72.6	100.0
1933	68.8	69.2	44.0	68.5	81.6
1934	62.4	61.5	37.9	61.7	59.6
1935	60.3	60.4	37.1	59.8	59.2
1936	64.5	64.8	38.8	63.8	62.4
1937	74.4	74.7	44.8	73.8	72.8
1938	73.8	73.6	44.8	73.2	72.8

Source: C.E.I. Vol. 6, Table 8.

As an independent country, Indonesia would probably not have pursued such a deflationary fiscal policy in the 1930s. It would certainly not have done so if it had been a Latin American country. By 1936, Indonesian prices had fallen to 44 per cent of their 1929 level, a much steeper decline than occurred in the Netherlands, the U.K., or India (Table 14.8). Fiscal revenue fell considerably in money terms, although not in relation to national income (Figure 10.5), and salaries were cut, but the public debt burden rose in real terms, even though the Dutch made a conversion issue which lowered the interest rate (Table 10.6). In addition, if Indonesia had been an independent country in the 1930s, it would probably have cut imports on a non-discriminatory basis by raising tariffs, whereas the Dutch used discriminatory quantitative restrictions, which favoured their exports rather than the cheaper ones available from Japan. This caused considerable discontent, particularly as the restrictions mainly concerned cheap items of mass consumption (Ranneft 1937).

In independent Latin American countries and China, the response to the crisis of the 1930s was debt default, but in Indonesia as in India and other colonies, the metropolitan power excluded such a solution. As a result the Indonesian depression was deeper than it need have been, though a considerable part of the deflation was absorbed by the very big fall in import volume. In 1929, Latin American countries were mostly without central banks, and their foreign transactions depended heavily on foreign banks as did those of Indonesia. However, in the 1930s they quickly acquired the instruments for autonomous economic policy. The exchange controls they imposed in those years increased

TABLE 14.8 Net Domestic Product Deflators

(1929=100)

	Netherlands	Indonesia	U.K.	India[a]
1921	114.3	132.8	138.0	126.1
1922	107.1	110.5	116.0	115.9
1923	100.0	108.8	106.6	109.6
1924	100.0	106.4	105.1	116.2
1925	100.0	104.5	105.5	113.6
1926	100.0	107.3	103.9	110.7
1927	100.0	100.2	101.4	108.2
1928	100.0	98.7	100.4	107.4
1929	100.0	100.0	100.0	100.0
1930	92.9	96.5	99.6	80.7
1931	85.7	73.1	97.2	71.9
1932	78.6	57.8	93.8	68.7
1933	78.6	47.6	92.6	65.0
1934	78.6	45.4	91.7	66.4
1935	78.6	45.8	92.7	66.9
1936	78.6	44.4	91.0	67.1
1937	78.6	48.6	96.6	68.9
1938	78.6	49.5	99.2	69.3
1939	85.7	48.1	101.7	74.1

[a] Indian figures are for fiscal years 1921/22 *et seq*.

Sources: Netherlands - Centraal Bureau voor de Statistiek (1979). Indonesia - Polak (1943). U.K. - Feinstein (1972). India - Sivasubramonian (1965).

their capacity to follow autonomous economic policy, and the strengthening of indigenous banks also weakened the role of foreign commercial interests in their economies. This cathartic process did not occur in Indonesia until after independence.

Notes

1. Estimates of the income and population of the Dutch in Indonesia and of Indonesian NDP are from Polak (1943). Estimates of Dutch NDP and income from abroad are from Centraal Bureau voor de Statistiek (1979). These results are confirmed by the findings of Derksen and Tinbergen (1945, p.213) that in the period from 1925 to 1934 income remitted from Indonesia was 8.3 per cent of Dutch NDP, and Dutch income retained in Indonesia was 4.6 per cent of Dutch NDP. For 1938 Derksen and Tinbergen show 7.6 and 3.2 per cent respectively.

Baudet and Wijers (1976) give a slightly revised figure for 1938 of 7.9 per cent instead of 7.6 percent of Dutch NDP for remitted income.

2. At its peak in the 1860s, the official revenue remittances *(batig slot)* to the Dutch exchequer averaged 32.4 million guilders per annum (C.E.I., Vol. 2, p.18). In addition there were smaller remittances by the limited group then in private business in Indonesia. In 1860, I estimate that Dutch NDP was around 840 million guilders, so that the total remittances from Indonesia at that time were probably running about 5 per cent of Dutch NDP. 1860 Dutch NDP estimates are interpolated from Maddison (1982) linked to the 1900 NDP level derived from Centraal Bureau voor de Statistiek (1979, p.144) and using van Stuivenberg's price index (1860 prices 24 per cent higher than 1900) cited by Griffiths and de Meere (1983).
3. See Remer (1933, p.185) who gives an estimate of the sources of Chinese emigrant remittances in 1930. Those from Indonesia came to about 25 million guilders or 5.8 per cent of foreign Asiatic income in Indonesia as given by Polak (1943, in C.E.I., Vol. 5, p.70) for that year.
4. The above description compares the "European" population of India with that of Indonesia, using the census definitions. The Indian census included about 30,000 persons of mixed race as part of the "European" total of 168,134 and noted that these were "Anglo-Indians who are not handicapped by excessive pigmentation." In addition, there were 138,395 persons who returned themselves as Anglo-Indians whom we have not treated as Europeans because, in British practice, they did not have "assimilated status"; see Hutton (1933).
5. See Maddison (1971, pp.63-67) for a discussion of the colonial burden in India and for net domestic product which was converted to current prices using the implicit deflator in Sivasubramonian (1965, pp.337-38). U.K. national product is derived from Feinstein (1972, pp. T 5-6 & T 15-16). Total U.K. income received from abroad in the period from 1921 to 1939 averaged 4.9 per cent of net domestic product at current prices.
6. The average trade surplus of Indonesia for the period from 1913 to 1938 equalled 75 per cent of imports, or, alternatively stated, 43 percent of exports (75/175), and exports in 1929 (taken as a rough proxy for the 1913-38 ratio) were 29 per cent of GDP. Therefore the export surplus was 12.4 per cent of GDP (i.e. 43 x 29).
7. Aye Hlaing (1964) estimates the share of exports in Burmese NDP at 38 per cent in 1929 and 48 per cent in 1938 and the Burmese export/import ratio at 142.3 in the years 1870 to 1915 and 193.0 between 1913 and 1938. This would suggest that the trade surplus was 18.3 per cent of NDP, i.e. bigger than the 12.4 per cent found for Indonesia. However, Burma was part of the Indian customs area until 1937 and had official estimates only for seaborne trade. Hlaing used unpublished trade estimates of U Chit Maung.
8. For trade balances from 1840 onwards see Table 14.2. For the period 1640 to 1840 see Prange (1935). There is an interesting article by Golay (1976) which reaches similar conclusions on the nature of the drain.
9. For a further analysis of policy in the 1930s, see Prince and Baudet (1983, Chapter II).

CHAPTER FIFTEEN

Directions for Further Research

Thee Kian-Wie and Anne Booth

In comparison with the enormous amount of work that has been published on the economic history of South Asia, for example, it is clear that the systematic study of Southeast Asian economic history has hardly begun. And even within Southeast Asia, Indonesia has been relatively neglected. As O'Malley argued in the first chapter of this volume, there are several reasons for expecting this situation to change over the next decade or two, particularly as the rich legacy of colonial statistics is republished in English in the ongoing *Changing Economy* series. The great merit of Creutzberg's work, now being continued by his associates at the Royal Tropical Institute, lies not only in the location and reclassification of the masses of statistics collected by many different parts of the colonial government over more than a century, but also in the adaptation and recombination of these data in a way which makes possible new measurement of economic variables and their comparison over time, across regions and, ultimately, across countries. The scope and comprehensiveness of this project can fittingly be compared with the work on the *Long Term Economic Statistics of Japan,* which since the 1960s have been prepared by Professor Kasushi Ohkawa and his associates at Hitotsubashi University in Tokyo (Yasuba 1972/3, pp.4-8), and which in turn have been used in a series of important studies of Japanese economic development (e.g. Ohkawa and Shinohara, 1979).

The ready availability of these long-term historical series will undoubtedly attract economists with an interest in the contemporary Indonesian economy to venture into economic history. Economic history has, of course, always had a quantitative orientation, as Clapham pointed out many years ago. But as the study of Indonesian economic history attracts the "new" economic historians and cliometricians, different questions will be posed of the data and different analytical tools used. There will be a more explicit and systematic application of economic theory, especially price theory, to historical data, a greater use of economic theory to remeasure historical processes, and a continuing reassessment of the past based on these fresh approaches to measurement and analysis (McCloskey 1978, pp.13-28).

The more systematic use of economic theory is thus likely to give fresh, if sometimes controversial, insights into Indonesian economic history in the same way as it has already done into North American and European economic history, and indeed into that of some developing countries (Feeny 1982b, pp.233-34). But it is unlikely that this development will be at the expense of historians, as a large part of the data of economic history are qualitative, and have always been the concern of "conventional" economic historians (Landes 1978, p.6). Moreover, many of the important questions which have to be dealt with in economic history do not, as yet, lend themselves easily to quantitative treatment. Sometimes the necessary data are lacking, or when they are available they do not tell us much (Landes 1978, pp.6-7). Furthermore, there are many issues on which we will probably never have the required quantitative data. In his introductory paper, O'Malley draws attention to the Java-centricity of much of the nineteenth- and early twentieth-century literature. Sadly this is unlikely to be fully rectified by further research as population, land area, and food production data simply were not collected in many parts of the outer islands until the 1920s, or in some areas, until after independence, and even then their quality was greatly inferior to data from Java. For Java too, the quantitative data become scarcer the further back in time one goes, and certainly for the period prior to the British interregnum, their collection and interpretation requires skills which only the trained historian is likely to possess.

In other words, while a more quantitative, and rigorously "economic" approach to the study of Indonesian economic history is likely to raise both its standards and substance, the economic historians who stray into the field from the economics side will continue to need the cooperation and assistance of their fellow economic historians who have approached, perhaps more deliberately, from the side of pure history, and who have invested much time in painstaking archival research. In addition, the special skills of other social scientists, such as demographers and anthropologists, will be of great value, both in directing attention to new sources of data and in asking different questions, and applying different analytical techniques from those which either the pure economist or the historian is likely to use. As was stressed in the first chapter, many of the most stimulating contributions to the study of Indonesian economic history have been made by people trained neither in economics nor in history, and this is likely to continue to be the case in the future.

While the labours of Creutzberg and his associates have served to draw the attention of a new generation of scholars to the rich legacy of the colonial era, it should not be forgotten that Indonesia has already acquired four decades of post-independence history, a period perhaps in more need of detailed analysis by economic historians than the late colonial era. Indeed, a recent survey by a distinguished American development economist of economic growth in the third world between 1850 and 1980 reaches the following, perhaps rather startling, conclusion about Indonesia:

> ...we know Indonesia's past better than its present. There have been several good studies of the colonial period, and we can give a convincing account of events up to 1940. There is no equally thorough study of the post-1945 period, and the statistical framework that would be needed for such a study is quite defective (Reynolds 1985, p.357).

Reynolds goes on to claim that, in Indonesia, a sustained increase in per capita income is relatively recent, and associated with the oil boom of the 1970s. This may seem a dubious proposition to students of the late colonial and post-independence eras, but to refute it, we would obviously have to continue the compilation of long-term time series on key indicators such as population, food production, export volume, money supply and government finance from where the Creutzberg team terminate in 1940. Only then would we be able to see whether the cycles in economic activity in Indonesia since the late nineteenth century have been around a rising, static, or even declining trend. While it is probably true, as Reynolds asserts, that the quality of the statistics in the immediate post-independence era is inferior to those of the inter-war years, there has been a significant improvement in both the quantity and the quality of official statistics since 1970. In addition, a number of surveys have been carried out by academics in both urban and rural areas which can be compared with similar studies done by colonial scholars, in order to assess the direction and magnitude of changes in a range of economic variables.

Although there are many exciting questions to be asked of the statistical record about Indonesia's development experience from the early nineteenth century to the present day, perhaps the most important topics for further research are in the domain of comparative economic history. The Netherlands Indies was by far the most important colony of the Netherlands, and as such the study of its economy and administration is useful not just for its own sake, but also as an input into comparative studies of different colonial regimes and their economic impact. Southeast Asia is probably the most suitable part of the world in which to study comparative colonialism, as all the major European colonial powers had colonies in the region; indeed, if we include Taiwan as part of Southeast Asia, then it is possible to examine, in a relatively compact geographical area, the colonial administrations of Britain, France, Spain, and the USA, the Netherlands, and Japan. An important start in this field was made by several colonial scholars, including Furnivall and Bousquet, before the Second World War, but very little has been done since their books were published in the 1940s. In the last few years, a major initiative has been taken by a group of scholars at Cambridge, Leiden, Delhi, and Gadjah Mada Universities, who have initiated a series of conferences on the comparative study of Indian and Indonesian history.[1] The time is ripe to follow this up with similar comparative studies of the Japanese, French, and American colonial systems.

That much challenging and important work remains to be done is indisputable. But who will do it? It is appropriate to end this chapter, and the collection, with a word about the study of Indonesian economic history within Indonesia. In the recent revival of interest in the field, Indonesian scholars have, on the whole, taken a back seat. The contrast with the South Asian situation is striking. Whereas the recently published *Cambridge Economic History of India* was edited and written largely by Indian scholars, there is among the overwhelming majority of Indonesian social scientists and historians an almost complete lack of interest in economic history, and even an unfortunate ignorance of what it is all about (Thee 1979). The lack of involvement on the part of Indonesian economists is particularly deplorable since economic history and its concern with explaining the performance and structure of economies through time (North 1978, p.77) could provide them with some valuable "lessons from history," both positive and negative. While this is not the place to dwell on the reasons for this lack of interest, the publication of this volume in Indonesian should prove a stimulus to a new generation of Indonesian historians and social scientists to take the study of their own economic history more seriously.

Notes

1. Papers from these conferences will be published in the journal *Itinerario*, beginning in 1986.

Bibliography and Author Index

Abdullah, Taufik (1971), *Schools and Politics: The Kaum Muda Movement in West Sumatra 1927-1933*, Cornell University Modern Indonesia Project Monograph Series, Ithaca, New York. 92

Aken, N. van (1923), *Rubber in the Netherlands East Indies*, New Jersey. 198

Alexander, J. and P. Alexander (1978), "Sugar, Rice and Irrigation in Colonial Java," *Ethnohistory* 25 (3), pp.207-23. 63, 290

Alexander, J. and P. Alexander (1979), "Labour Demands and the 'Involution' of Javanese Agriculture," *Social Analysis* 3, pp.22-24. 29, 63, 171

Allen, G.C. and A.G. Donnithorne (1954), *Western Enterprise in Indonesia and Malaysia*, Allen and Unwin. London. 10, 139, 156, 158, 160, 189

Anderson, B.R. O'G (1983), "Old State, New Society: Indonesia's New Order in Comparative Historical Perspective," *Journal of Asian Studies* 42 (3) pp.477-96. 321

Anon. (1849), "De residentie Madioen in het jaar 1846" [The Residency of Madium in 1846], *Tijdschrift voor Nederlandsch Indie* 11 (1), pp.169-83. 34

Anon. (1851), "De heer Launy over den toestand van Java" [Launy on the Situation in Java], *Tijdschrift voor Nederlandsch Indie* 13 (2), pp.35-42. 28

Anon. (1856), "Opgave den padi en rijst soorten welke gevonden worden in de residentie Tegal" [Statement of the Types of Padi and Rice Found in Tegal Residency], *Tijdschrift voor Nijverheid en Landbouw in Nederlandsch Indie* 3, pp.277-99. 66

Anon. (1858), "De toestand van Bagelen in 1830" [The Situation of Bagelen in 1830], *Tijdschrift voor Nederlandsch Indie* 20 (2), pp.65-84. 33

Anon. (1861), *Bijdragen tot de kennis van de voornaamste voortbrengselen van Nederlandsch Indie. II. De Koffij [Contributions to Understanding the Major Products of the Netherlands Indies: Coffee]*, uitgegeven door De Maatschappij tot nut van it algemeen, Fred. Muller, Amsterdam; J.H. de Langer, Deventer; A.W. Sijthoff, Leiden. 46

Anon. (1862), "Beknopt overzicht van de residentie Bagelen" [Short Survey of the Residency of Bagelen], *Tijdschrift voor Nederlandsch Indie* 24 (2), pp.129-40. 34

Anon. (1869), "Rijst", in P.J. Veth (ed.), *Aardrijkskundig en statistisch woordenboek van Nederlandsch Indie [Geographical and Statistical Lexicon of the Netherlands Indies]*, P.N. van Kampen, Amsterdam. 29

50 Anos (1963), *50 Anos de Revolucion Mexicana en Cifras* Nacional Financiera, Mexico. 327

Aye Hlaing (1964), "Trends of Economic Growth and Income Distribution in Burma, 1870-1940," *Journal of the Burma Research Society* 47 (1), pp.89-148. 234, 295, 324, 335

Baldwin, R. (1956), "Patterns of Development in Newly Settled Regions," *Manchester School of Economic and Social Studies* 24. 270

Banerji, A.K. (1963), *India's Balance of Payments*, Asia Publishing House, Bombay. 330

Barlow, C. (1978), *The Natural Rubber Industry: Its Development, Technology, and Economy in Malaysia*, Oxford University Press, Kuala Lumpur. 193

Barlow, C. and S.K. Jayasuriya (1984), "Bias Towards the Large Farm Subsector in Agricultural Research: The Case of Malaysia Rubber," paper presented to the Annual Conference of the Australian Agricultural Economics Society, Sydney, February. 199

Barlow, C. and Muharminto (1982), *Smallholder Rubber in South Sumatra: Towards Economic Improvement*, Balai Penelitian Perkebunan, Bogor, and Australian National University, Canberra. 208

Bastin, John (1954), *Raffles' Ideas on the Land Rent System in Java*, The Hague. 210

Baudet, M.J. and G.J. Wijers (1976), "De economische beteknis van Nederlands-Indie voor Nederland oude en nieuwe berekeningen" [The Economic Importance of the Netherlands Indies for Old and New Dutch Calculations], *Economische en Statistische Berichten*, 15 September. 335

Bauer, P.T. (1948), *The Rubber Industry: A Study in Competition and Monopoly*, Longmans, Green and Co., London. 195, 198, 202, 205, 206, 208

Beets, A.N.J. (1949), "Vorstenlandse Tabak" [Vorstenland Tobacco], in C.J.J. van Hall and C. van de Koppel (eds), *De landbouw in de Indische Archipel*, van Hoeve, The Hague, Vol. IIb, pp.414-86. 158, 168, 169

Bellwood, P. (1979), *Man's Conquest of the Pacific: The Prehistory of Southeast Asia and Oceania*, Oxford University Press, New York. 3

Benda-Beckmann, F. von (1979), *Property in Social Continuity: Continuity and Change in the Maintenance of Property Relationships Through Time in Minangkabau, West Sumatra*, Martinus Nijhoff, The Hague. 95, 104

Berg, N.P. van den (1879), "Historisch-statistische aanteekeningen over de voortbrenging en het verbruik van koffij" [Historical-Statistical Remarks on the Production and Consumption of Coffee], *Tijdschrift voor Nijverheid en Landbouw in Nederlandsch-Indie* 24, pp.427-518. 185

Berg, N.P. van den (1895), *The Financial and Economic Condition of Netherlands India Since 1870*, The Hague. 215, 216, 265

Berg, N.P. van den (1907), *Munt-, crediet-, en bankwezen, handel en scheepvaart in Nederlandsch-Indie: Historisch-statistische bijdragen [Currency, Credit and Banking Systems, Trade and Shipping in Netherlands India: Historical-Statistical Contributions]*, The Hague. 265

Berkhuysen, A.P.H. (1948), "De drainage theorie voor Indonesie" [The Drain Theory Applied to Indonesia], thesis, The Hague. 265

Bigalke, T. (1983), "Dynamics of the Torajan Slave Trade in South Sulawesi" in A.J.S. Reid (ed.), *Slavery, Bondage and Dependency in Southeast Asia*, University of Queensland Press, St. Lucia, pp.341-63. 14

Birnberg, Thomas B. and Stephen A. Resnick (1975), *Colonial Development: An Econometric Study*, Yale University Press, New Haven. 240, 279, 280, 281

Bleeker, P. (1849), "Fragmenten eener reis over Java" [Scraps from a Journey through Java], *Tijdschrift voor Nederlandsch Indie* 11 (2), pp.262-70. 34

Bleeker, P. (1866), "Statistiek der bevolking van het Gouvernment van Java's noordoostkust in het jaar 1802," *Tijdschrift voor Nederlandsch Indie* 22, pp.325-38. 130, 133

Bleeker, P. (1870), *Nieuwe bijdragen tot de kennis der bevolkingsstatistiek van Java*, The Hague. 113

Boeke, J.H. (1910), "Tropisch-koloniale staathuishoudkunde: het probleem" [Tropical-Colonial Political Economy: The Problem], Ph.D. thesis, University of Leiden. 4, 77

Boeke, J.H. (1926), "Inlandsche budgetten" [Indigenous Budgets], *Koloniale Studien*, 10 (2). 266

Boeke, J.H. (1942), *The Structure of the Netherlands-Indian Economy*, Institute of Pacific Relations, New York. 265

Boeke, J.H. (1946), *The Evolution of the Netherlands Indies Economy*, Institute of Pacific Relations, New York. 169, 315, 316, 318, 321

Boeke, J.H. (1953), *Economics and Economic Policy of Dual Societies as Exemplified by Indonesia*, Institute of Pacific Relations, New York. 132, 208, 232

Boeke, J.H. (1961), "Objective and Personal Elements in Colonial Welfare Policy" in *Indonesian Economics: The Concept of Dualism in Theory and Policy*, Selected Studies on Indonesia by Dutch Scholars Vol. 6, van Hoeve, The Hague. 242

Boomgaard, P. (1981), "Female labour and population growth in nineteenth-century Java," *Review of Indonesian and Malayan Affairs* 15, pp.1-31. 132, 171

Boomgaard, P. (1984), "Java's agricultural production, 1775-1875," paper for the conference on Economic Growth and Social Change in Indonesia, 1820-1940, Groningen. 23, 115, 122

Booth, Anne (1974), "Ipeda - Indonesia's Land Tax," *Bulletin of Indonesian Economic Studies* 10 (1), pp.58-81. 13

Booth, Anne (1977), "Irrigation in Indonesia, Parts I and II," *Bulletin of Indonesian Economic Studies* 13 (1), pp.33-74; 13 (2), pp.45-77. 13

Booth, Anne (1980), "The Burden of Taxation in Colonial Indonesia in the 20th Century," *Journal of Southeast Asian Studies* 11 (1). 242

Booth, Anne (1988), *Agricultural Development in Indonesia*. Sydney: George Allen and Unwin. 290

Bosch, W. (1851), *De vermeerdering van Java's bevolking, beschouwd als de grootste bron van rijkdom voor Nederland [The Growth of Java's Population, Considered as the Greatest Source of Wealth for Holland]* M. Wijt and Zonen, Rotterdam. 47

Bosch, W. (1868), "Is de welvaart der Javanen onder het Cultuurstelsel toegenomen?" [Has the Welfare of the Javanese Increased under the Cultivation System?], *Tidjschrfit voor Nederlandsch Indie* (3rd series) 2 (1), pp.21-26. 47

Bosse, J. van (1895), *Eenige beschouwingen omtrent de oorzaken van den achteruitgang van de koffiecultuur ter Sumatra's westkust benevens eenige onmerkingen omtrent de economische en politieke toestand aldaar [Some Observations About the Causes for the Decline of Coffee Growing on the West Coast of Sumatra and Some Remarks About the Economic and Political Conditions There]*, Martinus Nijhoff, The Hague. 100, 108

Bousquet, G.H. (1940), *A French View of the Netherlands Indies*, Oxford University Press, London. 231

Boutmij, G.A. (1868), "De siekete in het Padi-gewas in de Residentie Pekalongan" [Padi Sickness in Pekalongan Residency], *Tijdschrift voor Nijverheid en Landbouwin Nederlandsch Indie* 13, pp.129-33. 66

Bree, L. de (1928), *Gedenkboek van De Javasche Bank: 1828-24.1.1928 [Memorial Volume of the Java Bank]*, Parts 1 and 2, Weltevreden. 250, 253

Breman, J. (1980), "The Village on Java and the Early-Colonial State", CASP I, Erasmus University, Rotterdam. 74

Broek, J.O.M. (1942), *Economic Development of the Netherlands Indies*, Russell and Russell, New York. 8, 310, 318

Broersma, R. (1913), *Besoeki, een gewest in opkomst [Besoeki, a Rising Region]*, Scheltema Holkema, Amsterdam. 168

Burger, D.H. (1929), *Rapport over de desa Pekalongan in 1868 en 1928 [Report on the Village Pekalongan in 1868 and 1928]*, G. Kolff, Weltevreden. 5

Burger, D.H. (1930), *Vergelijking van den economischen toestand der districten Tajoe en Djakenan (regentschap Pati, afdeeling Rembang) [Comparison of the Economic Situation of Tajoe and Djakenan Districts (Pati Regency, Rembang)]*, G. Kolff, Weltevreden. 5

Burger, D.H. (1933), "De desa Ngablek in 1869 en 1929" [Ngablek Village in 1869 and 1929], *Koloniale Studien* 17, pp.226-40. 5

Burger, D.H. (1939), *De ontsluitung van Java's binnenland voor het wereldverkeer [The Opening of Java's Interior to World Commerce]*, Veenman, Wageningen. 5, 68, 185

Burger, D.H. (1948/50), "Structuurveranderingen in de Javanese samenleving" [Structural Change in Javanese Society], *Indonesie*" 2, 1948-49, pp.381-98; 521-37; 3, 1949/50, pp.1-18; 101-23; 225-50; 347-50; 381-89; 512-34. 9, 68

Burger, D.H. (1956), *Structural Changes in Javanese Society: The Supra- Village Sphere*, Modern Indonesia Project Translation Series, Cornell University, Ithaca, New York. 299

Burger, D.H. (1975), *Sociologisch-economische geschiedenis van Indonesie [Sociological-Economic History of Indonesia]*, Landbouwhogeschool, Wageningen. 2 vols. 8, 10, 68, 132

Burger, D.H. and Prajudi Atmosudirdjo (1957/58), *Sedjarah Ekonomis-Sosiologis Indonesia [Sociological-Economic History of Indonesia]*, J.B. Wolters, Jakarta. 2 vols. 10

Butlin, N.G. (1962), *Australian Domestic Product, Investment and Foreign Borrowing, 1861-1938/9*, Cambridge University Press, Cambridge. 237

Butlin, N.G., A. Barnard and J.J. Pincus (1982), *Government and Capitalism*, Allen and Unwin, Sydney. 238

Caldwell, J.A.M. (1964), "Indonesian Export and Production from the Decline of the Culture System to the First World War" in C.D. Cowan (ed.), *The Economic Development of South-East Asia*, Allen and Unwin, London, pp.72-101. 156, 274, 294

Caldwell, M. and Utrecht, E. (1979), *Indonesia: An Alternative History*, Alternative Publishing Cooperative Limited, Sydney. 14

Cator, W.J. (1936), *The Economic Position of the Chinese in the Netherlands Indies*, Oxford University Press, Kuala Lumpur. 195

C.E.I. (1975-80), *Changing Economy in Indonesia: A Selection of Statistical Source Materials from the Early 19th Century up to 1940*, initiated by W.M.F. Mansvelt, re-edited and continued by P. Creutzberg, and J.T.M. van Laanen (Vol. 6 only), Martinus Nijhoff. 49

Centraal Bureau voor de Statistiek Nederlands (1979), *Tachtig jaren statistiek in tijdreeksen [Eighty Years of Statistics in Time Series] 1899-1979*, C.B.S., The Hague. 334, 335

Centraal Kantoor voor de Statistiek (C.K.S. 161), *Handelsstatistiek Nederlandsch-Indie 1874-1937 [Trade Statistics, Netherlands Indies, 1874-1937]*, Mededeeling No.161, C.K.S., Batavia. 278, 284, 287

Central Bureau of Statistics (1941), *Statistical Pocketbook of Indonesia*, C.B.S., Batavia. 236, 279, 282, 287, 317, 324

Chandravarkar, A.G. (1980), "Monetisation of Developing Economies" in W.L. Coats and D.R. Khatkhate (eds), *Money and Monetary Policy in Less Developed Countries*, Pergamon Press, Oxford. 244

Chaudhuri, K.N. (1983), "Foreign Trade and Balance of Payments" in *Cambridge Economic History of India* Vol. 2, Cambridge University Press, Cambridge. 237, 294

Chayanov, A.V. (1966), *The Theory of Peasant Economy* (D. Thorner, B. Kerbley, R.E.F. Smith, eds), Richard D. Irwin Inc., Homewood, Illinois. 94

Chinese Economy Post-Mao (1978), Joint Economic Committee, U.S. Congress. 327, 328

Comercio Exterior de Mexico (1960), *Comercio Exterior de Mexico 1877-1911. Estadisticas Economicas del Porfiriato*, Colegio de Mexico. 327

Contador, C.R. and C.L. Haddad (1975), "Produto Real, Moeda e Precos: A Experiencia Brasileira no Periodo 1861-1970," *Revista Brasileira de Estatistica*, July/Sept. 328

Cornets de Groot van Kraayenburg, J.P. (1862), *Over het Beheer onzer Kolonien [Concerning the Administration of our Colonies]*, Belifante, The Hague. 30, 68

Cornwall, John (1977), *Modern Capitalism: Its Growth and Transformation*, Martin Robertson, Oxford. 269

Couperus, P.Th. (1856), "Aantekeningen omtrent de landbouwkundige nijverheid in de Residentie Padangsche bovenlanden" [Notes on Agriculture in the Residency of the Padang Highlands], *Tijdschrift voor Indische Taal-, Land-, en Volkenkunde* 5, pp.285-312. 95, 98, 103, 105, 110

Cramer, J.C.W. (1929), *Het volkskredietwezen in Nederlandsch-Indie [The People's Credit System in Netherlands India]*, Amsterdam. 262

Crawfurd, J. (1820), *The History of the Indies Archipelago*, A. Constable, Edinburgh. 3 vols. 4

Creutzberg, P. (ed.) (1972-75), *Het ekonomisch beleid in Nederlandsch-Indie [Economic Policy in the Netherlands Indies]*, issued by the Committee on the Publications of Source Material on the History of Indonesia, 1900-1942, of the Netherlands Historical Society, Wolters-Noordhoff, Groningen. 3 parts in 4 vols. 11, 69, 169, 219, 284

Daendels, H.W. (1814), *Staat der N.O.I. bezittingen onder het bestuur van den G.-G. Herman Williem Daendels ... [The Dutch East Indies Possessions during the Administration of Governor-General H.W. Daendels]*, n.p., The Hague. 4 vols. 80

Dalton, G. (ed.) (1967), *Tribal and Peasant Economies*, New York. 245

Day, Clive (1900), "The Dutch Colonial Fiscal System" in *Essays in Colonial Finance*, Publications of the American Economic Association, Third Series 1 (3). 210, 211, 217

Day, Clive (1904), *The Policy and Administration of the Dutch in Java*, Macmillan, New York. Reprinted in the Oxford in Asia Historical Reprints series, Oxford University Press, 1966. 4, 68, 166, 169, 171, 217

Deinum, Hk. (1941), "Bevolkingssuiker" [People' Sugar], in C.J.J. van Hall and C. van de Koppel (eds), *De landbouw in de Indische Archipel*, van Hoeve, The Hague, Volume IIa, pp. 405-26. 169

Dekker, W. (1978), "Tussen zelfvoorziening en commerciale landbouw" [Between Self-Sufficiency and Commercial Agriculture], Ph.D. thesis, University of Amsterdam. 59

Derksen, J.B.D. and J. Tinbergen (1945), "Berekeningen over de economische betekenis van Nederland" [Calculations on the Economic Importance of the Netherlands], *Maandschrift*, Centraal Bureau voor de Statistiek, The Hague, Oct/Dec. 334

Deventer, C.T. van (1904), "Overzicht van den economischen toestand der inlandsche bevolking van Java en Madoera" [Survey of the Economic Condition of the Indigenous Population of Java and Madura], *Koloniaal-economische Bijdragen*, Part I, The Hague. 266

Deventer, M.L. van (1891), *Het nederlandsch gezag over Java onderhoorigheden sedert 1811 [Dutch Rule in Java and its Dependence since 1811]*, Martinus Nijhoff, The Hague. 68

Deventer, S. van (1865/6), *Bijdragen tot de kennis van het landelijk stelsel op Java [Contributions to Understanding the Land Rent System in Java]*, Noman and Zoon, Zalt-Bommel. 3 vols. 31, 64, 65, 68, 185, 186

Dharma Kumar (1983), "The Fiscal System," *Cambridge Economic History of India* Vol. 2, Cambridge University Press, Cambridge. 234, 235, 236, 237

Diaz Alejandro, C.F. (1970), *Essays on the Economic History of the Argentine Republic*, Yale University Press, New Haven. 237, 327, 328

Dick, H.W. (1977), "The Indonesian Interisland Shipping Industry," Ph.D. thesis, Australian National University, Canberra. 320

Dijkman, M.J. (1951), *Hevea: Thirty Years of Research in the Far East*, University of Miami Press, Coral Gables. 202

Dobbin, C. (1972), "Tuanku Imam Bonjol (1772-1864)," *Indonesia* 13, pp.5-35. 91

Dobbin, C. (1974), "Islamic Revivalism in Minangkabau at the Turn of the Nineteenth Century," *Modern Asian Studies* 8 (3), pp.319-56. 13, 91

Dobbin, C. (1977), "Economic Change in Minangkabau as a Factor in the Rise of the Padri Movement, 1784-1830," *Indonesia* 23, pp.1-38. 13, 91, 93, 98

Dobbin, C. (1983), *Islamic Revivalism in a Changing Peasant Economy: Central Sumatra, 1784-1847*, Curzon Press, London. 13, 91, 92, 93, 95, 96, 97, 104, 109, 169

Doorn, C.L. van (1926), *Schets van de economische ontwikkeling der afdeeling Poerworedjo (Residentie Kedoe) [Sketch of the Economic Development of Poerworedjo (Kedu Residency)]*, G. Kolff, Weltevreden. 5

Douwes Dekker, E. [Multatuli] (1860), *Max Havelaar*, Amsterdam. 77

Drabble, J.H. (1973), *Rubber in Malaya 1876-1922: The Genesis of the Industry*, Oxford University Press, Kuala Lumpur. 187, 193, 197, 209

Drabble, J.H. (1981), "Survival of the Fittest: Estates and Smallholdings in the Malayan Rubber Industry before World War II," Department of Economic History, University of Sydney. 197

Drabble, J.H. and P.J. Drake (1974), "More on the Financing of Malayan Rubber, 1905-23." *Economic History Review*, Second series, XXVII, pp.108-20. 193

Earl, G.W. (1971 reprint), *The Eastern Seas*, Oxford University Press, London. 300

La Economia Mexicana en Cifras (1966), Nacional Financiera, Mexico. 327

An Economic Profile (1967), *An Economic Profile of Mainland China: Studies prepared for the Joint Economic Committee, U.S. Congress*, U.S. Government Printing Office, Washington, D.C. 2 vols. 328

Eindresume (1876-96), *Eindresume van het bij Gouvernements besluit van 10 June 1867 No. 2 bevolen onderzoek naar de rechten van den inlander op den grond op Java en Madoera ... [Final Summation of the Research into Native Land Rights in Java, Conducted in Accordance with Government Decision No. 2 of June 1867 ...]*, Ernst and Landsdrukkerij, Batavia. 78

Elson, R.E. (1978a), *The Cultivation System and Agricultural Involution*, Centre of Southeast Asian Studies, Monash University, Melbourne. 50, 51, 52

Elson, R.E. (1978b), "The Impact of the Government Sugar Cultivation in the Pasuruan Area, East Java, During the Cultivation System Period," *Review of Indonesian and Malayan Affairs* 12 (1), pp.26-55. 50, 51, 52

Elson, R.E. (1979), "Sugar and Peasants: The Social Impact of the Western Sugar Industry on the Peasantry of the Pasuruan Area, East Java, from the Cultivation System to the Great Depression," Ph.D. thesis, Monash University, Melbourne. 13, 83, 169, 171

Elson, R.E. (1982), "The Transition to 'Free Labour' in Java's Sugar Factories in the 19th Century," paper presented to the Eighth International Congress of Economic Historians, Budapest. Mimeograph. 76

Elson, R.E. (1984), "The Famine in Demak and Grobogan in 1849-50: Its Causes and Circumstances," paper presented to the Fifth National Conference of the Asian Studies Association of Australia, Adelaide. Mimeograph. 83, 283

Emden, J.H. van (1949), "De Theecultuur" [Tea Cultivation], in C.J.J. van Hall and C. van de Koppel, (eds.), *De landbouw in de Indische Archipel*, van Hoeve, The Hague, Volume IIb, pp.121-226. 158

Engelhard, N. (1816), *Overzicht van den Staat der N.O.I. Bezittingen ...[Survey of the Condition of the Dutch East Indies Possessions ...]*, Van Cleef, The Hague. 80

Evenson, R.E. and Yoav Kislev (1975), *Agricultural Research and Productivity*, Yale University Press, New Haven. 290

Fasseur, C. (1975), *Kultuurstelsel en koloniale baten: de Nederlandse exploitatie van Java, 1840-1860 [Cultivation System and Colonial Profits: Dutch Exploitation of Java, 1840-1860]*, Universitaire Pers, Leiden. 13, 26, 29, 30, 31, 45, 46, 49, 50, 69, 72, 169, 186

Fasseur, C. (1977a), *De Geest van het Gouvernement [The Spirit of the Government]*, Rede [Speech], Universitaire Pers, Leiden. 69

Fasseur, C. (1977b), "Organisatie en sociaal-economische betekenis van de gouvernements-suikerkultuur in enkele residenties op Java omstreeks 1850" [Organization and Socio-economic Significance of the Government Sugar Cultivation in some Residencies in Java around 1850], *Bijdragen tot de Taal-, Land- en Volkenkunde* 133, pp.261-93. 13, 50, 59

Fasseur, C. (1978), "Some Remarks on the Cultivation System in Java," *Acta Historiae Neerlandicae* 10, pp.1430-62. 25, 38, 51, 69

Fasseur, C. (1981), "The Cultivation System and its Impact on the Dutch Colonial Economy and the Indigenous Society in Nineteenth-Century Java," paper presented to the Second Anglo-Dutch Conference on Comparative Colonial History, Leiden. Mimeograph. 50, 51, 65, 69, 132

Federated Malay States (1932), Preliminary Note on Retrenchment, Statement 'A'. 209

Feeny, David (1982a), *The Political Economy of Productivity: Thai Agricultural Development*, 1880-1975, University of British Columbia Press, Vancouver. 238, 267, 269

Feeny, David (1982b), "Workshop Summary - Quantitative Third World Economic History," *The Journal of Economic History*, March, pp.233-34. 337

Feinstein, C.H. (1972), *National Income, Expenditure and Output of the United Kingdom, 1855-1965*, Cambridge University Press, Cambridge. 334, 335

Fernando, M.R. (1980), *Famine in Cirebon Residency, Java, 1844-1850*, Working Paper No. 21, Centre of Southeast Asian Studies, Monash University, Melbourne. 283

Fernando, M.R. (1982a), "Peasants and Plantation Economy: The Social Impact of the European Plantation Economy in Cirebon Residency from the Cultivation System to the End of the First Decade of the Twentieth Century," Ph.D. thesis, Monash University, Melbourne. 13, 83, 169, 171, 173, 178, 185, 186

Fernando, M.R. (1982b), "A Social History of Peasants in the Private Lands of Indramayu and Kandanghaur in the Late Nineteenth Century," paper presented to the Asian Studies Association of Australia. Mimeograph. 83

Ferns, H.S. (1960), *Britain and Argentina in the Nineteenth Century*, Oxford. 327

Feuerwerker, A. (1976), *The Foreign Establishment in China in the Early Twentieth Century*, Michigan. 324

Figart, D.M. (1925), *The Plantation Rubber Industry in the Middle East*, Trade Protection Series, No. 2, Department of Commerce, Government Printing Office, Washington. 188, 192, 194, 200, 205

Fitzgerald, E.V.K. (1984), "Restructuring through the Depression: The State and Capital Accumulation in Mexico, 1925-40" in R. Thorp (ed.), *Latin America in the 1930s: The Role of the Periphery in World Crisis*, Macmillan, London. 328

Fokkens, F. (1901/02), *Eindresume ... onderzoek naar de verplichte diensten der inlandsche bevolking op Java en Madoera [Final Summation of the Research into Obligatory Services among the Natives of Java and Madura]*, Smits-Jav. Boekh. en Drukkerij, Batavia. 84

Frank, A.G. (1976), "Multilateral Trade Imbalances and Uneven Economic Development," *Journal of European Economic History* 5. 270

Frijling, W. (1917), "Bestuurscontrole op de inlandsche rijstcultuur ter Sumatra's Westkust" [Government Supervision of Native Rice Cultivation on the West Coast of Sumatra], *Tijdschrift voor het Binnerlands Bestuur* 52, pp.95-97. 105

Fruin, Th.A. (1937), "Popular and Rural Credit in the Netherlands Indies," *Bulletin of the Colonial Institute of Amsterdam* 1 (2 and 3), February and May. 257

Furnivall, J.S. (1934a), "State and Private Money Lending in Netherlands India," *Studies in the Social and Economic Development of the Netherlands East Indies IIIb*, Rangoon: Burma Book Club. 265

Furnivall, J.S. (1934b), "State Pawnshops in Netherlands India," *Studies in the Social and Economic Development of the Netherlands East Indies IIIC*, Rangoon: Burma Book Club. 265

Furnivall, J.S. (1944), *Netherlands India: A Study of Plural Economy*, Cambridge University Press, Cambridge. 6, 26, 68, 101, 165, 171

Geertz, C. (1963), *Agricultural Involution: The Process of Ecological Change in Indonesia*, University of California Press, Berkeley. 10, 63, 78, 92, 132, 138, 171, 196, 296

Geertz, C. (1965), *The Social History of an Indonesian Town*, Massachusetts Institute of Technology Press, Cambridge. 10

Gelderen, J. van (1927), *Voorlezingen over tropisch-koloniale staathuishoudkunde [Lectures on Tropical-Colonial Economics]*, Haarlem. An English translation of three of these lectures is given in *Indonesian Economics: The Concept of Dualism in Theory and Policy*, van Hoeve, The Hague, 1961, pp.113-64. 248, 265

Gelderen, J. van (1939), *The Recent Development of Economic Foreign Policy in the Netherlands East Indies*, Longmans Green and Co., London. 294

Gelderen, J. van (1961), "The Economics of the Tropical Colony" in *Indonesian Economics: The Concept of Dualism in Theory and Policy*, Selected Studies on Indonesia by Dutch Scholars Vol. 6, van Hoeve, The Hague. 193, 196

Gerretson, C. (1938), "Historische inleiding" [Historical Introduction], in *De Sociaal-Economische Invloed van Nederlandsch-Indie op Nederland [The Social-Economic Influence of the Indies on The Netherlands]*, Veenman, Wageningen. 69

Gimbrère, E.G.J. (1928), *Eenige beschouwingen over de financiering van de suikerindustrie en den suikerhandel op Java [Some Considerations on the Financing of Java's Sugar Industry and Sugar Trade]*, H. Bergmans, Tilburg. 169, 250

Glamann, K. (1958), *Dutch-Asiatic Trade, 1620-1740*, Danish Science Press, Copenhagen. (2nd edition, Martinus Nijhoff, The Hague 1981). 22, 137, 185

Goedhart, A. (1948), *De onmogelijke vrijheid [Impossible Freedom]*, Universiteit Pers, Utrecht. 186

Golay, F.H. (1976), "Southeast Asia: The 'Colonial Drain' Revisited" in C.D. Cowan and O.W. Walters (eds.), *Southeast Asian History and Historiography*, Cornell University Press, Ithaca, New York. 265, 295, 325

Goldsmith, R.W. (1969), *Financial Structure and Development*, Studies in Comparative Economics No. 9, Yale University Press, New Haven. 244

Gonggrijp, G.L. (1928), *Schets eener economische geschiedenis van Nederlandsch-Indie [Sketch on an Economic History of the Netherlands Indies]*, Erven F. de Bohn, Haarlem. (2nd edition 1938; 3rd edition 1949; 4th edition 1957). 8

Gonggrijp, G. (1938), "Muntkorrektie voor Indie," [Coinage Regulations for Indonesia], *Koloniaal Tijdschrift* Vol. 22, Batavia. 265

Gough, H. (1927), *Practical Budgrafting and Seed Selecting of Hevea Brasiliensis*, Kelly and Walsh, Singapore. 202

De Gouvernements Koffiecultuur (1904), *De Gouvernements Koffiecultuur van 1898-1903: tweede gedeelte de Gouvernements Koffiecultuur in de buitenbezittingen [Coffee Cultivation for the Government from 1888 to 1903; Second Part, Coffee Cultivation for the Government in the Outer Islands]*, Landsdrukkerij, Batavia. 104

Graaf, S. de *et al.* (eds.) (1917-39), *Encyclopaedie van Nederlandsch-Indie*, Martinus Nijhoff and Brill, The Hague. 185

Graves, E.E. (1980), *The Minangkabau Response to Dutch Colonial Rule in the Nineteenth Century*, Cornell Modern Indonesia Project, Cornell University, Ithaca, New York. 96, 100, 109

Griffiths, R.T. and J.M.M. de Meere (1983), "The Growth of the Dutch Economy in the Nineteenth Century - Back to Basics," Vrije Universiteit, Amsterdam. Mimeograph. 335

Gurtoo, D.H.N. (1961), *India's Balance of Payments 1920-1960*, Chand, Delhi. 331

Haan, F. de (1910-12), *Priangan*, Landsdrukkerij, Batavia. 4 vols. 173

Haberler, G. (1959), *International Trade and Economic Development*, National Bank of Egypt, Cairo, as reprinted in G. Meier (ed.), *Leading Issues in Economic Development* (Third edition), Oxford University Press, New York, 1975. 268

Hall, C.J.J. van and C. van de Koppel (eds.), (1946-50), *De landbouw in de Indische Achipel [Agriculture in the Indies Archipelago]*, van Hoeve, The Hague. 3 vols. 66

Hansen, B. and G.A. Marzouk, G.A. (1965), *Development and Economic Policy in the U.A.R.* (Egypt), North Holland, Amsterdam. 328

Hanson, John R. (1980), *Trade in Transition: Exports from the Third World*, Academic Press, New York. 270, 271, 275, 293, 294

Hasselman, C.J. (1912), "Karakter van ons koloniaal beheer inzonderheid over Java" [Character of our Colonial Rule, Especially Concerning Java], in H. Colijn (ed.), *Neerlands Indie*, Elsevier, Amsterdam. 2 vols. 68

Hasselt, A.L. van (1882), *Volksbeschrijving van Midden Sumatra [An Ethnography of Central Sumatra]*, Brill, Leiden. 94, 95, 96, 98

Helsdingen, W.H. van (ed.) (1941), *Daar werd wat groots verricht ...[Something Great to be Accomplished There ...]*, Elsevier, Amsterdam. 169

Helfferich, C. (1914), *Die Niederlandisch-Indischen Kulturbanken [Netherlands-Indian Agricultural Banks]*, Jena. 265

Higgins, Benjamin (1959), *Economic Development: Principles, Problems and Policies*, W.W. Norton, New York. Revised edition, Constable and Co., London, 1968. 232

Hirschmann, A.O. (1977), "A Generalised Linkage Approach to Development with Special Reference to Staples," *Economic Development and Cultural Change* 25 (supplement), pp.67-98. 269, 270

Historical Statistics (1975), *Historical Statistics of the United States* Vol. 2, Bureau of the Census, U.S. Department of Commerce, Washington D.C. 327

Historische Nota (1905), *Historische nota over grondbeginselen van artikel 57 van het regeeringsreglement [Historical Note on the Basic Principle of Article 57 in the Government Regulation]*, Landsdrukkerij, Batavia. 84

Hoadley, M. (1983), "Slavery, Bondage and Dependency in Pre-Colonial Java: The Cirebon-Priangan Region, 1700," in Anthony Reid (ed.), *Slavery, Bondage and Dependency in Southeast Asia*, University of Queensland Press, St. Lucia. 80

Hoevell, W.R. van (1849-51), *Reis over Java, Madura en Bali, in het midden van 1847 [Journey through Java, Madura and Bali in the Middle of 1847]*, P.N. van Kampen, Amsterdam. 27, 29, 30, 34

Hoevell, W.R. van (1862-65), *Parlementaire redevoeringen over koloniale belangen [Parliamentary Speeches on Important Colonial Topics]*, Noman and Zoon, Zalt-Bommel. 31

Hsiao Liang-lin (1974), *China's Foreign Trade Statistics 1864-1949*, Harvard. 327

Huender, W. and Meyer Ranneft, J.W. (1926), *Onderzoek naar den belastingdruk op de inlandsche bevolking [An Inquiry into the Tax Burden of the Indigenous Population]*, Landsdrukkerij, Weltevreden. 265, 266

Hugo, G.J. (1980), "Population Movements in Indonesia During the Colonial Period" in J.J. Fox, R.G. Garnaut, P.T. McCawley and J.A.C. Mackie (eds.), *Indonesia: Australian Perspectives*, Vol.1, Research School of Pacific Studies, Australian National University, Canberra. 200, 323

Hutton, J.H. (1933), *Census of India, 1931*, Vol. I: *India*, Part I: *Report* and Part II: *Imperial Tables*, Delhi, 1933. 324, 335

Hymer, S.H. and S.A. Resnick (1971), "International Trade and Uneven Development" in J.N. Bhagwati *et al.* (eds.), *Trade, Balance of Payments and Growth*, North Holland, Amsterdam. 270

I.B.G.E. (1960), *O Brasil en Numeros*, Appendix to *Anuario Estatistico do Brasil 1960*, I.B.G.E., Rio de Janeiro. 327

Imlah, A.H. (1958), *Economic Elements in the Pax Britannica*, Harvard University Press, Cambridge. 327

Indonesian Economics (1961), *Indonesian Economics: The Concept of Dualism in Theory and Policy*, Selected Studies on Indonesia by Dutch Scholars Vol. 6, van Hoeve, The Hague. 5, 77

Ingram, J.C. (1971), *Economic Change in Thailand 1850-1970*, Stanford University Press, Stanford. 236, 237, 327

Jackson, J.C. (1968), *Planters and Speculators: Chinese and European Agricultural Enterprise in Malaya, 1786-1921*, University of Malaya Press, Kuala Lumpur. 193

Jaeggi, A.C. (1949), "De Tabakscultuur van de Residentie Besoeki" [Tobacco Cultivation in Besoeki Residency], in C.J.J. van Hall and C. van de Koppel (eds.), *De landbouw in de Indische Archipel*, van Hoeve, The Hague, Volume IIb, pp.486-521. 158, 168

Java Bank (n.d.), *The Java Bank: A Short Description of its Organisation, Operations and General Policy, Supplemented by Notes on the Monetary System of Netherlands India*, Batavia. 265

Johnson, Harry G. (1977), "Trade, Growth and Economic Stability" in *Trade and Employment in Asia and the Pacific*, Council for Asian Manpower Studies, Quezon City. 268

Jong, A.M. de (1946), "De Financieel-economische verhouding tusschen Nederland en Nederlandsch-Indie voor den tweeden wereldoorlog en de geschiednis van het indische geldwezen gedurende de jaaren 1900-39" [Financial and Economic Relations between the Netherlands and the Netherlands Indian Monetary System], *De Economist* 94, pp.663-714. 265

Jonge, J.K.J. de (1862-1888), *De Opkomst van het nederlandsch gezag over Java [The Rise of Dutch Rule on Java]*, Martinus Nijhoff, The Hague. 13 vols. 68

Joustra, M. (1923), *Minangkabau, overzicht van land, geschiedenis en volk [Minangkabau: A Survey of the Land, its History and People]*, Martinus Nijhoff, The Hague. 91

Kamerling, R.N.J. (1979), "De Copra-olie industrie in Nederlands-Indie gederende en kort na de eerste wereldoorlog" [The Copra-Oil Industry in the Netherlands Indies During and Shortly After the First World War] in F. van Anrooiy *et al.* (eds.), *Between People and Statistics*, Martinus Nijhoff, The Hague. 306, 317

Kamerling, Z.H. (1895), "De vroegere en tegenwoordige toestand van handel, nijverheid en landbouw op Sumatra's Westkust en de vooruitzichten daarvan voor de volgende jaren" [The Former and Present Situation of Trade, Industry and Agriculture on the West Coast of Sumatra and their Prospects in the Years Ahead], *De Indische Gids* 17 (2), pp.1059-88. 108

Kat Angelino, A.D.A. de (1929-30), *Staatkundig beleid en bestuurszorg in Nederlandsch-Indie [Political Policy and Governmental Concern in Netherlands Indies]*, Martinus Nijhoff, The Hague. 2 vols. 68

Kemp, P.H. van der (1916), *Java's landelijke stelsel, 1817-1819, naar vorspronkelijke stukken [Java's Land System, 1817-1819, according to the Original Sources]*, Martinus Nijhoff, The Hague. 185

Key, B.M. (1971), "The Role of Foreign Contributions in Japanese Capital Formation, 1868-1936," Ph.D. thesis, University of California. 237

Kielstra, E.B. (1888), "De Koffiecultuur ter Westkust van Sumatra" [Coffee Cultivation on the West Coast of Sumatra], *De Indische Gids* 10, pp.1437-86; pp.1609-74. 91, 97, 100, 103, 104

Kielstra, E.B. (1890), "Sumatra's Westkust 1836-1840" [Sumatra's West Coast from 1836 to 1840], *Bijdragen tot de Taal-, Land- en Volkenkunde* 39, pp.127-221; pp.263-348. 90

Kindleberger, C.P. (1962), *Foreign Trade and the National Economy*, Yale University Press, New Haven. 289

Kleiman, Ephraim (1980), "Exports and Growth: Definition, Measurement and Causality," seminar paper, Dept. of Economics, Australian National University, Canberra. Mimeograph. 269

Knight, G.R. (1980), "From Plantation to Padi-Field: The Origins of the Nineteenth-Century Transformation of Java's Sugar Industry," *Modern Asian Studies* 14, pp.177-204. 13, 49

Knight, G.R. (1982a), "Capitalism and Commodity Production in Java," in H. Alavi *et al.* (eds.), *Capitalism and Colonial Production*, Croom Helm, London, pp.119-58. 13, 48, 53, 55, 83, 171

Knight, G.R. (1982b), "The Indigo Industry and the Organization of Agricultural Production in Pekalongan Residency, North Java, 1800-1850," paper presented at the Fourth National Conference of the Asian Studies Association of Australia, Monash University, Melbourne. 28

Knight, G.R. (1984), "Rice and Second Crops in Pekalongan Residency, North Java, 1780-1870," paper presented to the Asian Studies Association of Australia. Mimeograph. 83

Knops, J. and P.H. Lawick van Pabst (1812), *Java zo als het is en zo als het kan zijn [Java As It Is and As It Can Be]*, India Office Library, Mackenzie Collection Private No. 56. 80

Kolff, G.H. van der (1925), *Bekolkingsrietcultuur in Nederlandsch-Indie [People's Cane Cultivation in the Netherlands Indies]*, Thieme, Nijmegen. 169

KPM (annual), *Jaarverslag van de directie in Nederlands-Indie [Annual Report of the Directorate in the Netherlands Indies]*, Batavia, (by permission of the Tweede Afdeeling, Alg., Rijksarchief, The Hague).

Kraan, A. van der (1980), *Lombok: Conquest, Colonization and Underdevelopment, 1870-1940*, Heinemann, Singapore. 13

Krueger, Anne O. (1980), "Trade Policy as an Input to Development," *American Economic Review* 70 (2), pp.288-92. 267

Kulke, H. (1980), "Early State Formation and Ritual Policy in East Java," paper presented to the Eighth Conference of the International Association of Historians of Asia, Kuala Lumpur. Mimeograph. 79

Kuznets, S. (1979), "Growth and Structural Shifts" in W. Galenson (ed.), *Economic Growth and Structural Change in Taiwan*, Cornell University Press, Ithaca, New York. 324

Laanen, J.T.M. van (1983), "Het archief van De Javasche Bank: 125 Jaar bedrijfs-, monetaire en algemeen economische geschiedenis van Nederlandsch-Indie" [The Archives of the Java Bank: 125 Years of Business, Monetary and General Economic History of Netherlands India], *Het Nederlands Archievenblad*, Part 3, Amsterdam. 250

Laanen, J.T.M. van (1984), "Per Capita Income Growth in Indonesia, 1850-1940," paper presented to the conference on Economic Growth and Social Change in Indonesia, 1820-1940, Rijksuniversiteit, Groningen, September. 280, 284, 294

Landes, D.S. (1978), "On Avoiding Babel," *The Journal of Economic History*, March, pp.3-12. 337

Lathan, A.J.H. (1978), "Merchandise Trade Imbalances and Uneven Economic Development in India and China," *Journal of European Economic History* 7, pp.33-60. 271

Leeuwen, R.J. van (1970), "Indonesia" in W.A. Lewis (ed.), *Tropical Development, 1880-1913*, Allen and Unwin, London. 294

Leff, Nathaniel H. (1982), *Underdevelopment and Development in Brazil*, Allen and Unwin, London. 2 vols. 240, 269, 283, 293

Legge, J.D. (1964), *Indonesia*, Prentice-Hall, Englewood Cliffs. 2

Leur, J.C. van (1955), *Indonesian Trade and Society: Essays in Asian Social and Economic History*, Selected Studies on Indonesia by Dutch Scholars Vol. 1, Van Hoeve, The Hague. 5, 298, 299, 320

Lewis, C. (1948), *The United States and Foreign Investment Problems*, Brookings, Washington, D.C. 331

Lewis, W.A. (1952), "World Production, Prices and Trade, 1870-1960," *Manchester School of Economics and Social Studies* 20 (2), pp.105-38. 276

Lewis, W.A. (1969), *Aspects of Tropical Trade: The Wicksell Lectures*, Almquist and Wiksell, Stockholm. 269, 270

Lewis, W.A. (1970), "The Export Stimulus" in W.A. Lewis (ed.), *Tropical Development, 1880-1913*, Allen and Unwin, London. 187, 269, 293

Lewis, W.A. (1976a), "Development and Distribution" in A. Cairncross and A. Puri (eds.), *Employment, Income Distribution and Development Strategy, Essays in Honour of H.W. Singer*, Macmillan, London. 271, 272

Lewis, W.A. (1976b), "The Diffusion of Development" in T. Wilson and Andrew Skinner (eds.), *The Market and the State: Essays in Honour of Adam Smith*, Clarendon Press, Oxford. 269

Lewis, W.A. (1978), *The Evolution of the International Economic Order*, Princeton University Press, Princeton. 270

Lim Chong-Yah (1967), *Economic Development of Modern Malaya*, Oxford University Press, Kuala Lumpur. 328

Lim, T.G. (1977), *Peasants and Their Agricultural Economy in Colonial Malaya, 1874-1941*, Oxford University Press, Kuala Lumpur. 199, 203, 205

Liu, T.C. and K.C. Yeh (1965), *The Economy of the Chinese Mainland*, Princeton University Press, Princeton. 328

Lockwood, W.W. (1954), *The Economic Development of Japan*, Princeton University Press, Princeton. 268

Lulofs, C. (1904), "Koffiecultuur en belasting ter Sumatra's Westkust" [Coffee Growing and Taxation on Sumatra's West Coast], *De Indische Gids* 26 (2), pp.1629-61, pp.1787-1815. 91, 97, 98, 100, 104, 105, 110

Maas, J.G.J.A. and F.T. Bokma (1950), "Rubbercultuur der ondernemingen" [Plantation Rubber Cultivation], in C.J.J. van Hall and C. van de Koppel (eds.), *De landbouw in de Indische Archipel*, van Hoeve, The Hague, Vol. III, pp.237-426. 159

McCloskey, D.N. (1978), "The Achievements of the Cliometric School," *The Journal of Economic History*, March, pp.12-28. 336

McFadyean, A. (1944), *The History of Rubber Regulation*, Allen and Unwin, London. 196, 202, 205

McVey, R. (1965), *The Rise of Indonesian Communism*, Cornell University Press, Ithaca, New York. 92

Maddison, A. (1971), *Class Structure and Economic Growth: India and Pakistan Since the Moghuls*, Allen and Unwin, London. 335

Maddison, A. (1982), *Phases of Capitalist Development*, Oxford University Press, Oxford. 335

Maddison, A. (1983), "Economic Stagnation Since 1973 - Its Nature and Causes: A Six-Country Survey," *De Economist*, December. 328

Malaya (1932-1941), *Rubber Statistics Handbooks, 1931-40,* Department of Statistics, Kuala Lumpur. 204

Malaya (1954), *Rubber Statistics Handbook, 1953*, Department of Statistics, Kuala Lumpur. 199

Mandere, H.Ch.G.J. van der (1928), *De Javasuikerindustrie in beden en verleden [The Java Sugar Industry Today and in the Past]*, Bureau Industra, Amsterdam. 169

Mansvelt, W.M.F. (1925-26), *Geschiedenis van de Nederlandsche Handel-Maatschappij [History of the Dutch Trading Company]*, Enschede and Zonen, Haarlem. 2 vols. 63

Mead, D.C. (1967), *Growth and Structural Change in the Egyptian Economy*, Irwin, Homewood, Illinois. 234, 235, 236, 237

Meier, G. (ed.) (1975), *Leading Issues in Economic Development* (Third edition), Oxford University Press, New York. 268

Meilink-Roelofsz, M.A.P. (1962), *Asian Trade and European Influence in the Indonesian Archipelago Between 1500 and About 1630*, Martinus Nijhoff, The Hague. 10, 137, 320

Meulen, W.A. van der (1940), "Irrigation in the Netherlands Indies," *Bulletin of the Colonial Institute of Amsterdam* 3, pp.142-59. 291

Mitchell, B.R. (1975), *European Historical Statistics 1750-1970*, Macmillan, London. 327

Mitchell, B.R. (1982), *International Historical Statistics: Africa and Asia*, Macmillan, London. 327, 328

Moertono, S. (1968), *State and Statecraft in Old Java*, Cornell Modern Indonesia Project, Ithaca, New York. 79

Mubyarto (1983), "Plantation Agriculture in Indonesia: Its Past and Future," paper delivered to the ARTEP-ILO meeting, Bangkok, October. 208

Muhlerin, B. (1970/71), "The 'Bekel' in Javanese History," *Review of Indonesian and Malaysian Affairs* 4/5, pp.1-28. 79

Muljatno (1960), "Perhitungan Pendapatan Nasional Indonesia untuk 1953 dan 1954" [Calculation of the National Income for Indonesia for 1953 and 1954], *Ekonomi dan Keuangan Indonesia* Tahun 13, March/April. 328

Musgrave, Richard A. (1969), *Fiscal Systems*, Yale University Press, New Haven. 235

Myint, Hla (1958), "The 'Classical Theory' of International Trade and Underdeveloped Countries," *Economic Journal* 48, pp.317-37. 325

Myint, Hla (1971), *Economic Theory and the Underdeveloped Countries*, Oxford University Press, New York. 268, 295

Myint, Hla (1973), *The Economics of the Developing Countries* (Fourth Revised Edition), Hutchinson, London. 268

Nahuijs van Burgst, H.G. Baron (1826), *Brieven over Bencoolen, Padang, het rijk van Menangkabau, Rhiouw, Sincapoera en Poelo-Pinang [Letters Concerning Bencoolen, Padang, the Kingdom of Minangkabau, Riau, Singapore and the Island of Penang]*, Hollingerus Pijpers, Breda. 96, 98

Nahuijs van Burgst, H.G. Baron (1847), *Beschouwingen over Nederlandsche-Indie*, The Hague. 116

Naerssen, F.H. van and R.C. de Iongh (1977), *The Economic and Administrative History of Early Indonesia*, Brill, Leiden. 3, 73, 77

Netherlands East Indies (1941), *Living Conditions of Plantation Workers and Peasants on Java*, Coolie Budget Commission, Batavia (English translation of original report in Dutch by R. Van Niel), Southeast Asian Program, Cornell University. 200

North, D.C. (1978), "Discussion on the Achievements of Three Influential Schools in Economic History," *The Journal of Economic History*, March, pp.77-80. 339

Nugent, J.A. (1973), "Exchange-Rate Movements and Economic Development in the Late Nineteenth Century," *Journal of Political Economy* 81 (5). 295

Ochse, J.J. *et al.* (1961), *Tropical and Subtropical Agriculture*, Vol. 2, Macmillan, New York. 110

Ohkawa, K. and M. Shinohara (eds.) (1979), *Patterns of Japanese Economic Development: A Quantitative Appraisal*, Yale University Press, New Haven. 234, 235, 237, 327, 336

Oki, Akira (1977), "Social Change in the West Sumatran Village; 1908-1945," Ph.D. thesis, Australian National University, Canberra. 100, 105

O'Malley, W.J. (1977), "Indonesia in the Great Depression," Ph.D. thesis, Cornell University, Ithaca, New York. 166, 169

Onghokham (1975), "The Residency of Madiun: Priyayi and Peasant in the Nineteenth Century," Ph.D. thesis, Yale University. 13

Ooi, J.B. (1963), *Land, People, and Economy in Malaya*, Longmans, Green and Co., London. 201

Oorschot, H.J. van (1956), *De ontwikkeling van de nijverheid in Indonesie [The Development of Industry in Indonesia]*, van Hoeve, The Hague. 310, 318, 319

Oshima, Harry T. (1965), "Meiji Fiscal Policy and Economic Progress," in W. Lockwood (ed.), *The State and Economic Enterprise in Japan*, Princeton University Press, Princeton, New Jersey. 236

Paauw, Douglas S. (1963), "From Colonial to Guided Economy" in T.R. McVey (ed.), *Indonesia*, HRAF Press, New Haven. 296, 307, 314

Paauw, Douglas S. (1969), "Economic Progress in Southeast Asia" in Robert O. Tilman (ed.), *Man, State and Society in Contemporary Southeast Asia*, Pall Mall Press, London. 328

Paerels, B.H. (1949), "Bevolkingskoffiecultuur" [Indigenous Coffee Cultivation], in C.J.J. van Hall and J. van de Koppel (eds.), *De landbouw in de Indische Archipel [Agriculture in the Indonesian Archipelago]*, Deel 2B, van Hoeve, The Hague. 101, 106

Parmer, J.N. (1960), *Colonial Land Policy and Administration: A History of Labour in the Rubber Plantation Industry of Malaya, 1910-1941*, Monographs of the Association for Asian Studies IX, J.J. Augustin, New York. 200

Pelzer, K.J. (1945), *Pioneer Settlement in the Asiatic Tropics*, American Geographical Society, New York. 290

Pelzer, K.J. (1978), *Planter and Peasant: Colonial Policy and the Agrarian Struggle in East Sumatra 1863-1947*, Martinus Nijhoff, The Hague. 13, 162, 168, 169, 198

Pelzer, K.J. (1982), *Planters Against Peasants: The Agrarian Struggle in East Sumatra, 1947-1958*, Martinus Nijhoff, The Hague. 13, 169

Personalia (1930/31), *Personalia en Verder Gegevens Betreffende de Suiker industrie in Nederlandsch-Indie Jaargang 1930-31*, Surabaya: van Ingen

Pierson, N.G. (1868), *Het Kultuurstelsel: zes voorlesingen [The Cultivation System: Six Lectures]*, Van Kampen, Amsterdam. 68

Pigeaud, T.G.T. and H.J. de Graaf (1976), *Islamic States in Java, 1500-1700*, KITLV Verhandelingen No. 70, Martinus Nijhoff, The Hague. 299

Polak, J.J. (1943), *The National Income of the Netherlands Indies, 1921- 1939*, Institute of Pacific Relations, New York. Reprinted in *Changing Economy in Indonesia, Vol. 5: National Income*, Martinus Nijhoff, The Hague, 1979. 234, 248, 280, 285, 334, 335

Prange, A.J.A. (1935), "De Nederlandsch Indische Betalingsbalans [The Netherlands Indies Balance of Payments]," Thesis, University of Leiden. 335

Prince, G.H.A. and H. Baudet (1983), Chapter II in H. Baudet and M. Fennema (eds.), *Het Nederlands Belang bij Indie [The Netherlands Interest in the Indies]*, Spectrum, Utrecht. 335

Raffles, S. (ed.) (1835), *Memoir of the Life and Public Services of Sir Thomas Stamford Raffles*, Duncan, London. 2 vols. 96

Raffles, T.S. (1817), *The History of Java*, Black, Parbury and Allen, London. 2 vols. Reprinted 1830. 4, 113, 125, 129, 133

Ranneft, J.W. Meyer (1937), "Hollands fout in Indie" [Holland's Mistake in the Indies, *De Gids* I. 333

Reid, A.J.S. (1980), "The Structure of Cities in Southeast Asia: Fifteenth to Seventeenth Centuries," *Journal of Southeast Asian Studies* 11 (2), pp.235-50. 272, 297

Reid, A.J.S. (ed.) (1983), *Slavery, Bondage and Dependency in Southeast Asia*, University of Queensland Press, St. Lucia. 14

Reid, A.J.S. (1984), "The Pre-Colonial Economy of Indonesia," *Bulletin of Indonesian Economic Studies* 20 (2), pp.151-67. 21, 272, 320

Reinsma, R. (1955), *Het verval van het Cultuurstelsel [The Decline of the Cultivation System]*, Van Keulen, The Hague. 10, 25, 41, 69, 75, 132, 185

Reinsma, R. (1980), "De kultuurprocenten in de praktijk en in de ogen der tijdgenoten" [Cultivation Percentage Payments in Practice and in the Eyes of

Contemporaries], in C. Fasseur (ed.), *Geld en geweten*, Martinus Nijhoff, The Hague. 31

Remer, C.F. (1933), *Foreign Investments in China*, Macmillan, New York. 335

Reynolds, Lloyd G. (1985), *Economic Growth in the Third World, 1850-1980*, Yale University Press, New Haven. 338

Ricklefs, M.C. (1981), *A History of Modern Indonesia*, Macmillan, London. 2, 24

Robequain, C. (1944), *The Economic Development of French Indo-China*, Oxford University Press, London. 324

Robequain, C. (1948), *Malaya, Indonesia, Borneo and the Philippines*, Longmans, Green and Co., London. (Second edition, 1958.) 156, 324

Roo, L.W.G. de (1909), *Documenten omtrent Herman Willem Daendels [Documents About Herman Willem Daendels]*, Martinus Nijhoff, The Hague. 68

Rothenbühler, F.J. (1798), "Extracten uit eene missive van den resident van Pekalongen ..." [Extracts from a Letter of the Resident of Pekalongan], *Endresume*, Vol. II, Bijlange JJ. 80

Rothenbühler, F.J. (1812a), "Rapport van den staat en gesteldheid van ... Sourabaija" [Report on the State and Condition of Surabaya], *Verhandelingen van het Bataviaasch Genootschap* Vol. XLI. 80

Rothenbühler, F.J. (1812b), "Vertoog ... omtrent het invoeren van een ander stelsel van handel en culture op Java" [Representation Concerning the Implementation of Another System of Trade and Cultivation in Java ...], ARA, The Hague. Archief J.C. Baud, No. 1002. 80

Rouffaer, G.P. (1906), "Vorstenlanden" [(Central Javanese) Principalities], *Encyclopaedie van Nederlandsch-Indie* Vol. IV. 79

Rowe, J.W.F. (1931), *Studies in the Artificial Control of Raw Material Supplies, No. 2: Rubber*, London School of Economics, London. 203

Rubber Research Institute of Malaya (1931-41), *Annual Reports*, Kuala Lumpur. 202

Rubber Research Institute of Malaya (1950), *Report for the period January 1941 to August 1945*, Kuala Lumpur. 202

Rubber Research Institute of Ceylon (1971), Private communication based on Institute records, Agalawatta. 191

Rudner, M.R. (1981), "Development Policies and Patterns of Agrarian Dominance in the Malaysian Rubber Export Economy," *Modern Asian Studies* 15. 198

Rush, J.R. (1977), "Opium Farms in Nineteenth-Century Java: Institutional Continuity and Change in a Colonial Society, 1860-1910," Ph.D. thesis, Yale University. 13

Salis, A.M.T. de (1809), *Korte aantooning van de notabelste verbeteringen en redressen ... [Short Demonstration of the Most Notable Improvements and Redresses ...]*, Gouvernments Drukkerij, Batavia. 80

Sang-Chul Suh (1978), *Growth and Structural Changes in the Korean Economy 1910-1940*, Harvard University Press, Cambridge. 324, 328, 331

Sartono Kartodirdjo (1972), "Agricultural Radicalism in Java" in C. Holt (ed.), *Culture and Politics in Indonesia*, Cornell University Press, Ithaca, New York. 79

Schadee, W.H.M. (1918), *Geschiedenis van Sumatra's Oostkust [History of Sumatra's East Coast]*, East Coast of Sumatra Institute, Amsterdam. 2 vols. 190, 201

Scheltema, A.M.P.A. (1936), *The Food Consumption of the Native Inhabitants of Java and Madura*, Institute of Pacific Studies, Batavia. 280, 284

Schoch, C.F. (1891), *De heerendiensten op Java en Madura [Corvée in Java and Madura]*, Van Stokum, The Hague. 75, 84

Scholz, U. (1977), *Minangkabau: Die Agrarstruktur in West-Sumatra und Möglichkeiten ihrer Entwicklung*, Giessener Geographische Schriften, Heft 41: Selbstverlag des Geographischen Instituts der Justus Liebig Universität, Giessen. 106

Schrieke, B. (1927), "Het probleem der bestuursorganisatie ter Sumatra's Westkust" [The Problem of the Organisation of Government on the West Coast of Sumatra], *Koloniale Studien* 11 (1), pp.57-106. 93

Schrieke, B. (ed.) (1929), *The Effect of Western Influence on Native Civilisations in the Malay Archipelago*, G. Kolff, Batavia. 23

Schrieke, B. (1955), *Indonesian Sociological Studies Part One*, van Hoeve, The Hague. 23, 92, 105

Schrieke, B. (1957), *Indonesian Sociological Studies Part Two: Ruler and Realm in Early Java*, van Hoeve, The Hague. 23

Scott, J.C. (1976), *The Moral Economy of the Peasant: Rebellion and Subsistence in Southeast Asia*, Yale University Press, New Haven. 103

Selo Soemardjan (1970), "The Influence of Social Structure on the Javanese Peasant Economy," in C.R. Wharton Jr. (ed.), *Subsistence Agriculture and Economic Development*, Aldine, Chicago. 80

Setten van der Meer, N.C. van (1979), *Sawah Cultivation in Ancient Java: Aspects of Development During the Indo-Javanese Period, 5th to 15th Century*, A.N.U. Press, Canberra. 3, 79

Shanin, T. (ed.) (1971), *Peasants and Peasant Societies*, Penguin, Harmondsworth. 94

Shein, Myint Thant and Tin Sein (1969), "Provincial Contract System," *Journal of the Burma Research Society* 52 (2). 234

Sibinga Mulder, J. (1929), *De rietsuikerindustrie on Java [The Sugar Cane Industry in Java]*, Tjeenk Willink, Haarlem. 169

Sitsen, Peter H.W. (1940), *Industrial Development of the Netherlands Indies* Bulletin 2, Netherlands and Netherlands Indies Council of the Institute of Pacific Relations. 232

Sivasubramonian, S. (1965), "National Incomes of India 1900-01 to 1946-47," Ph.D. thesis, Delhi School of Economics. 334, 335

Snodgrass, D.R. (1966), *Ceylon: An Export Economy in Transition*, Irwin, Illinois.

Soedjatmoko, M.A., G.J. Resink and G.McT. Kahin (eds.) (1964), *An Introduction to Indonesian Historiography*, Cornell University Press, Ithaca.

Soedersten, B. (1970), *International Economics*, Macmillan, London. 267

Soest, G.H. van (1869-71), *Geschiedenis van het Kultuurstelsel [History of the Cultivation System]*, Nijgh, Rotterdam. 3 vols. 25, 68, 185

Soetardjo Kartohadikoesoemo (1965), *Desa [Village]*, Sumur, Bangdung. 81

Spraos, J. (1980), "The Statistical Debate on the Net Barter Terms of Trade Between Primary Commodities and Manufactures," *Economic Journal* 90, pp.107-28, March. 279

Spalding, William F. (1918), *Eastern Exchange, Currency and Finance*, Isaac Pitman and Sons, London. 265

Steijn Parve, D.C. (1851), *Het koloniaal monopoliestelsel agetoetst aan geschiedenis en staathuishoudkunde, nader toegelicht door den schrijver [The Colonial Monopoly System, seen in the light of History and Political Economy]*, Noman and Zoon, Zaltbommel. 48

Steinberg, D.J. *et al.* (1971), *In Search of Southeast Asia*, Praeger, New York. 23

Steinbuch, W. (1917), "Bestuurs-controle op de inlandsche rijstcultuur ter Sumatra's Westkust" [Government Supervision of Native Rice Cultivation on the West Coast of Sumatra], *Tijdschrift voor het Binnenlands Bestuur* 51, pp.67-74. 105

Stibbe, S. (1884), "Werkvolk ter Sumatra's Westkust" [Labourers on the West Coast of Sumatra], *De Indische Gids* 6 (2), pp.697-700. 95

Stibbe, D.G. (1901-02) "Beschrijving der Onderafdeeling AlahanPanjang," *Tijdschrift voor het Binnenlands Bestuur,* Vol. 21, pp.218-42, pp. 298-322, pp.496-526; Vol. 22, pp. 324-44. 94, 95, 96, 105

Stivens, M. (1983), "Women's Economic Autonomy, Resistance and the Conservation of Matriliny: Women in the Rural Economy of Rembau, Negri Sembilan, Malaysia," paper presented to the Second Women in Asia Workshop, Monash University, Melbourne, July. 110

Stokvis, J.E. (1922), *Van wingewest naar zelfbestuur in Nederlandsch Indie [From Profit Area to Self-Government in the Netherlands Indies]*, Elsevier, Amsterdam. 68

Stoppelaar, J.W. de (1934), Het pandhuiscrediet [The Pawnshop Credit System], *Economisch Weekblad voor Neerlandsch Indie* 3 (14). 264

Sumitro Djojohadikoesomo (1943), *Het volkscredietwezen in de depressie [The People's Credit System in the Depression]*, Haarlem. 262

Sundrum, R.M. and Aye Hlaing (1961), *The Role of Agriculture in Economic Development: The Burmese Experience*, Economic Paper 6, Department of Economics, University of Rangoon, reprinted in *Proceedings of the Eleventh International Conference of Agricultural Economists*, pp.226-36. 267

Sutherland, H. (1975), "The Priyayi," *Indonesia* 19, pp.57-77. 50, 54

Sutherland, H. (1979), *The Making of a Bureaucratic Elite: The Colonial Transformation of the Javanese Priyayi*, Heinemann, Singapore. 50, 78

Sutherland, H. (1983), "Slavery and the Slave Trade in South Sulawesi, 1660s-1800s" in A.J.S. Reid (ed.), *Slavery, Bondage and Dependency in Southeast Asia*, University of Queensland Press, St. Lucia, pp.263-85. 14

Swieten, J. van (1863), "De invoering en weking van het koffiestelsel in het Gouvernement van Sumatra's Westkust" [The Introduction and Operation of the Coffee System in the Gubernatorial Province of Sumatra's West Coast], *Tijdschrift voor Nederlandsch Indie* 1, pp.201-24. 97, 103, 104, 110

Tan,F.J.E. (1964), "Aspects of an Indonesian Economic Historiography" in Soedjatmoko *et al.* (eds.), *An Introduction to Indonesian Historiography*, Cornell University Press, Ithaca, pp.395-403. 1, 2

Thee, Kian Wie (1977), *Plantation Agriculture and Export Growth: An Economic History of East Sumatra, 1863-1942*, National Institute of Economic and Social Research, Jakarta. 13, 162, 163, 190, 200, 204, 205, 207, 287, 290, 291

Thee, Kian Wie (1979), "The Study of Economic History in Indonesia" in F. van Anrooy *et al.* (eds.), *Between People and Statistics - Essays on Modern Indonesian History Presented to P. Creutzberg*, Martinus Nijhoff, The Hague.

Thomas, K.D. and J. Panglaykim (1976), "The Chinese in the South Sumatran Rubber Industry" in J.A.C. Mackie (ed.), *The Chinese in Indonesia: Five Essays*, Nelson, Melbourne. 291

Tichelaar, J.J. (1927), *De Java-suikerindustrie en hare beteekenis voor land en volk [The Java Sugar Industry and Its Significance for the Country and the People]*, Van Ingen, Surabaya. 169

Tichelman, F. (1980), *The Social Evolution of Indonesia: The Asiatic Mode of Production and its Legacy*, Martinus Nijhoff, The Hague. 14

Tio Poo Tjiong (1923), *De suikerhandel van Java [Java's Sugar Trade]*, de Bussy, Amsterdam. 169

Tunku Shamsul Bahrin (1965). "Indonesian Labour in Malaya," *Kajian Ekonomi Malaysia* II (1), p.53. 201

Ultee, A.J. (1949), "Koffiecultuur der ondernemingen" [Coffee Cultivation on Estates], in C.J.J. Hall and J. van de Koppel (eds.), *De landbouw in de Indische Archipel [Agriculture in the Indonesian Archipelago]*, Deel 2B, van Hoeve, The Hague. 106

United Nations (1948), *Public Debt, 1914-16*, Lake Success, New York. 237

United Nations (1950), *Public Finance Information Papers: Egypt*, Lake Success, New York. 236

Utrechtsche Bijdragen (1932?-1950?), *Utrechtsche Bijdragen tot de geschiedenis, het staatscrecht en de economie van Nederlandsch-Indie [Utrecht Contributions to the History, Constitutional Law, and Economy of the Netherlands Indies]*, under the direction of C. Gerretson and H. Westra. 69

Van Niel, R. (1964a), "The Alfred A. Reed Papers," *Bijdragen tot de Taal-, Land- en Volkenkunde* 120, pp.224-30. 72

Van Niel, R. (1964b), "Considerations on the Introduction of the Cultivation System in Pasuruan, Java," paper presented to the International Conference on Asian History, Hong Kong. 51, 52

Van Niel, R. (1964c), "The Function of Landrent under the Cultivation System in Java," *Journal of Asian Studies* 23 (3), pp.357-75. 10, 83, 169

Van Niel, R. (1966), "Nineteenth-Century Java: an Analysis of Historical Sources and Method," *Asian Studies* 4, pp.201-12. 25, 70

Van Niel (1969), "The Introduction of Government Sugar Cultivation in Pasuruan, Java, 1830," *Journal of Oriental Studies* 7 (2), pp.261-76. 10, 169

Van Niel, R. (1972), "The Measurement of Change under the Cultivation System in Java, 1837-1851," *Indonesia* 14, pp.89-109. 13, 52, 61, 69, 111, 114, 169, 171

Van Niel, R. (1976), "The Labour Component in the Forced Cultivation System in Java, 1830-1855," *Proceedings 30th ICHSANA*, El Colegio de Mexico, Mexico City. 69, 75

Van Niel, R. (1981), "The Effect of Exports Cultivations in Nineteenth-Century Java," *Modern Asian Studies* 15 (1), pp.25-58. 38, 50, 51, 52, 54, 69, 71, 78

Van Niel, R. (1982), "Landholding in Java," paper presented to the Eighth International Conference of Economic Historians, Budapest. Mimeograph. 69

Verkerk Pistorius, A.W.P. (1871), *Studien over de inlandsche huishouding in de Padangsche bovenlanden [Studies in the Indigenous Economy in the Padang Highlands]*, Noman and Zoon, Zalt-Bommel. 94, 95

Verrijn Stuart, G.M. (1923), *Het bankwezen in de Nederlandsche Kolonien [Banking in the Netherlands Colonies]*, Wassenaar. 254, 256, 265

Veth, P.J. (ed.) (1881), *Reizen in Midden-Sumatra 1877-79, door de leden der Sumatra Expeditie, uitgerust door het Aardrijkskundig Genootschap [Travels in Central Sumatra 1877-79, made by the Members of the Sumatran Expedition with the support of the Geographical Society]*, (Eerste gedelte beschreven door A.L. van Hasselt en J.F. Snelleman), Brill, Leiden. 95, 96, 104

Vinne, J. van der (1842), "Beknopte overzicht van den handel en scheepvaart te Padang gedurende het jaar 1841" [A Brief Survey of Trade and Shipping at Padang during the year 1841], *Tijdschrift voor Nederlandsch Indie* 4 (2), pp.373-84. 110

Vissering, G. (1920), *Muntwezen en circulatiebanken in Nederlandsch-Indie [Currency System and Bank of Issue in Netherlands India]*, Amsterdam. 265

Vitalis, L. (1851), *De invoering, werking en gebreken van het stelsel van kultures op Java [The Introduction, Operation and Defects of the Cultivation System in Java]*, The Hague. 29, 30

Vlieland, C.A. (1932), *British Malaya: a Report on the 1931 Census*, London. 324

Volker, T. (1928), *Van oerbosch tot cultuurgebied [From Jungle to Estate Region]*, D.P.V. Medan. 169

Volkstelling (1930), *Inheemsche Bevolking van Borneo, Celebes de Kleine Soenda Eilanden en de Molukken,* Department van Economische Zaken Batavia 1936.

Vollenhoven, C. van (1932), *De Indonesier en zijn grond [The Indonesian and His Land]*, Brill, Leiden. 68, 78, 198

Voon, P.K. (1976), *Western Rubber Planting Enterprise in Southeast Asia 1876-1921*, Penerbit Universiti Malaya, Kuala Lumpur. 187, 198

Vries, E. de (1931), *Landbouw en welvaart in het Regentschap Pasoeroean: bijdrage tot de kennis van de sociale economie van Java [Agriculture and Welfare in Pasuruan Residency: A Contribution to the Knowledge of Java's Social Economy]*, Veenman, Wageningen. 2 vols. 5, 265

Vriese, W.H. de (n.d.), *Rapport betrekkelijk de ziekte in het padigewas in de residentie Pekalongan [Report on the Padi-crop Disease in Pekalongan Residency]*, n.p., Batavia. 66

De Vrije Arbeid (1885), "De vrije arbeid en het soekoebestuur op Sumatra's Westkust" [Free Labour and Lineage Government in the West Coast of Sumatra], *Tijdschrift voor Nederlandsch Indie* 17, pp.91-103. 97

Waal, R. van de (1959), "Richtlijnen voor een ontwikkelingsplan voor de Oostkust van Sumatra [Guidelines for a Development Plan for Sumatra's East

Coast],'' Ph.D. thesis, Wageningen Agricultural University, Wageningen. 162, 164

Wardhana, Ali (1971), "The Indonesian Banking System: The Central Bank" in Bruce Glassburner (ed.), *The Economy of Indonesia: Selected Readings*, Cornell University Press, Ithaca, New York. 265

Waterloo, M. (1806), "Correspondentie Engelhard-Waterloo: de agrarische toestanden in des sultans landen" [Correspondence Between Engelhard and Waterloo: Agrarian Conditions in the Territories of the Sultans], KITLV, Leiden. Manuscript H69f, Stuk XIV. 80

Waterloo, M. (1811), *Memorial Relative to the Actual State of Cheribon*, India Office Library, Mackenzie Collection Private, No. 10 (2). 80

Wertheim, W.F. (1956), *Indonesian Society in Transition*, van Hoeve, The Hague. 10

Westendorp Boerma, J.J. (1956), *Briefwisseling tussen J. van den Bosch en J.C. Baud 1829-1832 en 1834-1836 [Correspondence between J. van den Bosch and J.C. Baud 1829-1832 and 1834-1836]*, Kemink and Zoon, Utrecht. 46

White, B. (1973), "Demand for labour and population growth in colonial Java," *Human Ecology* Vol. 1, pp.217-36. 132, 171

White, B. (1983), "'Agricultural Involution' and its Critics: Twenty Years Later," *Bulletin of Concerned Asian Scholars* 15 (2), pp.18-31. 12

Whitford, H.N. (1931), *Estate and Native Plantation Rubber in the Middle East, 1930*, Rubber Manufacturers Association, New York. 188, 195, 205

Whittlesey, C.R. (1931), *Governmental Control of Crude Rubber: The Stevenson Plan*, Princeton University Press, Princeton. 203

Wilde, A. de (1830), *De Preanger Regentschappen op Java gelegen [Priangan Regencies in Java]*, Amsterdam. 116

Williams, L.E. (1952), "Chinese Entrepreneurs in Indonesia," *Explorations in Entrepreneurial History* V (1), pp.34-60. 197

Wisseman, J. (1977), "Markets and Trade in Pre-Madjapahit Java," in Karl L. Hutterer (ed.), *Economic Change and Social Interaction in Southeast Asia* CSSEAS, Ann Arbor, Michigan. 79

Wolters, O.W. (1967), *Early Indonesian Commerce: A Study of the Origins of Srivijaya*, Cornell University Press, Ithaca, New York. 3

Wong, Lin-Ken (1960), "The Trade of Singapore, 1819-69," *Journal of the Malayasian Branch of the Royal Asiatic Society* 33 (4). 320

Wong, Lin-Ken (1965), *The Development of the Malayan Tin Industry to 1914*, Tucson, Arizona. 300, 320

Wong, Lin-Ken (1978), "Singapore: Its Growth as an Entrepôt Port, 1819-1941," *Journal of Southeast Asian Studies* 9 (1), pp.50-84. 301, 320

World Bank (1980), *World Tables*, World Bank, Washington, D.C. 328

Wycherley, P.R. (1959), "The Singapore Botanic Gardens and Rubber in Malaya," *Gardens' Bulletin* XVII (2), p.175. 202

Yasuba, Y. (1972/73), "Modern Economists' Views on the Japanese Economy: A Survey," *Japanese Economic Studies* 1 (2), pp.3-46. 336

Young, K.R. (1980), "The Late Nineteenth-Century Commodity Boom in West Sumatra," *Indonesia Circle* 22, pp.64-69. 107

Young, K.R. (1983), "The 1908 Anti-Tax Rebellion in Minangkabau (West Sumatra): A Socio-Economic Study of an Historical Case of Political Activism among Indonesian Peasants," Ph.D. thesis, University of London. 90, 96, 97, 109, 110

Ysseldyk, W.H. (1799), "Verslag" [Report], in J.K.J. de Jonge (comp.), *De Opkomst van het Nederlandsch Gezag over Java* Vol. XIII, pp.480-83. 80

Zimmerman, L.J. (1962), "The Distribution World Income, 1860-1960" in Egbert de Vries (ed.), *Essays on Unbalanced Growth*, Mouton and Co., The Hague. 226, 280

Published Colonial Statistical Sources

Koloniaal Verslagen (K.V.) [Colonial Reports]. These are the series of official reports published annually as appendices to the *Handelingen van de Tweede Kamer der Staten Generaal [Proceedings of the Second Chamber of the States General]*. The series runs from 1849 to 1930 (*C.E.I.* Vol 1, p.147). Each annual volume has numerous statistical appendices, covering a broad range of demographic and economic data. From 1931 to 1941 the *Koloniaal Verslag* was replaced by the *Indisch Verslag*, published annually in two volumes; the first volume was the official *Report on the Administration and the State of Netherlands India* while the second volume comprised the *Statistical Yearbook.*

Jaarcijfers voor het Koninkrijk der Nederlanden: Kolonien. [Annual Statistics for the Kingdom of the Netherlands: Colonies]. These annual statistical digests were first published in 1887 by the *Statistisch Instituut* of the *Vereeningung voor de Statistiek* in the Netherlands. After 1897 they were compiled by the Netherlands Central Bureau of Statistics. They rely heavily on data from the *Koloniaal Verslag* but also use other sources. After 1922 they were replaced by the *Statistisch Jaaroverzicht van Nederlandsch- Indie*, which after 1931 was in turn replaced by the second volume of the *Indisch Verslag*. These publications thus comprise a continuous statistical record for the last five decades of the colonial period. Up to 1922 the publications were in Dutch and French; after 1922 they were in Dutch and English.

Central Bureau of Statistics, *Statistical Pocketbook of Indonesia 1941*. During the 1930s several statistical pocketbooks were published in Dutch; the final one to appear was in English. They mainly published data appearing in the *Indisch Verslag, Vol. 2* but contained some other material as well.

Medeelingen van het Centraal Kantoor voor de Statistiek (C.K.S.). During the inter-war years the Central Bureau of Statistics in Batavia published a series of *Medeelingen [Bulletins]*, many of which carried valuable time series on particular topics, including trade, food production and prices. These culminated in the nine volumes initiated by W.M.F. Mansvelt (referred to in this volume as *C.K.S.* 160 to 168), which were intended to give a complete statistical record of the 19th and 20th centuries (*C.E.I.*, Vol. 1, p.7). Most were only published in mimeo form and few copies remain. The *Bulletins* cited in this volume are as follows:

C.K.S. 146: *Prices, Price Indexes and Exchange Rates in Java, 1913-37*

C.K.S. 160: *Trade Statistics, Java: 1823-73*

C.K.S. 161: *Trade Statistics, Indonesia: 1874-1937*

C.K.S. 162: *Trade with Singapore: 1825-1937*

C.K.S. 166: *Indonesian Prices: 1840-1937*

C.K.S. 167: *Indonesia's Economic Development: 1823-1937*

Changing Economy in Indonesia (C.E.I.). This series was begun in 1975 under the editorship of P. Creutzberg, and is intended to continue the series begun by Mansvelt before the war. The publications are in English. At the time of writing, six volumes have appeared:

C.E.I. Vol. 1:*Indonesia's Export Crops 1816-1949*

C.E.I. Vol. 2: *Public Finance 1816-1939*

C.E.I. Vol. 3: *Expenditure on Fixed Assets*

C.E.I. Vol. 4: *Rice Prices*

C.E.I. Vol. 5:*National Income*

C.E.I. Vol. 6: *Money and Banking 1816-1940*